JBuilder™ 7.0 EJB Programming

Chuck Easttom

Wordware Publishing, Inc.

Library of Congress Cataloging-in-Publication Data

Easttom, Chuck.
    JBuilder 7.0 EJB programming / by Chuck Easttom.
        p.   cm.
    Includes index.
    ISBN 1-55622-874-0
    1. Java (Computer program language).   2. JBuilder.   I. Title.

    QA76.73.J38 E23   2002
    005.2'762—dc21   2002008517
                                          CIP

ISBN 1-55622-874-0
10 9 8 7 6 5 4 3 2 1
0207

All inquiries for volume purchases of this book should be addressed to Wordware Publishing, Inc., at the above address. Telephone inquiries may be made by calling:

(972) 423-0090

Contents

Contents

Contents

Acknowledgments

This book has been a lot of work, but it was also a pleasure to do. I have several people to thank; without them this would never have happened. First of all, I would like to thank my wife, Misty, and my son, AJ, who are always so patient when I am working on a book. They are very understanding when I am sequestered away in my den writing. Next I wish to thank the wonderful people at Wordware Publishing. Jim Hill and Wes Beckwith have always been absolutely wonderful to work with. Without them, I would not be writing programming books today. Wes was unbelievably patient as I continuously revised the dates for milestones in this book. I also owe a great debt to Beth Kohler and Heather Hill, who edit the rough drafts and save me from embarrassing myself!

I also owe a tremendous debt to the remarkable people at Borland. They made available to me all the resource material I could possibly want about their product, including beta versions of JBuilder 6.0 and 7.0, documentation, and other resources. Their assistance allowed me to truly dive into their product and give it the coverage it deserves.

Finally, I want to thank my students and colleagues who occasionally lent a friendly ear to hear my thoughts on a particular topic or look over a piece of code for accuracy.

Introduction

Sun Microsystem's Java programming language has quickly become one of the most popular programming languages in use today. Its platform independence is only one reason for this success. Other reasons include its powerful object-oriented approach to programming and the fact that it is freely available from the Sun Microsystems web site. However, as many of you have undoubtedly discovered, programming from a text editor and a command line compiler is not always the most efficient way to develop professional applications. This is where the Borland JBuilder product comes in. JBuilder gives you 100% pure Java but in an easy-to-use environment. The JBuilder development environment is as easy to use as any of the popular RAD (rapid application development) tools available.

Java has become a very rich and powerful programming language with many different features. There exists a plethora of books on the various aspects of Java programming. This book's focus is on the development of JavaBeans and, more specifically, Enterprise JavaBeans (EJBs). Beans are reusable components that can be used to build applications or facilitate distributed computing design. The purpose of the volume you hold in your hands is to teach you how to develop Enterprise JavaBeans (EJBs) using both the Sun Java Development Kit and the Borland JBuilder 7.0 development kit. Each technique is first discussed and demonstrated using a standard text editor and command line compiling with Sun Microsystems Java tools, and then I show you how to do the same technique using JBuilder 7.0. My goal is to demonstrate the inner workings of Enterprise Bean development and, at the same time, show you how to develop them more efficiently using JBuilder 7.0. JBuilder 7.0 provides everything you could possibly want or need to develop both standard JavaBeans and Enterprise JavaBeans. It has a very rich set of easy-to-use tools that will assist in your development efforts. This book won't make you an Enterprise JavaBeans guru; no single book could achieve such an ambitious goal.

However, it can give you a solid fundamental understanding of Enterprise JavaBeans and related topics.

What Does This Book Assume about You?

It is assumed that you have a working knowledge of Java. This book does not purport to teach basic Java programming. However, I try not to assume any more knowledge than that: a basic working knowledge of Java. While some of you may have developed standard JavaBeans before, this knowledge is not assumed for this book. The first four chapters introduce the concept of standard JavaBeans and show how to develop these beans. Chapters 5 and 6 provide the knowledge base that will be required to understand how and why Enterprise JavaBeans work. The rest of the book expands upon this knowledge and teaches specifically how to develop Enterprise JavaBeans. If you are already familiar with standard JavaBeans, then feel free to skip over the first four chapters.

How Is the Information Presented?

This book is filled with examples. Some readers might even think there are too many examples, some of which may be redundant. I also use complete examples, not code snippets. Most readers find it helpful to have the code in a complete context. Obviously, someone who is experienced on the topic, and just looking for a refresher or a reference, may not need the complete code. It is my hope that by seeing some technique demonstrated several different ways, you will have a more thorough understanding of the topic. The complete code for the examples is available from the downloadable files. Each chapter also concludes with a list of key chapter terms and ten review questions. This is designed to facilitate the gaining of knowledge that you need from this book.

This book is about Enterprise JavaBeans. However, we cannot discuss that topic without first ensuring that you have a basic understanding of standard JavaBeans. That is why the first four chapters are devoted to that topic. The primary difference between the two is that a standard JavaBean is a component that is used to create applications, while an Enterprise JavaBean can be a stand-alone component. Essentially, Enterprise JavaBeans are deployable and standard JavaBeans are not. It should also be noted that you can use standard JavaBeans to build Enterprise JavaBeans, so that is another good reason to cover standard beans first.

Prerequisites

Before you embark on the reading of this book, I must stress to you that it assumes some knowledge. It presumes that you have had experience developing at least simple Java applications and that you have some basic knowledge of Borland JBuilder. If you require more basic knowledge of Java or JBuilder 7.0, I strongly recommend reading *Charlie Calvert's Learn JBuilder 7.0* by Charlie and Margie Calvert (from Wordware Publishing). Both Charles and Margie are excellent authors and experts in Java and JBuilder. Their book would be the perfect place to get a solid grounding in Java and JBuilder. However, I must also stress that this book does not assume any more than a basic working knowledge of Java. For this reason, some topics that are related to Enterprise JavaBeans, such as standard JavaBeans, exception handling, and distributed computing, are also given some basic coverage.

JBuilder

As the title suggests, this book emphasizes the use of Borland's JBuilder to create Enterprise JavaBeans. This leads to the obvious question of which version of JBuilder you will need. This book's focus is on the latest version, JBuilder 7.0. However, most of the examples in this book can be done in JBuilder 5.0 and 6.0. So if you happen to be utilizing an older version of JBuilder, you will still be able to use this book.

Example Files

The example files for this book can be downloaded from www.wordware.com/ejb.

Chapter 1

Introduction to Beans

Introduction

If you are reading this book, then you are probably aware that JavaBeans is one of the hottest topics in Java programming today. While doing the final revisions to this book, I scanned various computer job web sites and noted a plethora of ads that requested programmers who knew JavaBeans or Enterprise JavaBeans. The wide range of job opportunities associated with these skills alone is a strong reason for you to acquaint yourself with this topic. However, if you are reading this book, you are probably already aware of that fact.

Far more important than simply increasing your available job opportunities (at least from an academic or philosophical viewpoint) is the fact that JavaBeans represents what is perhaps the best implementation of the power of object-oriented programming available today. JavaBeans are completely self-contained object-oriented code that can be readily reused in a variety of programming contexts. In essence, JavaBeans (both standard JavaBeans and Enterprise JavaBeans) embody the most important aspects of object-oriented programming.

The primary purpose of this book is to teach you the essentials of Enterprise JavaBeans (EJB). Along the way, a few other closely related topics are introduced by necessity. Your education to Enterprise JavaBeans will include the theoretical underpinnings of EJBs, their structure, and how to create your own Enterprise JavaBeans. However, you cannot really learn Enterprise JavaBeans without a firm understanding of the standard JavaBeans. Therefore, the goal of this chapter, and the three subsequent chapters, is to provide you with a fundamental, working knowledge of JavaBeans. With this knowledge in hand, you should be able to master the Enterprise JavaBeans concepts presented throughout the rest of this book. Clearly, since you are reading this book, I don't have to tell you the importantance of JavaBeans knowledge. So why don't I just jump right to the topic?

Before I demonstrate how to build your own JavaBeans, or even how to utilize existing JavaBeans, two important questions should be answered: What exactly is a JavaBean? Why should you use JavaBeans?

Let me try to address that first question. Java is an object-oriented programming language, a fact you are undoubtedly already very familiar with. One of the hallmarks of object-oriented programming is code reusability. In fact, the entire reason that object-oriented programming was originally developed was to support code reusability. With procedural programming languages (BASIC, Pascal, C, COBOL, etc.) and techniques, reusing code was difficult and cumbersome. The advent of object-oriented programming allows the code to be very efficiently reused. The concept is quite simple. Once a programmer has spent significant time and effort developing a programming object, other programmers should be able to simply utilize this object in their own programs, provided it has the functionality they need. Another way to put this is simply to quote a popular piece of folk wisdom: "Don't reinvent the wheel." JavaBeans are, at least in my view, the ultimate expression of code reusability, at least as far as presently available technology is concerned. Beans are essentially fully functional, compiled code components that you can use in a variety of ways in your application development. You can even simply link JavaBeans together to create an application. It may be useful for you to think of beans as parts, which a Java programmer can then assemble into useful programs. So to answer the original question, a JavaBean is a self-contained, reusable Java code component. This is a working definition that we can use for now. As I explain more aspects of

JavaBeans, I will expand this definition one more time to include another key feature of JavaBeans that I have not yet shown you.

The second question is even simpler to answer than the first question. The main reason why a programmer might wish to use JavaBeans is to facilitate code reuse, thereby more efficiently utilizing his or her own programming time. Since JavaBeans are completely self-contained, they are very easy to reuse. In my opinion, JavaBeans are the best expression of the concept of reusable components that are currently available to a programmer. By understanding and implementing JavaBeans effectively, you will elevate your code reuse beyond the level of simply importing packages.

You may think to yourself that standard Java classes provide an adequate degree of code reusability. Why would you require any further technology? Classes do indeed provide a measure of code reusability. You can include classes that you, or even other programmers, have developed in your own programs, thereby reusing that code. In Java, there are two basic ways to do this. For simple classes, you could simply copy the requisite code into one of your program's source code files. That may not be an elegant solution, but it does work.

> **Note:**   I am certain that object-oriented purists reading this are simply wincing at the sight of my even mentioning it. However, in my defense, I did mention it, but I did not recommend it!

A better solution (and one that will make those object-oriented purists smile again!) is to simply import the package that contains this class. In fact, that is how all Java programming is done. All of the functionality of the Java language is contained in classes that are stored in packages. You just import the package that contains the class you need, and then you are free to instantiate that class and utilize its methods and properties. JavaBeans takes this concept to a new level: You need not even import packages into a project. You can simply link compiled objects into your application, or even link beans together to form an application, constructed totally out of JavaBeans. This is object orientation in its fully developed form. In fact, a programmer with minimal skills could, at least theoretically, link together JavaBeans and create a fully functional program.

JavaBeans vs. ActiveX

Now that you have some idea of what a JavaBean is, you may think that it seems to offer functionality that is strikingly similar to other technologies you have seen, like ActiveX components. If you have used rapid application development (RAD) tools, such as Borland's Delphi or Microsoft Visual Basic, you should be familiar with the idea of reusable components. Windows programmers frequently utilize ActiveX controls in their programming endeavors, and programmers who specifically use Microsoft Visual Basic as their Windows development tool of choice have much of their code based on the use of ActiveX components. It is true that ActiveX components are self-contained objects made of object-oriented code that are integrated into applications. So it is definitely true that ActiveX and JavaBeans share some common features. The underlying concept behind all reusable component architectures is essentially the same, only the implementation is different. A JavaBean is a reusable software component designed for use with Java. The JavaBean has a few advantages over an ActiveX component, the first being that it can be used on any operating system. ActiveX components can only be used in Microsoft Windows environments. With the widespread use of Unix, growing popularity of Linux, and the market share of Macintosh, it seems unwise to base your component programming on a single platform. Furthermore, ActiveX components are usually incorporated into applications.

> **Note:** There are ActiveX executables and DLLs that are distributed in a stand-alone fashion.

JavaBeans can be incorporated into applications, or you can simply link different beans together to form an application created entirely from JavaBeans.

Basics of JavaBeans

The first step for you to take is to develop a solid understanding of precisely what a JavaBean is. Previously, I gave you a working definition. After I explain a little more about JavaBeans, I will give you a final definition that you can use. To understand the precise meaning of a JavaBean, you must first understand the following terms:

- Software component
- Builder tool
- Visual manipulation

A software component is simply a self-contained piece of code that you can use to build applications. The component should be completely self-contained, which means two things: First, the component should not have any external dependencies. This requirement is frequently left unfulfilled by ActiveX components, since they often depend on other DLLs (dynamic linked libraries) in order to function properly. However, ideally, any component should be self-sufficient. Second, the internal mechanisms of the component should be completely irrelevant to the programmer utilizing the component. The programmer using the component should not need to know anything about the internal mechanisms of the component. He or she should merely have to manipulate properties and call methods to get the component to work. This concept is sometimes called the "black box." The component in question should be a black box to the programmer utilizing it. They need not concern themselves with the details of how the component implements its methods.

Builder tools are simply development/design tools that facilitate a visual manipulation of code components. In the context of JavaBeans, builder tools assist you in creating JavaBeans.

The term *visual manipulation* means that you can manipulate the bean in a visual/graphical manner, much like using any rapid application development tool. Usually, JavaBean builder tools provide you with a drag and drop graphical interface, wherein you can manipulate existing beans or even create new ones.

JavaBeans are, therefore, simply self-contained components you can use to build solutions. It is important to realize that JavaBeans are development components, not deployment components. This means that you use JavaBeans to create applications; they are not directly distributed <u>as</u> applications. You cannot simply distribute a standard JavaBean as if it were a stand-alone application. You can, however, link several beans together to create a stand-alone application. This technology has been an exciting tool for Java developers, allowing them to fully take advantage of the code reusability aspect of object-oriented programming. JavaBeans are pieces of code that you can plug into your application and use. Standard JavaBeans can only be used as building blocks for applications and cannot be deployed as stand-alone components. In contrast, Enterprise JavaBeans can be deployed as stand-alone components. For now, I will delay any further discussion of Enterprise JavaBeans. Chapters 5 and beyond in this book are solely concerned with acquainting you with the intricacies of Enterprise JavaBeans.

Another, more technical way to define a JavaBean would be to say that it is a collection of one or more Java classes that serves as a self-contained, reusable component. A JavaBean can be a component used in building a user interface or a non-GUI component, such as a data module. JavaBeans have properties, methods, and events that follow certain naming conventions. JavaBeans have some advantages over other components; they are pure Java, cross-platform components. If you are using JBuilder, you can even install them on the JBuilder component palette and use them in the construction and design of your other applications. JavaBeans can also be used with other application builder tools for Java.

Sun's Bean Development Kit

At this point, you should have a firm understanding of a JavaBean. The next, logical step is to show you how to use JavaBeans. You are undoubtedly already familiar with the Sun Microsystems Java Development Kit (JDK). If you are not, you are probably reading the wrong book! Sun Microsystems also provides a Bean Development Kit, or BDK. As of publication, the current version is BDK 1.1 and is available as a free download from the Sun Microsystems web site. This kit will provide everything you need to create standard JavaBeans, as well as a number of sample beans you can use to assist you in learning about beans. The kit can be downloaded for free from http://java.sun.com/products/javabeans/software/bdk_download.html. It contains several items. The following list is a brief summary of the items in the kit:

- README.html is the starting point for the entire bean development kit documentation. Starting with this web page, you can read the various documents that Sun Microsystems provides for bean development. I will warn you that, like most technical documentation, this makes for rather dry reading. But if you want to get the authoritative word on JavaBeans (or anything Java), the Sun Microsystems documentation is the place to go.

- LICENSE.html contains the bean development kit license agreement. Many developers never read the license agreement for free software tools. However, I highly recommend that you do indeed read this one. It outlines the ways in which you can legally use and distribute Java programs created with this development kit.

- GNUmakefile and Makefile are Unix and Windows makefiles (these files have .gmk and .mk extensions) for building the demos and the BeanBox and for running the BeanBox (and yes, that means exactly what you think it does). You can rebuild the BeanBox itself. You can modify the BeanBox and recompile it if you are so inclined, though I don't recommend that exercise for the faint of heart. You are far more likely to simply render your BeanBox unusable than you are to create any new enhancement to the BeanBox (but one never knows...).

- The folder Beans/apis has a subdirectory containing JavaBeans source files. These are the actual source files to many existing beans. If you want to see how Sun Microsystems programmers go about building JavaBeans, the source code can be found here.

- The folder Beans/BeanBox contains a classes directory containing the BeanBox class files, a lib directory containing a BeanBox support JAR file used by, and other files needed to run, the BeanBox.

- The folder Beans/demos has an HTML subfolder containing an applet wrapper demonstration that must be run in applet viewer or a JDK 1.1-compliant browser. This will allow you to see some of the incredible things you can do with JavaBeans. It might even be a good idea for you to take a look at this before you start creating your own beans.

- The folder Beans/doc contains various supporting documents. Again, I must confess that the documentation is somewhat dry, but it is the most technically accurate authority on JavaBeans. You probably won't wish to dive into this documentation right away. After all, that's why you bought this book! However, after you have some experience developing JavaBeans, you may find this documentation useful for finding information you might need.

- The folder Beans/JARs contains JAR files for demo beans. If you don't know what a JAR file is, don't panic. You will create one in Chapter 2. However, if you are simply too curious to wait that long to find out what a JAR file is, I will tell you: Essentially, it is an archive file that has a group of files that will be distributed together.

Fundamental JavaBean Concepts

Before I show you how to utilize JavaBeans, it would be prudent to first examine some critical JavaBean concepts. The JavaBeans API (application programming interface) enables the programmer to write component software using the Java programming language. These components are self-contained, reusable software units called JavaBeans. These beans can be composed into composite components used in applets or integrated into applications. The JavaBeans specification outlines how a bean interface should be designed. Adhering to this standardized interface is what allows beans created by different developers to communicate with each other. It is also what allows bean development tools, such as the BeanBox, to communicate with beans. The very first fact about bean development that you must remember is that you must follow the JavaBean specifications when developing a JavaBean. It is only by using a standardized interface and specifications that JavaBeans are able to communicate with one another and with builder tools.

Beans expose their features via public methods and events. In fact, a bean's methods and events can only be exposed because they adhere to specific design patterns. A JavaBeans-enabled builder tool can then examine the bean's patterns, and since they adhere to these predetermined design patterns, it can then expose those methods for manipulation. A Bean Builder tool maintains beans that it is aware of in a toolbox. You can then select a bean from the toolbox, place it in the work area provided, and modify its properties or link its events to other beans. The work area looks very much like the canvas in most graphics software, such as Adobe Photoshop or Microsoft Paint. The Sun Microsystems Bean Development Kit (BDK) comes with the BeanBox, which allows you to take beans, place them in the work area, and define their interactions and change their properties. The following image shows you what the BeanBox looks like:

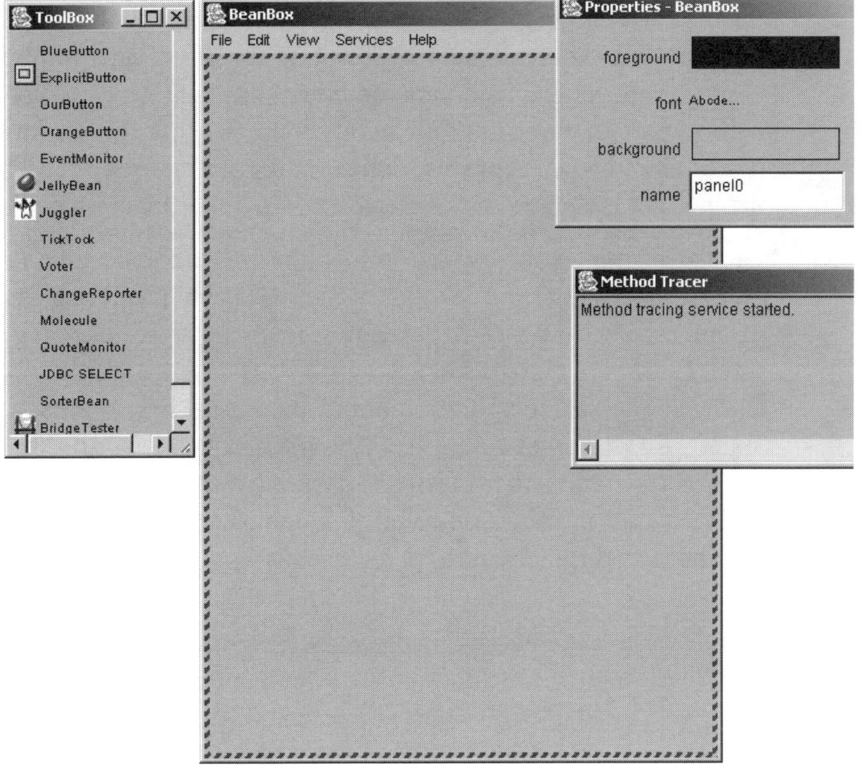

Later in this chapter, I will show you how to use the BeanBox and walk you through several examples that demonstrate how to utilize the BeanBox. You will find that the BeanBox is very easy to use and an intuitive tool that allows you to connect various beans together. I suspect that you will have very little trouble getting comfortable with the BeanBox.

Introspection

In the previous section, I mentioned that JavaBeans expose their properties and methods. You may wonder how they go about exposing these methods and properties. Bean Builder tools find out about a bean's members through a process known as *introspection*. Introspection is a process whereby external objects, be they bean development tools, applications, or other beans, can find out information about a bean's members. Each bean has a related bean information class, which provides information about the bean's properties, methods, and events. Each bean information class must implement the BeanInfo interface, which lists the bean features that are to be exposed. It is this interface that defines how beans communicate their information. If you are not already aware of this, you should note that many features through-out the Java language are utilized by implementing a particular interface.

Beans also support introspection by adhering to the specific rules, or design patterns, defined by the JavaBean standards when naming bean features. The Introspector Java class examines beans for these design patterns and thereby learns about the beans' members. The Introspector class provides a standard way for tools to learn about the properties, events, and methods supported by a target JavaBean. The Introspector will analyze each of the bean's classes and super-classes separately looking for the information, and it will use that information to build a BeanInfo object that comprehensively describes the target bean.

Communicating with Beans

JavaBeans require some method for communicating with the outside world. This communication is accomplished through the use of properties and events. Properties allow you, the developer, to send information into the bean. Events allow the bean to send information to the outside world. Properties are discussed in Chapter 2, and Chapter 3 discusses properties and events. However, I will provide you with a short definition of the two here. Properties are literally descriptive adjectives that tell you about a bean. Events are functions that the bean initiates in response to some action. If you have worked with AWT or Swing at all, then you have already had some experience using events.

You can alter a bean's internal information by manipulating its properties. Properties are characteristics that define a bean's appearance and behavior. These properties can also be changed at design time. Bean Builder tools use the previously described introspection methodology to find out about a bean's properties and expose those properties for manipulation.

Beans utilize events to communicate with other beans. A bean that wants to receive events registers its interest with the bean that fires the event. A bean that receives events is called a *receiver bean*. Beans that initiate events for other beans to receive are called *source beans*. Bean Builder tools can examine a bean and determine which events that bean can initiate (send) and which events it can receive. A single bean can be both a source and a receiver of events. In fact, it is common for a bean to serve as both a source of events for other beans and a receiver of events produced by other beans. Events will be covered in detail in Chapter 3 "Events and Properties."

Persistence is the process that enables a bean to save and restore its state. After you have changed a bean's properties, you may wish to save the state of the bean so that you can restore that bean and its properties the next time you use that bean. JavaBeans uses Java object serialization to support persistence. This topic will be discussed in much greater depth in Chapter 4 "JavaBean Persistence."

Bean Builder Tools

The primary purpose of beans is to enable the visual construction of applications. If you have previously used RAD tools, such as Delphi or Visual Basic, then you have already used a visual application tool. These tools are referred to as visual application builders, or *builder tools* for short. Usually, these tools are GUI (Graphical User Interface) applications, although it is possible to create a non-GUI builder tool. There is usually a palette of components available called a toolbox from which a program designer can drag items and place them on a client window or form.

One of the most popular tools for developing Java applications is JBuilder from Borland. This tool provides you with a very rich set of development tools for creating Java applications. Wizards within JBuilder take care of many of the details of JavaBean development and packaging. We will look briefly at JBuilder in Chapter 2 and use it extensively in Chapter 3 and in subsequent chapters.

Using the BeanBox

Next we will discuss the use of the BeanBox and the various bean operations. The beans/BeanBox directory contains Windows (run.bat) and Unix (run.sh) scripts that start the BeanBox. You can use either of these commands to start the BeanBox. If you are using any version of Windows, then start run.bat (either from a command prompt or from Window's Explorer). If you are using Unix, then start run.sh from your favorite shell.

We will use some of the sample beans that come with the BeanBox to show you how to use beans. In the next chapter, I will show you how to create your own JavaBeans. Please recall that if you do not have the Sun Standard Java Development Kit installed on your PC, you will not be able to use the BeanBox.

When you first start, the BeanBox displays three separate windows: the Tool-Box, the BeanBox window, and the Properties window. The ToolBox contains the beans available for use by the BeanBox. It initially contains the sample beans that ship with the bean development kit, but later it will contain the beans we create. In order to use a bean, you select it from the ToolBox and drop it on the BeanBox window. The BeanBox window is the area where you visually connect beans together. You can think of this window as a JavaBean workspace. You use this workspace to define how beans appear and interact with other beans. You may be interested to know that the BeanBox window itself is an instance of a BeanBox bean. You select among beans in the BeanBox window simply by clicking on the bean. The Properties sheet displays the properties for the bean currently selected within the BeanBox window. If you place another bean in the BeanBox window, the properties sheet will display that bean's properties.

Let's work with two of the existing beans so you can get a feel for how the BeanBox works. After we have done that, I will give you a more detailed look at the various components of the BeanBox.

Using the following example explicitly, you will be able to see how to use the BeanBox to manipulate JavaBeans. This tutorial is rather easy to follow, but it gives you a good first look at JavaBeans.

Step 1:

Start the BeanBox. This is accomplished by going to the beans/BeanBox directory and running either run.sh (a BASH shell script for Unix) or run.bat (a batch file for Microsoft operating systems). If you are using Windows, you should do this from the DOS shell (Win 95/98) or the command prompt (Win NT/2000/XP).

Step 2:

Locate the ToolBox. It will be displayed vertically on the left-hand side of the screen. Place your mouse over the Juggler bean in the BeanBox. Click once on this bean with your left mouse button.

Step 3:

Move the mouse into the canvas area and draw out a rectangle shape. When you let go of the mouse, you will see the juggler animated in the canvas window:

Step 4:

Now place your mouse over the OurButton bean in the BeanBox. This should be the third bean in the ToolBox. Then simply draw a small rectangle on the canvas above the Juggler bean.

Step 5:

Repeat the process in Step 4 to create a second button. Your canvas should now look like this:

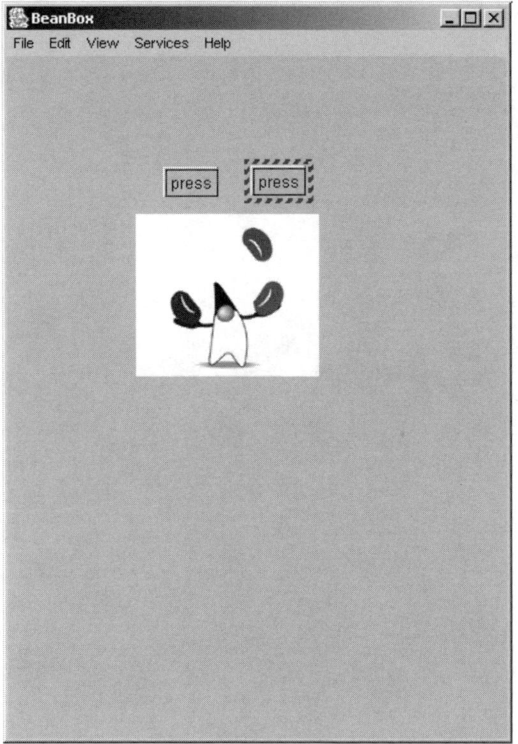

Step 6:

Now we are going to set a few properties of the two buttons. Note that when a button is highlighted (has focus) its properties are displayed in the Properties window. Change the caption property of one button to read "Start" and the other to read "Stop."

Step 7:

Now for the really exciting part about beans. We are going to connect the events of the buttons to the events of the juggler. Click once on the Start button and then go to the drop-down menu at the top of the canvas. Select Edit ▸ Events ▸ Action ▸ Action Performed. When you do this, a red line will appear. Drag your mouse into the Juggler bean and click.

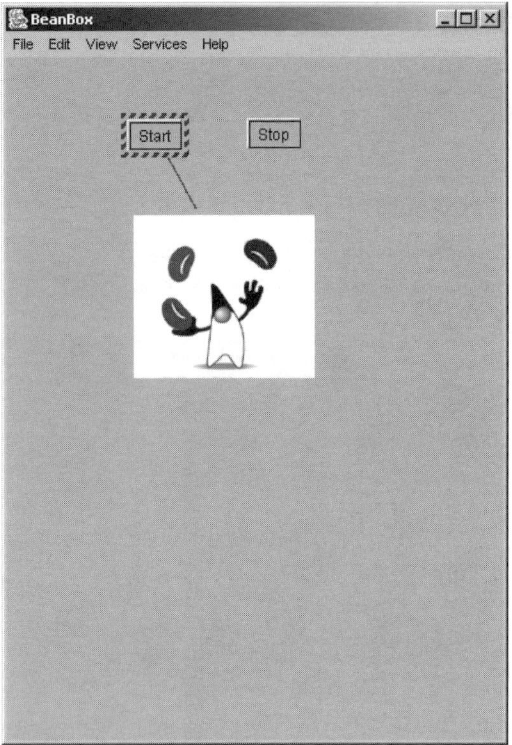

A dialog box will appear where you will select which juggler event you wish to connect to. Select startJuggling.

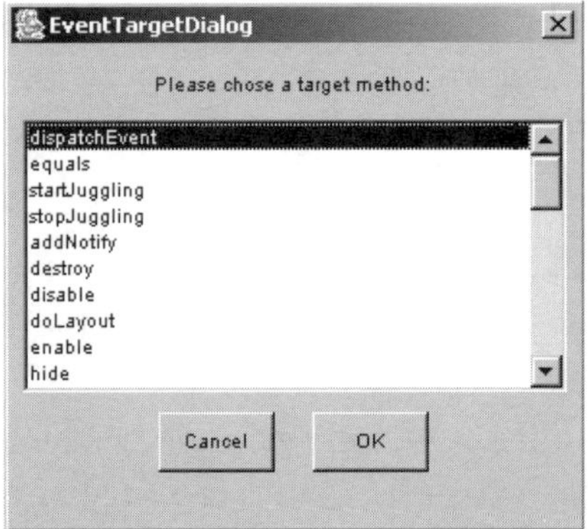

Now your start button action event is directly linked to the juggler's start juggling event.

Step 8:

The next step is to map the Stop button. Again, click once on the Stop button, and then choose Edit ▸ Events ▸ Action ▸ Action Performed. Drag your mouse into the Juggler bean and click once. You will again be presented with a dialog box; this time choose stopJuggling.

Now if you click on the stopJuggling button, the Juggler bean stops juggling. To start it up again, just click on the startJuggling button. What you have just witnessed is the beauty of bean development. You can connect events in one bean to events in another. By linking beans in this manner, you can create basic applications quickly and easily, without writing any code.

This rather simple example illustrates several points about bean development, the first being that once a bean is created, it can be utilized with little or no actual programming. In the preceding example, you did not write a single line of code. This example also shows you how easy it is to manipulate JavaBeans with an appropriate Bean Builder tool. You were able to literally drag one event in one bean to an event in another bean and cause the two events to be connected. The final lesson you should learn from this example is that it is indeed possible to create entire applications by simply assembling existing beans. In fact, you just did that!

It has been my experience, however, that a single example is rarely enough to ensure that a person has mastered a topic. With that in mind, let's take a look at another example:

Step 1:

Select File ▸ Clear from the drop-down menu to clear the canvas. This will clear the current content of the workspace and prepare the BeanBox to work with a new JavaBean.

Step 2:

Place one instance of the Molecule bean on the canvas and one instance of the TickTock bean. Recall that you do this by clicking once with your left mouse button on the bean you want in the ToolBox, and then use the mouse to "draw" out the area you wish the bean to occupy on the canvas.

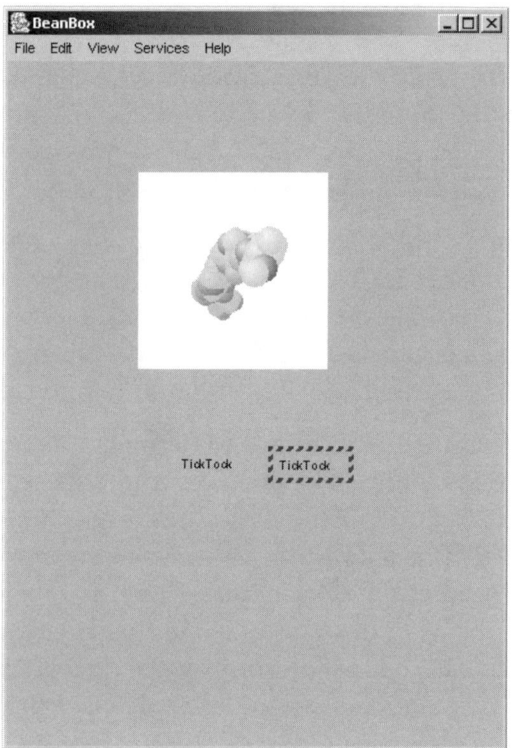

Step 3:

With the TickTock bean selected, go to the drop-down menu and select Edit ▸ Events ▸ Property Changed ▸ Property Changed and drag the resulting red line into the molecule box. When the Properties window pops up, select Rotate about the x axis. You will now see the molecule slowly rotating along the x-axis.

You can change the speed at which it rotates by changing the interval property of the TickTock bean. You can also add a second TickTock bean and set it to cause the molecule to rotate around the y-axis. This example is interesting for several reasons. The first is that it provides yet another example of the bean principles I already mentioned and showed you in the first example, but it is also interesting in that this bean actually has some practical use. It would not be a difficult task to make a collection of bean-based applications that would allow an introductory chemistry student to view a variety of molecules and rotate them in three dimensions. Again, recall that such an application could be created totally from manipulating existing beans, without writing any code!

These two simple examples should illustrate to you the basics of how to utilize the BeanBox and how to use existing beans. If you still don't feel completely comfortable with the BeanBox, I encourage you to take some time to experiment before you continue with the rest of this chapter. You may wish to simply open the BeanBox and place different beans on the canvas, experimenting with how to manipulate and connect them. However, if you are ready to continue, I would like to give you a more detailed look at the various options in the drop-down menu and the various windows the BeanBox provides you with:

Drop-down Menu	Purpose
File	
Save	This allows you to save the work you currently have on the canvas.
Serialize Component	This allows you to save the current property settings via serialization (more detail on that later in this book).
Make Applet	This allows you to create an applet from your bean configuration.
Load	This will allow you to load a bean.
Load Jar	This allows you to load a Java Archive file (JAR).
Print	This will print the current screen.
Clear	This option clears all work from the canvas.
Exit	This option exits the BeanBox.

Drop-down Menu	Purpose
Edit	
Cut	This menu option is for cutting the contents of the canvas and placing them on the system clipboard.
Copy	This option allows you to copy the contents of the canvas to the clipboard.
Paste	This allows you to paste from the clipboard.
Report	This causes a verbose report of everything that is occurring to appear in the command line window.
Events	This allows you to select an event from the bean that currently has focus.
Bind Property	This lets you bind a property of one bean to a property of another.
View	
Disable Design Mode	This will hide all of the design tools, leaving just the canvas. Note that once you select this, its caption will change to "View Design Mode."
Hide Invisible Beans	This will hide any invisible beans on the canvas. Note that once you select this, its caption will change to "View Invisible Beans."
Help	
About	This will give you information about the version of the BDK that you are using.
Documentation	This will point you to the web site for current BDK documentation.

This is simply a quick summary of the different drop-down menu items available. I am sure that most of them are relatively self-evident to you. However, one simple method for becoming familiar with the various options in the BeanBox is to simply experiment. I recommend that you take some time, before you move on to the next chapter, to try out the various beans available in the ToolBox and try out the various drop-down menu commands. Take the time to make certain that you are quite comfortable with the

BeanBox, since it will be an important tool in your JavaBean development. Now that I have given you a basic overview of the drop-down menu options available to you in the BeanBox, let's look at the various BeanBox windows and what they do.

The first, and most obvious, area you have is the canvas or workspace. It looks like the image you see here:

The workspace is the area on which you place beans and connect bean events. It is here that the real "action" of bean development takes place. The canvas is simply a blank space that you can use to place beans and work with them. If you have ever used Microsoft Windows Paint or Adobe Photoshop, this workspace looks very much like the canvas area in both of those graphics software packages, and for good reason, since it serves a similar purpose.

Next you have the ToolBox. It will look like this image:

The ToolBox contains the various beans that you have to work with. The JavaBean Development Kit ships with 16 different beans ready for you to use. As you create your own JavaBeans (starting in Chapter 2), I will show you how to add them to the ToolBox. Later in this chapter, I will discuss with you the use and features of most of these beans. I also have another example using yet another one of these beans.

Then you have the Properties window. This window should look like the image you see here:

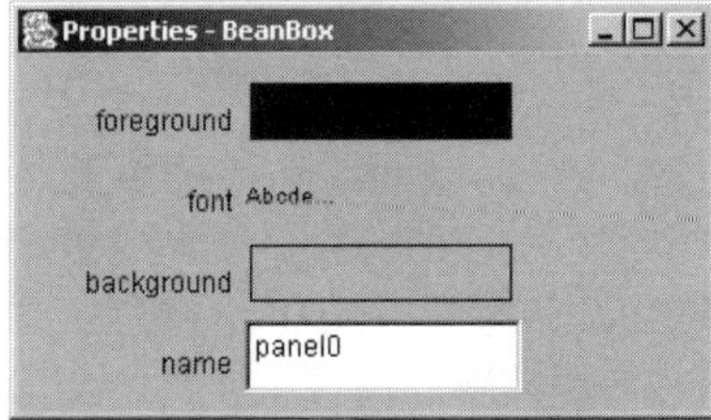

Each bean has different properties and, therefore, the Properties window will display different values for each bean. In this window, you can change the properties of any given bean and you will see the change take place immediately. For example, the Juggler bean has a property called "animation rate." This property determines how fast the juggler will juggle. By default, this property is set to 125. The lower the number, the faster he juggles. To verify this, you might try resetting that property, first to 35 and then up to 250, and watch the effect.

Finally, you have the Method Tracer window, which looks like the image you see here:

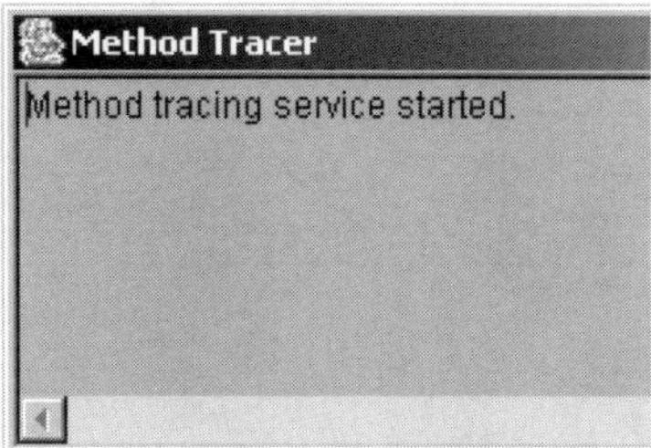

This window provides a tracing of what methods are actually being called. This can be quite useful if you are having problems with your bean.

Using the BeanBox you can easily work with beans, manipulate their properties, and connect their events. You will need to become familiar with the various windows and drop-down menus. It may also be useful for you to gain a basic understanding of the sample beans provided with the bean development kit. This may give you some insight into what types of functionality can be incorporated into a JavaBean. The following table summarizes some of the beans, which ship with the BDK 1.1:

Bean	Description
BlueButton	This creates a blue button that users can click.
ExplicitButton	This also creates a button; however, the background is simply gray.
OurButton	This creates a button very similar to the Explicit Button, but it has more property options you can set.
OrangeButton	This is exactly like the blue button, except it is orange.
Juggler	This displays a juggler who is juggling large coffee beans.

Bean	Description
TickTock	This is a timer that will count off seconds.
Voter	This displays a "Yes" or "No."
Molecule	This displays a particular organic molecule that can be rotated in three dimensions.
QuoteMonitor	This interesting little bean can display the current quote for a given stock.
JDBC SELECT	This bean gives you access to a database.
SorterBean	This bean sorts information according to some preset algorithm, such as Bubble Sort.

Many of these beans function best in conjunction with other beans, as we have already seen in two separate examples.

More JavaBean Concepts

Individual JavaBeans will certainly vary in functionality. However, they must have certain common defining features. These features are required in order to adhere to the JavaBean development standards that have been established by Sun Microsystems. These common characteristics, shared by all JavaBeans, are summarized here:

- Support for introspection, thereby allowing a builder tool to analyze a bean's methods, events, and properties. All JavaBeans must provide support for introspection. Without this, they will not be usable by any builder tools or other beans.

- Support for customization, allowing a user to alter the appearance and behavior of a bean. This is usually accomplished via properties. If your JavaBean has no properties to manipulate, it might still technically be a JavaBean, but it would be completely useless.

- Support for events allowing beans to initiate events, receive events, and inform builder tools about the events they can initiate and receive. Without event procedures, a bean cannot communicate with a builder tool or other beans. You already saw that simply linking bean events together can be a very useful tool.

- Support for properties, allowing beans to be manipulated programmatically, as well as to support the customization mentioned above.

- Support for persistence, allowing beans that have been customized in an application builder to have their state saved and restored. Often, persistence is implemented via an application builder's save command. The bean tool's load menu command is used to restore any work that has gone into constructing an application. Persistence will be discussed in more depth in Chapter 4. Right now, you merely need to remember that all beans support persistence.

Although JavaBeans are usually manipulated primarily with builder tools, this is not the only way to manipulate a JavaBean. JavaBeans can be manually manipulated by text tools through programmatic interfaces. All key APIs, including support for events, properties, and persistence, have been designed to be easily read and understood by human programmers as well as by builder tools. However, this is not the usual practice. JavaBean developers almost always use some development tool such as the Bean Builder or JBuilder to create, connect, and use JavaBeans. The graphical interfaces of these tools are more appropriate for JavaBeans, since the beans themselves are, in most cases, graphical objects.

Some may wonder why anyone would use a bean over a standard Java class file. The strongest argument for a bean over a class is that beans support introspection. That is, they allow the development environment to analyze the bean, determine its properties and methods, and manipulate the bean at design time instead of at run time. However, there are many other reasons to utilize JavaBeans. Unlike standard classes, they can be used outside of a programming environment. What I mean by that is that it is possible to utilize and link beans without doing any actual programming.

A new way to use beans is to create a bridge between Java and ActiveX. Several software companies are working on methods to quickly convert ActiveX controls to JavaBeans (IBM's Visual Age, for example). This allows Java developers to make use of ActiveX component functionality in a Java environment. To date, Microsoft has not provided any reverse functionality that would allow an ActiveX component to use Java or JavaBeans.

JBuilder and Beans

The focus of this book is to show you how to utilize JavaBeans and Enterprise JavaBeans using Borland's JBuilder. This example, and indeed most of those in this book, focus on JBuilder version 7.0. However, most of the techniques you will encounter work equally well in JBuilder 5.0 and 6.0. There are several reasons for this slant on bean development. The first is that JBuilder is the most powerful and most popular Java development tool on the market today. The second is that bean development is much easier and more efficient using JBuilder. I will demonstrate how to do the various tasks without JBuilder; however, you will find that using JBuilder makes virtually any Java task simpler and less prone to error.

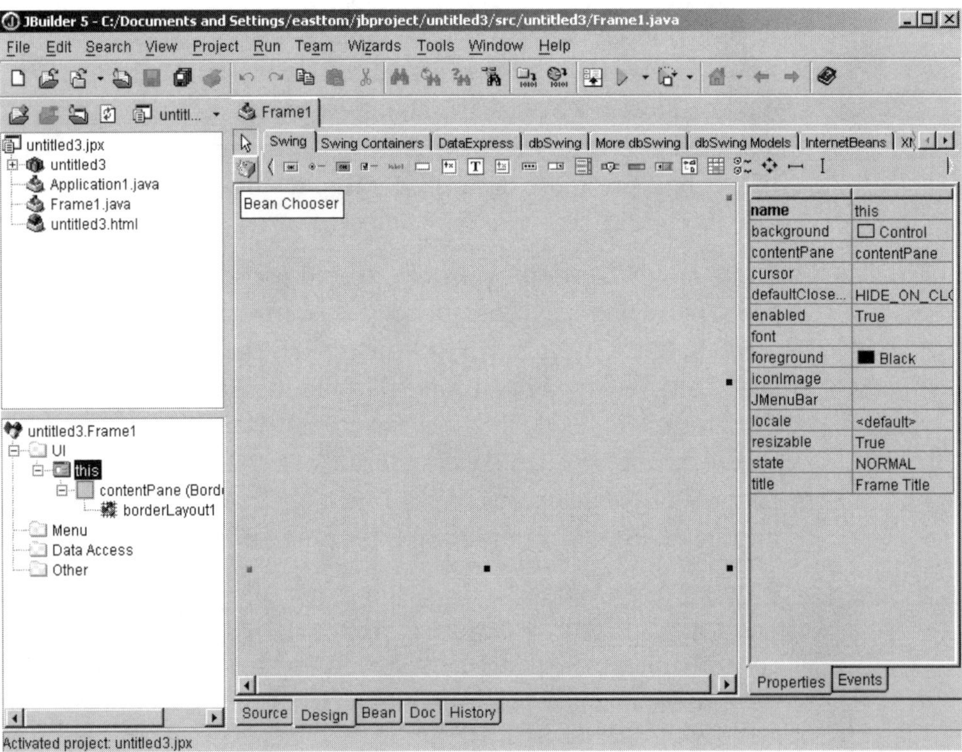

Borland's JBuilder comes with a variety of tools for creating and using beans. We will deal with most of these later in this book. Right now, I would like to show you how to utilize existing beans in any JBuilder project. It is also interesting to note that JBuilder ships with quite a few more beans than does the standard Sun JavaBean Development Kit. If you open any JBuilder project (either new projects or an existing one) and select the Design tab, you will notice an icon in the upper left-hand corner of the screen. This is the Bean Chooser icon and allows you to select from the available JavaBeans.

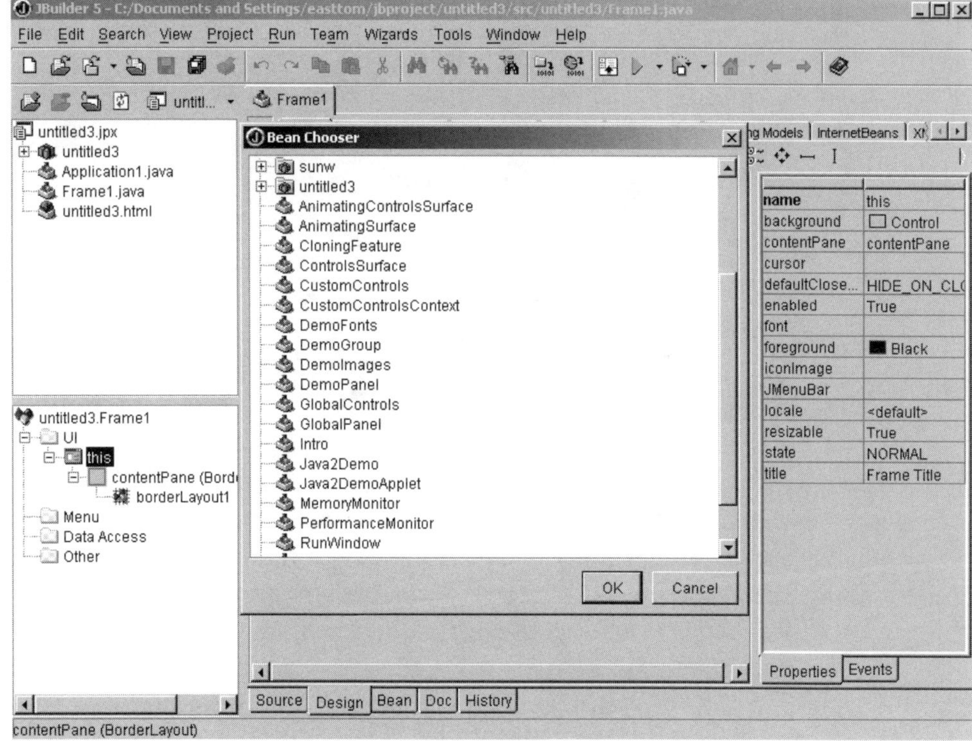

After you have selected any of the available beans, you will be returned to the main design screen where your mouse pointer will now be a simple cross hair. You can then draw that bean onto the design surface. If you happen to draw your bean in a place that you later decide is inappropriate, don't worry — you can simply drag it to another place.

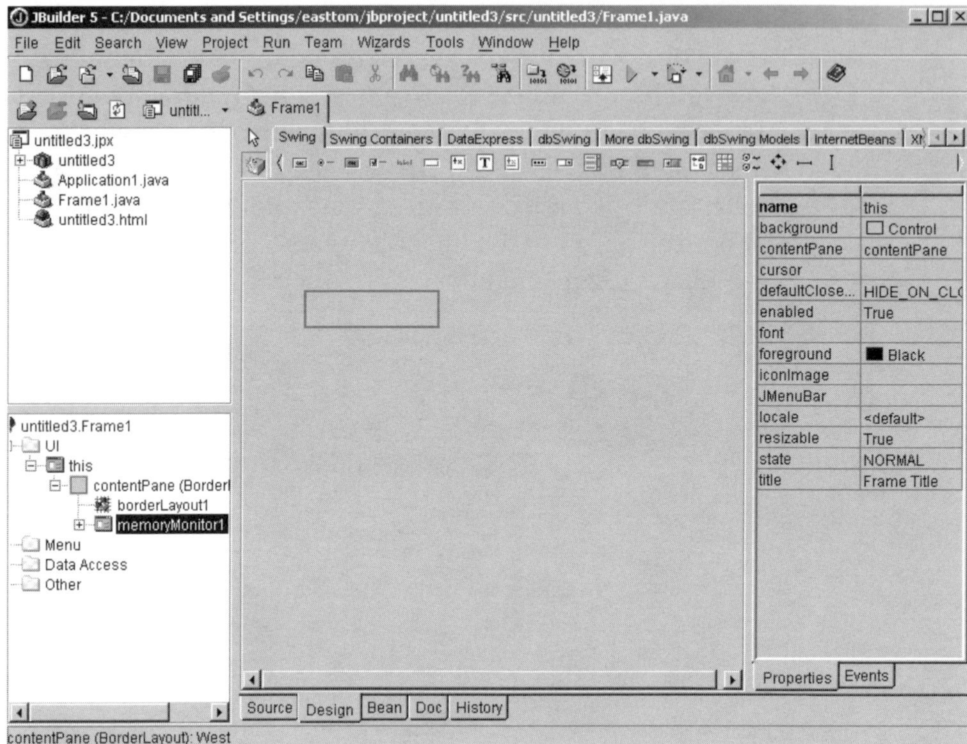

Using this tool, you can add JavaBeans to any of your projects. Earlier in this chapter, I showed you how to link one bean to another, which is a useful application of JavaBeans. However, the real utility of JavaBeans becomes clear when you consider their use as components inside larger applications. You can create a JavaBean that encapsulates a set of functions and then adds that functionality to any Java project you like. This is the real goal of JavaBeans in particular and object-oriented programming in general — code reusability. You will also find a variety of JavaBeans on the Internet, either as shareware or commercial products, which you can download and use in your own applications. The core concept of object-oriented programming is to make code that is easily portable and reusable in a variety of different application settings. JavaBeans takes this concept to a new level.

Summary

This chapter introduced you to the concept of JavaBeans. It also gave you your first look at the bean development kit. You saw how to connect the events of one bean to the events of another bean. This patching together of beans is the very heart of the JavaBean component architecture. I also presented you with a few examples of using beans and linking them together. With this information, you should have a basic understanding of how JavaBeans work, and you should be prepared to move on to Chapter 2 to begin creating your own beans.

This chapter is the foundation for bean development in general and our later excursions into Enterprise JavaBean development. You can find even more resources in Appendix A that will continue your exploration of JavaBeans. I also recommend, if you are using Borland JBuilder, that you avail yourself of the help file that is replete with example code.

Terms

JavaBean – A self-contained Java object that conforms to the JavaBean specification.

RAD – Rapid Application Development tool. Any tool used to ease software development by providing a graphical interface within which to program.

Builder Tool – Any tool which enables the bean developer to manipulate existing JavaBeans and create new JavaBeans.

JDK – Java Development Kit. The freely downloadable Java compiler and tools available from Sun Microsystems.

BDK – Bean Development Kit. The freely downloadable JavaBean Development Kit, complete with a builder tool, available from Sun Microsystems.

API – Application Programming Interface. A set of functions in one object that are exposed to the external environment and which a programmer can utilize.

GUI – Graphical User Interface.

Review Questions

1. What is the process whereby a JavaBean can reveal information about itself?

2. How do you start the BeanBox in a Microsoft Windows operating system?

3. What does the Serialize Component drop-down menu option do?

4. What is persistence?

5. Can standard JavaBeans be deployed as a stand-alone product?

6. How do beans expose their features?

7. How do you alter a bean's internal information?

8. What class provides a standard way for bean development tools to learn about a bean?

9. What is a JAR?

10. How do you remove all the beans from the canvas?

Chapter 2

Creating Your Own Beans

Introduction

The previous chapter was simply an introduction to JavaBeans. Essentially, it was meant to get you acclimated to this subject area by introducing you to the essential concepts behind JavaBeans. I also demonstrated how to use bean tools to manipulate existing beans. At this point, you should be comfortable with the essential features of JavaBeans and understand how to use existing JavaBeans. Now it is time to take the next step in your journey into the world of JavaBeans. This chapter will show you how to create your own JavaBeans and how to add them to the BeanBox. You will then be able to manipulate those beans in the same ways that you manipulated the standard beans that ship with your bean development tool.

In this chapter, you will learn how to:

- Create a simple bean
- Compile and save the bean into a Java Archive (JAR) file
- Load the bean into the bean tool's ToolBox

- Place an instance of a bean onto the BeanBox

- Inspect the bean's properties, methods, and events

It is important for you to keep in mind the essential requirements and the basic structure of a JavaBean. This basic knowledge is critical in order for you to successfully create your own beans. Please ensure that you are quite comfortable with the material in Chapter 1 before proceeding.

Using the BDK

In order to work with JavaBeans, you will need the JavaBean Development Kit, or BDK. This can be downloaded, free of charge, from http://java.sun .com/products/javabeans/software/bdk_download.html. For this kit to work you will also need the Java Development Kit, or JDK. It can be downloaded, for free, from http://java.sun.com/products/jdk/1.1/index.html.

> **Note:** If your JavaBean Development Kit does not work properly, it is most likely that you have more than one version of the JDK on your machine and there is some conflict. This sometimes happens with users of IBM's Visual Age or Borland's JBuilder, since those products also install a version of the JDK. This is due to the fact that the JavaBean Development Kit may not be able to determine which of the Java Virtual Machines (JVMs) on your machine to use. You may have to either alter your system class path settings or uninstall one of your JVMs. If you are using JBuilder or any other Java development tool, then you do not need to download the JDK to your machine. It is already there.

Of course, you could use other Bean Builder tools to create your own JavaBeans, but since the Sun Microsystems BDK is a free download, and thus available to all readers, we will start our study of bean development with the BDK. Later in this chapter, I will show you how to create JavaBeans using JBuilder. While JBuilder tools are not free of charge, they are much easier to use, and you can get a free trial version from the Borland web site: http://www.borland.com/jbuilder/offers/.

Basics of Bean Creation

For the most part, creating a JavaBean is not much different from creating a standard Java class. All the basic requirements of any Java class must still be met. In case you are a bit rusty on your Java development, let me summarize the main requirements for all Java programs:

- All Java source files have three sections. These are package declaration, import statements, and class declarations. You first declare the package name for the source file you are creating. Then you import any packages you will need to use in your code. Finally, you define your various classes. It is not required that the first class defined be the main class of the source file. However, it is quite common to see code written this way, and I recommend this approach for the sake of clarity. You will also see some code, occasionally, written without the package declaration line. However, if you do this, then your source file cannot be part of a package and therefore cannot be imported into another application.

- Your main class must have the same name as your source file. If the file is named mybean.java, then the main class must be named mybean. It is customary, though not required, that the class name have the first letter capitalized. I must confess that this is one convention I occasionally violate, but it is a very widely used convention. Again, however, this is just a convention, not a requirement.

- Remember your exception handling. All checked errors must have exception handling. My own personal feeling is that you cannot have too much exception handling.

As you can see, JavaBeans have a lot in common with standard Java programs. In fact, all Java classes share certain common structural similarities. However, there are certain development specifications that are required in order to make a class communicate with beans and bean containers (a prerequisite for that class being a JavaBean). These particular specifications are unique to JavaBeans. In fact, it is these specifications that make a bean a bean instead of just a normal class. In order to create a JavaBean, your code must adhere to these specifications. Like all Java specifications, these specifications have been established by Sun Microsystems, and they are quite clearly defined. I will cover the main points in this chapter. However, if you want a more in-depth look at the JavaBeans API, then I recommend you consult the Sun Microsystems documentation. You will find links to that documentation, as well as other resources, in Appendix A.

The reason that beans can communicate with each other and Bean Builder tools can understand and manipulate beans is that all JavaBeans adhere to these specific standards. These specifications are primarily concerned with how the bean will expose its interfaces to the external world. The main areas of JavaBean development that the specification is concerned with are class names, constructors, and introspection. The next few sections will be concerned with providing details on the JavaBean specifications. As you read these sections, keep in mind that not all of the specifications are absolute requirements. Some are merely recommended. However, if you wish for your JavaBean code to be readily understood by other developers, it would be wise to follow all of the specifications. You may also wish to consider the specifications that are merely "recommended," as these are recommended by the creators of JavaBeans. That should be sufficient reasoning for you to strongly consider following those suggestions.

Class Naming Conventions

One of the specifications that you will need to be cognizant of when creating your own JavaBeans is that of naming conventions. There are certain rules that bean developers follow when selecting the names for the classes that make up the bean. You should notice that, in most cases, bean classes include the word "Bean" in their name. Examples would include UserBean, JugglerBean, DataAccessBean, etc. This particular naming convention is not required in order for beans to function; however, it does make your code more readable. While the JavaBean API specification does not absolutely require you to name your beans in this fashion, using the industry standard naming conventions will enhance your bean's readability and maintainability. The more experienced reader will immediately see the value in any technique that increases code maintainability. If you are a novice programmer, then please take my word for it: Code maintainability is a valued prize sought after by all experienced programmers. Follow any specification that furthers that goal. It is the Holy Grail of software development!

Besides the aforementioned naming convention, JavaBeans follow the same class naming rules as any other Java class. They must start with an alphabetic character, contain only alphanumeric and underscore characters, and be case-sensitive. You cannot use any other characters (such as #, $, &, etc.). Also, like other Java classes, it is a common practice to start the name of a bean class with a capital letter. This naming convention is also not a requirement, but it is common throughout the Java community. If you want your code to be more easily read by other Java programmers, this is one more convention that will further that goal.

I must remind you that these naming conventions are not absolute requirements. You are certainly free to create beans that do not follow any of these naming conventions. However, this would make your bean code quite difficult to follow. Code that is hard to read is also code that is hard to maintain. Recall the supreme importance of maintainable code. If you fail to follow any of the standard naming conventions, you will probably expose yourself to the ire of your colleagues!

Required Bean Conventions

The following JavaBean conventions are absolutely vital to the development of JavaBeans. This is because they allow a bean container to analyze a Java class file and interpret its methods and properties, designating the class as a bean. A bean container is simply any tool that is able to contain and utilize a JavaBean. This would include bean development tools such as the BeanBox, as well as development tools such as JBuilder. These conventions proscribe the rules for defining a bean's constructor, methods, and properties. If you do not follow these conventions, a bean container will not recognize your product as a bean. Before you attempt to create any bean, make certain that you are following these conventions.

The Bean Constructor

One of the key rules of JavaBean development is that you must have a constructor that takes no arguments. The Bean Builder tool will use this constructor when you place an instance of the bean on the canvas. If you think about this, it makes perfect sense. The bean tool won't pass any argument to the bean when it instantiates it, so the class must have a no-arguments constructor. Every Java class has a constructor method that is used to create instances of that class. If a class does not explicitly specify any constructors, a default zero-argument constructor is assumed. Because of this default constructor rule, the following Java class is perfectly valid and technically satisfies the bean conventions:

```
public class SampleBean
{
}
```

This bean has no properties or methods and cannot do anything useful, but it still technically fulfills the no-arguments constructor requirement for a JavaBean. Remember that Java provides a default no-argument constructor; therefore, this class has a no-argument constructor. Let's look at a better example of a class suitable for bean usage. Note that it has a zero-argument constructor that sets the time to the minute it is instantiated.

```
import java.util.*;
public class nowBean
{
  private int hours;
  private int minutes;
  public nowBean()
  {
    Date now = new Date();
    this.hours = now.getHours();
    this.minutes = now.getMinutes();
  }
}
```

Note that the constructor is used to initialize the bean's instance variables hours and minutes to hold the current time at instantiation. Of course, this class is still not a bean, as it does not implement all of the necessary interfaces required by the JavaBean API. But this class does have the necessary constructor so that it could be used as a bean. Unlike the previous example, this class's constructor actually does something useful. You can see that each example I show you takes you, step by step, closer to the goal of creating your own JavaBean.

Introspection and Reflection

It is imperative that when your bean is running, the bean container can retrieve information about your bean's properties, events, and methods. If it cannot, then your bean cannot be accessed or manipulated and is hence completely useless. The process whereby this is accomplished is called introspection. Introspection is the process whereby a bean can learn about its own methods and properties and then expose those methods and properties to the external world. If you consider the everyday use of the word "introspection," its use in the context of JavaBeans should be abundantly clear to you.

With some component architectures (such as COM and CORBA), there is a separate interface definition language, which is independent of the programming language being used. Sun Microsystems wanted to ensure that all bean development is completely done in Java. For this reason, there is no separate interface definition language. All of a JavaBean's behavior is completely specifiable directly in Java. This is where introspection comes in. It handles the functionality that is done by interface definition languages in other component architectures (such as CORBA, COM, and DCOM).

The purpose of JavaBeans is to have a completely Java-based component architecture that is easy to use. However, it is also important that developers have total and precise control over what methods, events, and properties are exposed and how they are exposed. A low-level mechanism termed "reflection" is used to examine the methods supported by a target bean and determine what properties, events, and methods that bean supports. Remember that the only way any information can be determined about a bean's inner workings is by examining its public methods. Even the properties are actually public methods that provide access to instance variables of the bean.

If a bean developer provides a BeanInfo class describing the bean, then this BeanInfo class will be used to programmatically discover the bean's behavior.

To allow bean containers to analyze beans, an Introspector class is provided. This class understands the various design patterns and standard interfaces and provides a uniform way of introspecting on different beans.

Reflection is a process that allows the bean container to examine any class at run time to determine its set of properties. The bean container determines what properties a bean supports by analyzing its public methods for the presence of property access methods. These property access methods must, of course, meet certain specific criteria. These criteria are defined by the JavaBeans API. For a property to exist, its bean class must define an access method to return the value of the property, change the value of the property, or both. It is the presence of the specially named access methods that determines a bean class's properties. In essence, the access methods that provide a means for interacting with a bean's private member variables are the bean's properties.

To use an analogy, consider an automobile. It has a variety of private variables. These are items that you cannot directly access (well, at least not without a great deal of effort and some mechanical knowledge). One such private member variable of the car class would be fuel level. You cannot directly reach into the gas tank and alter the fuel level. However, there are access methods that allow you to manipulate the fuel level. One such method is the "put gas in tank" method. When you deposit fuel into the provided orifice, it is placed in the tank for you. You can think of the fuel you put in as a parameter you pass to the access property. If there is a filter preventing debris from being passed to your gas tank, you can think of that as data validation occurring in the property method. Hopefully, this analogy will help clarify the use of properties/access methods.

Design Patterns

In the previous section, I mentioned design patterns. The term "design pattern" simply refers to conventional names and type signatures for sets of methods and interfaces that are used for standard purposes. For example, consider the use of getX and setX methods used to retrieve and set the values of a property X. These are standard access methods/properties that all JavaBeans use to expose their instance variables. Get methods retrieve the current value of a given member variable. Set methods change that value. In the previously used gas tank analogy, the "put gas in tank" method would be more aptly named setGas.

Using these standardized design patterns serves two valuable purposes. First, they are a useful documentation aid for programmers. By allowing a programmer to quickly identify particular methods that fit standard design patterns, the developer can more quickly assimilate and use new classes. Secondly, developers can write tools and libraries that recognize design patterns and use them to analyze and understand components. Without these standardized design patterns, bean containers would not be able to discover a bean's properties, methods, and events. Finally, as with any convention, it will make your code more readable and hence more easily maintained.

Remember that in all the public interfaces of a bean, it is important to follow the JavaBean design patterns. However, within JavaBeans, the use of method and type names that match design patterns is optional. If you are prepared to explicitly specify your bean's properties, methods, and events using the BeanInfo interface, you can call their methods and types anything you prefer. However, these methods and types will still have to match the required type signatures, as this is essential to their operation. In short, it's possible to bend the design patterns, but doing so requires more work from you. I recommend you simply follow the design patterns. I will introduce you to specific design patterns as we encounter them. You have already seen the pattern for get and set properties.

Specifying a Bean's Properties

A bean's properties are defined simply by creating the appropriate access methods for them. Access methods are used to either retrieve a property's value or make changes to it. A method used to retrieve a property's value is called a get method, while a method that modifies its value is called a set method. This terminology is not unique to JavaBeans. It is the standard method for accessing properties in any object-oriented language. Programmers who use Visual Basic or C++ to write classes should be well acquainted with get and set methods. Together, these methods are referred to as *access methods*.

They provide access to values stored in the bean's private member variables. There should not be any public variables in your bean. All member variables should only be accessible using access methods.

To define properties for a bean, simply create a public method with the name of the property you wish to define prefixed with the word get or set, as appropriate. A get method should return the appropriate data type, while the corresponding set method should accept one argument of the appropriate type and set the property. Set methods usually have a void return type. It is the get or set prefix that allows Java to determine that you are defining a property. The format for property access methods, then, is as follows:

```
public void setPropertyName(PropertyType value);
public PropertyType getPropertyName();
```

For example, to define a property called age, which can be used to store a numeric value representing a person's age and is both readable and writeable, I would need to create the following methods:

```
public void setAge(Int age)
{
}
public String getAge()
{
}
```

A good way to illustrate this topic is to return to the previous example and add some property access methods. I will add a couple of properties to nowBean, called hours and minutes, that will allow us to reference the current time in the page. For Java to recognize these properties, they will have to follow the get method formats defined by the JavaBean's design patterns. These methods should look like this:

```
public int getHours()
{
}
public int getMinutes()
{
{
```

Notice that I created two get methods without any associated set methods. When this is done, the properties are read only. The person using the bean can retrieve values but cannot set them. Given that this bean is meant to return the current time, the read-only methods make perfect sense.

In the constructor, I will store the current time's hours and minutes in instance variables. I can have our properties reference these variables and return their value.

```java
Import java.util.*;
public class nowBean
{
  private int hours;
  private int minutes;
  public nowBean()
  {
    Date now = new Date();
    this.hours = now.getHours();
    this.minutes = now.getMinutes();
  }

  public int getHours()
  {
    return hours;
  }
  public int getMinutes()
  {
    return minutes();
  }
}
```

The two methods simply return the appropriate values as stored in the instance variables. Since these methods meet the bean conventions for naming access methods, I have just defined two properties that I can access through any bean container. Remember that these are read-only properties. If you wish, you can create set properties and use the values that the user passes to you to change the time value in the now object.

Bean properties should not be confused with instance variables, even though instance variables are often mapped directly to property names. The properties are methods that allow you to access data that is stored in instance variables. However, the properties of a bean are not required to correspond directly with instance variables. You can think of the property as the public interface that allows you to interact with the instance variable. Of course, not all instance variables are mapped to properties. A bean's properties are defined by the method names themselves, not the variables or implementation behind them. This leaves the bean designer free to alter the inner workings of the bean without altering the interface and collection of properties exposed to users of the bean. However, I usually recommend that you use property names that are close to the names of the instance variables they map too. This makes reading your code much easier and will improve the maintainability of your JavaBean code.

Serialization

JavaBeans save information about themselves through a process known as *serialization*. This process allows the bean to save its current status to a file on the machine. That file can be read in the next time the bean is instantiated, and the information contained therein can be used to restore the bean to its previous state. I will discuss more about serialization in Chapter 4, "JavaBean Persistence." For the time being, it is important that you realize that JavaBeans use serialization to store dates concerning their state. In order to do this, the bean must implement the Serializable interface. All JavaBeans are required to implement the Serializable interface.

JAR Files and Manifest Files

JAR files were briefly mentioned in Chapter 1, but only a cursory definition was given. A JAR is a Java Archive file. It is a standard way to compress and package your files for distribution. A single JAR file can contain the files for a single JavaBean or multiple JavaBeans. In the JAR file, you can package all the files your JavaBean will need. This can include any or all of the following types of files:

- The compiled JavaBean(s)

- .txt and .html files that provide documentation for the bean

- Images

- Audio or video clips

- Any supporting .class files

The elements in a JAR file are compressed using an industry standard ZIP compression algorithm. You can even associate a digital signature with a JAR file. This is especially useful if distributing your JAR over the Internet. A digital signature identifies the creator of the JAR's contents and can be used to determine if anyone has altered the contents.

The first element in a JAR file is the manifest file. This file is simply a plain text file that contains information about the contents of the JAR file. It will also indicate which of the .class files are JavaBeans. The Sun JDK ships with a JAR utility and allows you to create and manage JAR files. It will be located in the same directory as the javac compiler and operates from the command line. The syntax is:

Jar *options files*

The files section is a list of files that you wish to include in the JAR file. The options tag represents any of the various command line parameter options you can use. The following table summarizes them:

Option	Description
c	Creates an archive file.
f	The first element in *files* is the name of the archive.
t	Tabulates the contents of the archive file.
m	The second element in *files* is the name of the manifest file.
v	Provides verbose output.
x	Extracts the files from the JAR.
M	Do not create a manifest file.

Here is an example of creating a JAR file:

Jar cfm c:\bdk\jars\myBean.jar myBean*.mft myBean*.class

This will create an archive file in which the first element (myBean) is the name of the archive, and the second element is the name of the manifest. It will include all files in c:\bdk\jars\myBean that have the .mft (manifest) or .class extensions.

In order to extract these files from the JAR, you would create a folder (in our case "myfolder"). Copy the JAR file to the new folder, and then execute the following command:

```
Jar xvf myBean.jar
```

A manifest file is simply a plain text file that shows the contents of the JAR. It lists <u>all</u> the files contained in a JAR. If you do not create your own manifest and do not use the M option when creating your JAR file, a manifest file will be created for you.

I have shown you the basic concepts underlying JavaBean development and the specifications that determine how a bean should be written. You should now have the requisite knowledge to move to the next step. Now it's time to actually write a bean. The following example will create a simple JavaBean. Follow the steps exactly, and you will create your first JavaBean! This bean does not do much, but it is a good first example of creating one.

Step 1:

Create a folder or directory on your machine that has the same name you will give the source file (in this case "myBean").

Step 2:

Inside that folder or directory, you will use a text editor to write the following code:

```
import java.awt.*;
import java.io.Serializable;
public class myBean extends Canvas implements Serializable
{
  //Constructor sets inherited properties
  public myBean()
  {
    setSize(50,50);
    setBackground(Color.blue);
  }
}
```

MyBean extends the java.awt.Canvas component. MyBean also implements the interface; therefore, it can save its current state. Furthermore, since it does not define a constructor, Java will give it a default no-arguments constructor. Therefore, it fulfills all the requirements for a JavaBean.

Before you start trying to compile JavaBeans and add them to your BeanBox tool, you must make sure the CLASSPATH environment variable is set to point to all needed .class (or .jar) files. The JDK Tool Reference Page provides complete CLASSPATH information for both Windows and Solaris platforms.

Step 3:

That is all that is needed to write the code for our bean. Now you must compile your JavaBean. You compile it as you would any standard Java source code file:

```
javac myBean.java
```

This will produce the class file myBean.class.

Step 4:

Now you will need to create a manifest file. Remember that a manifest file is really a template file that is used when creating a JAR; it describes the contents of the JAR. You can use any text editor to create a manifest file. I will call this one manifest.mft that contains the following text:

```
Name: myBean.class
Java-Bean: True
```

Create the JAR file. The JAR file will contain the manifest and the myBean class file:

```
jar cfm myBean.jar manifest.tmp myBean.class
```

Step 5:

Now go to the folder that has the BeanBox tool and start the BeanBox tool. You should then load the JAR file into the ToolBox. You accomplish this by selecting the File ▸ Load Jar menu item. This will bring up a file browser dialog box. Navigate to the myBean.jar location and select it. MyBean will now appear at the bottom of the ToolBox.

Note that when the BeanBox is started, all beans in JAR files in the beans/jars directory are automatically loaded into the ToolBox. Therefore, if you wish for your bean to be automatically loaded into the ToolBox, simply place it in the beans/jars folder.

Place an instance of myBean onto the canvas. The myBean properties will appear in the Properties sheet. You can resize myBean by dragging a corner. You will see the cursor change to a right angle when over a corner. You can also reposition myBean on the canvas simply by dragging on any non-corner portion of the hatched border. You will see the cursor change to crossed arrows when in position to move the bean. That's all there is to it. You have just created your first bean!

This example was not particularly exciting, but it did illustrate the basics of creating a JavaBean. Let's move on to a more useful example, so you can get a second look at the process of creating a JavaBean. In this example, you will create a bean that checks the time of day and provides appropriate greetings.

Step 1:

Create a folder or directory on your machine that has the same name you will give the source file (in this case "greetingBean").

Step 2:

Inside that folder or directory, you will use a text editor to write the following code:

```java
import java.util.*;
import java.io.*;
public class greetingbeam extends Canvas implements Serializable
{
  private final static int XPAD = 5;
  private final static int YPAD = 5;
  private String morning, afternoon, evening;
  public greetingBean()
  {
    morning   = "Good morning.";
    afternoon = "Good afternoon.";
    evening   = "Good evening.";
  }
  public String getMorning()
```

```java
{
  return morning;
}

public void setMorning(String morning)
{
  this.morning = morning;
  adjustSize();
}

public String getAfternoon()
{
  return afternoon;
}

public void setAfternoon(String afternoon)
{
  this.afternoon = afternoon;
  adjustSize();
}

public String getEvening()
{
  return evening;
}

public void setEvening(String evening)
{
  this.evening = evening;
  adjustSize();
}

public void setFont(Font font)
{
  super.setFont(font);
  adjustSize();
}

public Dimension getPreferredSize()
{
  Graphics g = getGraphics();
  FontMetrics fm = g.getFontMetrics();
```

```java
    int w = fm.stringWidth(selectGreeting()) + 2*XPAD;
    int h = fm.getHeight() + 2*YPAD;
    return new Dimension(w, h);
  }

  private void adjustSize()
  {
    Dimension d = getPreferredSize();
    setSize(d.width, d.height);
    Component parent = getParent();
    if(parent != null)
    {
      parent.invalidate();
      parent.doLayout();
    }
  }

  public void paint(Graphics g)
  {
    String greeting = selectGreeting();
    Dimension d = getSize();
    FontMetrics fm = g.getFontMetrics();
    int x = (d.width - fm.stringWidth(greeting))/2;
    int y = (d.height + fm.getMaxAscent() -
      fm.getMaxDescent())/2;
    g.drawString(greeting, x, y);
    if(border) {
      g.drawRect(0, 0, d.width - 1, d.height - 1);
    }
  }

  private String selectGreeting()
  {
    Calendar calendar = Calendar.getInstance();
    int hour = calendar.get(Calendar.HOUR_OF_DAY);
    if(hour < 12)
    {
      return morning;
    }
    else if(hour < 17)
    {
      return afternoon;
```

```
        }
        else
        {
          return evening;
        }
    }
```

Step 3:

Now you can simply compile your JavaBean. You will do this as you
would compile any Java source file.

```
Javac greetingBean.java
```

Step 4:

Now you will need to create a manifest file. Remember that a manifest
file is really a template file that is used when creating a JAR, and it
describes the contents of the JAR. You can use any text editor to create a
manifest file.

```
Name: greetingBean.class
Java-Bean: True
```

Now create the JAR file. The JAR file will contain the manifest and the
greetingBean class file:

```
jar cfm greetingBean.jar manifest.mft greetingBean.class
```

Step 5:

Now go to the folder that has the BeanBox tool and start the BeanBox
tool. You should then load the JAR file into the ToolBox.

Hopefully, you found this bean a bit more exciting. It actually did something
useful. It presented a greeting that is appropriate for the specific time of day.
This also illustrates one of the reasons for doing JavaBeans. You can now
incorporate this bean into any application where you may wish to display
the time of day greeting. There is no need for you to rewrite this code or
even import packages to use in another application. This bean handles everything, including the visual presentation of the greeting.

Creating a Bean with JBuilder

Recall that I said JBuilder made Java programming much easier. It especially eases tasks such as compiling and creating the JAR file. In fact, it makes all aspects of bean programming easy. To illustrate this point, let's create a JavaBean using JBuilder.

Step 1:

Launch JBuilder.

Step 2:

After launching your copy of JBuilder, start a new project. Then, to add a file to the project, select File ► New. This will present you with the following screen:

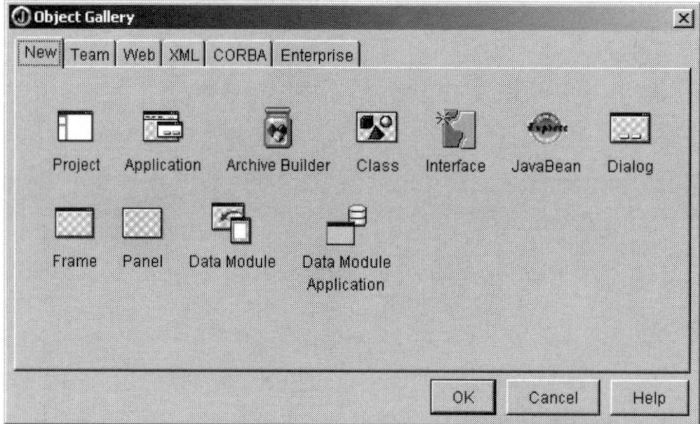

Step 3:

Select JavaBean as the type of item to add. This will start the JavaBean Wizard, seen in the figure at the top of the following page.

Notice that you have several options on this screen. The first two text fields allow you to set your bean's package name and the name of its main class. The third allows you to choose a base class for your JavaBean. The check boxes at the bottom of the screen allow you to set other items, such as having the wizard create a default no-argument constructor for you. For our purposes, we will leave everything as default except the package name and class name. Name the package "coolBean."

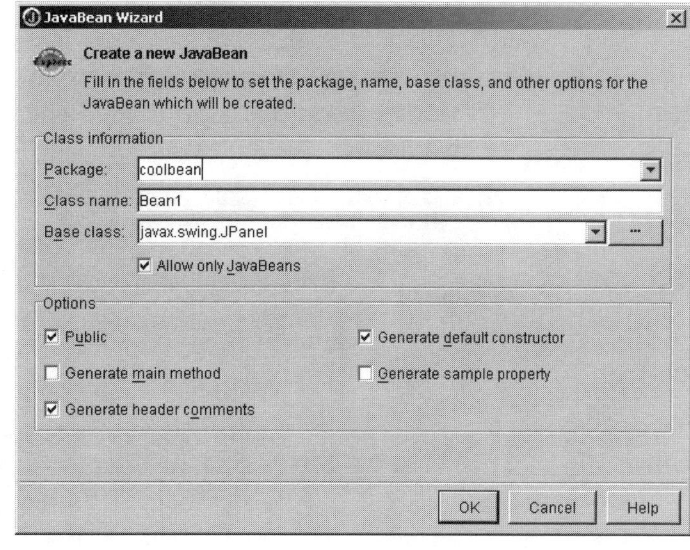

Step 4:

When you click OK on that screen, the wizard will finish and you will see the basic code for your JavaBean in a code window like this one:

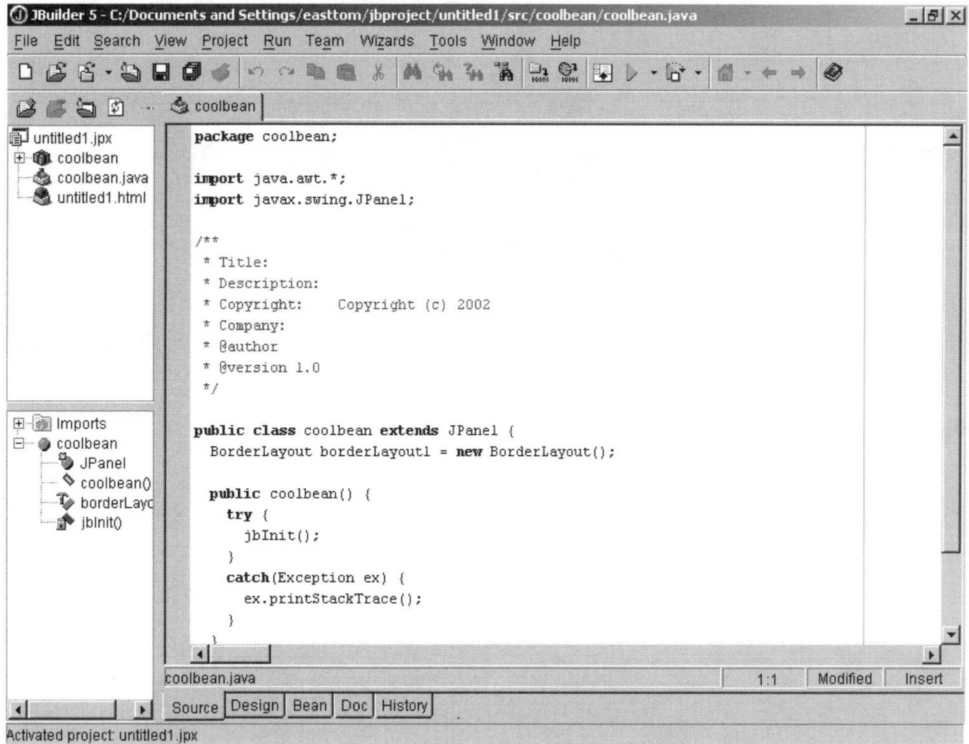


```
package coolbean;

import java.awt.*;
import javax.swing.JPanel;

/**
 * Title:
 * Description:
 * Copyright:    Copyright (c) 2002
 * Company:
 * @author
 * @version 1.0
 */

public class coolbean extends JPanel {
  BorderLayout borderLayout1 = new BorderLayout();

  public coolbean() {
    try {
      jbInit();
    }
    catch(Exception ex) {
      ex.printStackTrace();
    }
  }
```

Step 5:

You can edit the code right here in this window, or you can select the Design tab at the bottom. It will show you a visual representation of the way your JavaBean would look.

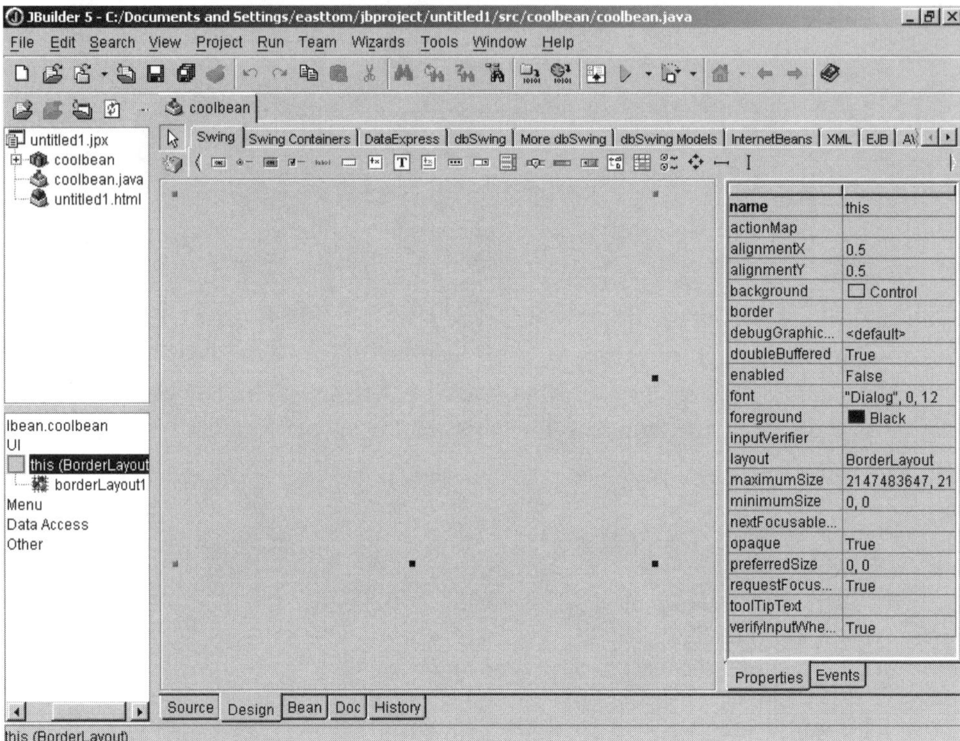

From this screen, you can add more visual elements and manipulate the visual interface.

Another tab you can select is the Bean tab. It will take you to a screen like this one:

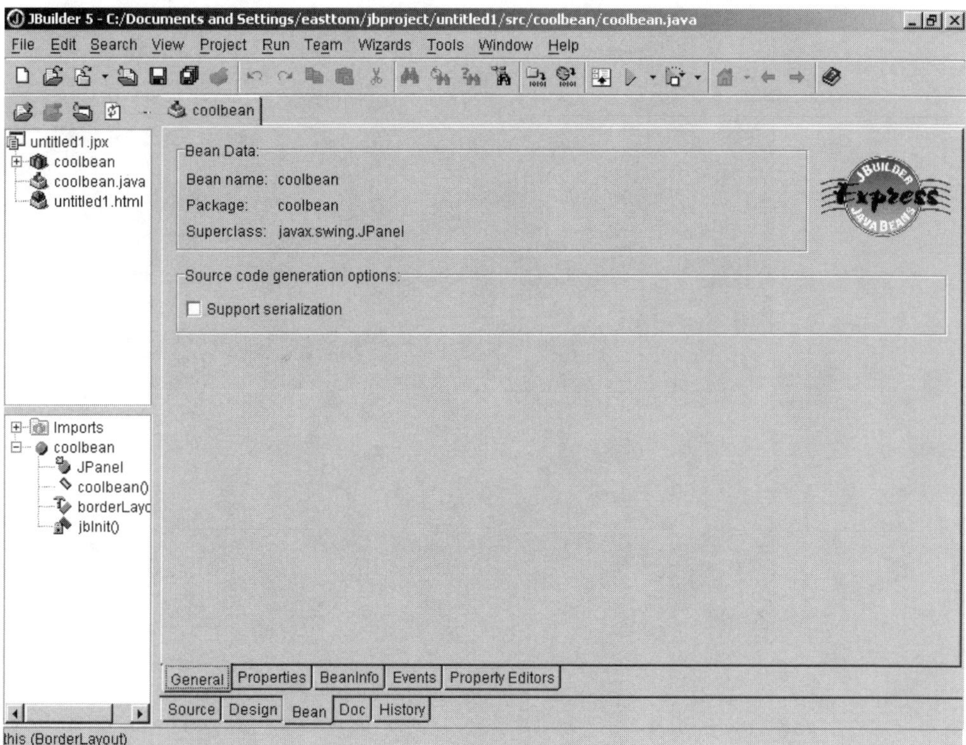

Note that here you have several options. On the primary screen, or General tab, you can set support serialization. If you select this, the implements serializable code will be added to your source code for you. You can also work with the other tabs to, for example, set the properties of a bean:

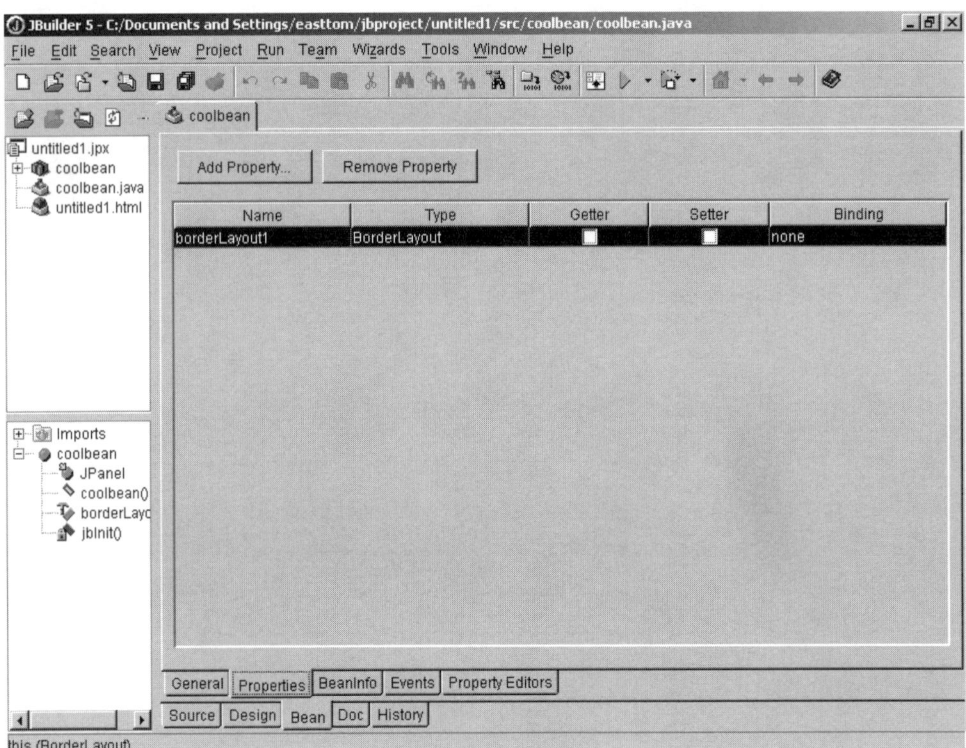

Generating the bean info:

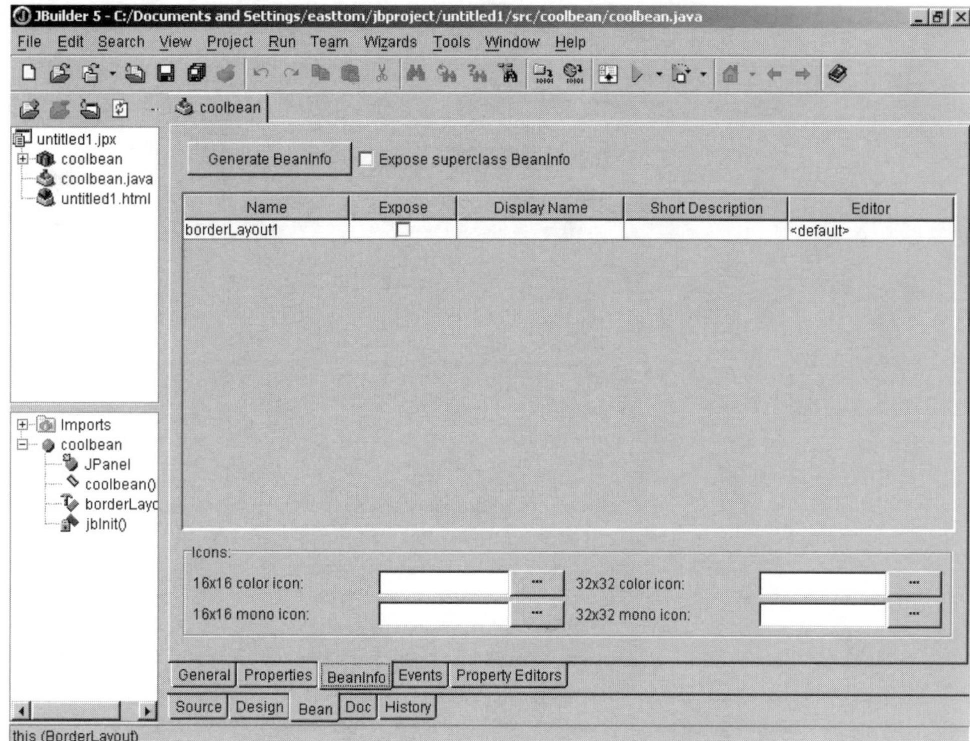

The events of your bean:

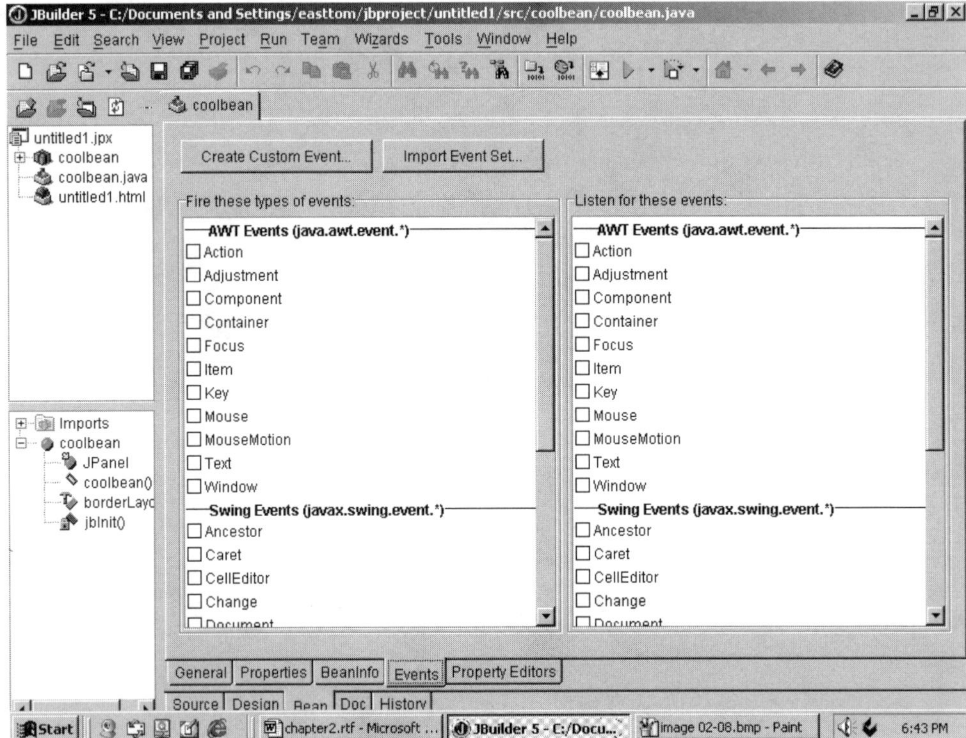

As you go through the next two chapters, you will become more familiar with these various tabs, but for now, let's just set a few items for our JavaBean.

Step 6:

On the General tab, select support serialization.

Step 7:

On the Properties tab, add a new property with the name text.

Step 8:

Run your bean. You can do this by clicking on the button in the toolbar that looks much like a CD play button or by choosing Run from the drop-down menu, then selecting Run Project. You can also use the short-cut key, F9. Whichever method you choose, you will then see a screen like this one:

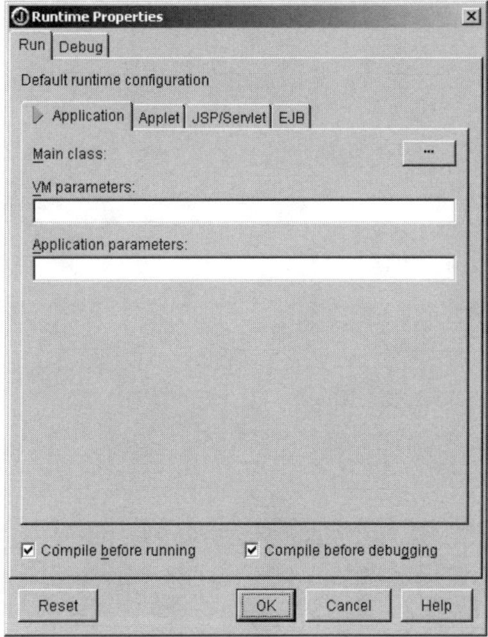

For our purposes, simply leave the default values and click on OK. Now your bean will run. However, since we did not add code to it, it won't do much. Later we will create some functional beans in JBuilder. For now, you can take the code from one of the previous beans and add it to our JBuilder bean code if you wish to see a functional bean. You can even create the JAR file from within JBuilder. Simply select Wizards ▶ Archive Builder, as shown in the following figure.

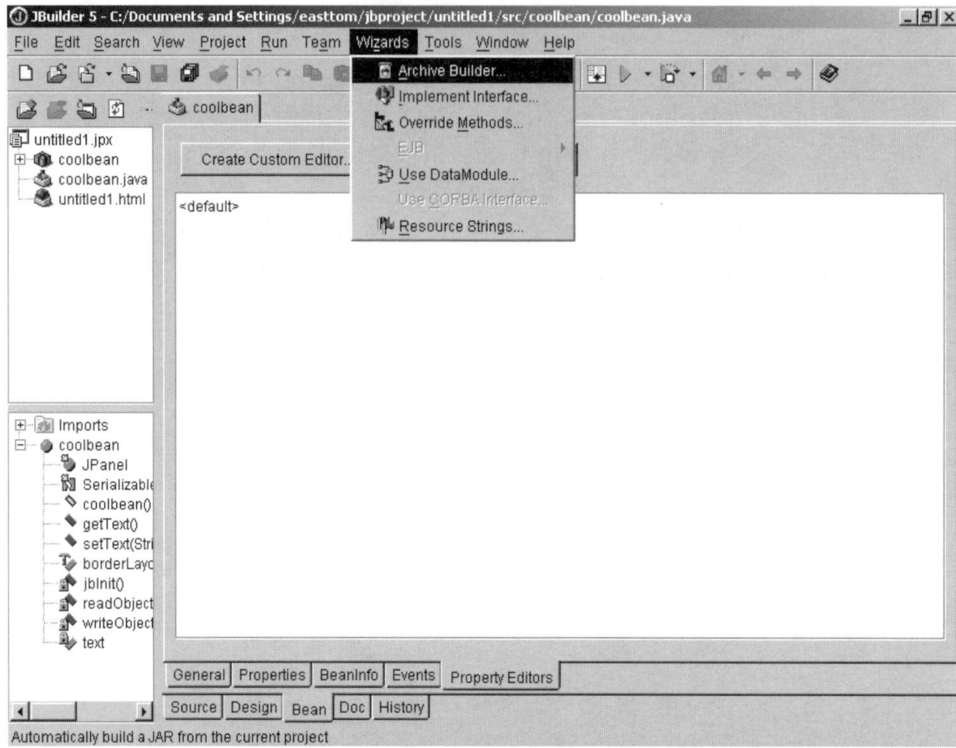

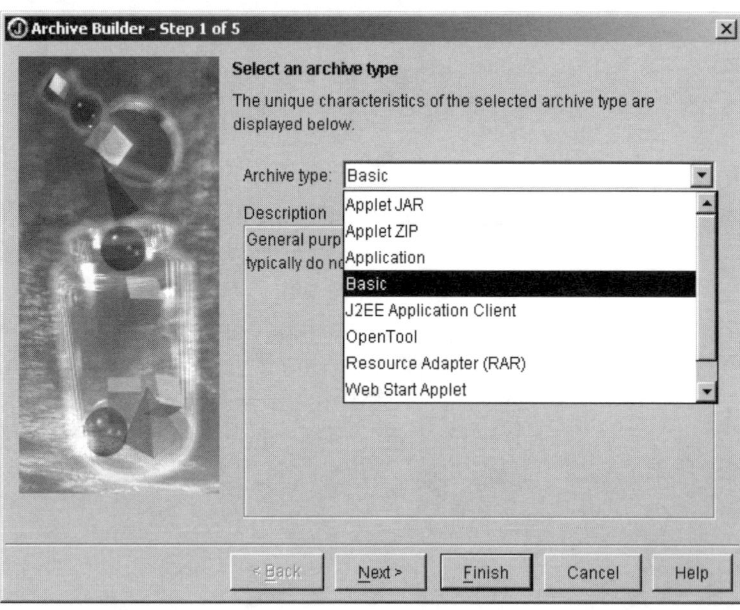

This will start a five-step wizard that will create the JAR file for you. For our purposes, simply choose the Basic type, but note that there are other types. We will use some of these later in this book.

After you press Next, you will be taken to step 2. Here you can choose the name of the archive file and whether or not you want it to compress the files.

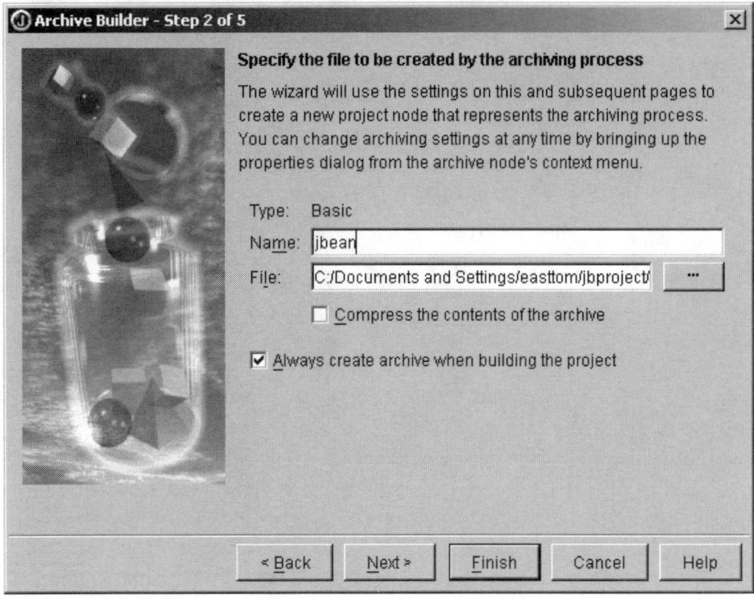

The next step, step 3, allows you to specify the files to include in this archive.

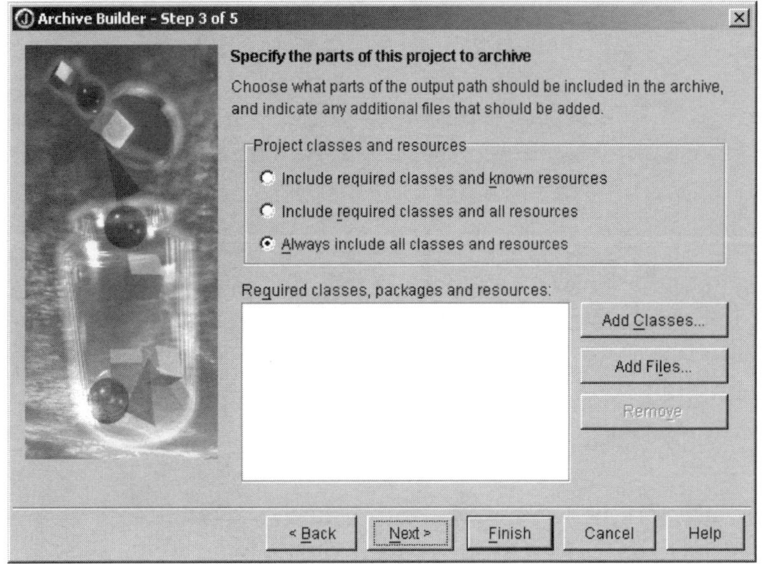

The fourth step allows you to decide how to handle the dependency files for the items you have included.

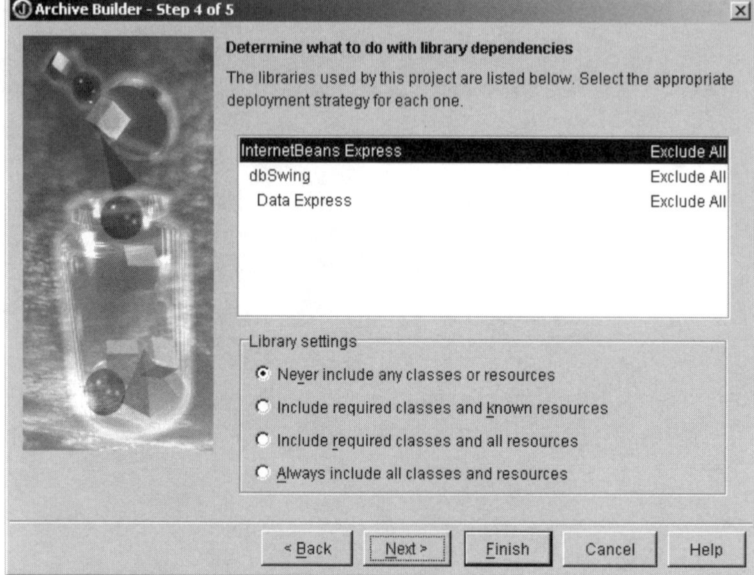

The fifth and final step will allow you to specify information about the manifest file.

Then simply press Finish, and your JAR file will be created for you.

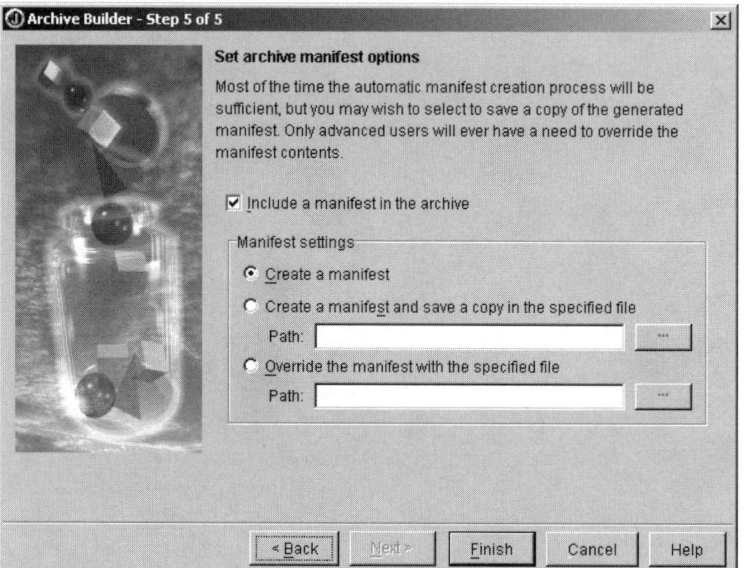

This example should give you the basic knowledge to utilize JBuilder to create JavaBeans. Throughout this book, I will show you how to perform tasks first using the standard Sun Microsystems development tools and then using JBuilder. I think that when you finish this book, you will agree that doing things with JBuilder is more efficient and much easier!

Summary

In this chapter, I showed you the standards that determine how a JavaBean should be developed. You have also seen how to create a simple JavaBean using the Sun Java SDK. This chapter also covered JavaBean requirements, such as how to define properties and design patterns. Finally, this chapter showed you how to create a JavaBean using Borland JBuilder. This should give you a basic understanding of how JavaBeans are created and allow us to move forward in our exploration of JavaBeans.

The most important concepts to retain from reading this chapter are the guidelines for creating a JavaBean and the various standards that your JavaBean must conform to in order to be a JavaBean. I recommend that you make certain that you have actually worked through the examples in this chapter at least once, and that you have thoroughly read the requirements for creating JavaBeans.

Terms

JAR – Java Archive file. This is a file that contains all the required objects that you will distribute with your JavaBean.

Manifest File – This file is simply a text file that delineates what is contained in the JAR file.

Introspection – The process whereby a bean exposes its functions for external use.

Reflection – The process whereby a bean discovers its functions to expose.

Serialization – The process of saving data to a file.

Review Questions

1. What interface must a bean implement in order to allow its properties to be saved?

2. What is a JAR file?

3. What is a manifest file?

4. What does the x option cause the JAR utility to do?

5. What is a property?

6. What is introspection?

7. What is a bean container?

8. What type of constructor must a JavaBean have?

9. What does option M cause the JAR utility to do?

10. What is the first file in a JAR file?

Chapter 3

Events and Properties

Introduction

If you will recall from Chapter 1, when I first introduced you to JavaBeans, I also gave you a brief introduction to the concept of events, in relation to JavaBeans. You were shown how to map the events in one bean to the events in another. Using the BeanBox, this was as simple as choosing an option from the drop-down menu and dragging the cursor to the next bean. Recall that you did not have to write any code at all to connect these bean events. In the first two chapters, you were given a cursory definition of an event and a few brief exercises connecting events. However, I have not yet addressed the question of what an event actually is. This chapter will rectify that deficiency in your JavaBean education.

Events are methods that the component in question, in this case a JavaBean, reveals to the outside world and represents some activity taking place. Events are methods that allow the JavaBean to communicate with the container. This is different from standard methods, which allow the programmer or the bean container to communicate with the JavaBean. Events are a central feature of the JavaBean's architecture. These events are triggered in response to some action. That action may be one taken by another bean, the user, or the system itself. JavaBean events are responses to activities that have occurred within the JavaBean.

Events provide more than just indications that certain actions have taken place. They provide a convenient mechanism for allowing components to be linked together in an application builder or a Bean Builder tool. An event is a method that occurs when some state changes in the source. An event can be generated by any such change. In Java applets, events are often generated in response to a user interacting with some graphical part of the applet. Using events, you can have an action taking place in relation to one bean trigger an action (event) in another bean. This linking allows activity occurring in the source bean to initiate code stored in the second bean. The ability to link together beans via their events is a cornerstone feature of JavaBeans. You can have an event that occurs in one JavaBean linked to another JavaBean, thus triggering a new event to occur in the second JavaBean.

A more technical definition of events would be: Events are a mechanism for propagating state change notifications between a source object and one or more target or listener objects. If you have ever worked with applets, you should be familiar with events. Applets frequently make use of the action event and the various mouse events.

Java implements an event architecture referred to as the Delegation Model. This model provides a standard mechanism for an event source to generate an event and send it to event listeners. Essentially, the event source "delegates" how the event should be dealt with to the event listener (thus the name "Delegation Model"). In order for a listener to receive an event, it must first register with the event source. An *event source* is any class that generates an event. An *event receiver* is any class that receives an event. The reception of events is accomplished via event listeners. *Event listeners* are classes that implement a specific interface. That interface identifies what events that event listener is interested in.

Event listeners must also register with the event source. This is accomplished by calling the appropriate method of the source. When the event listener calls the appropriate method of the event source, it is ready to receive any events that source may generate. Calling that specific method sets up a communication between the event listener and the event source. An example you may be familiar with from applet development is the ActionListener. The ActionListener interface provides one method that receives action events:

```
Void actionPerformed(ActionEvent ae)
```

As you can see, this method takes a single parameter. That parameter is an instance of the ActionEvent class. By receiving this object as a parameter, the method then has access to all the methods and properties of the event that occurred. You may write code within this method that utilizes these methods and properties to find out information about the event in question and to respond as you see fit.

Event Classes

There is a set of classes that represent AWT (Abstract Windowing Toolkit) events. These classes are part of a well-defined object hierarchy that inherits from the Object class. These AWT events represent most of the events you will use in JavaBean development. It is often helpful, though not essential, to have some experience working with AWT prior to embarking on learning JavaBeans. The reason is that there are many similarities between AWT programming and JavaBean programming. The most obvious, however, are events. In fact, as we will see throughout this book, AWT classes are often subclassed in the creation of JavaBeans. However, if you don't have much experience with AWT, don't worry. You will still be able to create JavaBeans. However, it will be an easier and more natural process for you if you have previously used AWT.

Key classes in AWT class hierarchy are shown here:

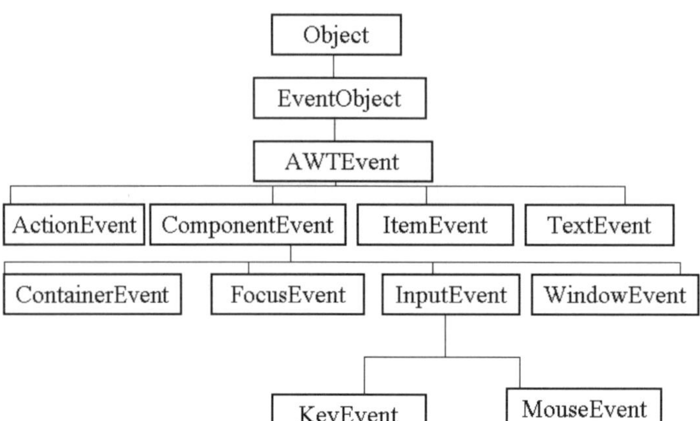

Before we continue in our exploration of events, I would like to give you a fuller explanation of some of the objects represented in the hierarchy shown above, as well as some important event classes not shown in the hierarchy. I will give particular attention to classes that are subclasses of the AWTEvent class. The reason for this is that these events are used extensively in JavaBeans.

The *EventObject* inherits from the Object class. EventObject has two methods:

- Object getSource() – returns a reference to the object that generated the event.

- String toString() – returns a string equivalent of the event.

The *AWTEvent* class is an abstract class. It inherits from EventObject and is found in the java.awt package. All of the AWT event classes are subclasses of this abstract class. It has a number of methods, which its child classes inherit. However, the two you will encounter most frequently are:

- int getId() – returns the type of event.

- String toString() – returns the string equivalent of an event.

I will describe for you all of the event classes that are in the AWTEventClass hierarchy, even though only a few are illustrated in the chart. The following table provides a summary of all of the event classes that inherit directly from AWTEventClass. This table also lists the associated listener interfaces for those classes. Listener interfaces are explained in the next section.

Event Class	Listener Interface(s)
ActionEvent	ActionListener
ComponentEvent	ComponentListener
ItemEvent	ItemListener
TextEvent	TextListener
FocusEvent	FocusListener
AdjustmentEvent	AdjustmentListener
InputEvent	InputListener
KeyEvent	KeyListener
MouseEvent	MouseListener and MouseMotionListener
WindowEvent	WindowListener

The ActionEvent class is called when a button is pressed, a menu item is clicked, or an item in a list is double-clicked. This class is a subclass of the AWTEvent class. This is an event you are probably familiar with, especially if you have ever developed applets. Java applets frequently must respond to the ActionEvent, and therefore, most texts on Java applets are replete with code examples using this event. There are also a few integer constants that help you determine what key was pressed in an ActionEvent. The most common are listed in the table below:

Integer Constant	Key Pressed
SHIFT_MASK	Shift key
META_MASK	Meta key
ALT_MASK	Alt key
CTRL_MASK	Ctrl key

The ComponentEvent class is triggered any time that a component is hidden, resized, shown, or moved. Like ActionEvent, this class is a subclass of the AWTEvent class. Also like the ActionEvent, it has integer constants that help you determine exactly what has transpired.

Integer Constant	Description
COMPONENT_HIDDEN	The component was hidden from view.
COMPONENT_SHOWN	The component became visible.
COMPONENT_RESIZED	The component's size has changed.
COMPONENT_MOVED	The component was moved.

The ItemEvent class is generated when the user selects an item from a choice, a checkable menu, or a list. This class is a subclass of the AWTEvent class. Like the previous event classes, the ItemEvent class specifies some integer constants that help you determine what has occurred.

Constant	Description
DESELECTED	The item has been deselected.
SELECTED	The item has been selected.
ITEM_STATE_CHANGED	The item's state has changed.

The TextEvent class is invoked when the text in a text field or text area changes. This class is a subclass of the AWTEvent class. This class, however, does not specify constants.

The FocusEvent class, which is a subclass of the ComponentEvent class, is invoked when a component gains or loses the focus of the keyboard. This class defines two integer constants that identify whether focus was gained or lost. These constants are, logically, FOCUS_GAINED and FOCUS_LOST.

The AdjustmentEvent class is associated with the movement of a scroll bar. This class is a subclass of the AWTEvent class. It also defines several integer constants that identify exactly what has occurred with the scroll bar.

Constant	Description
BLOCK_INCREMENT	The mouse was clicked in the region between the slider and the upper bound of the scroll bar, causing a block increment.
BLOCK_DECREMENT	The mouse was clicked in the region between the slider and the lower bound of the scroll bar, causing a block decrement.
UNIT_INCREMENT	The upper bound button was clicked.
UNIT_DECREMENT	The lower bound button was clicked.
TRACK	The slider is being dragged.

The InputEvent class, another subclass of the ComponentEvent class, has two important subclasses of its own: KeyEvent and MouseEvent. This class is used to handle various input functions. Its most commonly used methods are described in the following table:

Method	Description
Int getModifiers()	This method returns information about any modifiers that apply to this input event.
Boolean isAltDown()	This method returns true if the Alt key was pressed.
Boolean isControlDown()	This method returns true if the Ctrl key was pressed.
Boolean isMetaDown()	This method returns true if the Meta key was pressed.
Boolean isShiftDown()	This method returns true if the Shift key was pressed.

The KeyEvent class is invoked in response to a key being pressed or released. This class is a subclass of the InputEvent class. This class defines a wide range of integer constants to help determine exactly what key was pressed and which key it was associated with. The following table summarizes these constants:

Constant	Description
KEY_PRESSED	A key was pressed.
KEY_RELEASED	The key was released.
KEY_TYPED	A key has been typed.
VK_A, VK_B, VK_C, ...VK_Z	There is a constant for each letter from A to Z.
VK_0, VK_1, ...VK_9	There is a constant for all the decimal digits from 0 to 9.
VK_ENTER	The Enter key was pressed.
VK_DELETE	The Delete key was pressed.
VK_INSERT	The Insert key was pressed.
VK_TAB	The Tab key was pressed.
VK_ESCAPE	The Escape key was pressed.
VK_BACK_SPACE	The Backspace key was pressed.

The MouseEvent class is invoked in response to any use of the mouse, be it a mouse move, click, drag, or double-click. This class has several events. The most commonly used events are described in this table.

Method	Description
Point getPoint()	This method returns a point object that specifies the exact location of the mouse.
Int getX()	This method returns an integer that represents the x coordinate of the mouse.
Int getY()	This method returns an integer that represents the y coordinate of the mouse.

The WindowEvent class is invoked in response to a window being activated, deactivated, opened, closed, iconified, or de-iconified. This class is a subclass of the ComponentEvent class. The most commonly used method of this class is:

```
Window getWindow()
```

This method returns the window that was the source of the event in question. This class is also a child class of the AWTEvent class and defines a number of integer constants.

Constant	Description
WINDOW_ACTIVATED	The window has been activated.
WINDOW_DEACTIVATED	The window has been deactivated.
WINDOW_OPENED	The window has been opened.
WINDOW_CLOSING	A request to close the window has been received.
WINDOW_CLOSED	The window has closed.
WINDOW_ICONIFIED	The window has been iconified.
WINDOW_DEICONIFIED	The window has been de-iconified.

Each of these event classes is used to handle a certain set of events. These classes also provide a means, via their constants, to determine some specifics regarding the event that has transpired. These events are commonly used in applet development, so it is likely that you may have seen and used them before. You will also see that these events are also commonly used in the creation of JavaBeans.

Listener Interfaces

As previously stated, in order for a listener class to actually listen for events, it must implement an EventListener interface. The EventListener interface is found in the java.util package. It does not define any constants or methods; it simply identifies those interfaces that process events. All of the specific event listener classes for each of the event classes extend this class.

Event sources identify themselves as sourcing particular events by defining registration methods that conform to a specific design pattern and accept references to instances of particular EventListener interfaces. All event handling methods must be defined in EventListener interfaces (interfaces that inherit from java.util.EventListener). It has become a convention to give these EventListener interfaces names ending with the word "Listener." Any class that wants to handle any of the sets of events defined in a given EventListener interface must implement that interface.

Any event handling methods defined in an EventListener interface will usually conform to a standard design pattern. Writing event listener classes that conform to such a pattern aids in the utility and documentation of the event system, permits such interfaces to be determined by third parties programmatically, and allows the automatic construction of generic event adaptors. As mentioned earlier, the creation of JavaBeans is dependent upon the adherence to certain well-defined design patterns. Here is the design pattern which must be observed:

The signature of this design pattern is

```
void <eventOccurrenceMethodName>(<EventStateObjectType> evt);
```

The EventStateObjectType must be a subclass of java.util.EventObject.

Here is an example of a class that might work as a listener for a MouseMove event.

```
public class MyMouseMovedEvent extends java.util.EventObject
{
// code for the actual class goes here
}
interface MyMouseMovedListener extends java.util.EventListener
{
// This interface defines the listener methods that any event
// listeners for "MouseMovedExample" events must support.
    void mouseMoved(MyMouseMovedEvent mymouse);
}
```

Notice the method void mouseMoved(MyMouseMovedEvent mymouse). This function declaration adheres to the requirements for event listeners. It returns a void, has a name indicating what event has transpired, and takes as an argument an object of the event class type. This is a practical example of how event listeners are constructed.

In order to listen for that event, a class would have to implement the MyMouseMovedListener interface. Here is an example of a class doing just that:

```
class myexample implements MyMouseMovedListener
{
public void mouseMoved(MyMouseMovedEvent mymouse)
{
// place code here
}
}
```

In this example, the class in question can receive events of the type MyMouseMovedEvent. Inside this class's implementation of the mouseMoved event, the programmer writes whatever code she wishes to transpire in response to this particular event.

It is common practice to group related event handling methods in the same EventListener interface. For example, mouseEntered, mouseMoved, and mouseExited would be grouped in the same EventListener interface. In those situations where there may be a significant number of related kinds of events, a hierarchy of EventListeners may be defined so that the occurrences most commonly of interest to the majority of potential listeners are exposed in their own EventListener interface.

The usual practice concerning event handling methods and arguments is that event handling methods should have a single argument which is a subclass of java.util.EventObject. However, under certain specific circumstances, conformance to this standard method signature may not be appropriate. One such circumstance arises when forwarding event notifications to external environments that are implemented in different languages or with different conventions. In these circumstances, it may be necessary to express the notification method signature in a style more in keeping with the target environment. In these circumstances, it is permissible to allow method signatures containing one or more parameters of any arbitrary Java type.

The permitted signature for such circumstances is:

```
void event_method_name(parameter-list);
```

In order for potential EventListeners to register themselves with appropriate event source instances, event source classes must provide methods for registering and de-registering event listeners. As you may have guessed, there is a set of design patterns that define how such methods should be created, and yes, there are design patterns for almost all things in JavaBean development! The design pattern for EventListener registration is shown here:

```
public void addListenerType(ListenerType listener);
public void removeListenerType(ListenerType listener);
```

When a programmer uses the add*ListenerType* method, it adds the given listener to the set of event listeners registered for events associated with the ListenerType. As I hope you surmised, invoking the remove*ListenerType* method removes the given listener from the set of event listeners registered for events associated with the method.

So once you have created a class that implements a particular listener interface, you will need to invoke the event source add*ListenerType* method in order to register your class as an event listener for that event source. Once you have done this, your class will then receive events of that type that are generated from that event source.

Inner Classes

Adaptor classes frequently make use of inner classes, and it is entirely possible that some readers may not be familiar with this topic. For this reason, I will provide a brief introduction to inner classes here. If you are already familiar with inner classes, then feel free to skip to the next section, "Adaptor Classes."

Originally, Java supported only top-level classes. Top-level classes are simply the standard Java classes that you are familiar with and have used throughout this book and in your previous Java programming experience. Beginning with Java 1.1, you are now able to define inner classes as members of other classes locally within a block of statements. In essence, an inner class is simply a class that is defined within another class, thus the name.

Once you grasp the basic concept of what an inner class is, you may still be skeptical as to its utility. You might ask: Why even have inner classes? Well, there are a few interesting features of inner classes that are useful to programmers. To begin with, the inner class can use member variables and methods from the enclosing scope. This includes both class and instance members of enclosing classes and local variables of enclosing blocks. Notice that I used the terms "enclosing scope" and "enclosing block." Since an inner class might be defined within a method as well as within a class, it will have access to whatever its enclosing scope has access to, whether that enclosing scope is an entire class or a specific method. Another interesting point about inner classes is that they are not usable outside their scope. This means that this inner class is only used by the enclosing scope. That makes its functionality and its relationship to the other classes in the program exceedingly clear. If you would like more information on the details of inner classes, I recommend that you consult Appendix A at the end of this book. There are resources for this topic and many others.

Adaptor Classes

If, for any reason, an event listener cannot directly implement a particular interface, an instance of a custom adaptor class may be interposed between a source and one or more listeners in order to establish the relationship. Adaptor classes may also be used if some additional behavior is required. An adaptor class provides empty implementations of all the methods defined in a given EventListener interface. The following table summarizes some of the adaptor classes and their associated EventListener interfaces.

Adaptor Class	EventListener Interface
ComponentAdapter	ComponentListener
ContainerAdapter	ContainerListener
FocusAdapter	FocusListener
KeyAdapter	KeyListener
MouseAdapter	MouseListener
MouseMotionAdapter	MouseMotionListener

Adaptor Class	EventListener Interface
WindowAdapter	WindowListener

If you have used Java for some time, you are probably aware of the use of inner classes as adapter classes. An inner class is one which is wholly defined inside another class's definition. In the example shown here, class innerA is an inner class.

```
Class myclass
{
    class innerA
    {
    }
}
```

Let's take a look at a JavaBean example that uses events, listeners, and an inner class as an adapter. Hopefully, this example will make the concepts we have been discussing more clear. The first example uses Notepad, and then we will do another example with JBuilder.

Step 1:

Using Notepad, start a new project with a source file called mydot.java.

Step 2:

Enter the following code:

```
package mydot;
import java.awt.*;
import java.awt.event.*;
import java.util.*;
public class mydot extends Canvas implements java.io.Serializable,
    MouseListener, MouseMotionListener
{
    private Point a;
    public mydot()
    {
      setSize(300,300);
      a = new Point(150,150);
      addMouseListener(new MyMouseAdapter());
    }// end of constructor
```

```
public void changePoint(MouseEvent e)
{
  a = new Point(e.getX(),e.getY());
  repaint();
}  // end of changePoint
public void paint (Graphics g)
  {
  Dimension d = getSize();
  g.drawEllipse(0,0, d.width −1, d.height −1);
  g.fillRect(a.x −2, a.y −2, 4 , 4);
}
class MyMouseAdapter extends MouseAdapter
{
  public void mouseClicked(MouseEvent e)
  {
    changePoint(e);
  }
}// end of inner class adapter
}// end of class mydot
```

This example is not particularly exciting, as far as functionality, but it does illustrate all the concepts I have shown you so far. It uses an inner class and adaptor class as an event listener and then uses that event listener to receive events from an event source and respond to those events. You should also note that it has a no-arguments constructor, and it uses the addListener method to add the listener to the source. In short, it has all the qualities necessary for a JavaBean that is going to receive events from some event source.

As promised, I will now walk you through the same process with JBuilder. The code requirements are, of course, the same. However, you will quickly see that JBuilder generates a lot of the JavaBean required code for you. This allows you, the programmer, to concentrate on the code that is specific to your application.

Step 1:

The first step is, of course, to launch JBuilder.

Step 2:

After launching your copy of JBuilder, start a new project. Then to add a file to the project, select File ▸ New. This will present you with the following screen:

Step 3:

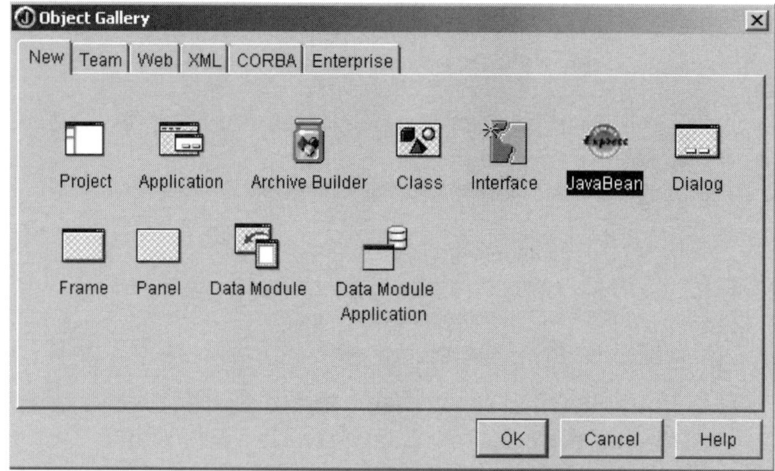

Select JavaBean as the type of item to add. This will start the JavaBean Wizard.

Step 4:

At this screen, choose the name of mydot. For the base class, enter "java.awt.Canvas."

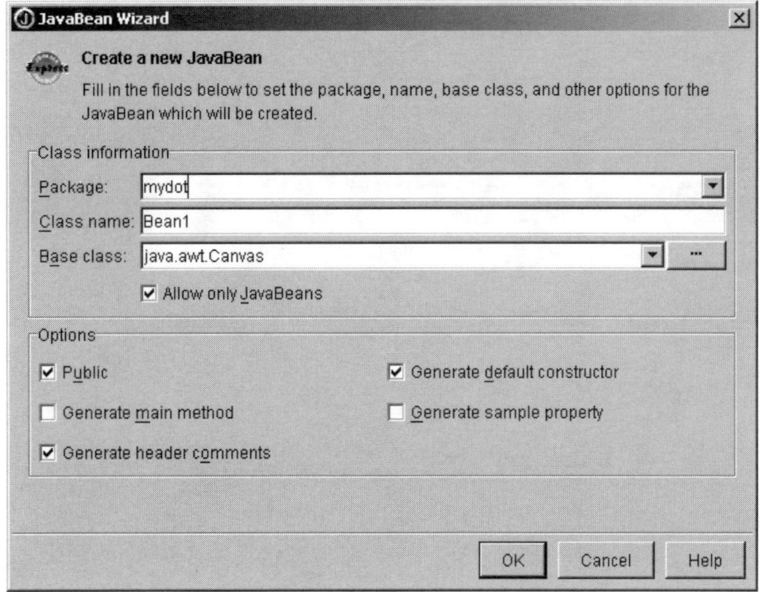

You will now see the code window for this bean:

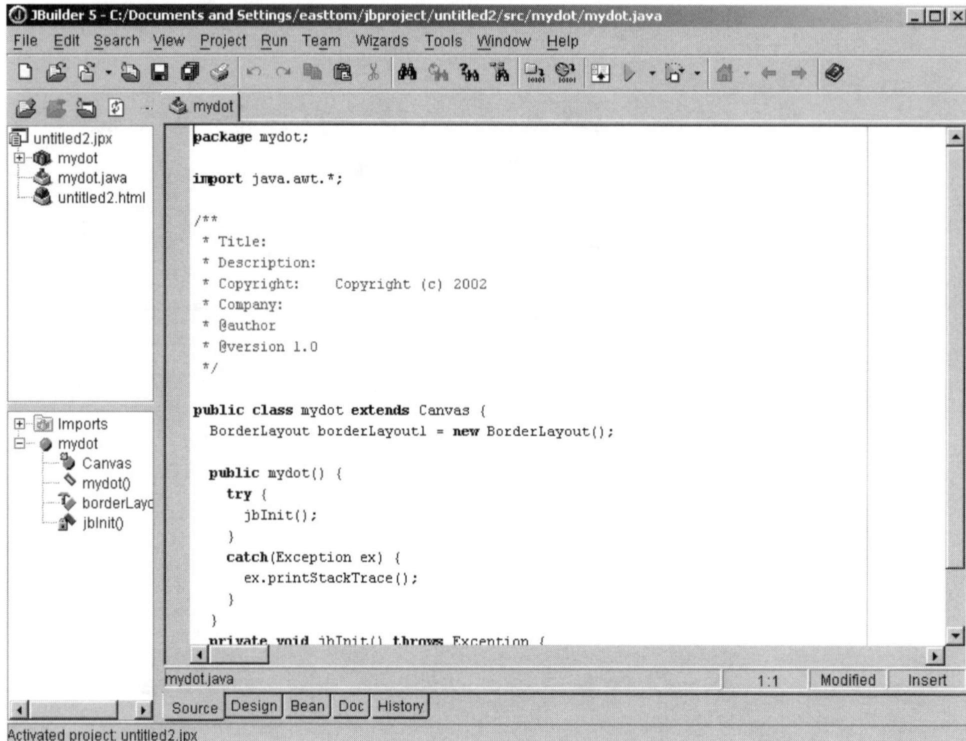

Notice that even comment sections are already provided for you.

Step 5:

You can manually type in the same bean code we used in the first example, or you can simply highlight the bean code in the code window of JBuilder and paste the other code over it, like you see here:

```
mydot

/**
 * Title:
 * Description:
 * Copyright:    Copyright (c) 2002
 * Company:
 * @author
 * @version 1.0
 */

public class mydot extends Canvas {
  BorderLayout borderLayout1 = new BorderLayout();

  public mydot() {
    try {
      jbInit();
    }
    catch(Exception ex) {
      ex.printStackTrace();
    }
  }
  private void jbInit() throws Exception {
    this.setLayout(borderLayout1);
  }
}
```

```
mydot

  {
    setSize(300,300);
    a = new Point(150,150);
    addMouseListener(new MyMouseAdapter);
  }// end of constructor
  public void changePoint(MouseEvent e)
  {
     a = new Point(e.getX(),e.getY());
     repaint();
  }  // end of changePoint
  public void paint (Graphics g_
   {
     Dimension d = getSize();
     g.drawEllipse(0,0, d.width □1, d.height □1);
     g.fillRect(a.x □2, a.y □2, 4 , 4);
   }
   class MyMouseAdapter extends MouseAdapter
   {
     public void mouseClicked(MouseEvent e)
     {
       changePoint(e);
     }
   }// end of inner class adapter
}// end of class mydot
```

Step 6:

Since we wish to use mouse events in this bean, select the Bean tab, and select its Event tab. Then check the boxes to listen for mouse events and mouse motion events.

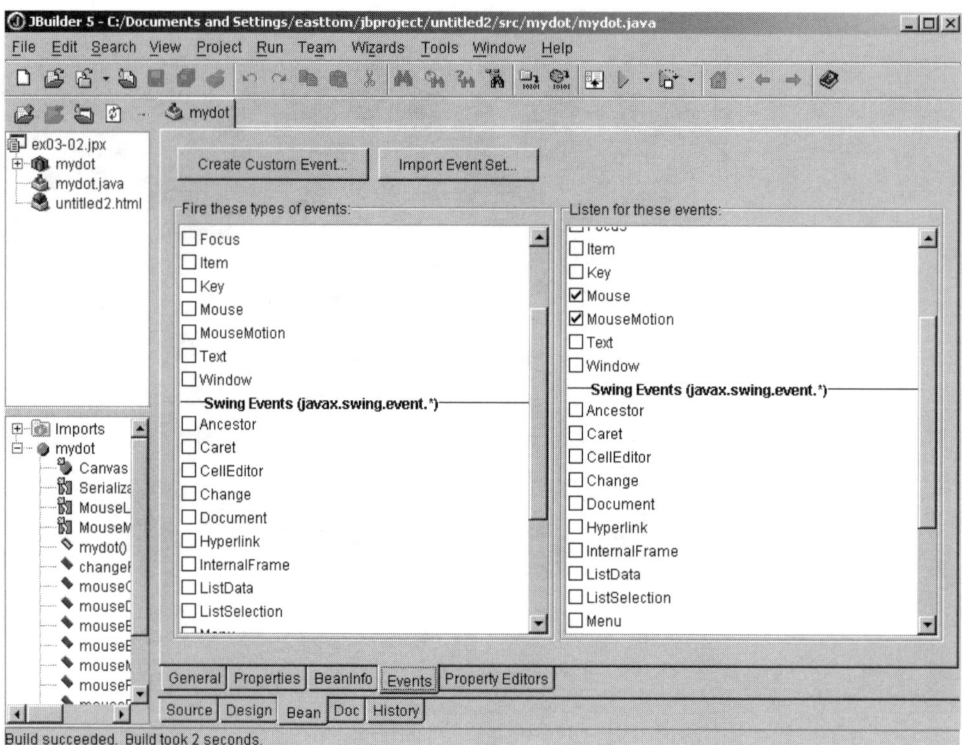

Step 7:

Now select Project ► Rebuild from the drop-down menu.

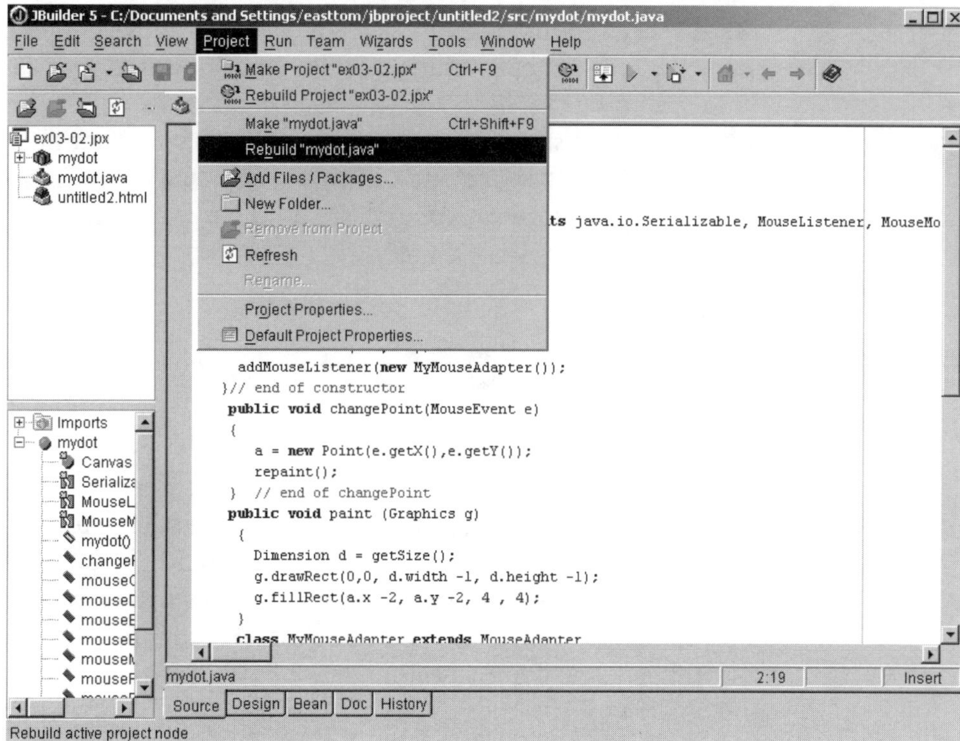

If you entered in all the code correctly, it will take just a second or two for this dialog box to appear, informing you that there were no errors or warnings:

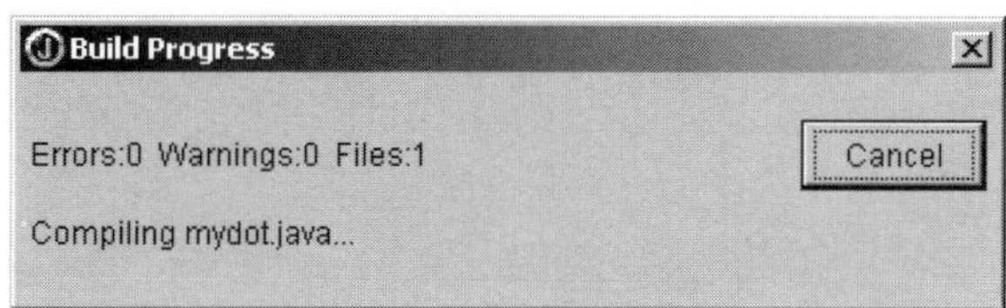

As you have probably noticed by now, it is significantly easier to create JavaBeans using JBuilder than it is using the JDK. In fact, the JBuilder environment will allow you to specify the interfaces you wish to implement, the class you need to inherit from, and the events you wish to support. It will then generate the appropriate code for you. It even allows you to specify whether your bean will generate these events or listen for them. It is also easier to debug using JBuilder, since it will tell you what the error was, and you can go directly to that error. I would also like to remind you that JBuilder has an extensive, searchable, and very readable help file that you should become acquainted with.

The Event State Object

If you were not fully aware before reading this book that everything in Java has an associated class, you should be aware of it by now. So it should be of no surprise to you that the state of events are associated with a class. There is an event state object that is used to encapsulate the state associated with a given event. This event state object inherits from java.util.EventObject. This object is the only argument passed to the event method. Information associated with a particular event notification is normally encapsulated in an event state object that is a subclass of java.util.EventObject. By convention, these event state classes are given names ending in "Event."

```
public class MyMouseMovedEvent extends java.util.EventObject
{
protected int x, y;
MyMouseMovedEvent(java.awt.Component source, Point location)
{
  super(source);
  x = location.x;
  y = location.y;
}// end of constructor
public Point getLocation()
{
  return new Point(x, y);
}// end of access method for location
public void translateLocation(int dx, int dy)
```

```
  {
    x += dx;
    y += dy;
  }
}// end of class
```

You can see in this example that the MyMouseEvent extends the
java.util.EventObject. Furthermore, note that the only access to the internal
variables of this MyMouseEvent class is via an accessor method. This is good
practice in any object-oriented development, but it is essential for developing
your own event classes. These classes are usually considered immutable.

Summary

This chapter has taken you deeper into JavaBean development by exposing
you to a deeper understanding of events. After studying this chapter, you
should understand the event object hierarchy and the relationship between
events in that hierarchy. You should also have an understanding of how
events are handled in Java in general and in JavaBeans in particular. I have
also given you an introduction to creating beans that support events. You
have seen an example done with both the JDK and JBuilder.

An understanding of Java events is crucial to understanding all JavaBean
development. If you are not yet comfortable with all of the material presented in this chapter, I suggest you reread the chapter. I also suggest that
you actually code the examples yourself and see how they work firsthand. If
you still require additional explanations, you might try some of the resources
listed in Appendix A.

Terms

Event Object – An object that represents an event and is used as an argument for event listeners.

AWT – Abstract Windowing Toolkit.

Inner Class – A class that is defined within another class.

AWTEventClass – The parent class for all of the specific AWT event classes. There are several AWT event classes to handle specific AWT events.

ListenerInterface – An interface that, when implemented, allows a class to be a listener for a specific type of event.

Delegation Model – The model that provides a standard mechanism for an event source to generate an event and send it to event listeners.

Review Questions

1. What is an event?

2. How are events received by a component?

3. What is the parent object of all events?

4. List the two subclasses of the InputEvent class.

5. List four subclasses of the AWTEvent class.

6. How do event sources identify themselves as sources for a particular event?

7. What class do all EventListener interfaces inherit from?

8. What is an adaptor class?

9. What is an inner class?

10. What is an event state object?

Chapter 4

JavaBean Persistence

Introduction

Earlier in this book I briefly introduced the topic of persistence. Persistence refers to a bean's ability to retain information about its current state. This information is then refreshed the next time the bean is invoked. The bean's state persists between invocations of the bean. A bean persists by having its properties, fields, and state information saved and restored. The mechanism that makes persistence possible is called serialization. When a bean instance is serialized, it is converted into a data stream and written to a flat file stored on the hard drive. Any applet, application, or tool that uses that bean can then restore that bean's state by de-serialization. This topic is not only important for standard JavaBeans, but it will play a prominent role in several types of Enterprise JavaBeans, which you will encounter later in this book. So I encourage you to pay particular attention to this chapter. You may even wish to read it twice!

All JavaBeans must support persistence. This is required by the JavaBean API specification, and it is not optional. To meet this requirement, however, the bean developer has two approaches that he or she can implement. A Java-

Bean can support serialization by implementing either the java.io.Serializable interface or the java.io.Externalizable interface. (Recall that in Chapter 1 I mentioned that much of the Java language functionality was accomplished by implementing specific interfaces. This is a good example of that fact. You will see more such examples throughout this book.) These interfaces offer you the choice between automatic serialization and customized serialization that is controlled by the programmer.

The Serializable interface will serialize all the variables that are eligible for serialization. When implementing the Serializable interface, the programmer is only required to implement the interface. No other coding or action is necessary to have the appropriate variables persist. The Externalizable interface requires you to decide which variables will be persisted. You must implement some code to have specific variables persisted. If you wish for your bean to use automatic serialization, then you would choose to implement Serializable. If you want to have control over what facets of your bean persist, then implement Externalizable.

For most situations, you don't really need the added control of the Externalizable interface, so you will usually just implement Serializable. When using serialization, at least one class in the bean classes hierarchy must be serializable. As long as one class in a class's inheritance hierarchy implements Serializable or Externalizable, that class is serializable. This means that not every class in your bean needs to directly implement the Serializable interface. However, the primary class in any JavaBean must be serializable.

When you choose to implement Serializable, all eligible instance variables in the class are persisted. This happens automatically without any need for you to write any code at all. This is probably the most compelling reason to use Serializable over Externalizable. You can, however, selectively exclude fields that you do not want serialized by marking with the transient modifier. The first way you can exclude a variable from being persisted is to mark it as transient. Transient variables are not persisted. The reason for this lies in the very nature of a transient variable. Its name alone should be a clear indication that it is meant to be temporary, or transient. A variable that is, by definition, temporary need not be persisted to permanent storage. The other way to exclude a variable from being persisted is to mark it as final. Like transient variables, final variables are also not serializable. The reason for this is that their values are constant and cannot change. Making a variable transient or final makes it ineligible for serialization. When the class is serialized, any variables that were defined as transient or final will be ignored, and their state will not be saved. However, all other member variables, those not declared as final or transient, will be persisted. You should also note that only member variables can be persisted; local variables cannot. Recall that member variables are members of the class, and their scope extends throughout the class. Local variables, on the other hand, are declared within a function and their scope is limited to that function.

If you want even more control over what items are serialized, then you should choose to implement Externalizable. When you implement the Externalizable interface, you will be required to add specific code to determine what variables will be persisted. This method of persistence is somewhat cumbersome. Also, if you consider that with the Serializable interface approach only member variables that are neither transient nor final get persisted, you realize that most programming situations can be adequately handled by using serialization as the mechanism for persistence. Throughout this book, I will use serialization as the mechanism for persisting JavaBean data.

Serialization and De-serialization

Serialization is the process whereby the state of an object is saved to a stream. The stream is then written to a file for storage. The file is just a standard flat file that could be read by any standard text editor. This is really not different from simply using the various Java.io classes to read and write from any standard flat file. Like most JavaBean code, serialization files follow a specific naming convention which consists of naming the file the same as the class that implemented the Serializable interface and giving the file a .ser extension. For example, if you have a class named myclass that implements serialization, the resulting file would be:

```
myclass.ser
```

De-serialization, as the name implies, is literally the process of reversing the serialization process. *De-serialization* is the process whereby the previous state of an object is restored from the file to which it was previously saved. When an object that implements the Serializable interface is instantiated, the .ser file is read (if one exists), placed in a stream, and the instance variables are restored from the data in the stream. No exception is generated if the .ser file is not found. The object simply assumes that there is no previously serialized data to de-serialize and continues. The combined processes of serialization and de-serialization permit objects to retain their state between invocations of the object.

Essentially, the entire process of serialization and de-serialization is merely a process of writing the value of variables to a plain text file and reading them back in the next time the class in instantiated. This process is automated for you by implementing the Serializable interface. That means that once you implement the Serializable interface, you will not need to write any additional code in order to have your class's state information serialized or de-serialized. Frankly, I feel that this feature alone makes the use of the Serializable interface a very desirable method to use.

Most JavaBeans that you encounter will simply implement the Serializable interface rather than implement the Externalizable interface. The Serializable interface provides automatic serialization by using the Java object serialization tools. Classes that implement Serializable must also implement a no-argument constructor. This constructor will be called when an object is restored from a .ser file. The reason for the no-argument constructor is that the bean is likely to be initialized by a bean tool (such as the BeanBox), which will not be able to pass any arguments to the constructor. If you recall from Chapter 2, all JavaBeans must utilize a no-argument constructor. Essentially, this simply means that your primary bean class must adhere to all the standard JavaBean requirements.

The Serializable interface needs to be present somewhere in a class's hierarchy in order for that class to support serialization. However, it need not be implemented by each and every class in that hierarchy. If serialization is implemented in a parent class, you don't need to implement it in the child classes. The data for all these classes that inherit from a class implementing serialization will also be saved. Any objects that the class references will also be serialized. In fact, all member variables in all referenced classes that have not been declared as final or transient are serialized by default when the object is unloaded. Remember, if you do not want a particular field to be serialized, you must use the transient modifier or the final modifier to specify member variables that you do not want to have serialized.

Before we discuss persistence any further, let's first look at an example where persistence is used in a JavaBean. By studying this example, you will get a look at serialization from an external view. You will see what serialization and de-serialization accomplish for you. I encourage you to not only thoroughly read this example but to actually perform the tasks given. Simply follow each of the steps given exactly and you will see serialization and de-serialization in action.

Step 1:

The first step will be for you to launch the BeanBox. You can do this by simply locating the folder where you installed the BeanBox and selecting the appropriate file to launch the BeanBox (run.sh for Unix, run.bat for Windows), and then execute that file.

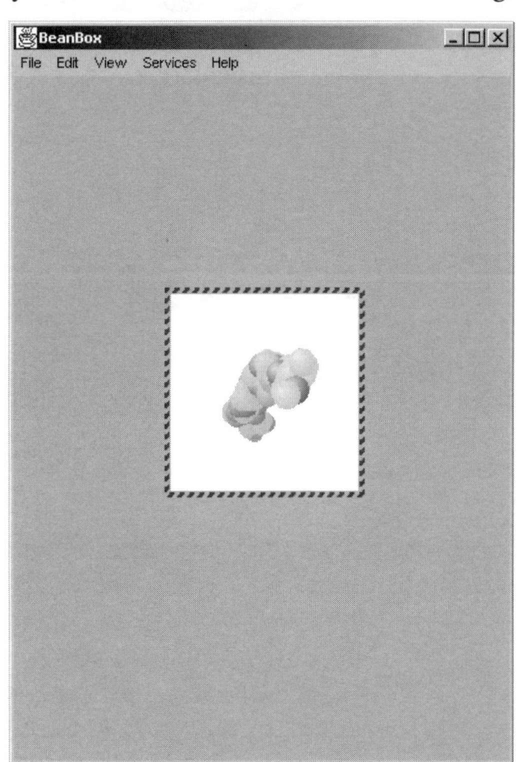

Step 2:

Place an instance of the Molecule bean on the work area. You can do this by finding the Molecule bean in the ToolBox to the left side of your screen and clicking on the Molecule bean. You will then move your mouse over the work area and "draw" out the area the bean is to occupy.

Step 3:

This bean only has one property, moleculeName. You will use the Properties window, to the right of your screen, to change that property to the buckminsterfullerine molecule. (I chose the buckminsterfullerine bean for personal reasons. I did a research paper on fullerenes for an analytical chemistry class in college. Yes, before you e-mail, I do realize it's a bit odd to have sentimental feelings for a molecular structure; what can I say?) Feel free to choose any molecule you wish.

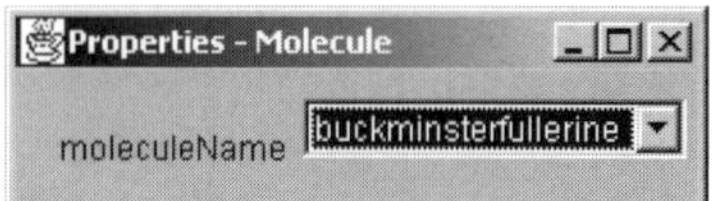

You should notice that the molecule displayed on the canvas is immediately changed. This is one of the wonderful things about the BeanBox. When you make changes to bean properties, you can see the effect of these changes immediately.

Step 4:

Now it's time to serialize this component. Don't worry, it won't hurt a bit. Just select File ▸ Serialize Component from the drop-down menu. You will then be presented with a dialog box prompting you to name the file in which you wish to save the state data. You can actually choose any file name you like; however, I recommend that you select molecule.ser.

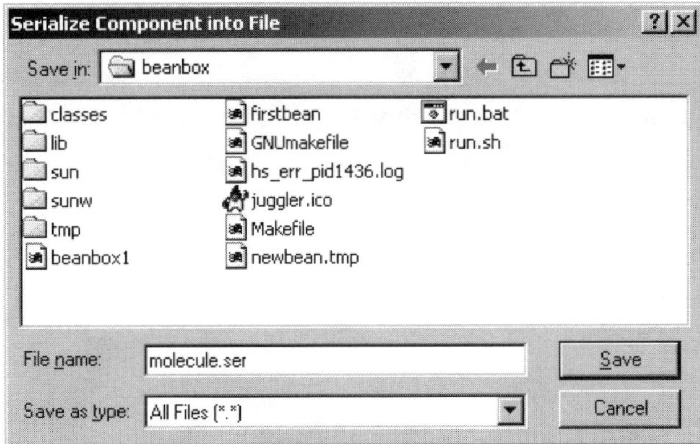

Step 5:

There's only one more step left to serialize this. Choose File ▸ Save from the drop-down menu. This will save the entire bean. Your bean and the property changes you effected are now serialized. What? You don't believe me? Press on, and the next two steps will make a believer out of you!

Step 6:

Clear the work area. You can do this by choosing File ▸ Clear from the drop-down menu to clear the canvas

Step 7:

Now for the moment of truth. Select File ▸ Load to reload your bean. You should notice that it is completely restored to its previous state.

Voilà! You have just used serialization and de-serialization. This won't quite compete with a David Copperfield show, but it is exciting nonetheless. At least, it is exciting to me, but then again, I have sentimental feelings for molecular structures.

I think that the most important thing you should notice about the preceding example is that the entire process of serialization and de-serialization happened in the background and was completely transparent to you, the bean developer. All you did was choose the Save option. What this did, however, was cause the bean to serialize itself. However, if you will look in the directory where the bean is located on your hard drive, you will now notice a molecule.ser file. There really is no reason for you to actually open that file in a text editor, but I am sure that at least some of my readers will (you are a mischievous bunch!). If you do open it in a text editor, don't be surprised; most of it will be incomprehensible. This does not indicate any problem and is exactly as it should be. The reason for the data appearing in this manner is that the data is in a specific format that the JavaBean expects when it de-serializes the bean.

The Serializable Interface

Now that you have had an introduction, albeit brief, to the concept of persistence via serialization, it is time to take a closer look at the serialization interface. Since this interface enables you to perform serialization, it seems prudent that you have some understanding of how it works, what it can do, and what it cannot do.

The Serializable interface is located in the java.io package. This interface does not define any methods or constants. Its only purpose is to identify that the class that implements it wishes to have its state serialized. The Serializable interface is hardly the only one that has no implementation code. Interfaces that define no methods or constants are often called *marker interfaces*. Their purpose is simply to identify the class that implements them as being a certain type of class. In order to use serialization, a class, or its parent class, the java.io.serializable interface must be implemented. If you attempt to serialize an object that does not implement this interface, a java.io.NotSerializableException is thrown.

It is important to note that not all classes are serializable. Fortunately, most of the classes frequently used with graphical interfaces are serializable. This is fortunate because most standard JavaBeans (the type of JavaBeans we have been discussing in these first four chapters) implement graphical interfaces, either from AWT or from Swing (pardon my shameless plug here, but if you wish to know more about Swing, you can check out my book, *JBuilder JFC and Swing Programming* due out in late 2002). For example, the component class, and hence all of its subclasses, is serializable. This means that all the various AWT (Abstract Windowing Toolkit) components (text field, button, etc.) are serializable.

However, as I mentioned, not all classes are serializable. For example, the thread class is not serializable. The reason for this is that the actual implementation of threading is tied to the particular implementation of the Java Virtual Machine (JVM). The sheer complexity of trying to serialize groups of threads on diverse platforms is a daunting task. Therefore, that class is simply not serializable. I am also not aware of any plans to make it serializable in a future version of Java.

Some of the classes in java.io are not serializable. This may seem a bit peculiar to you, considering that java.io is the package that contains the Serializable interface. However, due to the way some of these classes function, serialization becomes impractical. Since file access classes, such as FileInputStream, have transient states, depending on the amount of a file that has been written in or out, it can be very difficult to persist their state at a given moment. Therefore, many of the java.io classes are simply not serializable. It is for similar reasons that many of the classes in Java.net, such as Socket and ServerSocket, are also not serializable.

Foundations of Java 2 Persistence

The JavaBeans API specification details the specifics of the JavaBean serialization mechanism. For those readers who wish to pursue this topic to a greater depth than this book provides, you should refer to the Java API specification (URLs are provided for this and other resources in Appendix A). However, in the next few paragraphs, I will endeavor to give you a glimpse at what is happening behind the scenes with JavaBean persistence. It is certainly possible to be a competent JavaBean developer without this knowledge, but I feel that it is always better to have a more complete understanding of any technology one wishes to utilize. Besides, I am certain that my readers would never be satisfied with merely being competent!

Persistence, as it is implemented in Java 2, is not an entirely new technology. JavaBeans persistence in Java 2 is actually built on the framework of two Java 1.1 features: object serialization and introspection. As I will show you later in this chapter, you can still override the Java 2 serialization and implement object serializations if you so desire.

In order to support persistence in Java 2, it was necessary to add several classes and interfaces to the java.io package. These new classes and interfaces can, of course, read and write all of Java's built-in data types (int, float, double, etc.). The interfaces that describe how to read and write these data types are specified in java.io.DataOutput and java.io.DataInput.

Serialization Streams

As I have already mentioned, serialization is accomplished by writing the data regarding a particular object to a simple flat file on the machine. This file ends with the suffix .ser. As you should be aware, Java files are read from and written to via stream classes found in the java.io. So it should come as no surprise that there are stream classes that are essential to the process of serialization. The three stream classes of particular relevance to the topic of persistence are ObjectOutputStream, ObjectInputStream, and ObjectStreamClass. These three are essential to the process of serialization and will be discussed thoroughly in this section.

The ObjectOutputStream class is concerned, obviously, with serialization (as opposed to de-serialization, which is handled by the ObjectInputStream class). This class is used to serialize simple data types, arrays, and even objects. It has a number of methods, several of which are used in the serialization process. All methods of this class can throw an IOException. The methods of the ObjectOutputStream class are summarized in the following table:

Method	Description
Void close()	This method closes the stream.
Void flush()	This method flushes the stream.
Void reset()	This method resets the stream.
Void write(int I)	This method writes an integer to the stream.
Void write(byte b[])	This method writes a byte array to the stream.
Void write(byte b[], int index, int num)	This method writes a certain number of bytes in an array to the stream. It starts at the index provided.
Void writeBoolean(Boolean b)	This method writes a Boolean value to the stream.
Void writeByte(int b)	This method writes a single byte to the stream.
Void writeByte(string str)	This method writes a series of bytes to the stream.
Void writeChar(int chr)	This method writes a single character to the stream.
Void writeChars(string str)	This method writes a series of characters to the stream.
Void writeDouble(double d)	This method writes a double to the stream.
Void writeFloat(float f)	This method writes a float to the stream.
Void writeInt(int I)	This method writes an int to the stream.
Void writeLong(long l)	This method writes a long to the stream.
Void WriteObject(object o)	This method writes an object to the stream.
Void defaultWriteObject()	This method writes the non-static and non-transient values of the class to the stream.

If you are busy trying to memorize the preceding table, you need not expend that effort. It is not critical that you have an in-depth knowledge of all of these methods. It is merely important that you have a basic familiarity with the methods. However, you should pay particular attention to the last two methods. The defaultWriteObject() method handles standard persistence. As you might guess, the WriteObject() method is used to persist an entire object and is used with object serialization.

The ObjectInputStream class is used to de-serialize an object. Remember that de-serialization is the process of restoring an object's previous state when that object is re-instantiated. The ObjectInputStream class is responsible for reading the state information from the file to which it was saved. The following table summarizes the methods of this class.

Method	Description
Int available()	This method returns the number of bytes that are available to be read in.
Void close()	This method closes the stream.
Void defaultReadObject()	This method reads in all the non-static and non-transient fields of a class.
Int read()	This method returns a single byte from the stream. It blocks if no data is available.
Int read(byte b[], int index, int num)	This method reads a number of bytes (num) from the stream into an array, beginning at the index provided.
Boolean readBoolean()	This method reads a Boolean value from the stream.
Byte readByte()	This method reads a single byte from the stream.
Char readChar()	This method reads a single char from the stream.
Double readDouble()	This method reads a double from the stream.
Float readFloat()	This method reads a float from the stream.
Int readInt()	This method reads an int from the stream.
Long readLong()	This method reads a long from the stream.
Int skipBytes(int num)	This method skips a certain number of bytes in the stream.

Again, you may stop memorizing this table. As with the previous table, it is not critical that you understand each and every one of these methods. However, you should have a basic familiarity with the methods and the process used. This table is provided, primarily, as a reference tool to assist you in understanding de-serialization. You may wish to refer to it when writing your own JavaBeans (surely you keep this book on your desk, never more than an arm's length away!).

Object Persistence

You have seen that it is possible to persist individual variables. Often, you will have member variables that are primitive data types, such as integer, long, float, etc. These primitive data types can easily be persisted using standard serialization techniques. Simply make them member variables, and do not declare them as transient or final. However, this is not the limit of member variable persistence. It is even possible to persist an entire object. As you may have guessed, this is referred to as object persistence. Object persistence may seem like a novel or even a daunting concept; however, it is really no more difficult to grasp and utilize than standard serialization. By implementing and using two particular methods in your class, you can override the default serialization and will instead use object persistence.

If, in your class that implements the Serializable interface, you provide implementations for either of the following two methods, then the default serialization will not take place. Instead, these methods will be used to perform object serialization.

The methods in question are listed here:

```
private void WriteObject(java.io.ObjectOutputStream out)
   throws IOException;
private void ReadObject(java.io.ObjectInputStream in)
   throws IOException, ClassNotFoundException;
```

The presence of these methods will automatically override the default serialization mechanisms. You will then use those methods to implement object serialization. You can utilize both of these objects to handle the serialization of more complex objects. Recall that normally, serialization simply stores the values of the instance variables of a class. However, when the values you wish to store are complex objects, you will need a different method for serialization.

You can control how more complex objects are serialized by writing your own implementations of the WriteObject and ReadObject methods. You use the WriteObject method when you need to exercise greater control over what data gets serialized. When you need to serialize objects that default serialization cannot handle, object serialization is the methodology to use. You can then implement ReadObject to reconstruct the data stream you wrote with WriteObject. It is unlikely that you will need to utilize object serialization frequently. I can even guarantee that you will not need it to complete this book. If you are looking for more in-depth information on that topic, I suggest you refer to either the Sun Microsystems documentation or the JBuilder help files.

The Externalizable Interface

As previously mentioned, the Serializable interface is only one method for achieving object persistence, albeit the most commonly used method. The Externalizable interface is another methodology you can use, one which affords you greater control over the persistence process. You should consider using the Externalizable interface when you need complete control over your bean's persistence. In order to make this interface work, you will need to implement two methods: readExternal and writeExternal. Just like serializable classes, externalizable classes must also implement a no-arguments constructor.

Unlike serialization, each individual variable is not written into the stream with externalization. Only the identity of the class of an externalizable instance is written in the serialization stream. The responsibility of saving and restoring the contents of instance variables must be handled by the class itself. The writeExternal and readExternal methods of the Externalizable interface are implemented by a class that wishes to use externalization. These methods give the class complete control over the contents of the stream for an object. They also provide control over the format, and this is one of the primary reasons to choose externalization rather than serialization.

When an externalizable object is reconstructed, an instance is created using the public no-argument constructor. The readExternal method is then called to read in the state information that has been stored.

Object serialization can use either the Serializable or Externalizable interface. Each object to be stored is tested for the Externalizable interface. If the object supports externalizable, the writeExternal method is called. However, if the object does not support externalizable but does implement serializable, the object is saved using ObjectOutputStream.

Clearly, object serialization has some complexities that standard serialization does not involve. As I stated earlier, in most situations you will simply use the standard serialization, since it is far easier to implement. However, there may be occasions where you will require object serialization.

Serialization in JBuilder

As with everything else in Java, serialization is much easier to implement with JBuilder. Let's look at a JavaBean example and add serialization to that bean using JBuilder.

Once you have a bean that you wish to serialize, doing so is simple. Recall that in JBuilder when you choose File ▶ New, you can choose for the new code to be a JavaBean, illustrated in the following figure:

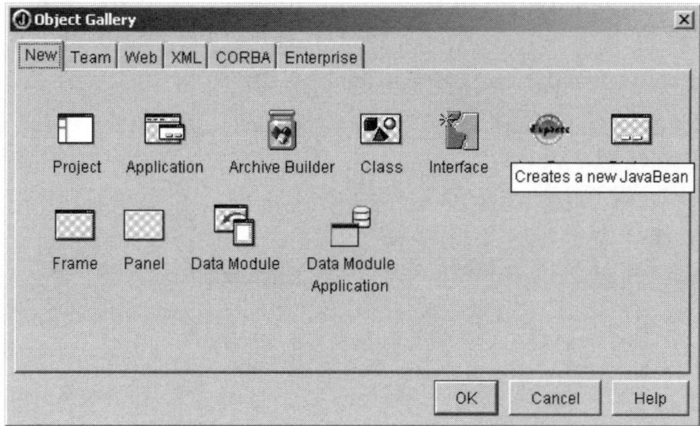

Select the Bean tab at the bottom, and then select the General tab. All that's left is to check the Support Serialization box:

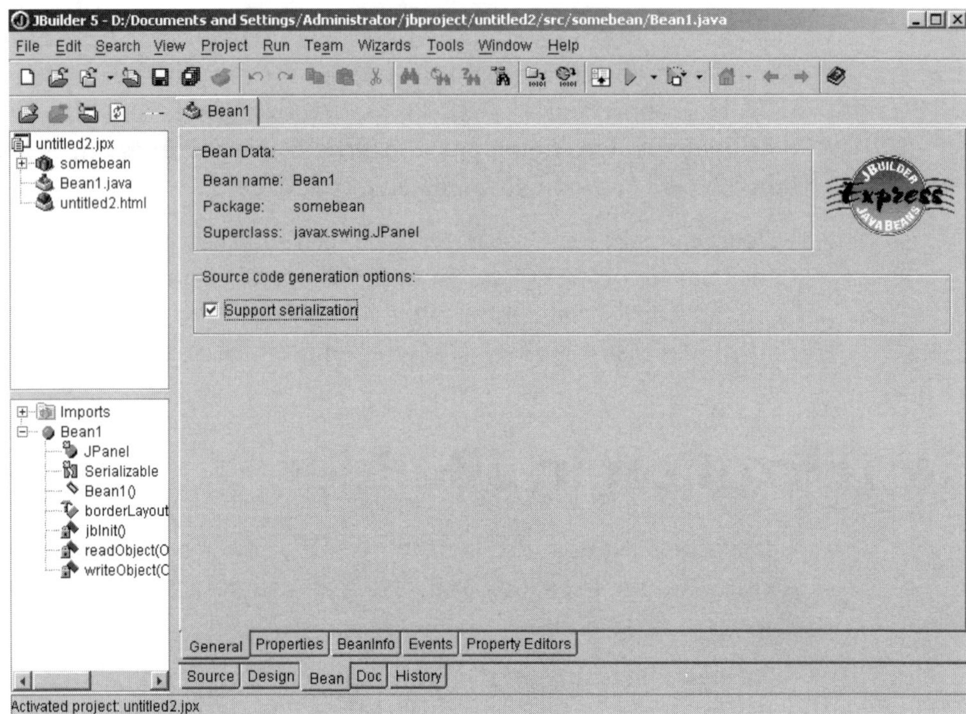

When you do this, the implements serializable code will automatically be added to your bean class. If you then return to the Source tab to view the source code, you will see something like this:

```java
package somebean;
import java.awt.*;
import javax.swing.JPanel;
import java.io.*;
public class Bean1 extends JPanel implements Serializable
{
  BorderLayout borderLayout1 = new BorderLayout();
  public Bean1()
  {
    try
    {
```

```java
      jbInit();
    }
    catch(Exception ex)
    {
      ex.printStackTrace();
    }
  }
  private void jbInit() throws Exception
  {
    this.setLayout(borderLayout1);
  }
  private void WriteObject(ObjectOutputStream oos) throws IOException
  {
    oos.defaultWriteObject();
  }
  private void ReadObject(ObjectInputStream ois) throws
      ClassNotFoundException, IOException
  {
    ois.defaultReadObject();
  }
}
```

Notice that the source code generated for you has all the necessary items for a valid JavaBean. It imports java.io and implements java.io.Serializable. There is a no-arguments constructor provided. You should also notice two methods: WriteObject() and ReadObject(). As you can see, JBuilder takes a lot of the work out of creating JavaBeans.

You should also note that the various methods that JBuilder has generated for you all throw the appropriate exceptions. You may have to write some exception handling in your bean, but only at a higher level, since all the methods throw the appropriate exceptions. However, you should note that there is a generic try-catch block in the main method (the one that initiates all the other code). So you can use the code directly as it is.

Summary

This chapter introduced you to a key subject in JavaBeans and Enterprise JavaBeans — persistence. You saw that there are two different interfaces that allow you to implement persistence, and each has its own advantages and disadvantages. You should recall that the vast majority of JavaBeans use automatic persistence with the serialization interface. This chapter also marks the end of the section on standard JavaBeans. These four chapters were, by no means, intended to make you an expert in JavaBeans. However, if you lack a background in JavaBean development or needed a refresher, then these chapters should have given you the requisite understanding to continue on with the study of Enterprise JavaBeans, the primary focus of this book. Please make certain that you are fully comfortable with the concepts of these first four chapters before continuing. Let me stress, however, that serialization will be a critical concept later in this book. Please make certain that you have a firm grasp on that topic before continuing.

Terms

Externalizable – A form of persistence that gives the programmer more control over what variables are persisted.

Java.io.NotSerializableException – The exception that is thrown if you attempt to serialize an object from a class that does not support serialization.

Serialization Stream – The stream that is used to read and write serialization data to and from the flat file that the data is stored in.

.ser Files – The flat files used to store serialization data.

De-serialization – The process of restoring data to an object from a flat file.

Object Serialization – The process of serializing object variables.

Review Questions

1. What is persistence?

2. What two interfaces allow you to implement persistence?

3. How would you make a particular instance variable not persist in a class that implemented Serializable?

4. What type of constructor must be used by classes that implement the Serializable interface?

5. Are thread objects serializable?

6. What package is the Serializable interface found in?

7. What two methods are used in object serialization?

8. When should you implement Externalizable rather than Serializable?

9. What advantage does Externalizable have?

10. Are socket classes serializable?

Chapter 5

Introduction to Enterprise JavaBeans

Introduction

Now that you have had an introduction to the basic concepts and uses of JavaBeans, you should be ready to move forward to Enterprise JavaBeans. This chapter is meant to be a bridge from the first four chapters on standard JavaBeans to the topic of Enterprise JavaBeans. For this reason, it is essential that you have a firm grasp on the topics presented in those first four chapters before continuing. Obviously, if you have a background developing JavaBeans, then you should be ready to move right into Enterprise JavaBeans. If not, you should study the first four chapters of this book. In this chapter, I will endeavor to provide you with the foundational working and conceptual knowledge base of Enterprise JavaBeans, which you will need throughout the rest of this book. I strongly recommend that you ensure that you are very familiar with this chapter and understand it thoroughly before moving on to Chapter 6.

The previous four chapters have taken you step by step through the fundamental concepts of JavaBeans. Those chapters introduced you to the concepts behind JavaBeans, the purpose of JavaBeans, and the creation of simple JavaBeans. However, this book's primary focus is *Enterprise JavaBeans*. This chapter will summarize the uses, characteristics, and types of Enterprise JavaBeans. The material in this chapter provides an important overview of much of the material in the rest of this book. In fact, Chapters 6 through 12 are really just expansions of topics you will be briefly introduced to in this chapter. Some readers may be tempted to skip this overview and move straight on to the next chapter. I strongly advise against this, since the overview provided in this chapter will give you the foundation necessary to fully master the topics presented in the subsequent chapters.

Before you continue with this book, I need to address a basic question. That question is simply: What are Enterprise JavaBeans and how do they differ from standard JavaBeans? Obviously, both are JavaBeans, and therefore have some similar characteristics. However, I assure you that the functionality of the two is quite different. An enterprise bean is a server-side component that runs inside an application server. It has some significant differences from a standard JavaBean. To begin with, it is not used as a building block for other applications. Instead, it is itself a deployable component. In fact, it will always be deployed into an EJB container before it can be used. An EJB will never be used as a building block for an application, though it is frequently a component in a multi-layered system.

The most common use of Enterprise JavaBeans is to encapsulate the business logic of a multi-tiered application. The business logic is the code that fulfills the primary function of the application. You can think of the business logic as the "engine" of a multi-tiered application. For example, if you had a sales application, you might create an Enterprise JavaBean that would encapsulate various sales rules, such as verifying inventory, computing sales tax, and totaling commissions. Enterprise JavaBeans are the preferred Java method for creating multi-tiered applications. An overview of distributed applications is provided in the next section, and a more detailed examination of distributed applications is provided later in this book.

Since Enterprise JavaBeans (EJB) are not components for building applications, they are not applets, and they are not console applications, you may wonder how and where they run. They run on the server and are hosted by an EJB container called an application server. Many EJB developers use BEA Web Logic for this purpose. However, users of Borland's JBuilder already have a fully functional application server when they purchase the Enterprise edition of JBuilder. That edition of JBuilder comes with an application server, as well as many other interesting and useful tools. This application server, whatever specific brand you use, does more than simply provide a container for the Enterprise JavaBean. It handles a number of services necessary for distibuted applications. For example, the EJB container is responsible for system-level services, such as transaction management and security authorization.

Enterprise JavaBeans can significantly simplify the development of distributed applications. Enterprise JavaBeans can simplify your development because they run in an application server. This EJB container provides a number of services to the enterprise beans, thus allowing the bean developer to concentrate on solving business problems rather than on the details of implementing and maintaining the business layer. Enterprise JavaBeans can also simplify distributed application development due to the fact that the business logic is contained in the EJB, allowing the client developer to focus on the presentation of the client. This also means that the clients are thinner. A thinner client means one that requires less resources (i.e., takes up less RAM). Since the business logic is actually on the EJB, which resides on an application server, the client side can be rather small with useless resources. While this can be a benefit in any development situation, it is particularly useful for clients that run on low-resource devices. Thin, or lightweight clients, make deploying the client simpler as well. The less resources and dependencies a client has, the less you will have to distribute and configure. It also means that modifications to the business logic don't require a re-writing and re-deployment of the client.

Distributed Applications

Since Enterprise JavaBeans are used in the development of distributed applications, it seems prudent to have a brief discussion about distributed applications. Many readers will already be familiar with distributed applications. This section is provided for those of you who are not or who simply want a brief refresher on the topic. Distributed applications have become the norm in modern business development, and it is therefore imperative that any developer become thoroughly acquainted with the topic.

In the past, most applications were single-component monolithic applications. Everything from mainframe applications written in COBOL to desktop applications written in C were formed from a single monolithic component. If any portion of the process changed, the entire application had to be recompiled and redistributed. This single-layer approach also stifled scalability. If a business grew, as all businesses wish to, single-unit software could not easily be scaled to handle increased demand. This type of architectural design is referred to as single tiered.

Eventually, the concept of client-server applications became prominent. In a client-server architecture, there is a centralized server component where the data is stored. Business rules may also be implemented at this layer, or they can be implemented in the client. The client layer is located on individual machines and provides the interface for users to interact with the system. This interface is often graphical in nature. When you use a web page, you are interacting with a client-server system. Your web browser is the client, and the web server you are connecting too is the server.

While this architecture is a significant improvement over single-unit applications, it still has some serious limitations. Scalability is still arduous to implement. A problem also arises if you have multiple types of clients, such as a desktop application client or a web interface client. However, this type of architecture is distributed, and it is referred to as two-tiered architecture.

The next stage in the development of distributed architectures was the n-tiered architecture. The n simply stands for some number, usually greater than two. Three- and four-tiered architectures are quite common. In this system, additional layers are interposed between the client and the database.

You might find a business layer that handles all the business rules of an organization. You might also find a database layer that handles all the actual communication with the database.

N-tiered architectures lend themselves to scalability and maintainability. If a particular portion of the system becomes a bottleneck for performance, then that layer can be distributed to multiple servers or simply moved to a more powerful server. Either method can be completely transparent to the client applications. Furthermore, the client's applications themselves need only handle the presentation of the interface to the user and the communication with the next tier. This means that you can create very lightweight clients.

Enterprise JavaBeans are particular well suited to *n*-tiered architecture. They are most often used to create the business layer, but they can also create the database layer. In fact, they are appropriate for any tier other than the actual user interface. The entire purpose of EJBs is to provide you with the middle layers in a multi-tiered architecture. They may function as the data layer, business layer, or some other intermediate layer in your distributed architecture. However, they are never used for the presentation layer. The presentation layer is almost always a GUI (Graphical User Interface) client. EJBs are simply not appropriate for this particular task. More appropriate technologies for the presentation layer include applets, HTML documents, Java server pages, and standard Java applications.

When Should You Use EJBs?

While I happen to think that Enterprise JavaBeans are a wonderful tool for developers, no tool is perfect for every situation. Before you embark on creating your own Enterprise JavaBeans, it is important that you understand the most appropriate situations in which to use these beans. Of course, you could use an EJB in virtually any situation. However, like any tool, using it in ways it was not designed for will certainly reduce the efficacy of the tool in question. You should probably consider using Enterprise JavaBeans if your application requirements include either of the following items:

- The application may have diverse clients. An EJB can be accessed, concurrently, from a variety of clients. You might have a standard

Java application and a Java server page, but acting as separate types of presentation layers for the same EJB.

- The application needs to be scalable. Scalability is a concern that should be on the mind of anyone developing an enterprise solution. EJBs can be moved to different machines, and the location is transparent to the client. This means that if you need to upgrade to a better machine or distribute components across more machines, it can be done with relative ease.

Types of EJBs

Now that you have a basic understanding of what an Enterprise JavaBean is and in what situations it is best used, it is time to begin to describe EJBs in more detail. The first step in describing any object is classification. Enterprise JavaBeans come in more than one variety, and these varieties of EJBs are classified according to their functionality. There are three types of Enterprise JavaBeans: session, entity, and message-driven. Each of these types serves a different purpose and behaves somewhat differently than the others. Each will be discussed in this chapter and more fully explored in subsequent chapters. In fact, each type of EJB has an entire chapter devoted to it, and in some cases, two chapters. The following table lists the three different types of enterprise beans:

Type	Purpose
Session	Performs a task for a client application.
Entity	Represents a business entity object that exists in persistent storage.
Message-Driven	Acts as a listener for the Java Message Service API, processing messages asynchronously.

Session Beans

The first type of bean, a session bean, is perhaps the most commonly encountered type of EJB. A session bean, as the name should imply, represents a single session with a client. Of course, this leads to the obvious question of, what, exactly, is a session? A *session* is a sequence of events that occur in a given time frame. Once the client disconnects from the server, the session ends. Another term for a session, a more generic term, is a conversation. You might think of a session as a finite conversation between a client and an Enterprise JavaBean. Each conversation will cover only one topic, and when the conversation is over, both parties disconnect.

A session bean represents a single client inside the application server. To access an application that is deployed on the server, the client utilizes the session bean's public methods and properties. The session bean performs tasks for its client and returns results to the client. It represents a single interactive session with a client. A session bean cannot be shared by multiple clients simultaneously; it can only have one user at a time. However, a session bean can have an unlimited number of sequential clients. Put another way, a session bean can only handle one client at a time, but it can handle a virtually unlimited number of clients in sequence.

An important feature of session beans is that they are not persistent (recall Chapter 4's discussion of persistence). When the client terminates, its session bean appears to terminate and is no longer associated with the client. None of its state information is retained. Its data is not saved to any type of permanent storage. However, it should be noted that it is likely that the session bean has merely been returned to a pool of session beans in the application server and not really destroyed. Usually, the EJB container will keep available session beans in a pool. When a client requests the services of a session bean, one of the available EJBs is taken from the pool and made available for the client. Once the session is over, the bean is returned to the pool.

There are actually two subtypes of session beans: stateful and stateless.

The state of an object essentially consists of the values in its instance variables. In a stateful session bean, these instance variables represent the state of a particular client-bean session. Since the client interacts with its bean, this state is sometimes referred to as the conversational state. The state of all session beans is retained for the duration of the client-bean session. If the client removes the bean or terminates the connection, the session ends and the state disappears. A stateful session bean is essentially one which retains the current state of its dialog with the client until the session ends. It is important that you do not confuse this with persistence, which is storing the state between sessions, something session beans do not do. A stateful session bean may continue its "conversation" with the client for a period of time that includes several different method calls. The fact that the client-bean session may last through multiple method calls is why stateful session beans retain state information between method calls.

A stateless session bean is simply a session bean that does not maintain any conversational state for a client. When a client invokes the method of a stateless bean, the bean's instance variables may contain a state, but only for as long as it takes for that method to complete. When the method is finished, the state is no longer retained. While stateful session beans retain the state for the entire session, stateless session beans only retain a given state for as long as it takes to execute a method. No conversation is maintained beyond the time it takes to execute a single method. So essentially, stateless session beans are appropriate for single-method invocation conversations, and if more then one method will be invoked during the session, then a stateful session bean is the appropriate choice.

You might wonder why one would wish to have a stateless session bean. Why not simply always retain the client state? Since a stateless bean does not retain the client's state throughout the entire session, it can support multiple simultaneous clients. Because stateless session beans can concurrently support multiple clients, they can offer better scalability for applications that require large numbers of clients. Because you do not require a one-to-one ratio between stateless session beans and clients, an application requires fewer stateless session beans than stateful session beans to support the same number of clients.

It is important to address the question of when to use session beans as opposed to entity beans or message-driven beans. Even though I have not yet explained these other EJB types to you, I can still give you an adequate answer to this question. There are several circumstances that lend themselves to session beans over other types of beans. If at any given time, more than one client has access to the bean instance, then a session bean might be preferred. If it is not important for the state of the bean to be persistent, existing only for a short period of time, a session bean is more appropriate. Or simply put, if you don't need persistence, are not trying to represent a database table, and wish several clients to interact with a single EJB, then session beans are the logical choice.

Once you have decided that session beans are the appropriate choice for your situation, you will still need to make another decision. You will then need to determine whether stateful or stateless session beans are more appropriate for your situation. A stateful bean is simply one that maintains state information for the duration of a given session. A stateless bean does not even retain state information between method calls.

If the bean's state represents the interaction between the bean and a single specific client, you may wish to use a stateful bean. Or if the client-EJB inter-action will require more than one method call to complete, a stateful session bean may be your best choice. If, however, your bean needs to work with more than one client simultaneously, you will need to use a stateless bean. If the bean needs to hold information about the client between method invoca-tions, you will need a stateless session bean. Carefully consider the circumstances of your development project before choosing what type of ses-sion bean you will use. Chapters 7 and 8 discuss stateless and stateful session beans at length. Those chapters also show you how to create your own session beans.

You will notice that Chapters 7 and 8 are devoted completely to session beans. The reason that session beans receive coverage in two entire chapters is simple: Session beans are the most common type of bean used. They are also perhaps the simplest to create and implement. For these reasons, they warrant a bit more thorough coverage than other types of Enterprise JavaBeans.

Entity Beans

The next type of Enterprise JavaBean I would like to introduce is the entity bean. Entity beans represent a particular business object or entity, thus their name. They are frequently closely tied to an underlying database and may represent an actual table in a database. Since they represent a specific business object, rather than a particular session, they support persistence. This should be rather obvious given that a particular business object will probably exist independently of specific client sessions interacting with it. In short, an entity bean represents some business object with a persistent storage mechanism. In the Java 2 Enterprise Edition Software Development Kit (SDK), the mechanism for persistent storage is a relational database. Each entity bean has an associated table in a relational database. Since you may have multiple instances of an entity bean active at any given time, each instance of the bean is stored in a separate row in that table. The database is simply a standard relational database. You can use any database system that you are comfortable with. In this book, I use Microsoft Access examples simply because Microsoft Access is so common, and readers are likely to have access to it. However, the techniques shown would work equally well with Oracle, DB2, or Microsoft SQL Server.

There are several differences between entity beans and session beans, but the most obvious is that entity beans support persistence. Session beans cannot retain their state between sessions; however, entity beans can and do retain their state. In fact, an entity bean not only can retain its state, it <u>must</u> retain its state. It must retain that state for as long as the business object it is representing is a valid and accessible business object. In addition to supporting persistence, entity beans allow shared access. This means that multiple clients may access the same entity bean simultaneously. Remember that an entity bean represents some business object, not a particular session. Therefore, support for simultaneous multiple clients makes perfect sense.

Persistence was discussed at some length in Chapter 4. If you require a refresher on that topic, please reread that chapter. However, in the case of an entity bean, the meaning of persistence can be summarized as follows: Persistence means that the entity bean's state exists beyond the lifetime of the application or the application server process. There are certainly times when this will be necessary.

For entity beans, there are actually two types of persistence: bean-managed and container-managed. The essential difference between bean-managed persistence and container-managed persistence is simply whether or not the bean itself is responsible for the underlying mechanism of persistence. With bean-managed persistence, the entity bean code contains the calls that access the database. The mechanism for persistence is managed within the bean itself. This means that you, the EJB programmer, will be required to write the actual database access code within your entity bean. However, with container-managed persistence, the EJB container automatically generates the necessary database access calls. The container, usually an application server, handles the mechanisms for persistence.

Entity beans can be shared by multiple clients. However, it is possible that different clients may wish to work with the same underlying data. How to handle this issue is of paramount importance, not just for EJB development, but for any distributed development. For this reason, entity beans work within *transactions*. A transaction is a cohesive set of actions, usually method calls and returns, that work together, often in their own thread. You will receive a thorough coverage of transactions later in this book. For now though, only a basic working knowledge is required. The reason you don't require an in-depth knowledge of transactions is that the Enterprise JavaBean container will handle most of the transaction details for you. Typically, the EJB container is responsible for managing the transaction; the developer does not need to directly handle the coding for transaction management. The programmer simply has to specify the transaction attributes in the bean's deployment descriptor.

Recall that entity beans store their state information in an underlying relational database management system. This means that entity beans share some commonalities with the structure of RDBMS, such as primary keys. Each entity bean has a unique object identifier, or primary key, which is used to identify that bean. The unique identifier enables the client to locate a particular entity bean.

Another important characteristic that entity beans share with relational database systems is the ability to have well established relationships between objects. In a relational database, a record or set of records in one database table can be related to, or linked to, one or more records residing in one or more other database tables. In fact, the entire term "relational database," refers to the fact that the various elements of the database have well-defined relationships. What this fact means for EJB development is that an entity bean may be related to other entity beans. For example, in an employee application, the EmployeeEJB and JobDescriptionEJB beans could be related.

The handling of relationships is one key difference between bean-managed persistence and container-managed persistence. In bean-managed persistence, the programmer has to write the code that manages the persistence. However, with container-managed persistence, the EJB container handles the relationship. For this reason, relationships in entity beans with container-managed persistence are often referred to as container-managed relationships.

Remember that container-managed persistence means that the EJB container handles all database access required by the entity bean. The bean's code contains no code to access the database. The advantage to this is that the container-managed entity bean is not tied to a particular database platform, making it more portable.

In order to generate the code to handle data access calls, the container needs information that you provide in the entity bean's abstract schema.

The abstract schema is part of an entity bean's deployment descriptor. It defines the bean's persistent fields and relationships. The term "abstract" is meant to illustrate the difference between this schema and the physical schema of the underlying database. For example, in a relational database, the physical schema is made up of structures such as tables, records, and columns. The name of an abstract schema is specified in the deployment descriptor. For an entity bean with container-managed persistence, you must define an EJB query language query for all finder methods (except findByPrimaryKey). The EJB query determines the query that is executed by the EJB container when the finder method is invoked. We will discuss this query language in more depth in later chapters.

Interfaces

I have discussed, briefly, the interaction of clients with both session and entity Enterprise JavaBeans. You may be curious to know exactly how clients interact with Enterprise JavaBeans. Clients do not directly interact with EJBs. In fact, the client is not even aware of what machine the EJB is on. The client is, however, aware of what application server the enterprise is using. That application server handles the specifics of communicating with the EJBs. This is accomplished by providing the client with interfaces. The interface communicates with the application server, which locates the EJB needed. A client can only access a session or an entity bean through the methods defined in the bean's interfaces. These interfaces define how the client will view the bean. All other aspects of the bean are hidden from the client.

It will be important when we move on to actually developing Enterprise JavaBeans to give great consideration to how you design your interfaces. Ideally, in any distributed architecture, the interface should be immutable, regardless of any changes made to the underlying mechanisms. This means that once you have designed your interface and deployed it, it will not change. You may change the underlying code inside an interface, but the actual method declarations, parameters, and return types should not change. If the interface is changed, then any client applications will have to be modified as well. Well-designed interfaces simplify the development and maintenance of J2EE applications. For example, even if you change your entity beans from bean-managed to container-managed persistence, you should not have to alter the client code. If your interfaces are well designed, this will be the case. In fact most changes in the business layer should be completely transparent to the client layer. However, if you do not design your EJBs properly, maintenance can be a very cumbersome task.

Message-Driven Beans

As you might suspect, a message-driven bean works via the passage of messages. If you have experience doing Windows programming with C++, especially Visual C++, you should be experienced with the concept of messages. For those readers who lack such a background, here is a simple explanation. A message is much like an event, but one that is directed at a particular target. That target then has code to respond to a given message. Whereas events are general and any component may listen for a given event, messages are targeted at a particular object. A message-driven bean is an enterprise bean that allows applications to process messages asynchronously. It acts as a message listener, which is similar to an event listener except it receives messages instead of events. The messages may be sent by any Java 2 Enterprise component, be it an application client, another enterprise bean, or a web component. In some cases, a message-driven bean can even receive messages from non-J2EE components, provided they are sent in a compliant fashion. Message-driven beans rely on Java Message Service (JMS) technology. For this reason, message-driven beans can currently process only JMS messages.

The message is sent to a message-driven EJB and when the message arrives, the container calls the message-driven bean's onMessage method to process the message. The onMessage method will normally cast the message to one of the five JMS message types and handles it in accordance with the application's business logic. The onMessage method may, of course, call additional helper methods. It may even invoke a session or entity bean to process the information in the message or store it in a database.

A message may be delivered to a message-driven bean within a transaction context. This would mean that all operations within the onMessage method are part of a single transaction.

The obvious question at this point would be, what are the essential differences between message-driven beans and session or entity beans? The most noticeable difference between message-driven beans and session and entity beans is that clients do not access message-driven beans through interfaces. Unlike a session or entity bean, a message-driven bean has only a bean class. In some ways, a message-driven bean resembles a stateless session bean.

A message-driven bean's instances do not retain their state. Since the message-driven beans have no state, all instances of a message-driven bean are equivalent. This means that the EJB container assigns a message to any message-driven bean instance. The container can pool these instances to allow streams of messages to be processed concurrently. The instance variables of the message-driven bean instance can contain some very limited state data across the handling of client messages (for example, an open database connection). A single message-driven bean can process messages from multiple clients.

Now, of course, we come to the question of when to use message-driven beans rather than session beans or entity beans. Session beans and entity beans will also allow you to send and receive JMS messages. However, messages sent and received by session or entity beans must be processed synchronously, not asynchronously. If you wish to receive messages asynchronously, use a message-driven bean. In any distributed architecture system, asynchronous operations can be vital. They allow a client to initiate some process in the business layer without tying the client up, waiting for the process to conclude.

All Enterprise JavaBeans must implement the javax.ejb.EnterpriseBeans interface or one of the interfaces that inherit from it, such as javax.ejb.SessionBean or javax.ejb.EntityBean. This interface is simply a marker interface (it has no implementation code) and is simply used to identify the class as an EJB class. You should note that the javax.ejb.EnterpriseBeans interface implements Serializable. This is required for any class that wishes to serialize its data. This means that all EJBs are capable of serialization.

EJB Clients

I have spent the bulk of this chapter introducing you to the basics of Enterprise JavaBeans and their role in the business tier of a multi-tiered enterprise system. However, no system is of much use without a client tier that users can interact with. For this reason, it is important for me to take a moment to provide you with an overview of the interactions of the client tier, with respect to the Enterprise JavaBean business tier. When you design a J2EE application, one of the first decisions you make is the type of client access allowed by the enterprise beans. Clients have only two access options: remote or local.

A client that uses remote access to interact with an Enterprise JavaBean may run on a different machine and a different Java Virtual Machine (JVM) than the enterprise bean it accesses. It may be a web component, a J2EE application client, or even another enterprise bean. The location of the Enterprise JavaBean should be completely transparent to the remote client.

Creating an enterprise bean with remote access requires that you actually create two interfaces. You will need to create a remote interface and a home interface. The remote interface defines the business methods that are specific to the bean. It is the remote interface that the user will be calling in order to actually access the bean's functionality. The home interface will define the life cycle methods of the bean. These life cycle methods are create and remove. Essentially, the remote interface is the one that defines the actual interactions with the EJB, whereas the home interface simply allows the client to create and destroy instances of the EJB. For entity beans, the home interface must also define the finder methods and home methods. Finder methods are used to locate entity beans. Home methods are business methods that are invoked on all instances of an entity bean class.

Local access clients must run in the same JVM as the enterprise bean it accesses. It will most likely be web components or another enterprise bean. Local clients are often entity beans that have a container-managed relationship with another entity bean. The location of the enterprise bean it accesses is not transparent to a local client.

If an entity bean is the target of a container-managed relationship, it must have local interfaces. The direction of the relationship determines whether or not a bean is the target. Since they require local access, entity beans that participate in a container-managed relationship must reside in the same EJB JAR file. One significant benefit of this local interface method is increased performance. Local calls are almost always faster than remote calls.

This adds one more decision that you have to make before you create your Enterprise JavaBeans. That decision is whether to use local or remote access. If an entity bean is the target of a container-managed relationship, then the decision is made for you; it must use local access. If an enterprise bean is accessed by J2EE application clients, then it should allow remote access. Note that I said _allow_ remote access. That does not mean that it cannot also have, and even primarily use, local access. These clients almost always run on different machines than the J2EE server. If an enterprise bean's clients are web components or other enterprise beans, then the type of access depends on how you want to distribute your components. If the web server and application server are on the same machine, local access might be appropriate.

Another important factor in deciding on what type of interface to implement is the type of coupling you wish to have between the EJB and the client. Tightly coupled beans depend on one another. If a bean is tightly coupled to another bean, then it cannot function without the other bean. If you are using tightly coupled beans, you should at least consider local access. Since these components work together as a logical unit, they are likely to call each other often and would benefit from the increased performance that is possible with local access. The decision of coupling is particularly important when the client is another EJB.

If you are not sure which type of client access an EJB should have, use remote access. This decision gives you more flexibility and scalability. In the future, you can distribute your components to accommodate growing demands on your application. Although uncommon, it is actually possible for an enterprise bean to allow both remote and local access. However, such a bean would require both remote and local interfaces.

An important thing for any EJB programmer to realize is how arguments are passed with different interfaces. An argument in a remote call is passed by value, but an argument in a local call is passed by reference, just like a normal method call in the Java programming language. Passing by value means that the value contained in some variable is copied from the calling function to the parameter. In a call by reference, all that is passed is a reference to the location in memory where that variable in the calling function is. If you give this some thought, passing by value should seem very logical. It is not possible to pass values by reference to a component residing on a different machine in a different JVM. The reference to an address in memory would be meaningless on the other machine.

Since parameters in remote calls are passed by value, the parameters of remote calls are more isolated than those of local calls. If the client changes the value of the object, the value of the copy in the bean does not change. This layer of isolation can lend itself easily to improved data validation. Remember that with passing by value, the client and bean operate on different copies of a parameter object. When passing by reference, as in a local interface, both the client and the bean may modify the same object.

The Life Cycles of Enterprise Beans

Like any software component, an EJB has a well-defined life cycle. Before you begin developing your own Enterprise JavaBeans, you should become acquainted with this life cycle. Each type of enterprise bean has a different life cycle. The life cycle of each type of EJB is discussed in this section.

In the life cycle of a stateful session bean, the client initiates the life cycle by invoking the create method. The EJB container then instantiates the bean and invokes the setSessionContext and ejbCreate methods in that session bean. The bean is now fully invoked and ready to have its business methods invoked. The EJB container may decide to deactivate, or passivate, the bean by moving it from memory to secondary storage. This is accomplished by invoking the bean's ejbPassivate method immediately before passivating it. If a client invokes a business method on the bean while it is in the passive stage, the EJB container will activate the bean, moving it back to the ready stage, and then call the bean's ejbActivate method. When the client is done with the bean, it can invoke the remove method and the EJB container calls the bean's ejbRemove method. This marks the end of the stateful bean's life cycle, and the bean's instance is now ready for garbage collection.

A stateless session bean is never passivated. Therefore, its life cycle has just two stages: nonexistent and ready for the invocation. In short, the stateless session bean is either ready for use or removed from memory.

An entity bean life cycle is a bit different from the session bean. After the EJB container creates the instance, it calls the setEntityContext method of the entity bean class. The setEntityContext method passes the entity context to the bean. It essentially establishes what context this business object is operating within. Once an entity bean is instantiated, it moves to a pool of available instances. While in this pooled stage, the instance is not associated with any particular EJB object identity. All instances in the pool are identical. When moving it to the ready stage, the EJB container assigns an identity to an instance. One way that the instance may move from the pooled state is by the client invoking the create method. This causes the EJB container to call the ejbCreate and ejbPostCreate methods. The EJB container can also move the instance from the pooled status to the ready status by invoking the ejbActivate method. While in the ready stage, an entity bean's business methods may be invoked.

As you might suspect, the client and the container can also move the instance from the ready status back to the pooled status. A client can invoke the remove method, which causes the EJB container to call the ejbRemove method. The EJB container can also invoke the ejbPassivate method. When the EJB container removes the instance from the pool and invokes the unsetEntityContext method, the life cycle is ended.

The EJB container will usually create a pool of message-driven bean instances. For each instance, the EJB container instantiates the bean and performs several tasks. To begin with, it lets the bean know what its context is. It does this by calling the setMessageDrivenContext method to pass the context object to the instance.

The EJB container also calls the instance's ejbCreate method. Like a stateless session bean, a message-driven bean is never passivated, and it has only two states: nonexistent and ready to receive messages. At the end of the life cycle, the container calls the ejbRemove method. The bean's instance is ready for garbage collection.

Passivation and Activation

There are only two more terms I need to introduce you to so that you can have a theoretical understanding of how Enterprise JavaBeans work. Those terms are *passivation* and *activation*. Passivation and activation are two phases of a resource management technique that reduces the number of bean instances required to service all clients. Passivation is the process whereby a bean instance is dissociated from its EJB object so that the instance can be reused by another client or simply removed from memory. Activation is the opposite process. Passivation literally means to make the bean passive, or inactive. Activation is the process of associating a bean instance with an EJB object so that it can service client requests. Activation literally means to activate a bean, or to make it ready for some action. When the EJB object receives a request, the bean is activated. When a bean has been idle for a period of time, it is passivated. This process is completely transparent to the programmer.

Both session beans and entity beans support activation and passivation. They do this through methods in the interfaces they implement. The java.ejb.SessionBean and javax.ejb.EntityBean interfaces both include a call-back method that notifies a bean instance when it is about to be passivated or activated. The ejbPassivate() method notifies a bean that it is about to passivated, and, as you probably guessed, the ejbActivate() method notifies a bean that it is about to be activated. You can, of course, write code to respond to these events; however, the process is automatic and generally works best if you leave it alone!

Exactly what happens when a bean is activated or passivated depends on the type of EJB in question. For example, when a stateful session bean is passivated, it is usually removed from memory, while entity beans and stateless session beans are pooled for future use.

Using Borland JBuilder and EJB

The goal of this book is to teach you to create and use Enterprise JavaBeans. Throughout this book, I will continue the practice I began in Chapter 1, showing you how something is done using the standard Sun Java Development tools and then showing you how to do it more efficiently with Borland's JBuilder. You will find, starting in Chapter 7, that EJBs are much more efficiently developed using Borland JBuilder. However, before you can enable the enterprise development tools inside JBuilder, you must make sure you installed the Borland Application Server. It is on the same CD as your JBuilder Enterprise. If you did not install it when you installed JBuilder, stop now and install the application server. Once it is installed, you can enable enterprise development tools by following these simple steps:

Step 1:

From the drop-down menu in JBuilder, select Tools ▸ Enterprise Setup as shown in the following figure.

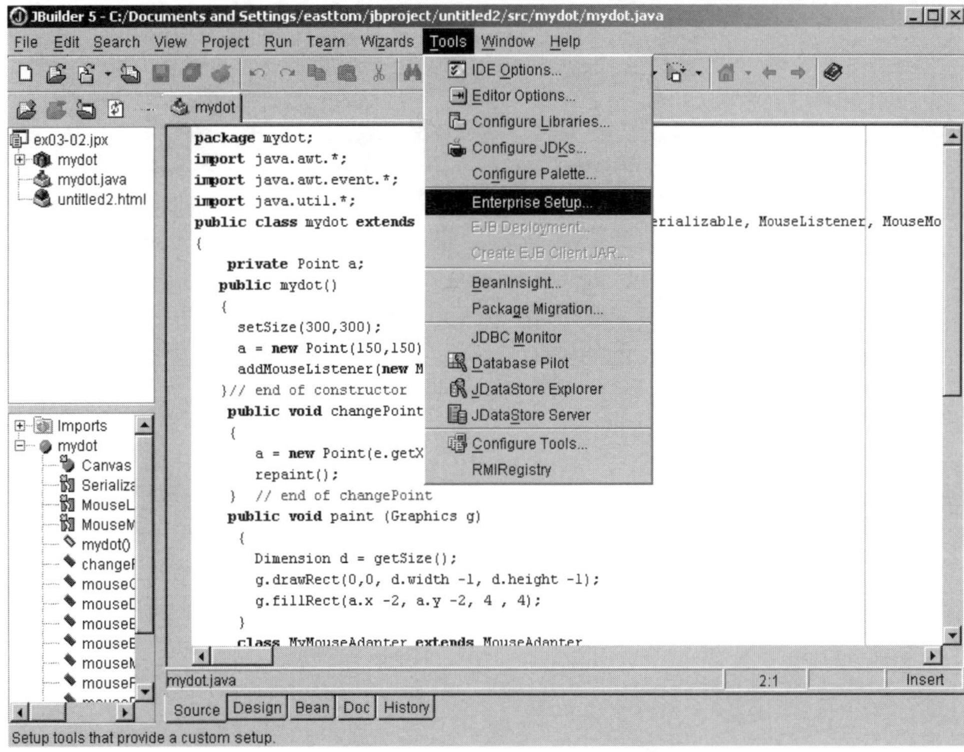

Step 2:

This will take you to a screen where you select the application server you wish to use.

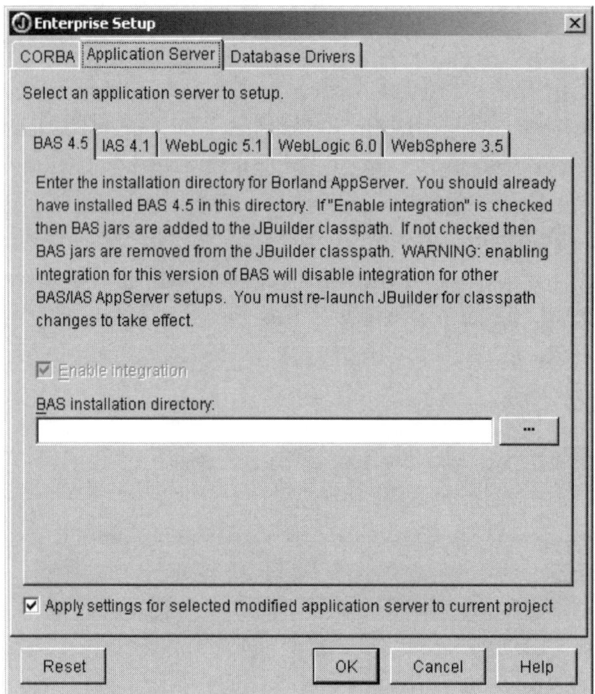

Borland allows you to integrate other vendor application servers into your JBuilder; however, we will use the Borland Application Server. So click on the small button next to the text field, and you will be presented with a dialog box.

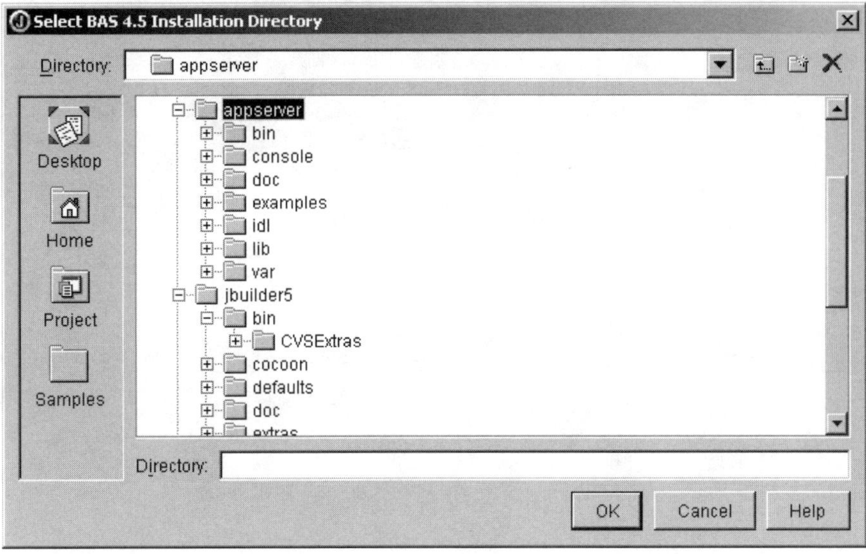

Step 3:

Use this dialog box to locate the directory in which you installed the Borland Application Server.

Step 4:

Then click OK, and the Application Server will be integrated with JBuilder.

You will have to restart JBuilder to see all the changes. When you do restart you will notice several fascinating new options in the drop-down menu. You will notice a new wizard for creating EJBs, shown in the following figure. This wizard is a tool we will use frequently later in this book.

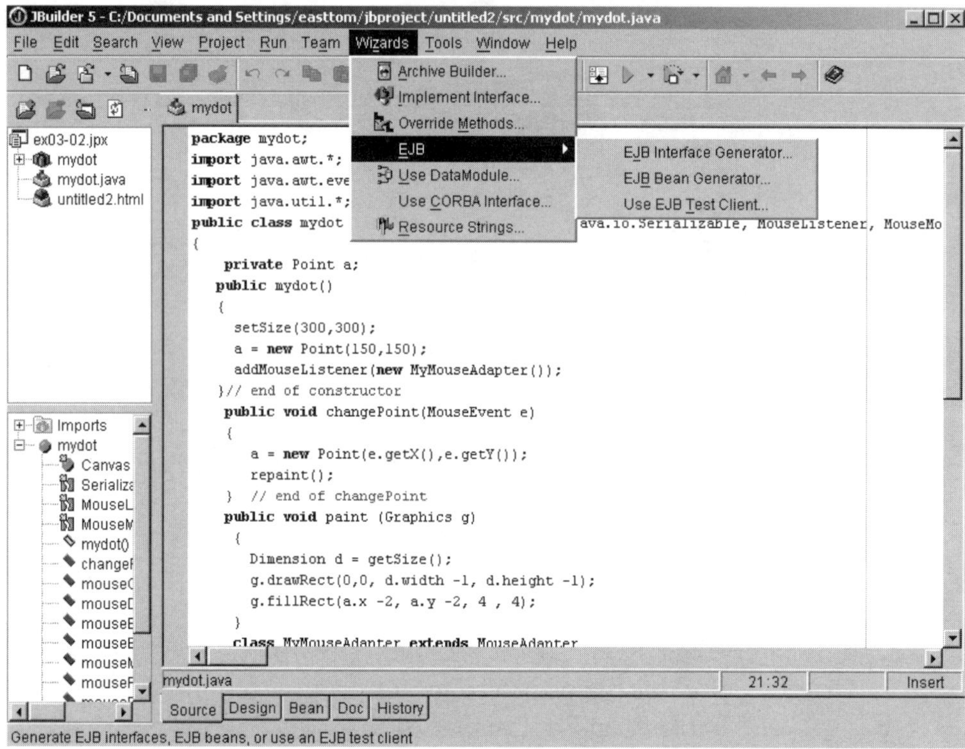

You should also notice that when you select File ▸ New, you have some new options on the Enterprise tab.

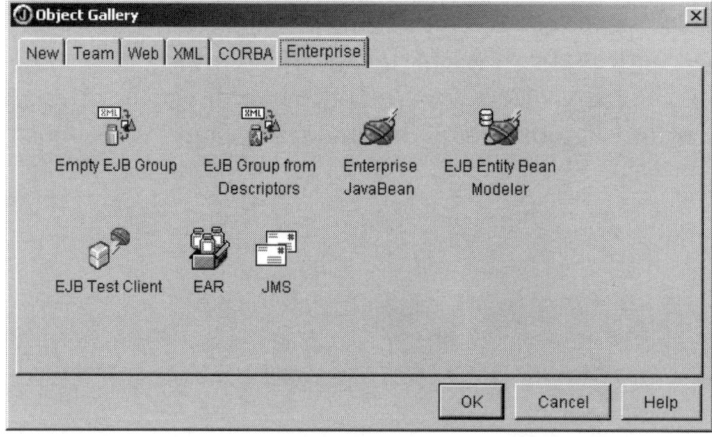

Summary

In this chapter, I established a basic conceptual foundation for Enterprise JavaBeans. You have been shown the essential differences between standard JavaBeans and Enterprise JavaBeans. I have also shown you the three different types of Enterprise JavaBeans, how they operate, and their life cycles. Another important facet of EJB development discussed in this chapter is how to determine which type of EJB is correct for a given situation. Reading and understanding the concepts of this chapter will set the groundwork necessary for you to move through the rest of this book.

Terms

n-tiered Application – An application that consists of more than one layer. The letter *n* represents the number of layers actually present.

Session Bean – A bean that represents a single session with a client. These beans can be either stateful or stateless.

Entity Bean – A bean that represents an underlying data object. These beans are persistent, and their structure is similar to a database.

Message-driven Bean – A bean that is used to process messages.

Interfaces – The interfaces used for clients to create instances of Enterprise JavaBeans and to access those beans. There are two such interfaces: home and remote.

Passivation – The process of moving an Enterprise JavaBean to an inactive state and, if required, storing state information.

Activation – The process of reactivating a previously passivated bean and, if required, restoring state information.

Review Questions

1. What is the primary difference between a standard JavaBean and an Enterprise JavaBean?

2. Where do Enterprise JavaBeans run?

3. List the three types of Enterprise JavaBeans.

4. How do remote clients pass parameters?

5. How do local clients pass parameters?

6. Give a brief definition of a session bean.

7. What are the two mechanisms for handling persistence with entity beans?

8. Do message-driven beans retain their state?

9. Can an entity bean handle more than one client simultaneously?

10. Can a session bean handle multiple clients?

Chapter 6

Remote Calls with EJB

Introduction

Now that you have acquainted yourself with the basics of JavaBeans and the fundamental concepts of Enterprise JavaBeans (EJBs), it is time to move into the intricacies that allow EJBs to communicate. Given that Enterprise JavaBeans are designed specifically for distributed software design, understanding how distributed components communicate is pivotal. One important concept that you should have noted in Chapter 5 is the fact that the location of an Enterprise JavaBean is completely transparent to the client. This means that the client should not know, or even care, where that EJB is located. It will most likely be on another machine running in a different Java Virtual Machine (JVM).

The question that is probably on your mind now is, how does an EJB call a function that resides in a different JVM on an entirely different machine? Well, the problem of how to call remote procedures is not limited to Enterprise JavaBean. In fact, it is common to all distributed application architectures. Each distributed architecture takes its own approach to solving this problem. Enterprise JavaBeans solve this problem with the use of

Remote Method Invocation (RMI). Remote Method Invocation allows a programmer to access methods that are on a remote location, thus the name. The term "remote" simply means that the procedure lies in a different machine than the client. This means that remote procedures are not only on other machines or instances of the Java Virtual Machine. It might simply refer to other components on the same machine. The methods in that component are remote to the client component that is calling them. In Java, any object whose methods can be called from another JVM is a remote object.

Before you continue with this book, where you will learn step by step how to create your own Enterprise JavaBeans, I feel that it is important that you gain a basic knowledge about the technology underlying the communication mechanisms of EJBs. While it is certainly possible to create Enterprise JavaBeans with little knowledge of RMI, it is not the best approach. I firmly believe that the more complete your understanding of the technologies underlying Enterprise JavaBeans, the more successful you will be at understanding and utilizing EJBs. However, for those of you that just want a "quick and dirty" how-to on Enterprise JavaBeans, you should feel free to simply skim this chapter or perhaps even skip it altogether. However, I feel confident that none of my readers will be satisfied with anything less than a complete mastery of the topics at hand!

RPCs and Marshalling

A Remote Procedure Call, or RPC, is a call to a procedure that is running in some other component (i.e., it is "remote" to the client). This could be a JavaBean, another application on the same machine, or even an application running on another machine. This is a common occurrence with all distributed architectures. In order to accomplish an RPC, there must be some mechanism to handle the inter-object communication. There must be some mechanism for passing data to and from the remote object. The process of passing data back and forth between objects is usually referred to as marshalling. The concepts of remote procedure calls and marshalling are by no means unique to EJBs. They are common problems for all distributed architectures to overcome. In all distributed architectures, a methodology is required to find remote procedures, pass them any required parameters, and receive back any return values.

In order to use a remote method, you have to find some way of getting data from the client to the server and vice versa. Even calling a single function requires you to take the parameters from the client to the server. You will then have to get the return value back from the server to the client. The process that does this is referred to as *marshalling*. Marshalling refers to the process of gathering data from one or more applications or sources in computer storage and making the data available to another application. This is accomplished by placing the data into a message and then organizing or converting the data into a format that is appropriate for a particular receiver. Marshalling may be required when passing the output parameters of a program written in one language as input to a program written in another language. Marshalling is simply the process of gathering data, such as parameters, to pass to a remote procedure. It is also the methodology used by distributed architectures, such as EJB and COM, to make remote functions available to clients.

> **Note:**　COM (Component Object Model) is primarily a Microsoft architecture and is not natively available with Java. However, you can use the JNI (Java Native Interface) to communicate with COM objects. The details of that process, however, are beyond the scope of this book. There are some fundamental characteristics that all distributed architectures share, so you will find some similarities between Enterprise JavaBeans, COM, DCOM, and CORBA.

The use of the term "marshalling" derives from the use of the same word in military jargon. In the military, marshalling is the gathering and ordering of military forces in preparation for battle (i.e., to "marshal one's forces for battle"). RMI utilizes object serialization to marshal and unmarshal a function's parameters. You should recall the topic of serialization from Chapter 4. The same process is used to get the parameters from the client object and the object it is attempting to pass the parameters to.

RMI

Remote Method Invocation is literally a methodology for invoking methods located remotely, thus the name. By remote, I simply mean in a different process. This could be in a different object on the same machine, on a different Java Virtual Machine, or on a different machine. If the procedure exists in a different memory process, then it is remote. Remote Method Invocation enables programmers to create distributed Java solutions in which the methods of remote Java objects can be invoked from other Java objects, regardless of the location of the objects.

Before you can use RMI to make a call to a remote object, you have to obtain reference to the remote object. This can be done in one of two ways. The first is by receiving the reference as an argument or as a return value. Simply put, this would mean that some other function that the client object called returned a reference to the object containing the remote procedure. This is actually a rather common way to obtain a reference to the remote procedure. You are certainly familiar with Java functions that have objects as their return type. This is exactly the same thing. The only difference is that the object that is returned is remote. Another way to obtain a reference is by looking up the remote object in the bootstrap naming service provided by RMI (more about the bootstrap naming service later in this chapter). Regardless of how the client obtains the reference, once it is obtained, a client can call a remote object in a server and use its methods, regardless of the relative locations of the client and server components. In short, Remote Method Invocation is Java's mechanism for communicating with remote objects.

RMI applications are usually comprised of at least two separate components: a server and a client. A typical server component creates a number of remote objects, makes references to these objects accessible to clients, and responds to client requests. A typical client application obtains a remote reference to one or more remote objects in the server and uses methods in those objects. RMI provides the mechanism by which the server and the client exchange information. This distributed architecture is becoming the norm for business. As you saw in Chapter 5, distributed architectures and *n*-tier software are now commonplace.

As previously mentioned, there must be some method for client components to get a reference to remote objects. An application can register its remote objects with RMI's naming facility, the rmiregistry. The application can also pass and return remote object references as part of its methods. However it is accomplished, the details of communication between remote objects are handled by RMI. The process is entirely transparent to the programmer. This should be rather good news to you. That means that in this chapter, you will have some concepts to master, but you will not be required to acquire new coding techniques. To the developer using an RMI, remote communication looks like a standard method invocation. This is one of the best features of RMI. The application developer can concentrate on solving the business problem at hand without being overly concerned with the details of how the remote procedure communication will be handled.

Remember that in Java, all classes are compiled to byte code. This is somewhat important to RMI communication. You should also be aware that RMI allows a client to pass objects to remote objects, as well as simple data types. RMI provides the necessary mechanisms for loading an object's code as well as for transmitting its data. RMI can load class byte codes using any URL protocol that is supported by the Java platform. This includes FTP and HTTP. This allows the programmer a great deal of flexibility in locating the objects used. This is also perfectly suited for distributed applications, where the web is one of the mediums through which the application layers are distributed.

Remote Interfaces

Remote objects are accessed via remote interfaces. A *remote* interface is an interface that declares a set of methods that can be called from a remote Java Virtual Machine. A valid remote interface must satisfy several requirements. The most important requirement is that a remote interface must extend the interface java.rmi.Remote. Now it is possible that the interface in question extends another interface that is in turn extending java.rmi.Remote. As long as somewhere in the interface's inheritance hierarchy it is either implementing java.rmi.Remote or inheriting another interface that does so, the requirement is met. It is also important that the method declarations in a remote interface meet certain requirements.

There are several requirements for remote interface method declarations. A remote method declaration must throw the exception java.rmi.Remote-Exception. It may, of course, throw other exceptions as well. It is also important to note that if the interface's parent class throws java.rmi.Remote-Exception, this requirement is satisfied. The requirement is also satisfied if the interface throws a parent class of java.rmi.RemoteException, such as Exception. Another requirement is that in a remote method declaration, a remote object declared as a parameter or return value must be declared as the remote *interface*. Declaring it as the implementation class of that interface will not satisfy this requirement.

Now that we have discussed the requirements of remote interfaces, perhaps it would be prudent to examine the java.rmi.Remote interface itself. The interface java.rmi.Remote is an interface that defines no methods.

```
public interface Remote
{
}
```

This interface is provided solely to mark the class that implements it as a remote object. The only purpose of this interface is to allow the creation of remote objects. Such an interface is referred to as a *marker interface*. You have probably seen other interfaces like this in Java, such as java.io.serializable. Also note that the new Java SDK 1.4 is reported to include some new marker interfaces, such as java.util.RandomAccess. What this means to you, a Java programmer, is that marker interfaces are common with the current version of Java and their use will continue and be expanded with the next version, so you should probably get comfortable with them.

Bootstrapping

I have previously mentioned that there are two ways to obtain a reference to a remote object, but so far I have only explained one to you. Recall that earlier I mentioned that you could get a reference to a remote object either by having it passed as a return type/parameter or by using the RMI bootstrap method. A simple bootstrap name server is provided for storing named references to remote objects. A remote object reference can be stored using the URL-based methods of the class.java.rmi.Naming. The RMI registry is itself a remote object, which in turn is used by clients for bootstrapping. Remote objects register themselves with this registry, and it, in turn, provides the required information to clients so that they can invoke the objects they need. Bootstrapping is essentially the mechanism whereby the client and the remote object begin their dialog. Fortunately, most of this process is completely transparent to the programmer working with the client.

The RemoteObject Class

I have discussed the mechanisms whereby Remote Server Invocation can be used by the client to communicate with the server. Obviously, this only works if there exists an RMI compliant server object to communicate with. The next obvious question would be, what makes an RMI compliant object? In other words, what criteria must be met in order for an object to participate in Remote Method Invocation? This is where the RemoteObject class comes in. All RMI server functions are provided by java.rmi.server.RemoteObject or one of its subclasses:

- java.rmi.server.RemoteServer

- java.rmi.server.UnicastRemoteObject

- java.rmi.activation.Activatable

The methods that are required to create remote objects and to make them available to remote clients are provided by the classes UnicastRemoteObject and Activatable. These subclasses identify whether the server is a simple remote object or an activatable remote object. An activatable remote object is one that executes when invoked. A simple remote object is one that does not immediately execute when it is invoked. After it is instantiated, you must call one of its methods in order to cause it to execute.

The java.rmi.server.UnicastRemoteObject class defines a remote object whose references are valid only while the server process is alive.

The java.rmi.activation.Activatable class is an abstract class that defines an *activatable* remote object that starts executing when its remote methods are invoked and will shut itself down.

Recall that in order for a client to invoke a method on a remote object, that client must first obtain a reference to the remote object. A reference to a remote object can be obtained as a parameter or return value in a method call. Also recall that RMI provides a simple bootstrap name server from which to obtain remote objects on a given host. The java.rmi.Naming class provides Uniform Resource Locator (URL)-based methods to look up, bind, rebind, unbind, and list the name-object pairings maintained on a particular host and port.

The following table lists the various classes, interfaces, and exceptions:

Class/Interface	Purpose
Remote	The Remote interface identifies interfaces whose methods may be invoked from a non-local JVM.
Naming	The Naming class provides methods for storing and obtaining references to remote objects in the remote object registry.
MarshalledObject	This class contains a byte stream with the serialized representation of an object given to its constructor.
AccessException	An AccessException is thrown by certain methods of the java.rmi.Naming class as well as methods of the java.rmi.activation.ActivationSystem interface. It is used to indicate that the caller does not have permission to perform the action requested by the method.
AlreadyBoundException	An AlreadyBoundException is thrown if an attempt is made to bind an object in the registry to a name that is already bound.
ConnectException	A ConnectException is thrown if a connection is refused to the remote host for a remote method call.
ConnectIOException	A ConnectIOException is thrown if an IOException occurs while making a connection to the remote host.
MarshalException	A MarshalException is thrown if a java.io.IOException occurs while marshalling the remote method call.
NotBoundException	A NotBoundException is thrown if an attempt is made to look up or unbind in the registry a name that is not bound.

Class/Interface	Purpose
NoSuchObjectException	A NoSuchObjectException is thrown if an attempt is made to invoke a method on an object that does not exist in the remote JVM.
RemoteException	A RemoteException is the common superclass for a number of communication-related exceptions that may occur during the execution of a remote method call.
StubNotFoundException	A StubNotFoundException is thrown if a valid stub class could not be found for a remote object when it is exported.
UnexpectedException	An UnexpectedException is thrown if the client of a remote method call receives a checked exception that is not among the checked exception types declared in the throws clause of the method in the remote interface.
ServerError	A ServerError is thrown as a result of a remote method call if the execution of the remote method on the server machine throws a java.lang.Error.
ServerException	A ServerException is thrown as a result of a remote method call if the execution of the remote method on the server machine throws a RemoteException.

These classes, exceptions, and interfaces are the ones that are most pertinent to the discussion for Remote Method Invocation. While it is certainly not vital that you have an in-depth understanding of each one, it is important that you have a basic familiarity with them. The most important concept for you to remember is that the RemoteObject class, and its subclasses, is integral to creating remote objects. I do recommend that you read through this list a couple of times until you have a basic familiarity with it.

The RemoteException Class

You are probably aware of the fact that Java defines a number of specific error handling classes for specific issues. In fact, there is a rather extensive hierarchy of exception classes, each tailor-made for specific types of exceptions. These various exception classes fit with particular types of errors. Remote Method Invocation is no exception to this rule. As mentioned in the section regarding RMI interfaces, these interfaces must throw the java.rmi.RemoteException error. This section will examine this particular class in some detail. The java.rmi.RemoteException class is the parent class of exceptions thrown by RMI during a remote method call. Each remote method declared in a remote interface must throw java.rmi.Remote-Exception (or one of its parent classes, such as java.io.IOException or java.lang.Exception).

This exception is thrown anytime a remote method invocation fails for any reason. You might ask what types of situations would lead to a remote call failing. The class RemoteException is a checked exception, not a run-time exception. This means that it must be handled by the caller of a remote method and is checked by the compiler. Remember that you cannot success-fully compile a class if its checked exceptions do not have some type of exception handling coded for them. There are several situations that might lead to an exception; some of the more common are listed here:

- Failure during parameter or return value marshalling or unmarshalling

- The remote server is unreachable.

- The remote server is refusing connections.

- The connection has been closed by the server.

- Protocol errors

Any of these situations can lead to an exception. By far, the problem with the remote server being unreachable is perhaps the most common. If, for any reason, access to the remote server is interrupted, an exception will occur. This can be caused by anything from network problems to issues with the server hosting the objects.

RMI Example

Throughout this chapter, I have shown you the specific requirements of Remote Method Invocation. I have also described the various interfaces, classes, and exceptions involved in the RMI process. Given that the RMI process is transparent to an EJB developer, this information is probably adequate to give you a basic understanding of how RMI works. However, I feel that it would be useful to show you an example of RMI being used directly in code. This is not an EJB example. The reason is that with EJB, the application container takes care of all the RMI details and hides them from you, the programmer. By writing the RMI code directly, you will get to see exactly what is happening behind the scenes with Remote Method Invocation. Let me warn you that coding the RMI directly can be rather tedious. If nothing else, examining this code should make you glad that with Enterprise JavaBeans, this is all taken care of for you!

This may not be particularly original, but I will use a variation of the ubiquitous "Hello World" example in order to demonstrate the coding of RMI. However, there will be two variations. The first is that I currently reside in Texas. Therefore, I feel compelled to honor my state by using the local vernacular of "Howdy" rather than "Hello." So you will now be taken through the process of creating the "Howdy Y'all" example program. I hope you find this example at least mildly amusing, since I use similar examples later in this book to illustrate other techniques. In this example an applet is the client, and when it runs, it displays "Howdy Y'all." The second variation is that in order to display this text, it must make a remote procedure call to a server.

During this process, we are going to create three separate files (I warned you that doing RMI by hand was quite tedious!).

- Howdy.java — a remote interface

- HowdyApplet.java — the client applet that displays Hello World

- howdy.html — the HTML page that hosts the aforementioned applet

Before we begin, you should recall from your previous Java programming experience that Java requires a mapping between the fully-qualified package name of a class and the directory path to that class. This means that the package name needs to reflect the directory that the package is in. On my PC, this means that the package name is rmi.howdy, and the source directory is c:/ejbbook/rmi/howdy. It might be very different on your PC.

Remember that in Java, a remote object is simply an instance of a class that implements a remote interface. Your remote interface will declare each of the methods that you would like to call from other JVMs. All remote interfaces share the following characteristics:

- The remote interface must be declared public. This should be pretty obvious. If it's not public, how will the client access it?

- The remote interface extends the java.rmi.Remote interface. As with many things in Java, an interface must be implemented or extended in order to achieve certain functionality.

- The data type of any remote object that is either passed as an argument or returned from the method must be declared as the remote interface type, not the implementation class (in our example, this means Howdy and not HowdyImp).

- Each method must declare java.rmi.RemoteException in its throws clause. Of course, it can also declare other application-specific exceptions.

I would like to begin by showing you the actual remote interface rmi.Howdy. This interface has only one method, sayHowdy, which returns a string to the caller:

```
package rmi.Howdy;
import java.rmi.Remote;
import java.rmi.RemoteException;
public interface Howdy extends Remote
{
  String sayHowdy() throws RemoteException;
}
```

That's all there is to the interface portion. Remote methods can fail in ways that local methods cannot. They can fail due to network problems, server response problems, etc. For this reason, remote methods will report communication failures by throwing a java.rmi.RemoteException.

Now let's look at the actual implementation class. This is the class that actually has the methods for that remote interface. As you might guess, it has to implement that interface. It must also have implementations for the methods defined in that interface and have a constructor for the remote object.

I will also show you the server class. A server class is the class which has a main method that creates an instance of the remote object implementation and binds that instance to a name in the rmiregistry. The class that contains this main method can be the implementation class itself, or it can even be another class entirely.

```
package rmi.HowdyImp;
import java.rmi.Naming;
import java.rmi.RemoteException;
import java.rmi.RMISecurityManager;
import java.rmi.server.UnicastRemoteObject;
public class HowdyImp extends UnicastRemoteObject implements Howdy
{
  public HelloImpl() throws RemoteException
  {
    super();
  }
  public String sayHowdy()
    {
      return "Howdy Yall!";
    }
  public static void main(String args[])
    {
// Create and install a security manager
if (System.getSecurityManager() == null)
{
  System.setSecurityManager(new RMISecurityManager());
}
try
{
  HowdyImp obj = new HowdyImp();
```

```
      // Bind this object instance to the name "HowdyServer"
      Naming.rebind("//myhost/HowdyServer", obj);
      System.out.println("HowdyServer bound in registry");
    }
    catch (Exception e)
    {
      System.out.println("Oops: " + e.getMessage());
      e.printStackTrace();
    }
  }
}
```

Now you may be feeling a bit perplexed by this. At this point in your reading, you probably anticipated the first several lines of code. The fact that this class extends UnicastRemoteObject, implements Howdy, and throws a RemoteException probably came as no surprise to you. However, once we got into the main function there was probably a lot of new code there for you to digest. That code is where the Remote Method Invocation action takes place. I will show you, in more detail, what each line of code is doing.

First, let me direct your attention to this segment of code:

```
// Create and install a security manager
   if (System.getSecurityManager() == null)
   {
       System.setSecurityManager(new RMISecurityManager());
   }
```

Also recall that at the beginning of this source file, in the imports section, I imported java.rmi.RMISecurityManager. All RMI transactions take place in some security context, and for this reason, the systems security manager must be invoked.

Next I would like to call your attention to the code that actually registered this object in the rmiregistry.

```
HowdyImp obj = new HowdyImp();
Naming.rebind("//myhost/HowdyServer", obj);
System.out.println("HowdyServer bound in registry");
```

You should recall from earlier in this chapter that an RMI interface needs to be registered with the rmiregistry in order to be called remotely. The code you see above is doing exactly that. First, an instance of the implementation object is created. That object is then bound with the rmiregistry using the Naming object's rebind method. Now other objects can look up the Howdy object in the rmiregistry under the name "HowdyServer" and then utilize that object.

Now that I have shown you how to build the server side, it's time to take a look at the client side. Next, I will show you how to create an applet that will use the server object in order to display "Howdy Y'all."

```java
package rmi.HowdyClient;
import java.applet.Applet;
import java.awt.Graphics;
import java.rmi.Naming;
import java.rmi.RemoteException;
public class HowdyApplet extends Applet
{
  String texasgreeting = "None"; // default value
  Howdy howdyobj = null;  //initial instance of the Howdy object
  public void init()
  {
    try
      {
      howdyobj = (Howdy)Naming.lookup("//" + getCodeBase().getHost() +
      "/HowdyServer");
      texasgreeting = howdyobj.sayHowdy();
    }
    catch (Exception e)
      {
      System.out.println("Oops: " + e.getMessage());
      e.printStackTrace();
      }
  }
  public void paint(Graphics g)
  {
    g.drawString(texasgreeting, 25, 50);
  }
}
```

This applet is pretty straightforward, and most of it should be familiar to you. Only a small section of it is new. First take note of the import statements and the beginning. You should notice that several packages are being imported that are not usually imported with applets. These packages are for use with the Remote Method Invocation. The actual code segment in question is quite small:

```
howdyobj = (Howdy)Naming.lookup("//" + getCodeBase().getHost() +
    "/HowdyServer");
texasgreeting = howdyobj.sayHowdy();
```

A call is made to the rmiregistry and an attempt is made to look up HowdyServer. If that object is found in the registry, its method sayHowdy is called.

Finally, we have the code to display the applet from within a standard HTML page. This code is really straightforward and is simply standard HTML.

```
<HTML>
  <head>
    <title>Hello World</title>
  </head>
  <body bgcolor = white>
    <center> <h1>Howdy World</h1> </center>
    <applet codebase="myclasses/"
      code="rmi.howdy.HowdyApplet" width=500 height=120>
    </applet>
  </body>
</HTML>
```

Obviously, there needs to be an HTTP server running on the machine from which you want to download classes. If not, then you won't be able to run the web page, and therefore the applet. The codebase in the HTML file specifies a directory below the directory from which the web page was itself loaded. Using this kind of relative path is a very common practice. The applet's code attribute specifies the fully-qualified package name of the applet (in this example, rmi.howdy.HowdyApplet).

If you found all this code a lot of trouble simply to display "Howdy Y'all," you are correct. To begin with, no programmer would ever do all of this just to display a greeting. At least, no sane programmer would! However, this code provides a simple and easy-to-follow example of how Remote Method Invocation works. The second thing to recall is that when using Enterprise JavaBeans, the RMI calls are handled for you by the application server. You don't have to write this code yourself. As I said previously, if nothing else, this example should make you appreciate all that the EJB application server is doing for you!

Summary

This chapter has given you a behind-the-scenes look at the remote method invocation process. This process is the backbone of communicating with Enterprise JavaBeans. You have seen the essential mechanisms of RMI and been introduced to concepts like remote procedure calls (RPC) and marshalling. In addition to this, I have shown you the basic classes involved in RMI and the exception classes thrown. You have also seen the basis for remote objects in the RemoteObject class. This chapter, combined with Chapter 5, should give you the requisite knowledge to completely understand the rest of this book and to fully grasp the concepts and techniques involved in Enterprise JavaBean development.

Terms

RMI – Remote Method Invocation. This is the process of invoking methods that exist in a separate memory process. These methods may exist in a different object on the same machine or on a different machine.

RPC – Remote Procedure Call. The generic term for calling a procedure that exists in another object. It is remote to the process calling it.

Marshalling – This is the process whereby a component gathers the arguments it wishes to send to a remote object.

JNI – Java Native Interface. This a method whereby Java can communicate with COM objects.

java.rmi.Remote Interface – This is the interface that is required for all use of RMI in Java.

Bootstrapping – The process of obtaining a reference to a remote object.

RemoteException – This is the exception thrown by all remote procedure calls in Java.

Review Questions

1. What is RMI?

2. What is marshalling?

3. What is an RPC?

4. What interface must be implemented to use RMI?

5. What causes a ServerException to be thrown?

6. What methods are found in the RMI interface?

7. List one method for obtaining a reference to a remote object.

8. What exception must all RMI objects throw?

9. What is the purpose of the remote interface?

10. What is the purpose of the marshalled object?

Chapter 7

Stateless Session Beans

Introduction

The first six chapters of this book built the requisite framework for you to be able to master the topic of Enterprise JavaBeans. Chapters 1 through 4 gave you a solid working knowledge of standard JavaBeans. Chapters 5 and 6 should have provided you with a firm theoretical understanding of the underlying mechanisms that are used by Enterprise JavaBeans. Now it is time to start studying specific types of Enterprise JavaBeans and to actually create some EJBs. In Chapter 5, you were introduced to the various types of JavaBeans, including the session bean. Recall that a session bean is essentially an EJB that provides a service to a particular user session. Session beans typically model specific business processes. Relative to entity beans, session beans are short-lived. Recall that a session bean can be either stateless or stateful.

Recall from Chapter 5 that a stateless bean does not retain any information about its state, even between method calls. These EJBs are useful for simple interactions between the client and some application service. Any interaction that is complete in a single method invocation can be used with a stateless session bean. A common example is an EJB that processes orders. Each order can be processed by a call to a single method, such as processOrder(). Since this operation is completed with a single call, it is perfectly suited to a stateless session bean.

Regardless of what type of session bean you wish to create, there are some common points that all session beans share. Each session bean is composed of certain parts. These parts must be developed by the enterprise bean programmer. The first, and most obvious, is the remote interface. It is this remote interface that provides the client's view of the bean. The home interface is also developed by the EJB provider. It contains all the methods for the bean life cycle used by the client application.

It should also be apparent that the EJB developer will have to create the actual bean implementation class. This is the class which provides the actual bean functionality you are trying to implement. It is also this class which must support items such as serialization. Finally, the EJB developer must develop the deployment descriptor, which contains the bean properties that may be edited at assembly or deployment time.

The Remote Interface

Before I show you how to create a remote interface, it would probably be prudent to define a remote interface. In the simplest terms, the remote interface is simply an interface that allows the client to use the EJB object. Since the interface the client interacts with is to a remote object, it is therefore called a remote interface. This interface will duplicate the method names of the EJB. It literally provides an interface for the client to the remote EJB object. This is the interface which will provide the client its view of the session bean. This interface contains the actual business methods of the enterprise bean. It is here that the client will call the actual methods that it is interested in invoking in order to perform the tasks it requires. The most important requirement for a remote interface is that it must extend the javax.ejb.EJBObject interface. This is an absolute requirement for all remote interfaces. You may find it useful to see the actual code for the javax.ejb.EJBObject interface so that you can have a better understanding of its functionality. Here is the source code for the javax.ejb.EJBObject interface:

```
public interface javax.ejb.EJBObject extends java.rmi.Remote
{
   public abstract javax.ejb.EJBHome getEJBHome()
     throws java.rmi.RemoteException;
   public abstract java.lang.Object getPrimaryKey()
     throws java.rmi.remoteException;
   public abstract void remove();
     throws java.rmi.RemoteException, java.ejb.RemoveException;
   public abstract javax.ejb.Handle getHandle()
     throws java.rmi.RemoteException;
   public abstract Boolean isIdentical(javax.ejb.EJBObject)
     throws java.rmi.RemoteException;
}
```

Notice that this interface utilizes several Remote Method Invocation classes. In fact, it extends the java.rmi.Remote class. Recall from Chapter 6 that RMI is responsible for facilitating the communication with remote objects. However, you should also recall that most of the RMI code is actually handled for you. Part of the reason for this is that interfaces, like this one, inherit from RMI objects. It is also important that the methods defined in this interface follow the rules for Java RMI. Among other things, this means that these methods must throw the java.rmi.RemoteException. You will recall that in Chapters 5 and 6, these issues were discussed at some length. If you need a refresher, then please reread those chapters. For each method defined in the remote interface, there must be a matching method in the enterprise bean's class. The method must have the same name, arguments, return type, and exception list. The only difference would be that the interface would throw the RemoteException.

Let's take a look at an example for an interface:

```
public interface myremote extends EJBObject
{
       public void somemethod (int x)  throws RemoteException;
       public int  someothermethod ()  throws RemoteException;
   }
```

Notice that the interface defines some methods without any implementation. These method declarations should match exactly the method declarations used in the actual EJBObject. The implementation will actually be done in the EJBObject in question. You should also note that these methods both throw the RemoteException. As was previously mentioned in Chapter 6, remote procedure calls can fail in ways that local procedure calls cannot; therefore, they must throw the RemoteException.

The Home Interface

The home interface is the interface that provides methods for creating instances of the EJB. The home interface and remote interface work in conjunction to provide the client with access to the Enterprise JavaBean. A session bean's home interface defines one or more create() methods. Each create method must be named create and must match one of the ejbCreate methods defined in the Enterprise JavaBean class. The create methods allow the client to create instances of the EJB's classes and utilize them. The home interface of a stateless session bean must have one create method that takes no arguments. The return type of the create method must be the enterprise bean's remote interface type. Essentially, the create method for a stateless session bean will take no arguments and return the remote interface for an EJB object. This will allow the client to create instances of the remote interface, thereby utilizing the methods of the EJB. Hopefully, you are beginning to see how these different classes and interfaces work together to allow programmers to use remote procedures contained in Enterprise JavaBeans.

All the exceptions defined in the throws clause of an ejbCreate method must be defined in the throws clause of the matching create method of the home interface.

Let's consider a home interface that uses the previous remote interface example as a return type:

```
public interface myhome extends EJBHome
{
  myremote create() throws CreateException, RemoteException;
  }
```

Notice that, as per the requirements I gave you, the home interface returns the remote interface previously defined. It also has a create method that takes no arguments. Notice also that this create method throws two exceptions, the first being a CreateException. This will occur if there is some problem preventing the interface from being able to create the object in question. The second exception thrown is the RemoteException. The reason for this exception has already been explained.

The Enterprise Bean Class

Creating interfaces is an integral part of being able to access an EJB; however, we must also have an actual Enterprise JavaBean to access. The enterprise bean class is the actual heart of the Enterprise JavaBean. The other classes are merely "helper" classes that facilitate remote access of the enterprise bean class methods. That brings us to the topic of the Enterprise JavaBean class itself. This class implements the bean's business methods and those methods of the bean which are dedicated to the EJB environment. By "dedicated to the EJB environment," I mean those methods used to allow the EJB to integrate with the application server that is hosting it. Remember that the application server is key to the entire EJB architecture.

As with all classes we have discussed, this one has certain requirements which must be met. To begin with, the class must be defined as public. It should be fairly obvious that if it is not public, it will not be accessible. Any EJB that is not accessible is a waste of time and of no use to anyone. Furthermore, other classes will need to make instances of this class. Therefore, it may not be declared as abstract. Remember that an abstract class cannot be directly instantiated but must be inherited. The session bean interface also requires certain methods, described in the following table.

Method	Purpose
public void setSessionContext(SessionContext ic)	This method is used by the container to pass a reference from the SessionContext to the bean instance. The container invokes this method on an instance after the instance has been created.
public void ejbRemove()	This method is invoked by the container during the process of removing an instance of a bean from the container.
public void ejbPassivate()	This method is invoked by the container when it is attempting to passivate the instance. After this method completes, the instance must be in a state that allows the container to use the Java serialization protocol to externalize and store away the instance's state.
public void ejbActivate()	This method is invoked by the container just after the instance of the bean has been reactivated. The instance will re-acquire any resources that were released earlier in the ejbPassivate() method.
public void afterBegin()	This method notifies a session bean instance that a new transaction has started.
public void afterCompletion(boolean committed)	This method notifies a session bean instance that a transaction commit protocol has completed and tells the instance whether the transaction has been committed or rolled back.
public void beforeCompletion()	This method notifies a session bean instance that a transaction is about to be committed.

It won't be necessary for you to commit this table to memory. However, you should take some time to familiarize yourself with these methods and their purpose. It is not important that you memorize them verbatim, but you should be familiar with them.

A summary of the requirements for all session beans is listed here:

- It implements the SessionBean interface.
- The class is defined as public.
- The class cannot be defined as abstract or final.
- It implements one or more ejbCreate methods.
- It implements the business methods.
- It contains a public constructor with no parameters.
- It must not define the finalize method.

These requirements are essential for creating a session bean. They are absolute and must be followed in all cases. Before you even attempt to compile a session bean, you would be wise to first compare your code with this list to ensure that you have met all the requirements for a session bean.

The ejbCreate Methods

In the previous section, I introduced you to the requirements for building a session bean. One of those requirements was a create method. This method is somewhat crucial to the use of session beans, so it seems prudent to give it a closer look. Because an enterprise bean runs inside an EJB container, a client cannot directly instantiate the bean. Only the EJB container can instantiate an enterprise bean. This involves a few steps:

1. The client invokes a create method on the home object.

2. The EJB container creates an instance of the enterprise bean.

3. The EJB container invokes the ejbCreate method in bean.

It is customary for the ejbCreate method to initialize the bean to some default state. An enterprise bean must have at least one ejbCreate method. The required create method takes no arguments. However, an EJB may overload this create method, and those other versions of the create method may indeed take parameters. However, all create methods must return void. The signatures of the methods must meet the following requirements:

- The access modifier must be public.

- If the bean allows remote access, the arguments must be legal types for the Java Remote Method Invocation (RMI) API.

- The special modifier may not be static or final.

Again, these requirements are inviolable; they must be strictly adhered to. When you write your own create methods, I suggest you check them against this checklist to see that you have met all the requirements before you even attempt to compile the class.

Business Methods

So far we have discussed how to set up methods for a bean that are primarily interested in creating instances of the bean and allowing remote access. In all of this discussion on these basic maintenance issues, it may seem that we have lost sight of the purpose of having an EJB. Remember that the whole reason for creating this bean is to run business tasks for the client. The client invokes business methods on the remote object reference that is returned by the create method.

These business methods also have certain requirements they must meet. Those requirements are:

- The method name must not conflict with one defined by the EJB architecture.

- The access modifier must be public.

- If the bean allows remote access, the arguments and return types must be legal types for the Java RMI API.

- The special modifier must not be static or final.

- The throws clause may include exceptions that you define for your application.

To indicate a system-level problem, such as the inability to connect to a database, a business method should throw the javax.ejb.EJBException. The reason for this is that when a business method throws an EJBException, the container wraps it in a RemoteException, which is caught by the client. The container will not wrap application exceptions. Therefore, those exceptions will not be returned to the client. It is vital that the client be aware of errors. Because EJBException is a subclass of RuntimeException, you do not need to include it in the throws clause of the business method.

More about the Home Interface

A home interface extends the javax.ejb.EJBHome interface. For a session bean, the purpose of the home interface is to define the create methods that a remote client may invoke.

The method definitions in a remote interface must follow these rules:

- Each method in the remote interface must match a method implemented in the enterprise bean class.

- The signatures of the methods in the remote interface must be identical to the signatures of the corresponding methods in the enterprise bean class.

- The arguments and return values must be valid RMI types.

- The throws clause must include the java.rmi.RemoteException.

Deployment Descriptors

You should recall from our discussions in the first four chapters the use of manifest files. You can still use those in your JAR file for EJBs. However, EJBs require a file called a deployment descriptor. This descriptor is actually a Java object that is itself serializable. These descriptors are generated using either your EJB container or your development environment (I will discuss how to do this with JBuilder later in this chapter). The file is used to allow a certain level of customization. A person can use this file to set certain attributes of an Enterprise JavaBean. Some of the settings in a deployment descriptor file are described in the following table.

Setting	Description
Home interface class name	The fully qualified name of the home interface.
Remote interface class name	The fully qualified name of the remote interface.
Bean home name	The "nickname" that clients use to look up your bean.
Enterprise bean class name	The fully qualified name of the EJB class.
Session timeout	The number of seconds before a client should time out when calling methods on your bean.
Stateful or stateless	Whether or not the bean is a stateful session bean or a stateless session bean.

Let me remind you that these settings will be done for you using a utility provided with either your EJB container or your development tool of choice. So all you need, for now, is to become comfortable with what these settings are for. Don't worry about how to implement the settings. Descriptor files are actually XML files; you will see an example later in this chapter.

System Properties and Context

There is one remaining issue for me to discuss before I can take you right into creating stateless session beans. I have talked a lot about a client obtaining a reference to the home interface, that home interface being used to create instances of the EJB, and other details of EJB-client communication. However, there is a really big unanswered question: How does the client gain access to the application server and request a copy of the home interface?

It actually begins with a rather common Java class, the system class. You have probably used this class in the past to find out the operating system, current user, and other information. It can provide even more information about the client system. The system class method getProperties() returns a properties object that represents the main properties of the system. One of those properties will identify the currently running application server that the client machine is using. You can then use a context variable to store a reference to this application server. That server is the "context" in which your client is operating. Here is a code snippet showing you what I mean:

```
Properties myprop = system.getProperties;
Context cont = new InitialContext(myprop);
SomeHomeInterface myhome = (SomeHomeInterface
    cont.lookup("SomeHomeInterface");
```

You first obtain a reference to the system's properties, and then you use that to get the context (a reference to the application server). Now that you have that context, you can query it for your home interface.

Building a Stateless Session Bean

I have spent the past several pages inundating you with the various details of stateless session beans. I think it is definitely time to actually write one, don't you? This first bean is not going to be anything earth-shattering, and that is totally intentional. I want you to focus on the code for implementing a stateless session bean rather than get bogged down in the business method implementation. It seems obligatory for every programming book to do the "Hello World" application, so I am going to do the Hello World stateless session bean. First, we will create our bean the hard way, using the standard Sun Java tools and a text editor. Then we will repeat the process using JBuilder. Don't panic, however, because this Hello World program is somewhat simpler than the Howdy Y'all program you saw in Chapter 6!

To create this code yourself, all you need is any standard text editor. Windows users will probably want to use Notepad. Most operating systems come with a text editor of some sort. For Linux users that are using the KDE interface, you will find the advanced text editor to be more than adequate for this task.

Step 1:

Create the remote interface. The code is fairly simple. I placed the code in a file named Hello.java.

```
import javax.ejb.*;
import java.rmi.*;
public interface Hello extends EJBObject
{
  public String hello() throws java.rmi.RemoteException;
}// end of interface
```

Notice that we do import javax.ejb and java.rmi. Also notice that our interface extends EJBObject and our single method throws the java.rmi.RemoteException. These are essential requirements for any remote interface.

Step 2:

Now we need the code for the actual bean. I placed this code in a file named HelloBean.java.

```
Package projects.ejb.chp7.helloworld
import javax.ejb.*;
public class HelloBean implements SessionBean
{
  public void ejbCreate()
  {
  }
  public void ejbRemove()
  {

  }
  public void ejbActivate()
  {
  }
  public void ejbPassivate()
  {
  }
  public void setSessionContext(SessionContext ct)
  {
  }
```

```
    public String hello()
    {
      return "Hello World";
    }
  } // end of HelloBean
```

I want you to notice several things about this code. First of all, it implements SessionBean. This is critical and all session beans must implement this particular interface. Also notice that there are several methods with no actual code in them. Your stateless session bean will not actually do any passivating or activating, so you don't need any code in those methods, but you must have the methods there for it. For instructional purposes, you may want to write in a System.out.println in each method, indicating that the method was called. This would allow you to watch the bean used throughout its life cycle.

Step 3:

We have a bean, we have a remote interface, and now we need a home interface. Recall that the home interface is what the client will use to create instances of the EJB, so this is a very important interface. I will place my code in a file called HelloHome.java.

```
Package projects.ejb.chp7.helloworld
import javax.ejb.*;
import java.rmi.RemoteException;
public interface HelloHome extends EJBHome
{
  Hello create() throws RemoteException, CreateException;
}// end of Home Interface
```

Notice first of all that the create method returns a Hello object. Also note that it throws two exceptions, The RemoteException and the CreateException. Finally, notice that the interface extends EJBHome. These are all core requirements for any home interface.

Now when you create your ejb-JAR file, you will need to include the bean class (compiled), the remote interface, and the home interface. You will also need a deployment descriptor. Recall that deployment descriptors are essentially a more up-to-date version of the manifest file.

Once you have assembled all the parts, you simply create your JAR file:

```
Jar cmf helloworld.jar *
```

This assumes that all files are in the current folder.

Now we come to the final leg in our journey — the creation of client code that uses the Enterprise JavaBean. Recall that you must have an application server established, and you must have loaded your bean into the application server. You will need to refer to your application server for details on how to do that. I will cover using the Borland Application Server later in this chapter.

Step 4:

I place the client code in a file named helloclient.java.

```
import javax.ejb.*;
import javax.naming.*;
import java.rmi.*;
import java.util.*;
public class helloclient
{
  public static void main(String args[])
  {
    try
    {
      Properties myprop = system.getProperties;
      Context cont = new InitialContext(myprop);
      HelloHome myhome = (HelloHome cont.lookup("HelloHome");
      Hello hello = myhome.create();
      System.out.println(hello.hello());
      hello.remove();
    }// end of try
    catch(exception e)
    {
      e.printStackTrace();
    }// end of catch
  }// end of main
}// end of class helloclient
```

There are several interesting items in this client code for us to examine. First of all, notice the two lines:

```
Properties myprop = system.getProperties;
Context cont = new InitialContext(myprop);
```

Recall the earlier discussion regarding system properties and context. These two lines of code give your client access to the application server. Now, obviously, if your application server is not running, you will get an error.

The next line of code I want you to look at is closely related to these.

```
HelloHome myhome = (HelloHome cont.lookup("HelloHome");
```

This uses the context object previously created to go find the HelloHome interface and give us an instance of that home interface that we call "myhome." We can now use that home interface to create an instance of our "Hello World EJB."

```
Hello hello = myhome.create();
```

While nothing in this example will go down in the annals of computer science history, it does illustrate all the essential parts to creating and using stateless session beans. The <u>only</u> difference between this bean and most real-world beans are the business methods. Our bean only has a single simple business method. Real-world beans usually have several methods, each performing some relevant business task.

Building a Stateless Session Bean with JBuilder

Well, as promised, it's now time to show you how to do things the easy way, the JBuilder way. As with everything else I have shown you, JBuilder makes creating a stateless session bean a snap. It will handle all facets of the development for you. Just open up your copy of JBuilder (these examples will all work with versions 5.0 and 6.0; I cannot guarantee how they will work with earlier versions), and follow these steps:

Step 1:

Choose a new project. In the dialog box that appears, name your project HelloWorld and select a directory to store it in.

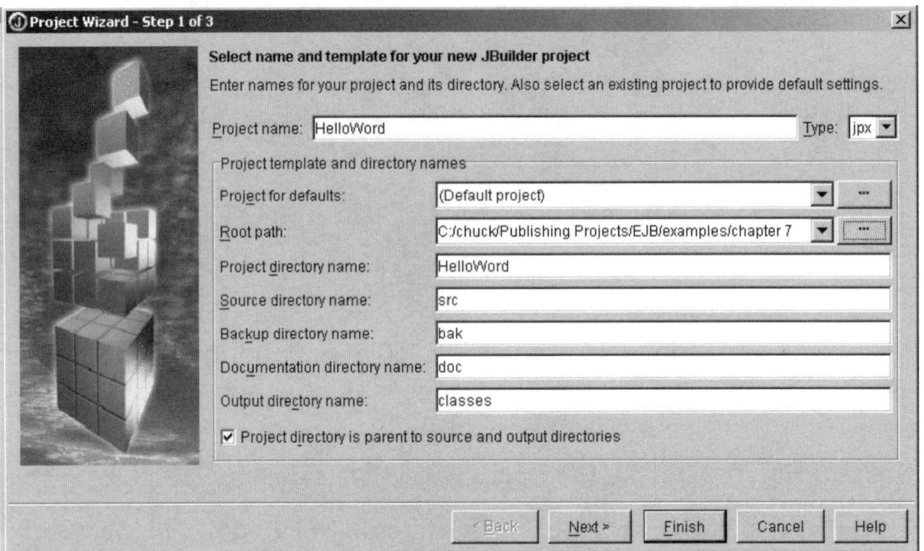

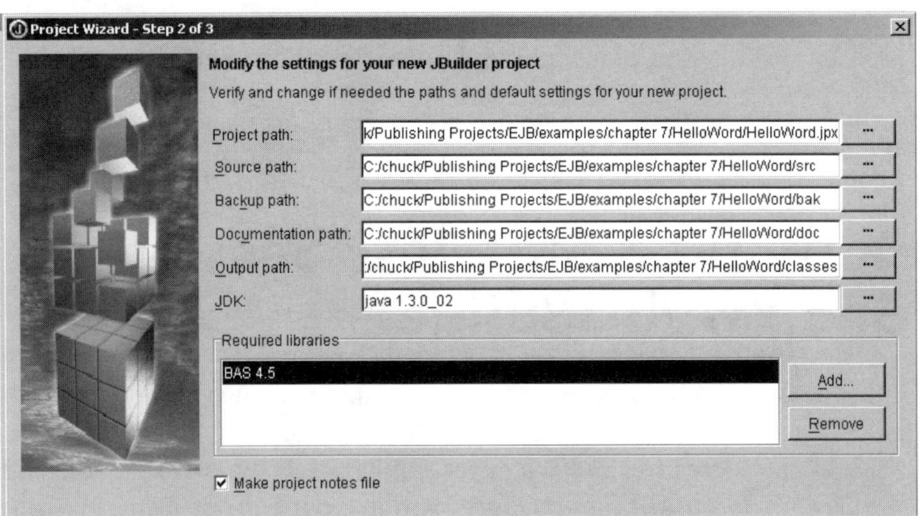

Step 2:

Now you can choose New and the Enterprise tab. Then select Enterprise JavaBean.

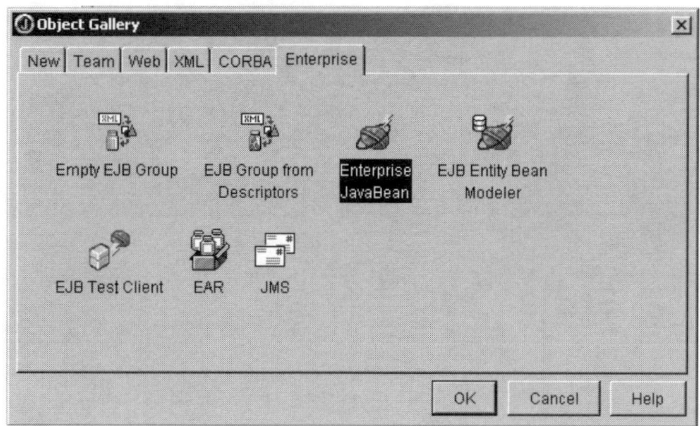

Step 3:

This will bring you to our next screen where we can choose our EJB group. We don't currently have one, so we will choose New and create one.

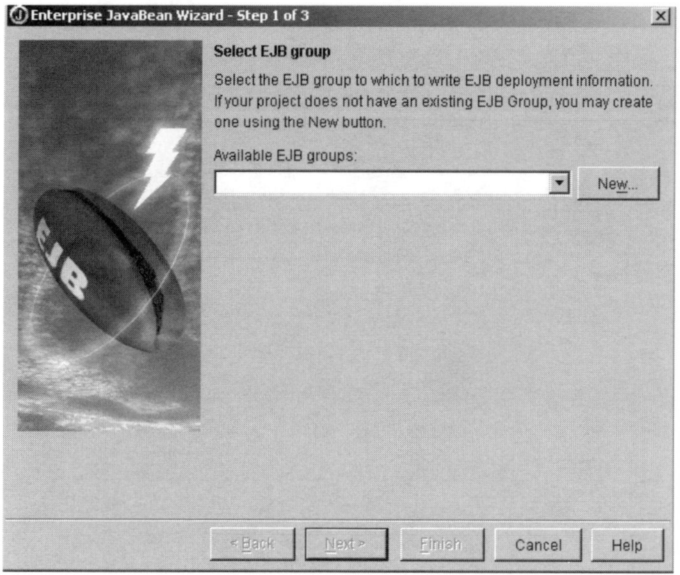

Step 4:

We then simply select a name, and JBuilder will create an EJB group for us.

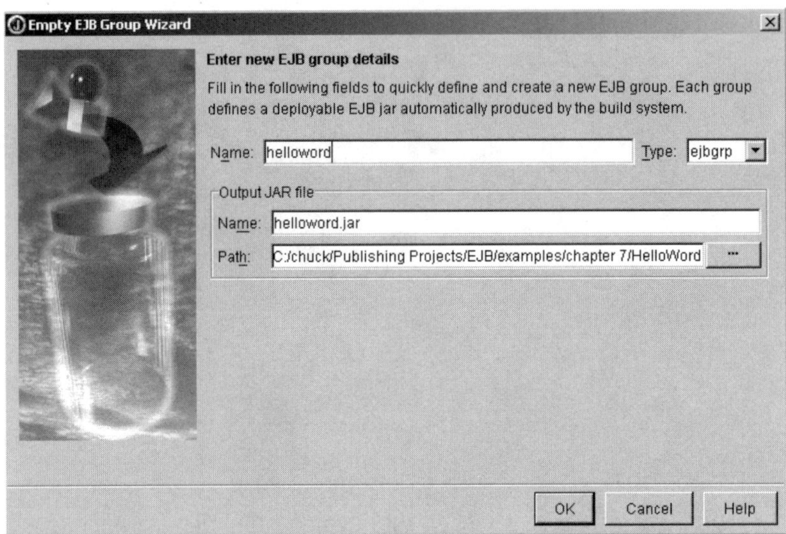

Step 5:

The next screen allows us to select several other options.

Notice that this screen gives you several options you can set for EJBs. You can select what type of bean, how to manage persistence, and what to use as a base class. I am calling my EJB class HelloWorld. Then click Next.

Step 6:

The next screen shows the class names that will be generated.

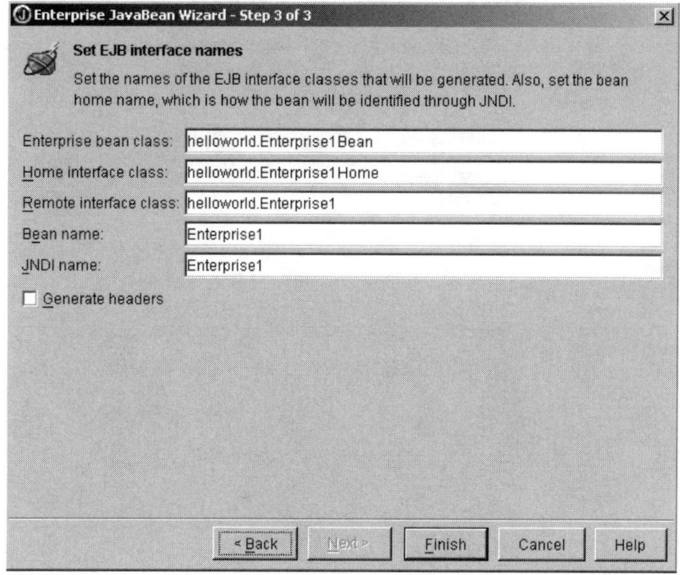

Step 7:

The following screen will set up the previously mentioned descriptor file for you.

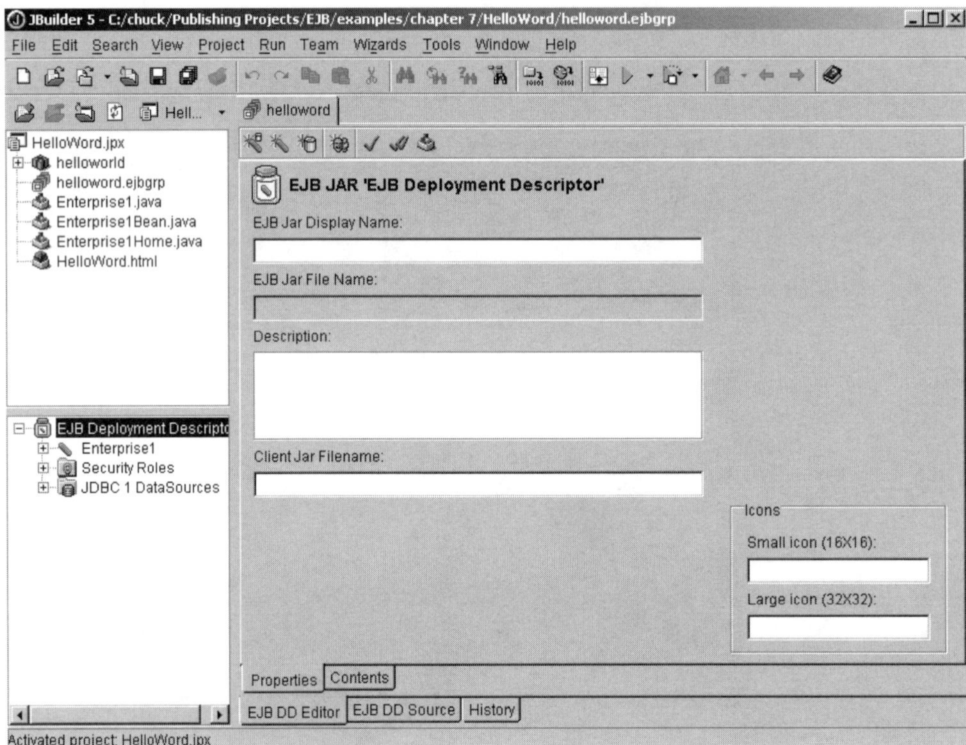

On this screen, you simply fill in the names you wish to use for your files.

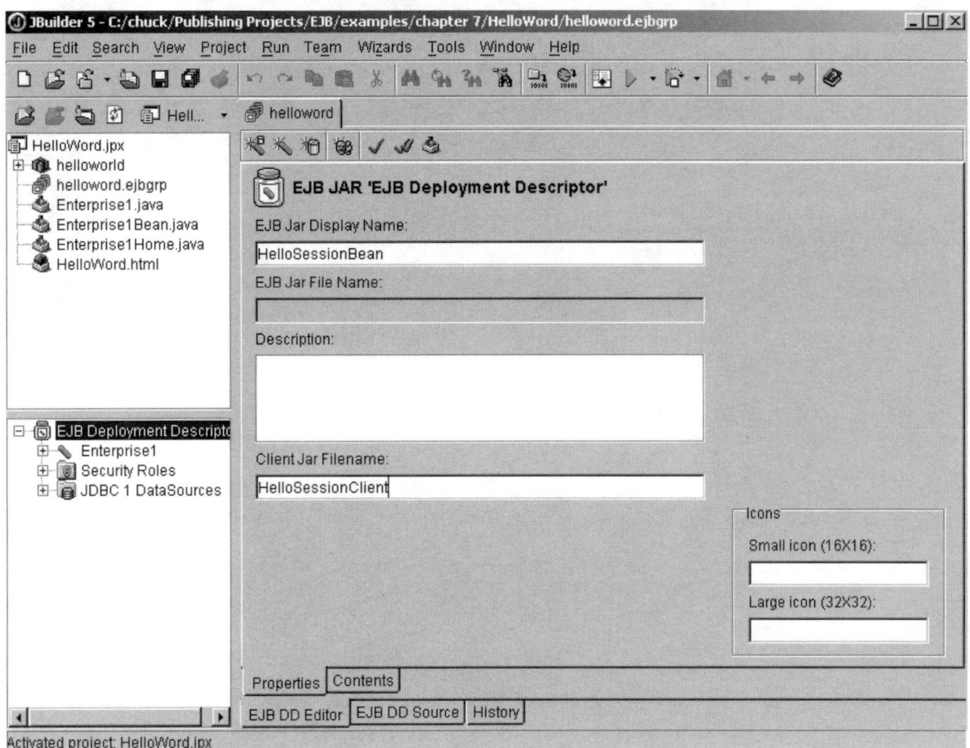

The second tab, Contents, lists the current contents of the EJB JAR.

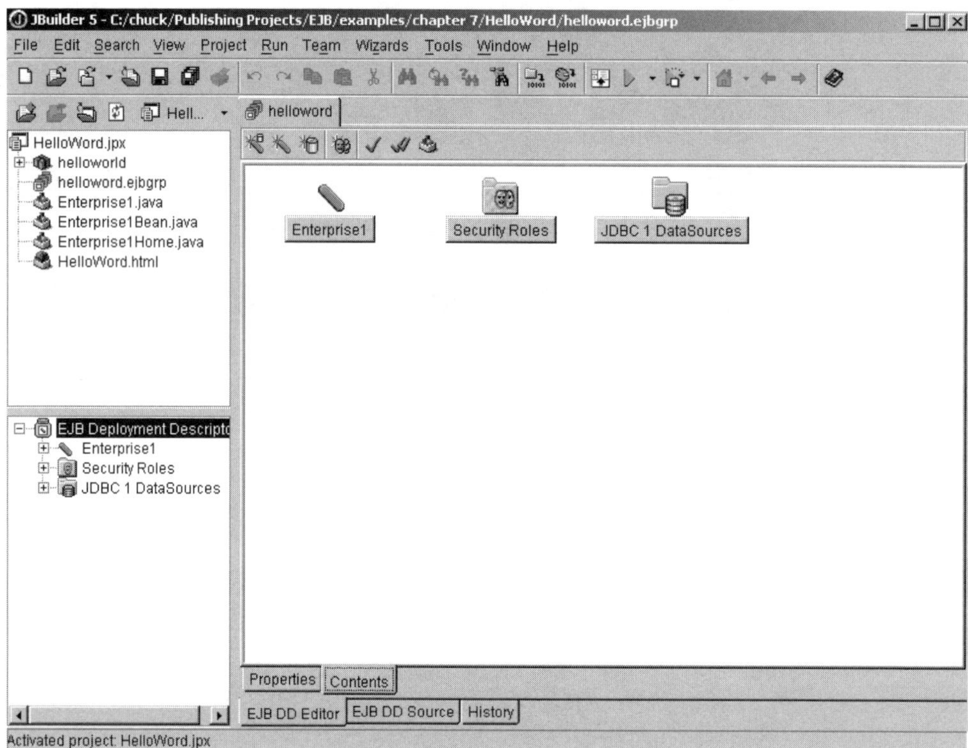

If you choose to view the Source tab, you will see the actual source for
the descriptor file. Remember that it is actually an XML file.

```xml
<?xml version="1.0" encoding="Cp1252"?>
<!DOCTYPE ejb-jar PUBLIC '-//Sun Microsystems, Inc.//DTD Enterprise
JavaBeans 1.1//EN' 'http://java.sun.com/j2ee/dtds/ejb-jar_1_1.dtd'>
<ejb-jar>
  <description>This is my hello world EJB Jar!</description>
  <display-name>HelloWorld</display-name>
  <enterprise-beans>
    <session>
      <ejb-name>HelloWorld</ejb-name>
      <home>helloword.HelloWorldHome</home>
      <remote>helloword.HelloWorldRemote</remote>
      <ejb-class>helloword.HelloWorld</ejb-class>
      <session-type>Stateless</session-type>
```

```
      <transaction-type>Container</transaction-type>
    </session>
  </enterprise-beans>
  <assembly-descriptor>
    <container-transaction>
      <method>
<ejb-name>HelloWorld</ejb-name>
<method-name>*</method-name>
      </method>
      <trans-attribute>Required</trans-attribute>
    </container-transaction>
  </assembly-descriptor>
  <ejb-client-jar>HelloClient</ejb-client-jar>
</ejb-jar>
```

Step 8:

If you look at the tab in the upper left-hand side of the IDE, you will
notice that all of the files you need (the EJB bean code, the remote interface, and the home interface) are already there for you. All you need to
do is add in the single business method in the HelloWorld.java file.

```
public String hello()
{
   return "Hello World";
}
```

You are now done coding your bean. Before I continue, I want you to
notice several advantages to using JBuilder over coding by hand. The
first advantage is that you only had to write the business method(s). This
means that as an EJB developer, you can concentrate on the actual business processes you are attempting to implement, rather than concerning
yourself with the simple details of creating an EJB. The other major
advantage is that since JBuilder generates the required code for you,
there is no chance of overlooking any minor details.

Step 9:

Now for the last phase, deploying your EJB. This can be tricky when done manually, since with JBuilder it is a trivial matter. Select Tools ▸ EJB Deployment.

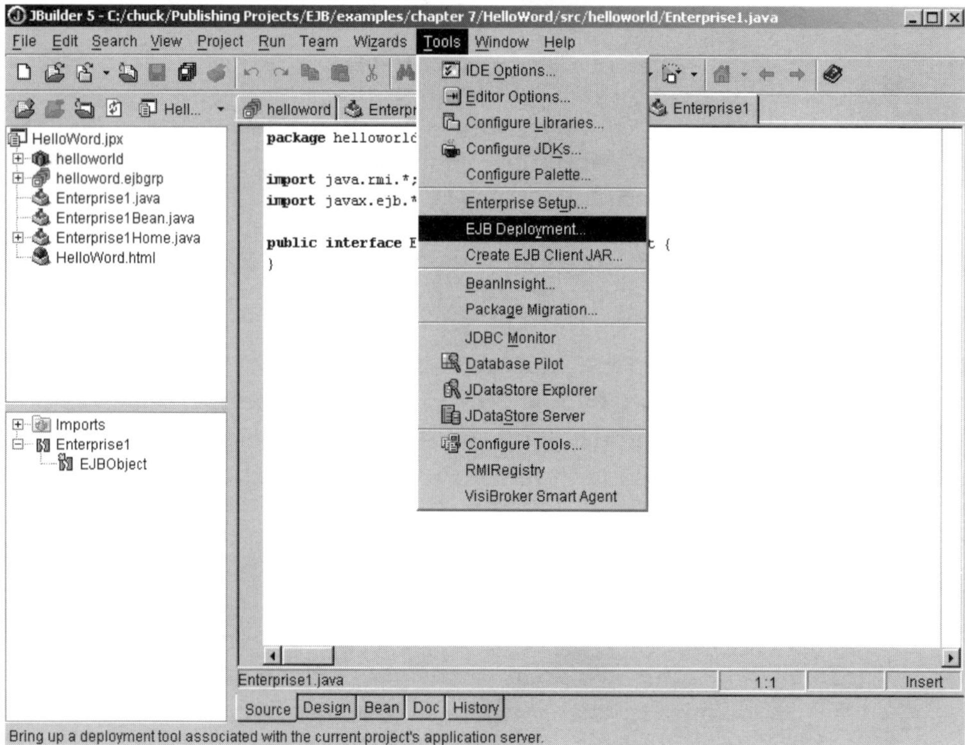

Note: The EJB Deployment option won't be enabled unless you have compiled your bean.

This will launch a wizard that will walk you through the process of deploying your EJB.

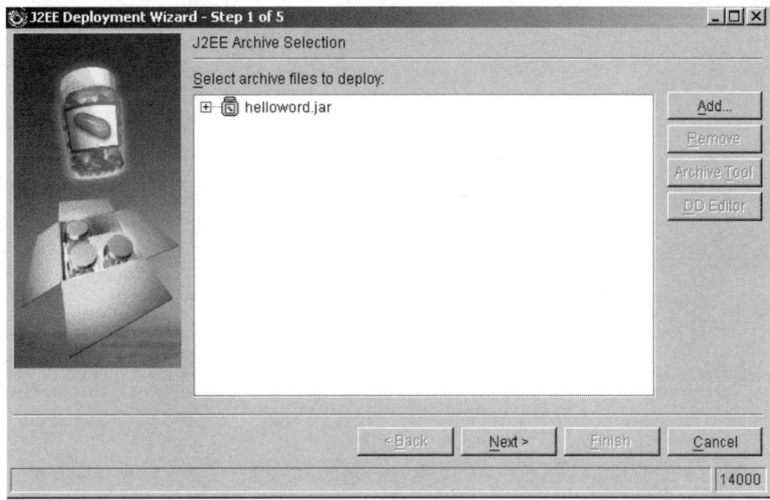

You can usually go with the default settings through each of the screens of the wizard, until you reach the fourth screen, which allows you to pick what EJB container you wish to deploy to.

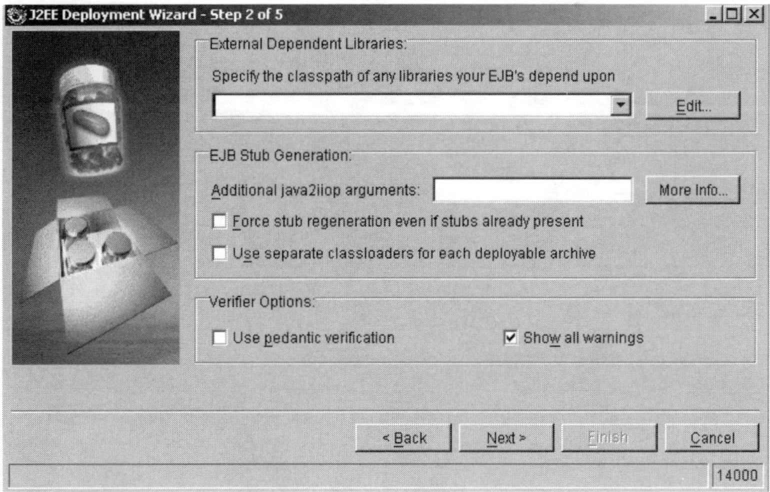

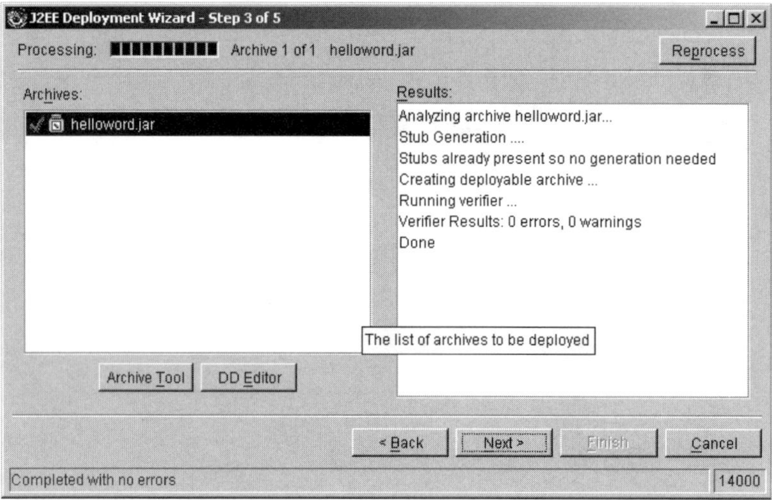

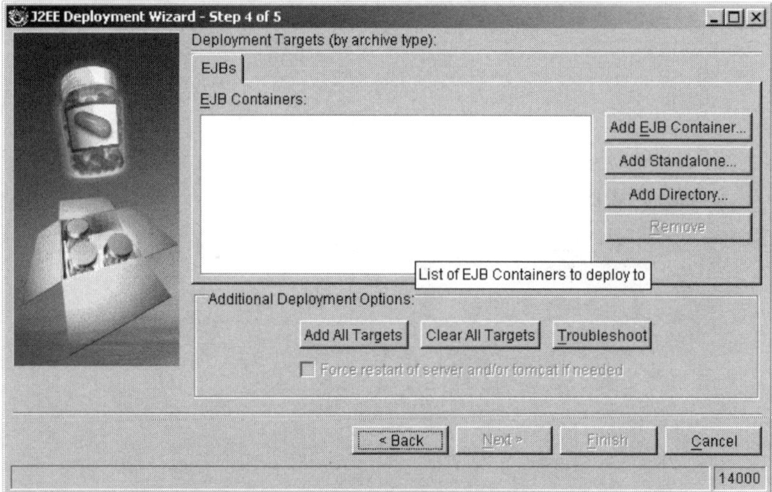

Your EJB is now created and deployed! As you can see, using the Borland JBuilder development tools makes creating and deploying EJBs much easier.

Summary

This chapter gave an introduction to stateless session beans. After studying this chapter, you should be aware of the various requirements for creating a stateless session bean. You should also understand that stateless session beans do not retain any state between method calls. This allows any client to use any stateless session beans. Stateless session beans are often kept in pools from which the application server can initiate any bean it needs. You should also recall that since these EJBs are stateless, they do not require passivation or activation.

Terms

Stateless – A session bean that does not retain any state information at all.

Home Interface – The home interface is the interface that provides methods for creating instances of the EJB.

Deployment Descriptors – This is a replacement for the manifest file. It describes all things needed for deploying Enterprise JavaBeans.

Review Questions

1. What interface must all remote interfaces extend?

2. What access modifiers can you use with the EJB class?

3. Each method in the remote interface must match a method in what class?

4. What object is responsible for creating client instances of the EJB object?

5. What does an ejbCreate method return?

6. What object must the home interface extend?

7. What exception must all remote interfaces throw?

8. Does a stateless session bean create method usually take arguments?

9. What exception must all business methods throw?

10. Is it possible to have an abstract session bean?

Chapter 8

Stateful Session Beans

Introduction

In Chapter 7, I showed you stateless session beans and discussed the theory behind them, how to create them, and how to use them. However, there are times when it is necessary for the EJB and client to have a multi-method conversation. Stateful session beans are session beans that retain information throughout a client conversation that may span multiple method calls. These EJBs are useful for business processes that require an interaction between client and application service that lasts longer than a single method invocation and requires maintenance of state about the interaction. A common example is an online shopping cart. The end user can order a number of items. The ordering of each item will probably be a separate method call. However, you would definitely want to have some connection between these various orders. The stateful session bean managing the interaction must accumulate all the orders until the end user is done placing orders. The stateful EJB would have to hold the unprocessed orders while allowing end users to add more orders.

Activation and Passivation

Recall from Chapter 5 that activation is the process of activating a bean that has previously been passivated. In other words, activation is the process of taking a JavaBean that is currently in an idle state and bringing it up to an active state. Passivation is, essentially, the process of putting a bean on idle. This information is not applicable to stateless session beans, as they do not use activation or passivation. Since they retained no state information, it was not necessary. Recall that with stateless beans, any client could access any bean. Since they retained no state information, it really did not matter. All stateless session beans were in an active state and ready to accept client calls at all times.

Activation and passivation have serious implications for stateful session beans. However, there can be only one stateful session bean per EJB client. Since they do retain some state information, each client must lock into a specific stateful session bean at the beginning of the conversation and maintain that lock until the entire conversation is completed, regardless of how many method calls are involved in that single conversation. Since stateful session beans can be persisted, they are sometimes referred to as persistent session beans. There are two specific methods that allow you to implement a type of persistence in stateful session beans. The getHandle() method returns a bean object's instance handle, which can be used to save the bean's state. To restore a bean from persistent storage, you use the getEJBObject() method.

Stateful session beans are linked to a particular client for the duration of the client conversation. Unlike entity beans or stateless session beans, they are not swapped among various EJB objects. Since there can be periods of inactivity between method invocations, stateful session beans can be passivated to preserve system resources and still retain state information. When this is done, the bean's serializable fields are serialized to a secondary storage. These fields can be restored when the bean is activated. Remember from Chapter 4 that any variable declared as transient will not be serialized.

The current state of a stateful session bean is stored in instance variables. If the bean is passivated, then those variables are serialized. Unlike entity beans and stateless session beans, stateful session beans are usually removed from memory when they are passivated. Not all application servers will do this, but most do. When a stateful bean experiences a long period of idle time, the container may choose to passivate the stateful bean instance. Remember, however, that it is up to the application server to determine how your application server handles this. Passivating an idle bean is the most common method. To conserve system resources, the bean instance is removed from memory by the EJB container. This means the bean is de-referenced and garbage collected. When the EJB object receives a new client request, a new stateful instance is instantiated and associated with the EJB object to handle that request. This means that passivation is an important technique that Enterprise JavaBean containers use for resource management.

Stateful session beans maintain a conversational state, which must be preserved before the bean instance is removed from memory. To accomplish this, the container will write the conversational state of the bean instance to a secondary storage. Remember that the method used for preserving the state information is serialization. This means that only the non-transient instance variables are preserved. When the bean is activated, the new instance variables are populated with the preserved state. The previous state information is de-serialized.

Recall from Chapter 7 that all session beans must implement the javax.ejb.SessionBean interface. This interface provides two callback methods that notify the bean instance that it is about to be passivated or was just activated. The ejbPassivate() method notifies the bean instance that it is about to be removed from memory and its instance variables will be serialized. Within this method, the bean developer can perform any operations the bean may require just prior to passivation, like closing open resources. This might include disconnecting from a database source, closing a file, or releasing any resource of which it has control. The ejbActivate() method is executed just after a new bean instance has been instantiated and populated with state information from secondary storage. The bean developer can use the ejbActivate() method to perform operations just prior to servicing the client request. This might include reopening files, reestablishing database connections, or activating any resource that it requires.

Stateful Session Bean Life Cycle

The life of a stateful session bean begins when the client calls the create()
method of the session bean's home interface. The container then creates a
new instance of the session bean. It will then initialize that instance and
return an object reference to the client. During the creation process, the container invokes the setSessionContext() method of the SessionBean interface
and calls the ejbCreate() method of the session bean implementation. Inside
the ejbCreate() and setSessionContext() methods, you can write any code
that you wish. If there is some resource you would like to access as soon as
the bean is instantiated, this would be an appropriate place for that code
(for example, if you need to access a database, or perhaps you need to open
a TCP socket). The session bean is now ready to be used. Some people refer
to this as "method ready," meaning that it is ready for you to call its
methods.

The bean will remain in this ready status until the bean enters a transaction,
is passivated, or is removed. When a client calls the remove() method of the
remote or home interface, the container invokes the corresponding
ejbRemove() method on the session bean object. This ejbRemove() method
is where you would place any application-specific clean-up code (for example, if you wish to disconnect from some resource like a database, or perhaps
you wish to close a TCP socket). In the ejbRemove() method, you could disconnect from the resource in question and release the objects utilized, thus
making them eligible for garbage collection.

After the ejbRemove() method is completed, that bean object is no longer
available for use. If a client attempts to call a method in a bean object after
the ejbRemove() method has been invoked, the container throws the
java.rmi.NoSuchObjectException.

The most common way to deactivate a bean is for the client to call the
appropriate method. However, this is not the only way a bean can be deactivated. The container can deactivate the session bean; this can occur when
the bean instance has been idle for a period of time and system resources are
getting low. The container determines that it must free memory, so it deactivates those bean instances that it deems have been idle for a long enough
period of time. It is important that you remember, however, that the

container still passivates the bean in the same manner as the client does. The container deactivates the bean by calling the bean's ejbPassivate() method. When a bean instance is passivated, the container stores the state of the session object on disk and frees the memory allocated to the bean. The container can, of course, reactivate the bean by calling the ejbActivate() method. If a client calls a method on a bean instance that has been passivated, the container will simply activate the bean. This activity is completely transparent to the client.

During the process of reactivation, the container recreates the session object in memory and restores the previously serialized state. It essentially mimics much of what was done in the ejbCreate() method. You can, of course, add code to the ejbActivate() method in order to accomplish any initialization procedures. You will often use similar items to what you might place in the ejbCreate() method. This might include opening TCP sockets or connecting to a data source.

Stateful Session Beans and Transactions

As pointed out previously in this text, beans may run in a transactional context. That simply means that the bean itself is currently part of a larger series of operations referred to as a transaction. When a client calls a method on a session bean object in a transactional context, the container will either start a new transaction or include the bean within an existing transaction. As with everything else you have learned about Enterprise JavaBeans, there are stages in a transaction's life cycle. Each of these stages are referred to as *transaction synchronization points*. At each of these transaction synchronization points, a session bean can be notified of upcoming transaction events, and the object can take whatever action may be required

As you might have guessed, based on what you have learned so far, a session bean will need to implement a specific interface in order to participate in this transaction synchronization. A session bean must implement the SessionSynchronization interface if it wishes to be informed about any changes in the state of any transaction in which it is involved. Stateful session beans don't have to implement this interface; it is optional. However, you should note that only stateful session beans using container-managed transactions can implement SessionSynchronization. The methods of SessionSynchronization are callback methods made by the container into the bean. These methods represent specific points within the transaction. Here is the source code for the SessionSynchronization interface:

```
public interface javax.ejb.SessionSynchronization
{
  public abstract void afterBegin() throws RemoteException;
  public abstract void beforeCompletion() throws RemoteException;
  public abstract void afterCompletion(boolean completionStatus) throws
    RemoteException;
}
```

The following table summarizes the methods needed for the Session-Synchronization interface:

Method	Description
afterBegin()	Notifies the bean instance that it is about to be used in a transaction
beforeCompletion()	Notifies the bean instance that the transaction is about to commit
afterCompletion()	Notifies the bean instance that the transaction has completed. If the transaction was committed, the parameter completionStatus is set to TRUE. If the transaction was rolled back, the parameter is set to FALSE.

As you might guess, using JBuilder to create your Enterprise JavaBeans will greatly facilitate coding. The Enterprise JavaBean Wizard can add these methods to your bean class for you. Using the wizard, you simply have to check the Session Synchronization check box, and the wizard declares the three methods with empty bodies in your bean class. Let's take a look at an example.

This example will show you how to create a simple stateless session bean. The steps are relatively simple, and you may be surprised at just how much work that JBuilder does for you.

Step 1:

The first step, of course, is to launch JBuilder Enterprise and start a new project.

For step 2 of the wizard, you can simply keep the default values.

Of course, the third page of the wizard is merely for you to add some documentation, if you should desire.

Step 2:

Now you will select File ▸ New and choose Enterprise JavaBean.

This will start the EJB Wizard. It will ask you what group this EJB should belong to; you should select New and give it some appropriate name.

Step 3:

The second screen of the EJB Wizard will ask you to select what type of bean you wish to create. Choose Stateful Session Bean and Session Synchronization.

We will leave the third screen of the EJB Wizard with the default settings, but you should notice that JBuilder is creating all the required interfaces and classes for you.

Now that JBuilder has created all the required classes, you can define the EJB JAR name and any other parameters you like, as shown in the following figure.

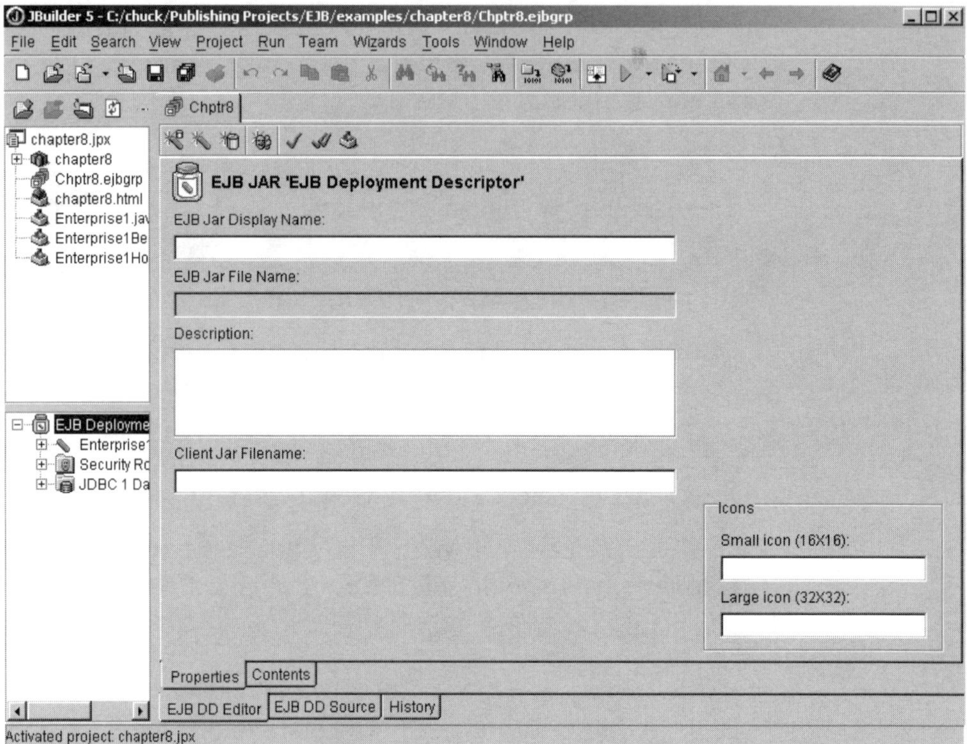

As I pointed out to you previously, JBuilder will create all the necessary classes and methods required for the EJB. You can then concentrate on simply implementing the business methods that you require. Below is the code that JBuilder generated for you on this example:

First the actual Bean class:

```
package chapter8;
import java.rmi.*;
import javax.ejb.*;
public class Enterprise1Bean implements SessionBean, SessionSynchronization
{
  private SessionContext sessionContext;
  public void ejbCreate()
  {
  }
  public void ejbRemove() throws RemoteException
  {
```

```java
    }
    public void ejbActivate() throws RemoteException
    {
    }
    public void ejbPassivate() throws RemoteException
    {
    }
    public void setSessionContext(SessionContext sessionContext) throws
        RemoteException
    {
      this.sessionContext = sessionContext;
    }
    public void afterBegin()
      {
      }
    public void beforeCompletion()
      {
      }
    public void afterCompletion(boolean committed)
      {
      }
    }
```

Notice that the ejbCreate(), ejbPassivate(), and ejbRemove() methods are all created for you. All session beans require this. You should also note that the required code for session synchronization is already created for you, including the afterBegin(), beforeCompletion(), and afterCompletion() methods, as well as the implements SessionSynchronization declaration.

The home interface is also created for you:

```java
package chapter8;
import java.rmi.*;
import javax.ejb.*;
public interface Enterprise1Home extends EJBHome
{
  public Enterprise1 create() throws RemoteException, CreateException;
}
```

Of course, you may choose to manually write this code in any text editor you choose and do command line compilation using the freely downloadable Java Development Kit. However, I think you will find that generating the code is much faster, and less prone to error, when you let JBuilder do it for you.

I have shown you how you can use JBuilder to create the basic code. However, what we have done so far is not particularly useful. It would indeed be a session bean, with synchronization, but it would not accomplish any business tasks. Next I will show you a bean that does perform some useful task. This bean is a shopping cart bean. Most EJB books will at some point show you a shopping cart bean, and in fact, the JBuilder help files show you one. It is such a useful product that it seems to have become the de facto standard in bean examples.

The following example has two purposes. The first is to provide you with another example of the essentials of creating stateful session beans. The other purpose is to show you an example of a stateful session bean with some business methods (in other words, a stateful session bean that accomplishes some useful or interesting task).

Step 1:

You can use JBuilder to create the bean, as you did in the first example, or you can create the code manually. In either case, you will be slightly modifying the code, generated as follows:

```java
import java.rmi.*;
import javax.ejb.*;
public class ShoppingCartBean implements SessionBean
{
  private SessionContext sessionContext;
  private Vector items = new Vector();
  private String cardHolderName;
  private String creditCardNumber;
  private Date expirationDate;

public void ejbCreate(String sz_cardholdername, String sz_cardnumber,
    Date dtexpiredate) throws CreateException
  {
    _cardHolderName = cardholdername;
    _creditCardNumber = sz_cardnumber;
    expirationDate = dtexpiredate;
  }
```

```java
    public void ejbRemove() throws RemoteException
    {
    }

    public void ejbActivate() throws RemoteException
    {
    }

    public void ejbPassivate() throws RemoteException
    {
    }
      public void setSessionContext(SessionContext context) throws
          RemoteException
    {
        sessionContext = context;
    }
public void addItem(Item item)
{
        items.addElement(item);
}
public void removeItem(Item item) throws ItemNotFoundException
{
  Enumeration elements = items.elements();
  while(elements.hasMoreElements())
{
        Item current = (Item) elements.nextElement();
        // items are equal if they have the same class and title
            if(item.getClass().equals(current.getClass())&&
            item.getTitle().equals(current.getTitle())) {
            items.removeElement(current);
            return;
    }
}
public float getTotalPrice()
{
    float totalPrice = 0.00f;
    Enumeration elements = items.elements();
    while(elements.hasMoreElements())
    {
      Item current = (Item) elements.nextElement();
```

```
        totalPrice += current.getPrice();
      }
    // round price to the nearest lower penny
    return (long) (totalPrice * 100) / 100f;
}
public java.util.Enumeration getContents()
{
return new com.inprise.ejb.util.VectorEnumeration(items);
}
public void purchase() throws PurchaseProblemException
{
// make sure the credit card has not expired
    Date today = Calendar.getInstance().getTime();
    if(_expirationDate.before(today))
    {
      throw new CardExpiredException("Expiration date: " + _expirationDate);
    }
}
  public String toString()
    {
    return "ShoppingCartBean[name=" + cardHolderName + "]";
  }
}
```

The ShoppingCartBean example uses an Item class. This class represents a
given item in the shopping cart.

```
package shoppingcart;
public class Item implements java.io.Serializable
{
  private String sz_title;
  private float f_price;
  public Item(String title, float price)
{
    sz_title = title;
    f_price = price;
  }
  public String getTitle()
{
    return sz_title;
  }
```

```
    public float getPrice()
{

   return f_price;
}
}
```

There are three custom exception classes used in the ShoppingCart example.
All are extensions of the Java class Exception.

```
    public class ItemNotFoundException extends Exception
{

   public ItemNotFoundException(String message)
{

   super(message);
}
}
public class PurchaseProblemException extends Exception
{

   public PurchaseProblemException(String message)
{

   super(message);
}
}
public class CardExpiredException extends Exception
{

   public CardExpiredException(String message)
{

   super(message);
}
}
```

Notice that our ShoppingCart example conforms to all the required EJB specifications. Remember that a session bean class must be defined as public. You
should also keep in mind that it cannot be defined as final or abstract.
Finally, recall that the bean class must implement the SessionBean interface.
Both of the beans we have created comply with these rules. However, in
order to have functionality, we will need to add some things. You should
notice the member variables at the beginning of this class. The names should
indicate their purpose. The items variable holds the items currently in the
shopping cart object. I used a vector here because I can then add as many
items as I might require. The other three member variables hold the credit

card information of the online shopper. (You do want the customer to pay, don't you?)

Our shopping cart bean works much like any other stateful session bean. The container calls the setSessionContext() method to associate the bean instance with its session context. The bean can then retain this session context reference as part of its conversational state. If you used the JBuilder EJB Wizard, the session context reference is held. The session bean can use the session context to get information about itself. Information that it may retrieve would include environment variables or its home interface. The container calls the ejbPassivate() method on the bean instance when it needs to place the bean instance into a passive state. The container writes the bean's current state to secondary storage when the bean is passivated. This allows the container to restore this state when it later activates the bean.

Remember that while a session bean isn't required to implement a constructor, it must implement at least one ejbCreate() method. This method can be used in much the same way as a constructor to create a new bean instance. A stateful session can implement more than one ejbCreate() method. Each ejbCreate() method would differ only in its parameters. Again, this is much like a constructor. The ShoppingCartBean example declares one ejbCreate() method that takes three parameters. These three parameters are used to initialize the bean to the context of a given shopper.

Of course, our ShoppingCartBean has some additional methods, the business methods. There are a few rules that all business methods must follow: None of the method names should start with the prefix "ejb" to avoid conflict with names reserved by the EJB architecture. Each method must be declared as public. No method can be declared as final or static. The throws clause may include the javax.ejb.EJBException exception, and it may define arbitrary exceptions specific to the application. In the ShoppingCartBean example, five business methods are implemented. It is imperative that you remember that the signatures (i.e., the method name, number of parameters, parameter types, and return type) of the session bean class methods must match those of the remote interface. To ensure that this happens, you can use the bean designer to move the business methods you add to the bean class to the bean's remote interface.

The methods we added should be fairly straightforward and easy to understand. The additem() method is used to add items to the shopping cart, whereas the removeitem() method is used to remove an item from the shopping cart. The getTotalprice() method is used to total up the purchase.

You should also bear in mind that all data types passed between a client and a server must be serializable. Therefore, they must implement the java.io.Serializable interface. In the ShoppingCart example, the bean returns a list of items to the client. If there were no serializable restrictions, you could use items.elements() to return the contents of the item vector. However, items.elements() returns a Java Enumeration object, which is not serializable. To avoid this problem, the program implements a class called com.inprise.ejb.util.VectorEnumeration(_items). This class takes a vector and returns an actual enumeration, which is serializable, for the contents of that vector. That class is a creation of the good people at Borland (the makers of JBuilder) and one more good reason to use JBuilder for your Java development! The ShoppingCartBean object passes this serializable vector to the client and receives a serializable vector passed from the client side. The getContents() method does the conversion between a Java Enumeration and a serializable VectorEnumeration.

The purchase() method should do the following: Get the current time and compare the expiration date of the credit card with the current time. If the expiration date is prior to the current time, the method throws the CardExpiredException application exception. It will also complete the purchasing process, including updating inventory, posting the charge to the credit card company, and initiating shipment of the item. (None of this has actually been implemented in the cart example.) If an error occurs at any point, the purchase process does not complete and the method throws a PurchaseProblemException exception. ShoppingCartBean also includes a toString() method to print out the ShoppingCartBean and the name of the card holder.

Of course, our ShoppingCartBean, like all EJBs, must have a home interface. The following is the code for the home interface. Remember that the ejbCreate() methods here must exactly match the signatures of the ejbCreate() methods in the actual bean class.

```
public interface ShoppingCartHome extends javax.ejb.EJBHome
{
  Cart create(String cardHolderName, String creditCardNumber,
              java.util.Date expirationDate)
  throws java.rmi.RemoteException,javax.ejb.CreateException;
}
```

Recall that our EJB must also have a deployment descriptor. If you are using JBuilder, it will generate one for you. However, for those of you who insist on doing things the hard way, here is the deployment descriptor file for the shopping cart session bean:

```
<ejb-jar>
  <enterprise-beans>
    <session>
      <description>
        XML deployment descriptor cart session bean
      <description>
      <ejb-name>cart</ejb-name>
      <home>ShoppingCartHome</home>
      <remote>Cart</remote>
      <ejb-class>ShoppingCartBean</ejb-class>
      <session-type>Stateful</session-type>
      <transaction-type>Container</transaction-type>
    <session>
  <enterprise-beans>
  <assembly-descriptor>
    <container-transaction>
      <method>
        <ejb-name>cart</ejb-name>
      <method-name>*</method-name>
      </method>
      <trans-attribute>NotSupported</trans-attribute>
    </container-transaction>
    <container-transaction>
      <method>
        <ejb-name>cart</ejb-name>
        <method-name>purchase</method-name>
      </method>
        <trans-attribute>Required</trans-attribute>
      </container-transaction>
```

```
</assembly-descriptor>
</ejb-jar>
```

A Client for Our EJB

No matter how well you design your EJB, it is not much use without a client. The following text will first describe and then show you a client application for this ShoppingCartBean. Its main() routine includes elements that all enterprise bean client applications must implement. This client also provides an example of how to use JNDI to locate the bean's home interface. It then uses the home interface's create() method to create a new remote cart object. Finally, it invokes methods declared in the Shopping Cart object.

```
public static void main(String args[]) throws Exception
{
// get a JNDI context using the Naming service
javax.naming.Context context = new javax.naming.InitialContext();
Object objref = context.lookup("cart");
ShoppingCartHome home =
    (ShoppingCartHome)javax.rmi.PortableRemoteObject.narrow(objref,
     CartHome.class);
ShoppingCart cart;
{
    String cardHolderName = "Jack B. Quick";
    String creditCardNumber = "1234-5678-9012-3456";
    Date expirationDate = new GregorianCalendar(2001,
        Calendar.JULY,1).getTime();
    cart = home home.create(cardHolderName, creditCardNumber,
        expirationDate);
}
Item  widget = new Item("The Ubiquitous Widget", 19.95f)
cart.addItem(widget)
    ... // create compact disc and add it to cart, then list cart contents
summarize(cart)
cart.removeItem(widget)
    ... // add a different book and summarize cart contents
try
{
```

```
        cart.purchase();
        }
      catch(PurchaseProblemException e)
  {

        System.out.println("Could not purchase the items:\n\t" + e);
      }
  cart.remove();
  }
```

The main() routine begins with a JNDI context to look up objects. It constructs an initial context (a Java-naming context). This is standard JNDI code. main() looks up the CartHome object called cart. Looking up a name with JNDI invokes a call from the client to the CosNaming service to look up the name in CosNaming. The CosNaming service returns an object reference to the client. In this example, it returns a CORBA object reference. The program must perform a PortableRemoteObject.narrow() operation on the object reference, cast the returned object to the type CartHome, and assign it to the variable home. This call is typical for distributed applications. The call uses CORBA and IIOP to do the following:

- Talk to a server

- Perform a CosNaming lookup

- Obtain a CORBA object reference

- Return the object reference to the client

The program declares a reference to the remote cart object, initializes three create() parameter variables, and creates a new cart remote object. The program creates two shopping cart items, a book and a compact disc, and adds these items to the shopping cart using the cart's addItem() method. The routine then lists the items currently in the cart by calling the summarize() function. summarize() retrieves the elements or items in the cart using the cart's getContents() method, which returns a Java enumeration. It then uses the Java Enumeration interface methods to read each element in the enumeration, extracting the title and price for each one. Here is the summarize() function code:

```
  static void summarize(Cart cart) throws Exception
    {
      System.out.println("======== Cart Summary =========")'
```

```
        Enumeration elements = cart.getContents();
        while(elements.hasMoreElements())
    {

            Item current = (Item) elements.nextElement():
            System.out.println("Price: $" + current.getPrice() + "\t" +
                current.getClass().getName() + " title: " + current.getTitle());
        }
        System.out.println("Total: $" + cart.getTotalPrice());
        System.out.println("=================================");
    }
```

The program then calls cart's removeItem() method to remove an item from the cart. It adds a different item and summarizes the cart contents again. Finally, the program attempts to purchase the items. The purchase operation fails because it is not implemented on the server, and a PurchaseProblem-Exception is thrown. Because the user is finished with the shopping session, the program removes the cart. It's not necessary to remove the cart, although it is good programming practice to do so. A session bean exists for the client that created it. When the client ends the session, the container automatically removes the session bean object. The container also removes the session bean object when it times out, although this doesn't happen immediately. ShoppingCartClient also includes code that extends the generic Item class with two types of items: a book and a compact disc.

Summary

In this chapter, your knowledge of Enterprise JavaBeans was expanded to include basic coverage of stateful session beans. After reading this chapter, you should be familiar with the basic requirements for any stateful session bean. The chapter concluded with a demonstration of a stateful session bean, using a shopping cart example. You should have a firm understanding of the requirements of a stateful session bean, the advantages and disadvantages of a stateful session bean, as well as the life cycle of a stateful session bean.

Terms

Conversation – The complete list of transactions between a client and an Enterprise JavaBean

Stateful – A session bean that retains state information between method calls

Stateless – This is a session bean that does not retain any state information. It only interacts with a client for the duration of a single method call.

Transactions – An individual operation between a client and an Enterprise JavaBean

Remote Interface – The interface that the client will actually interact with

Home Interface – The interface used to get a reference to the remote interface

SessionContext – The context within which the session bean interacts

Activation – This refers to moving a JavaBean from an idle state to an active state.

Passivation – This term refers to taking an active JavaBean and moving it to an idle state. This is often done by the EJB container to conserve resources.

Review Questions

1. What method do you use to restore an EJB from persistent storage?

2. What interface must all stateful session beans implement?

3. What method is executed just after a new bean instance has been instantiated and populated with state information from secondary storage?

4. What are stages in a transaction's life cycle referred to as?

5. What three methods are required for session synchronization?

6. What method notifies the bean instance that it is about to be removed from memory and its instance variables will be serialized?

7. During what process does the container recreate the session object in memory and restore the previously serialized state?

8. What interface must a session bean implement if it wishes to be informed about changes in the state of any transaction in which it is involved?

9. The bean will remain in this "ready" status until one of three actions occurs. What are the three actions?

10. Only stateful session beans using what type of transaction can implement SessionSynchronization?

Chapter 9

Java and Database Programming

Introduction

Now that you have read up on standard JavaBeans and session JavaBeans, you will be moving on to entity JavaBeans in Chapter 10. However, as I mentioned in Chapter 5, entity beans represent some data entity. It will be impossible for you to understand and use entity beans without a firm grasp of basic database programming in Java. It will also be impossible for you to complete the examples in Chapter 11 without this knowledge. Many readers may already have this skill. If you are already comfortable with Java database programming, then feel free to skip this chapter. However, if you are unfamiliar with database programming in Java, or if you require a brief refresher, then this chapter is just for you.

Database Concepts

Storing data in permanent secondary storage (i.e., to a hard drive, CD, diskette, etc.) is a common activity for all programmers. You could store the data in any of a number of formats. In the past, data was often stored in flat files (like a text file) in a sequential manner. You had to start at the beginning and search through until you found the data you were seeking. However, just as important as storing the data is being able to efficiently retrieve it. Relational databases provide you with an organized way to store data so that it can be more easily organized, manipulated, and retrieved. As the name suggests, relational databases are databases wherein different units of data are related. Specifically, database tables are related to each other. There are a number of database terms you will need to be familiar with. Those terms are described in the following table:

Term	Definition
Record	This is all the fields for a particular entry. For example, all the fields that make up a single employee's file are a record.
Field	This is a particular piece of data, like last name, address, phone, etc. In SQL Server or Oracle, this is referred to as a column.
Table	These are related records stored together. For example, all the records of all the employees might be stored in an employee table.
Database	These are related tables stored together. For example, the employee table, inventory table, and finance table might be stored together in a common small business database.
Primary Key	This is a field that is meant to uniquely identify a record in a database table. This field must hold unique values. A good example of a primary key would be using a social security number as the primary key for an employee table.

The Relational Database Management System (RDBMS) refers to units of data that are related. Let's say you have a database that included employee data. For each employee you would want a job description. What if you have

20 people with the same job description (20 Java programmers, for example)? Do you really want to rewrite the job description 20 times? In the relational database model, you simply have a table of job descriptions, and each employee's record in the employee table is related or linked to their job description. This drastically reduces the amount of overhead that a database requires. It also makes for a very logical layout to your database. There are a variety of commercial relational database management systems, all of which provide some type of tool that allows you to create relationships between tables.

This method of storing data is significantly different from the previously described flat file. A flat file simply stores information one record after another in a sequential manner. There is no relationship between records or fields. This makes for an inordinately large data file and one that has a lot of duplication. It is also quite difficult to perform searches. In fact, the only way to search through a flat file is to start at the beginning and cycle through each and every record until you have retrieved the data you are looking for.

Today, most data is stored in relational databases, not in flat files. In order to implement a relational database, you will require a relational database management system. There are a wide range of relational database systems on the market today. The most popular are:

- Oracle

- Microsoft SQL Server

- Microsoft Access (for small desktop databases)

- IBM DB2

- Sybase SQL Anywhere

If you are serious about database programming, you should take the time to become proficient in at least one, preferably two, of these database systems. In Appendix A, I list a few good books and online web tutorials that will assist you in getting up to speed with the relational database system of your choice. If you do not already have a firm grasp of at least one relational database management system, you should be aware that it is difficult to navigate very far in a programming career without at least a moderate level of skill with some commercial database system. After all, virtually all business programming is, at some level, database programming. Fortunately, you will find that all of these database systems share many common features; it is simply their individual implementations of those features, coupled with their storage capacity and the extra tools they offer, that differentiate one from the other.

SQL

Once a database has been built, there must be some method of interacting with it. This will include the following activities:

- Adding new records

- Deleting records

- Editing current records

- Finding records based on some criteria

In the early days of database programming, each relational database system had its own proprietary method for accomplishing these tasks. This posed two serious difficulties. The first was that skills learned with one commercial database system where virtually irrelevant in another system. Secondly, and perhaps more problematically, was the fact that these proprietary schemes were closely tied to the underlying database architecture. Most modern database programmers, or even database administrators, never have to work with, or even be aware of, the underlying mechanisms whereby the database system stores and accesses data. However, with the various proprietary mechanisms, it was often necessary to be very cognizant of these details. Hence, a great deal more knowledge and effort was required in order to effect any database manipulations

With modern commercial database systems, this is no longer the case. Virtually all database systems available today utilize Structured Query Language for all of their database access and manipulation. This means that a database query written for Microsoft's SQL Server 2000 will work with an Oracle 8i database. This is a tremendous advance for business programming. Now database programmers can use skill acquired with one database platform in a completely different product. Programmers need not concern themselves with the intricate details of the data storage and access architecture implemented by the relational database system.

SQL (usually pronounced S-Q-L or "sequel"), or Structured Query Language, is the language used to talk to relational databases. This system is now almost universal for database methodologies. In fact, I am not aware of any database system that does not utilize SQL. However, since there certainly could be some system of which I am not aware, I use the phrase "almost universal." The relational database model for database design was invented by Dr. E.F. Codd in 1969 and published in *Computer World* in 1985.

SQL was first implemented in 1974 at the IBM San Jose Research Laboratory. SQL is essentially a non-procedural language that uses English-like words to talk to a database. The American National Standards Institute (ANSI) is continually updating its versions of SQL standards. SQL is independent of the individual database. This means that SQL queries work equally well on MS Access, MS SQL Server, IBM DB2, Oracle, or any other relational database system. An SQL statement is simply a string variable that is usually passed to the database. Below is an example of an SQL query that retrieves all the data from a table named MYTABLE.

```
"SELECT * FROM [MYTABLE]"
```

Note: The brackets are used to denote a table within the database. The asterisk (*) symbol is computer shorthand for "everything." The capitalization is not absolutely necessary but is an often used convention for the SQL commands themselves.

The following table lists the most commonly encountered SQL statements and their purpose. There are certainly many more SQL commands than the ones you see here, but these fundamental commands are ubiquitous throughout the worlds of relational database administration and database programming.

Command	Purpose	Example
SELECT	Retrieves data	"SELECT * FROM [MYTABLE]"
FROM	Denotes what table to retrieve data from	"SELECT * FROM [MYTABLE]"
WHERE	Defines some criteria for selecting data	"SELECT [field1],[field2],.... FROM [sometable] WHERE [somefield] = SomeCriteria"
ORDER BY	This statement simply orders the records based on a particular field you wish to order by.	"SELECT * FROM [MYTABLE] ORDER BY[SomeField]"
DISTINCT	If there are multiple copies, it will only return the first.	"SELECT DISTINCT FROM [MYTABLE] ORDER BY[SomeField]"
INNER JOIN	Joins data from two separate tables	"SELECT * FROM [TABLE1] INNER JOIN [TABLE2 ON table1.fieldname=table2. fieldname"
OUTER JOIN	Joins data from two separate tables	"SELECT * FROM [TABLE1] OUTER JOIN [TABLE2 ON table1.fieldname=table2. fieldname"

Let's look at some examples of how you might want to utilize SQL statements. For demonstration purposes, we will assume that you have a database with a table named EMPLOYEE. This table has the following fields:

- Last Name
- First Name
- Phone Number
- Position
- Hire Date
- Salary

Using this configuration, I will show you how to extract various types of data from this table using SQL statements. As you have already seen, you can retrieve all fields from all records with this statement:

```
"SELECT * FROM [EMPLOYEE]"
```

However, if you simply need to retrieve a list of employee names, there is no reason to also retrieve the other four fields. That is a waste of resources. In that case, you can retrieve just the fields you need by using this SQL statement:

```
"SELECT [Last Name], [First Name] FROM [EMPLOYEE]"
```

Of course, both of these SQL statements return all records from a given table. In many cases, you only want records that meet a certain criteria. For example, you might want only those employees whose last name is Jones. Alternatively, you may wish to retrieve all employees whose salary is in excess of $50,000 per year. The following SQL statements do just that for you:

```
"SELECT * FROM [TABLE] WHERE [Last Name] = 'Smith'"
"SELECT * FROM [TABLE] WHERE [Salary] > 50000"
```

In both cases, only the records that match your criteria are returned to you. You can even select those records that are close to your criteria. For example, what if you wanted all employees whose last name started with "Smi":

```
"SELECT * FROM [Employees] WHERE [Last Name] LIKE 'Smi*'"
```

There are a number of other SQL commands with a variety of purposes. INNER JOIN and OUTER JOIN both take data from two tables and bring it together into a single result set. Commands like INSERT and DELETE have obvious purposes. A thorough coverage of Structured Query Language is beyond the scope of this book.

This has simply been a brief introduction to database concepts and SQL. If this material is new to you, then I strongly recommend you take the time to learn more about databases and SQL. You will find several resources, including books and online tutorials, in Appendix A at the end of this book. For now, however, these concepts should be enough for you to comprehend the rest of this book.

JDBC

Now that you have seen basic database concepts and a little about Structured Query Language, it's time to take a look at how data access code is done in Java. JDBC is an acronym for Java Database Connectivity. JDBC is the set of Java drivers that connect to data sources. The concept is very similar to ODBC (Open Database Connectivity) drivers that you may be familiar with.

Inside the java.sql package, there is a rich set of classes that will allow you to perform any database activities you may require. The java.sql package contains classes that provide the API (application programming interface) for accessing and processing data from a data source. The java.sql package is sometimes referred to as the JDBC 2.0 API. JDBC is a standard that allows Java to connect with almost any database. The java.sql package includes classes, interfaces, and methods for making database connections, sending SQL statements to a database, retrieving query results, providing information about a database, and throwing exceptions. There are several classes in java.sql, but a few are of primary importance. The following table summarizes these classes and their functionality:

Class	Functionality
Connection	This class represents a connection to an actual database. You use objects of this class to select a data source, drivers, and database location, and to open a connection. You also use methods of this class to close the connection when you are finished.
Statement	Objects of this class allow you to execute any valid SQL statement on your data source. This will be of particular value to you.
ResultSet	Objects of this class represent the set of records that are returned from executing a statement. This is very much like the recordset object in Microsoft's ADO technology.

Class	Functionality
DriverManager	During its initialization, this class will attempt to load the driver classes referenced in the "jdbc.drivers" system property. That means that all JDBC drivers that it can locate on the system. This allows a user to customize the JDBC drivers used by their applications.

It is important for any Java programmer to be comfortable with JDBC and the various classes used with JDBC programming. It is absolutely critical that a programmer who wishes to develop entity beans have a working knowledge of these classes and their use. Let's look at an example class that handles basic data access in Java. After the example, I will provide some detailed explanation of exactly what is occurring.

```java
import java.sql.*;
class sql
{
  // The URL is the location of the data source
  static String url = "jdbc:odbc:mysource";
  // Connection objects represent the actual connection to
  // some data source.
  static Connection connection;
  public static void main(String args[])
  {
    String sz_field;  // This will hold a single field/column returned
                      // from a database

    String sqlquery;  // This will hold any valid SQL Query
    try
    {

      // These statements make the initial connection to
      // The data source
      Class.forName("sun.jdbc.odbc.JdbcOdbcDriver");
      connection = DriverManager.getConnection(url);
      // Build an sql query that will be passed to the data source
      sqlquery = "SELECT * FROM bank";
      // The statement object represents any valid sql statement
      Statement statement = connection.createStatement();
      // Execute the sql and get back the recordset
```

```java
        ResultSet rs = statement.executeQuery(sqlquery);
        // move to the first record
        rs.next();
        // retrieve and display the first field
        sz_field= rs.getString(1);
        System.out.println("The account number " + sz_field);
        // retrieve and display the second field
        sz_field= rs.getString(2);
        System.out.println("The checking balance is " + sz_field);
        // retrieve and display the third field
        sz_field= rs.getString(3);
        System.out.println("The savings balance is " + sz_field);
        // close the connection
        connection.close();
    }
    catch(Exception e)
    {
        System.out.println("Error! " + e.toString());
    }


    }
  }
```

This is the exact code that I present to students who are taking their first
Java course and trying to learn about Java database programming. It may
not be particularly impressive, but experience has shown it to be effective at
demonstrating the fundamental concepts of database programming in Java.
Most of the code presented is standard Java code. The main function, exception trapping, and other facets of this code are simply standard Java code.
However, parts of this example are specific and unique to JDBC database
programming. The first part of the code that might seem a bit odd to you is
the string declaration of:

```java
    static String url = "jdbc:odbc:mysource";
```

This string provides the location of the data source; in this case it is a DSN
(Data Source Name) representing an Access database. It also indicates that a
JDBC "wrapper" around ODBC drivers will be used. Notice that the string
name is "url." This is intentional. With the Java JDBC API, you can access

database resources over the Internet. So, in some cases, the database location may indeed be a URL, or uniform resource locator (i.e., web address).

The next item that may not be immediately clear to you is the two lines of code that actually establish a connection to the data source:

```
Class.forName("sun.jdbc.odbc.JdbcOdbcDriver");
connection = DriverManager.getConnection(url);
```

The first line of this code snippet is simply identifying what set of drivers to use. In our case, we are using the Sun Microsystems JDBC drivers. The next line of code sets the connection object equal to a valid connection to the data source location previously specified. The DriverManager class literally manages the use of the various JDBC drivers.

Next, we have the code that will execute the appropriate SQL statement to retrieve the items in a particular table. The table, in our example, is named "bank."

```
sqlquery = "SELECT * FROM [bank]";
Statement statement = connection.createStatement();
ResultSet rs = statement.executeQuery(sqlquery);
```

First you see a string that is set equal to a particular SQL statement. This can be any valid SQL statement. If you are not already familiar with SQL, there are a number of excellent tutorials available on the web that you may wish to reference (see Appendix A for a few such resources). Then we set that statement equal to the return value of the connection object's createStatement() method. That method will return a statement object. Finally, we set the resultset object equal to the return value of the statement object's executeQuery() statement.

This last item simply causes the resultset to point at the first record that is returned. If you do not execute this line of code, subsequent actions with the resultset object will generate an error.

```
rs.next();
```

This is fundamentally all you need to access a database using the Java JDBC API. As you can see, the code is not overly difficult, provided you have a solid grasp of database fundamentals and a working knowledge of Structured Query Language.

Database Connectivity Using JBuilder

As I have shown you throughout this book, most tasks in Java can be accomplished more efficiently with JBuilder. Database connectivity is no exception. At this point, let's walk through an example and see how it works.

This is a rather simple example, but it will demonstrate how easy creating database applications with JBuilder can be. If you follow the steps given exactly, you will produce a Java database application.

Step 1:

Start a new project, and pick an appropriate name. You can choose any name you wish. In the downloadable files, I simply called the project example 09_01, but I am certain you can come up with a more creative name for your project.

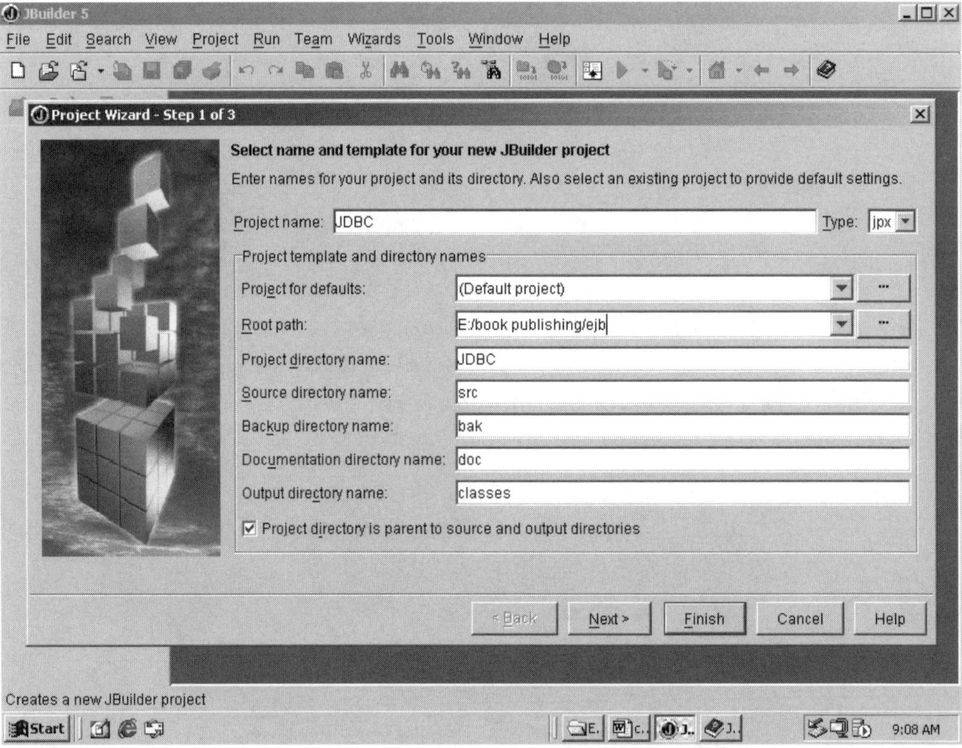

Simply use the default values on steps 2 and 3 of the Project Wizard.

Step 2:

Now you will need to actually add a data module. To do this, you must select File ▸ New and then choose Data Module.

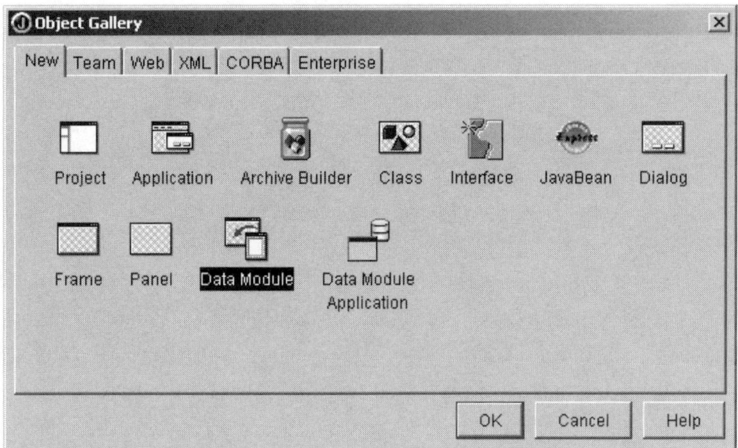

Step 3:

Next you will have to set the name of this data module.

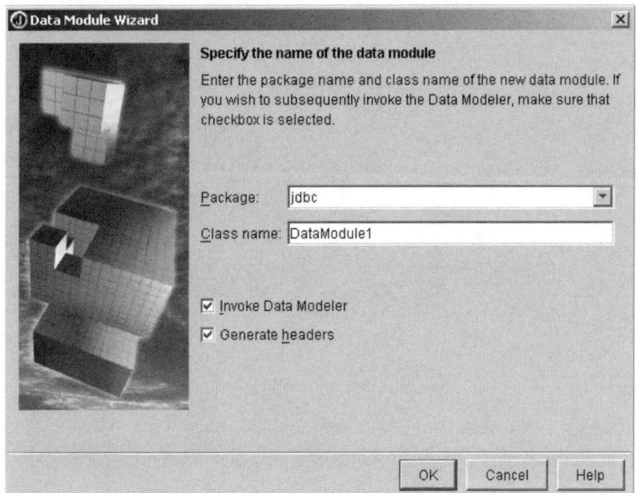

Step 4:

The next screen allows you to build queries and generate the required database code via a GUI (graphical user interface).

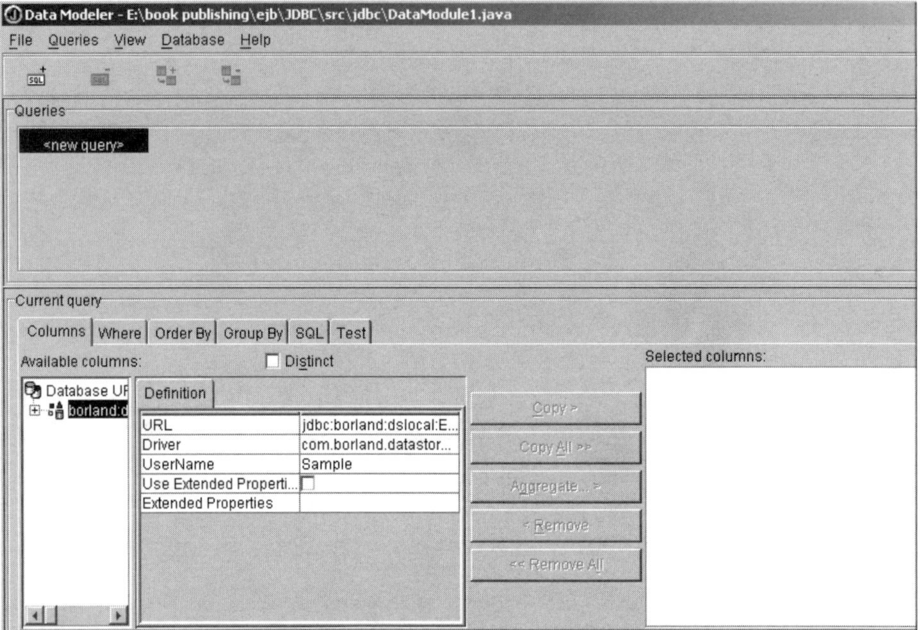

Step 5:

We will now add a connection URL.

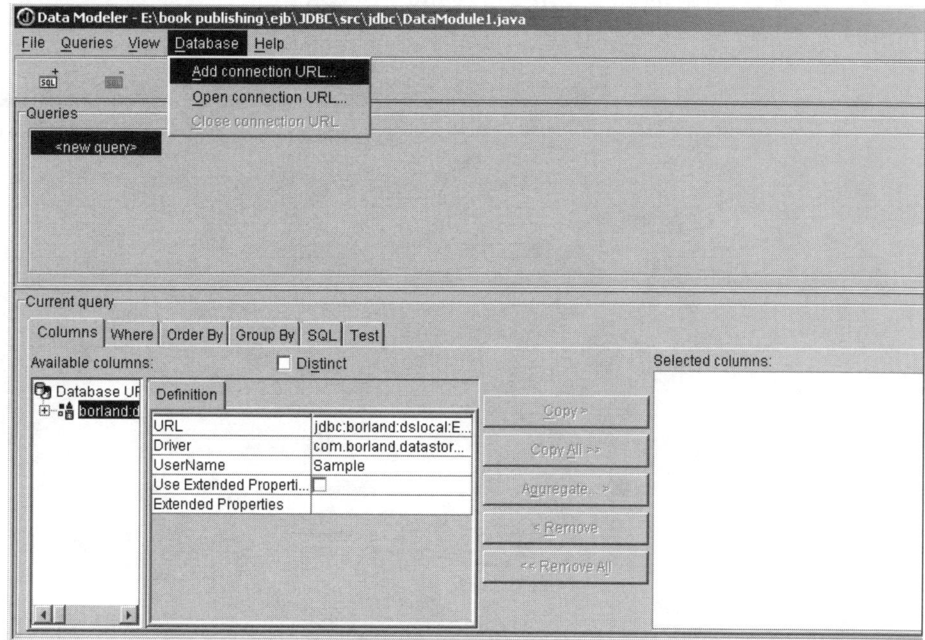

Step 6:

You can now choose any driver and any valid data source on your machine. I am choosing the sun.jdbc.odbc.JdbcOdbcDriver driver and a test MS Access database located on my PC.

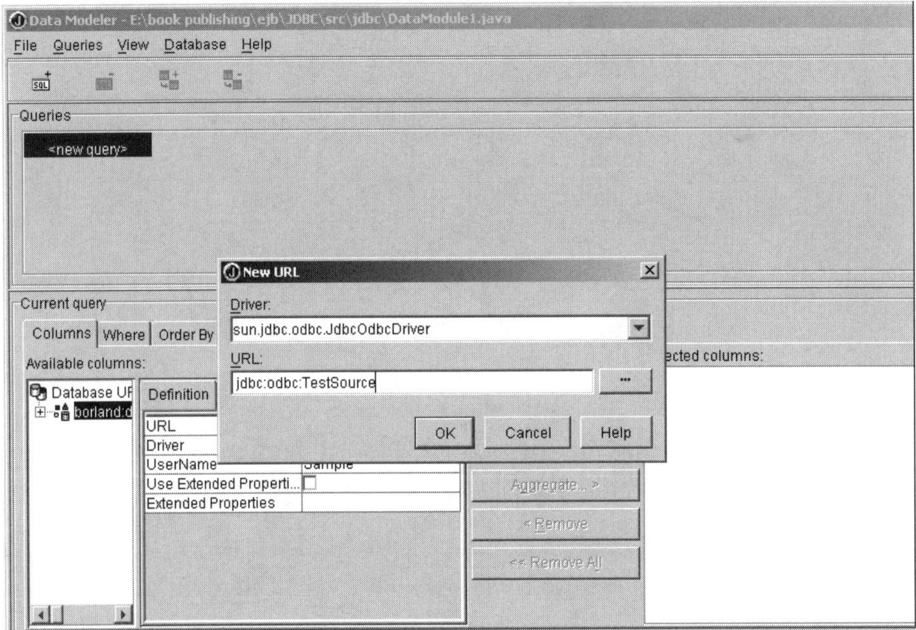

Step 7:

Opening the database connection is easy:

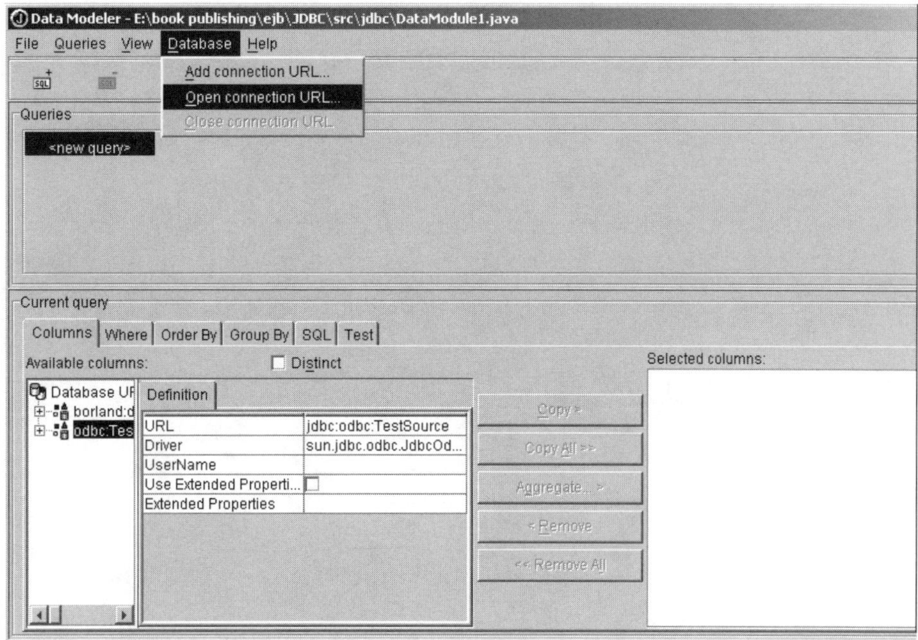

Step 8:

Building an SQL query is as simple as clicking on the table and the fields you want.

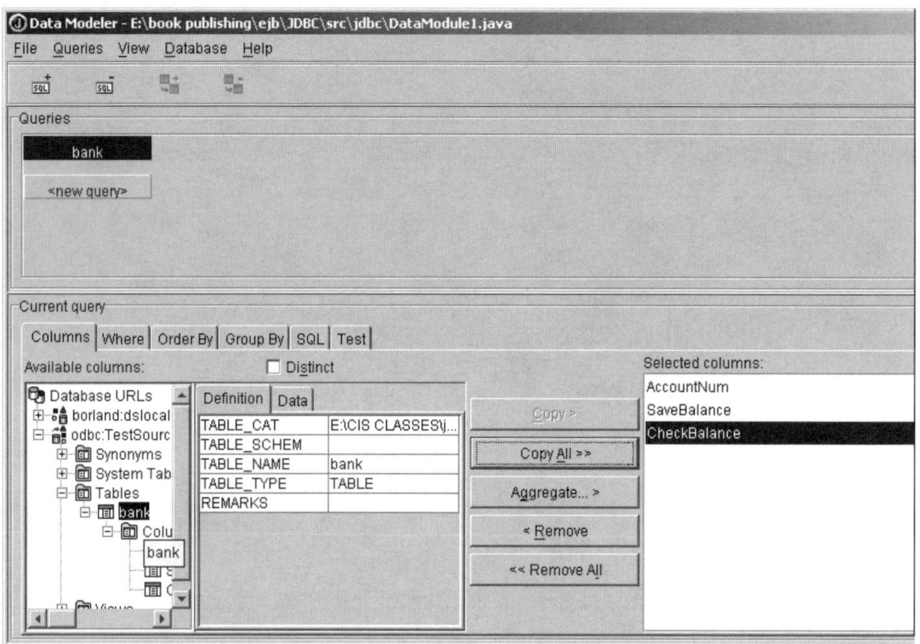

Step 9:

Now save your data module and exit the wizard. JBuilder has produced the following source code for you. Examine this code carefully; it is completely functional database code, with all the basics done for you:

```java
package jdbc;
import java.awt.*;
import java.awt.event.*;
import com.borland.dx.dataset.*;
import com.borland.dx.sql.dataset.*;
public class DataModule1 implements DataModule
  {
  private static DataModule1 myDM;
  Database database1 = new Database();
  QueryDataSet bank = new QueryDataSet();
  public static DataModule1 getDataModule()
```

```
    {
      if (myDM == null)
    {
      myDM = new DataModule1();
    }
      return myDM;
    }
    public DataModule1()
    {
      try
      {
        jbInit();
      }
      catch(Exception e)
      {
        e.printStackTrace();
      }
    }
    private void jbInit() throws Exception
  {
      bank.setQuery(new com.borland.dx.sql.dataset.QueryDescriptor
        (database1, "SELECT bank.AccountNum,bank.SaveBalance,bank.
        CheckBalance FROM\"E:\\CIS " + "CLASSES\\javaclass\\Sample
        Code\\db1\".bank", null, true, Load.ALL));
      database1.setConnection(new com.borland.dx.sql.dataset.Connection
        Descriptor("jdbc:odbc:TestSource", "", "", false, "sun.jdbc.
        odbc.JdbcOdbcDriver"));
    }
    public Database getDatabase1()
    {
      return database1;
    }
    public QueryDataSet getBank()
    {
      return bank;
    }
  }
```

Some of this code, particularly in jbInit(), may seem a bit more complex than the code we did by hand earlier. Don't let that trouble you. This is simply because JBuilder has chosen a different approach to database connectivity than I did in the previous example. It is important that you realize that most coding problems have more than one possible solution. Since JBuilder generates all the necessary code for you, it should not be a problem.

JBuilder Data Tools

In addition to the wizards that enable you to create database code with relative ease, JBuilder also ships with a set of tools for creating the databases themselves and managing the connections. Anyone who has used Microsoft's Visual Basic and its Data Manager will be familiar with development tools that provide rich graphical database management utilities. However, JBuilder offers the most complete tools for this purpose that I have seen.

Database Pilot

The first such tool we will look at is the Database Pilot. You can find this tool by choosing Tools ▶ Database Pilot.

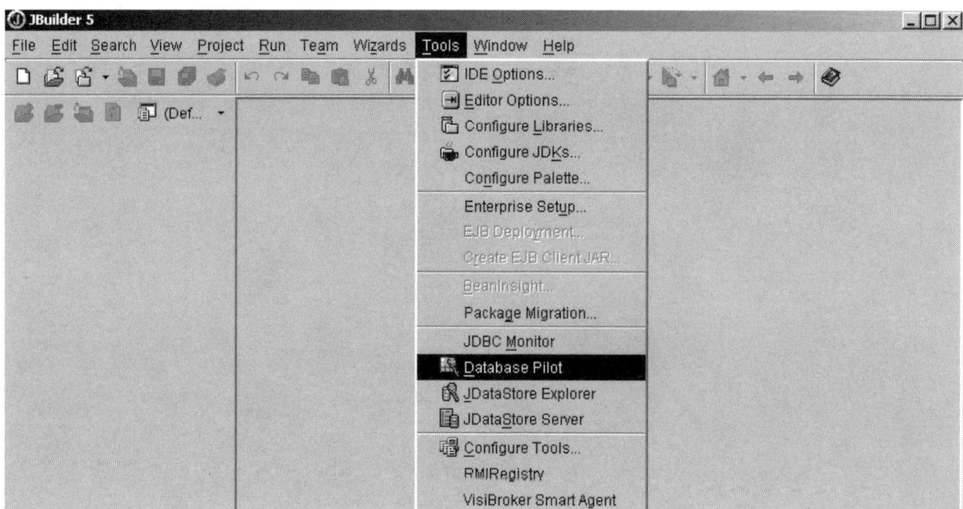

Once you have done this, you will see the primary Database Pilot screen.

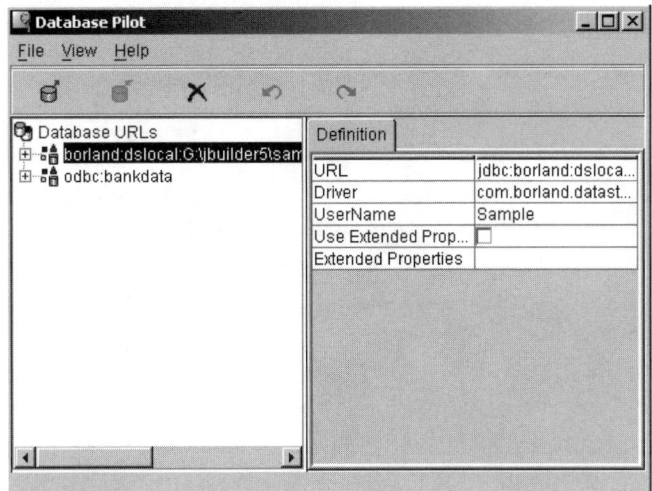

The Database Pilot is essentially a database browser. It presents the data in a hierarchical "tree-like" format, and it allows you to edit the data in the database as well. It presents JDBC-based meta-database information in a two-paned window. In the left pane, you should see a tree that displays a set of databases and their associated tables, views, stored procedures, and metadata. The right pane is a multi-page display of information about each node of the tree. In certain cases, you can edit data in the right pane as well.

You can use the Database Pilot to create, view, or edit data in an existing database table. You can also enter and execute SQL statements. Let's walk through a few simple examples with the Database Pilot.

In this example, I will show you how to connect to an existing database and table using the Database Pilot.

Step 1:

From the Database Pilot, double-click on the sample database provided.

You can see that the tree expanded to show you the tables and the stored procedures. You should also note that in the left-hand pane, you can see any other data sources on this machine, including the one created earlier for the previous database example.

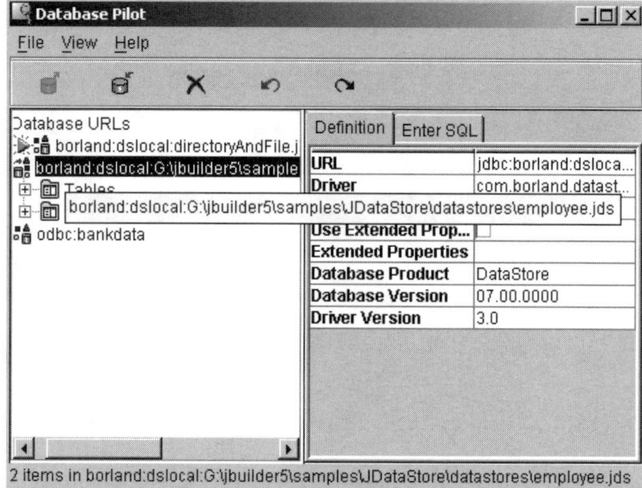

Step 2:

I selected the Addresses table so that I could view the data in that table. When you double-click on a table, you will see its contents displayed in the right-hand pane.

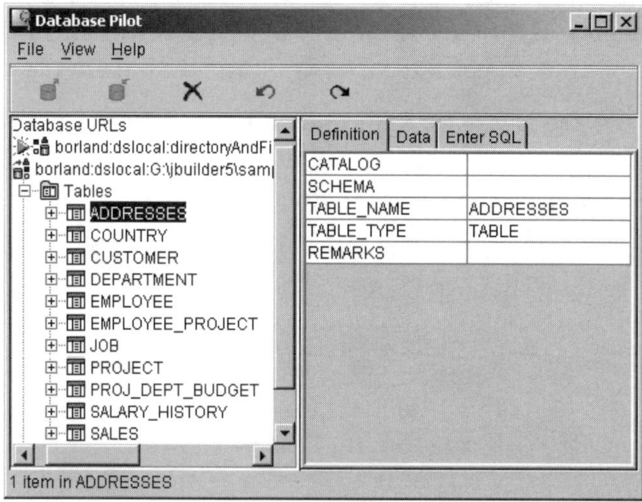

Notice that the first tab, or Definition tab, simply tells you about the tab. The second tab, or Data tab, shows you the actual data in that table. You can actually enter new data, delete data, or edit data right in this screen.

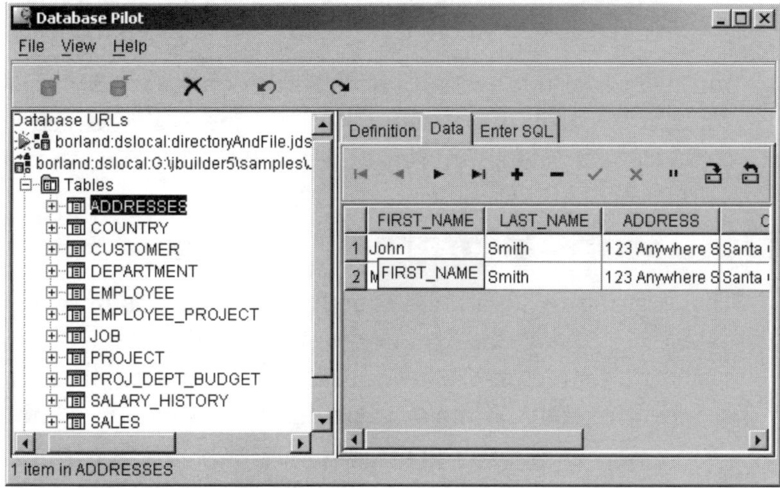

The third tab, or Enter SQL tab, allows you to directly type in SQL statements and execute them.

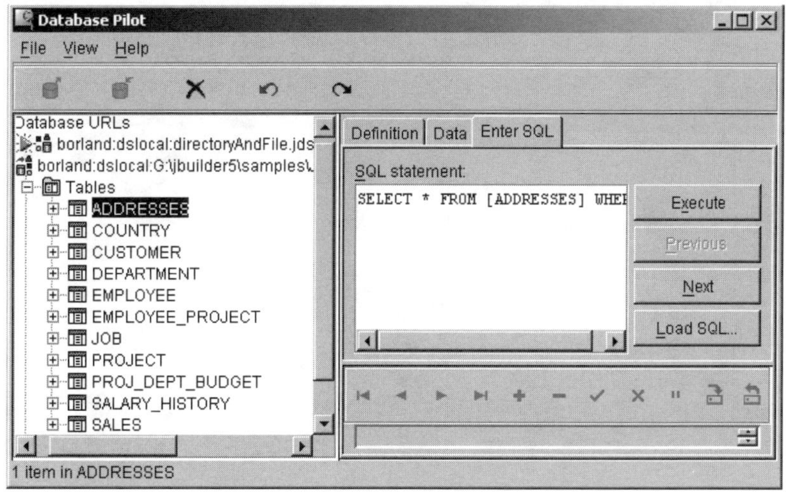

This is just a brief introduction to the Database Pilot. However, even with a brief introduction you should be able to see that it is a very versatile and powerful database tool. If you intend to do a significant amount of database programming with JBuilder, I strongly recommend that you take the time to more thoroughly acquaint yourself with this tool.

You will also find the JDataStore Server and JDataStore Explorer under Tools in the drop-down menu. Both of these offer a rich set of tools that facilitate your database work. I will briefly describe each of them here.

JDataStore Explorer

The JDataStore Explorer is exactly what its name implies, an explorer for datastores. Using this explorer, you can examine the contents of a datastore. The store's directory is shown in a tree, with each data set and its indexes grouped together. When a particular data stream is selected, its contents are displayed. Using the JDataStore Explorer, you can perform many store operations without writing any code at all. You can create a new JDataStore, import files, delete data, edit the data sets, and save changes back to server tables. The JDataStore Explorer looks like the image you see here:

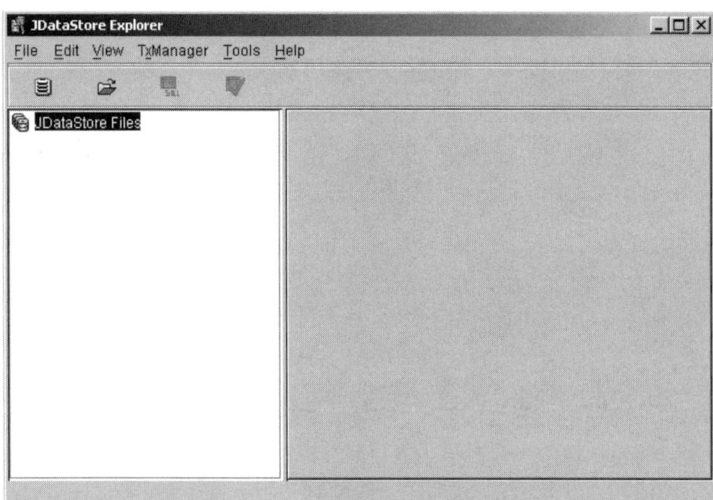

JDataStore Server

Once you have completed development of a database application and are ready to move to production, you will need to have a database server. JDataStore is such a server. It will allow you to make your datastores available across an entire network or even over the Internet. The JDatastore Server window looks like the image you see here:

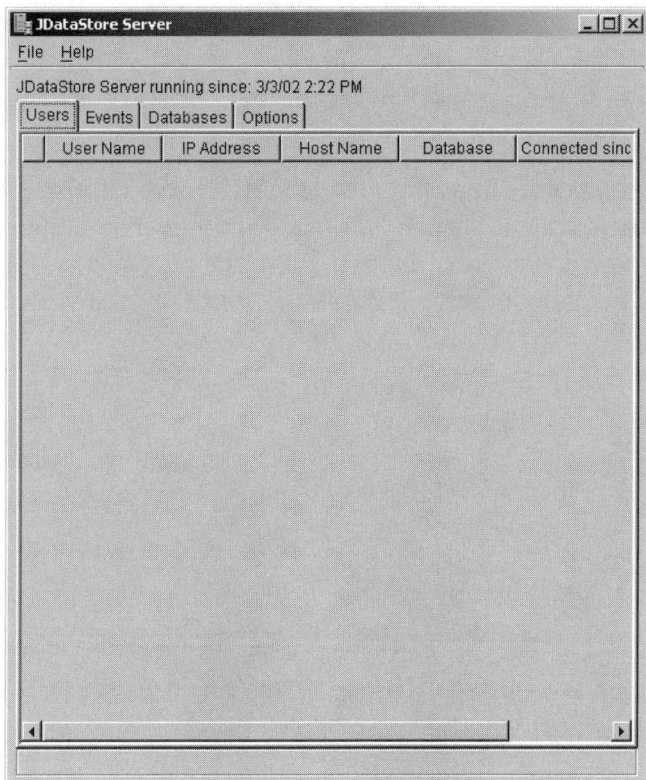

For a more thorough coverage of JBuilder database programming, I suggest you look at *Charlie Calvert's Learn JBuilder 7* listed in Appendix A. You will also find a lot of useful information in the JBuilder help files. In addition to these resources, I have provided you with some pretty solid online tutorial links, also found in Appendix A.

Summary

In this chapter, I have shown you the basic concepts of relational databases and Structured Query Language. I have also shown you the basics of accessing data from within Java. The chapter has covered the fundamental classes found in java.sql, such as the DriverManager, connection, resultset, and statement classes. You have also seen how to leverage JBuilder to help you create database applications with relative ease. The fundamental concepts presented in this chapter should allow you to do basic database programming in Java. Make certain that you are comfortable with all of the topics in this chapter before continuing.

This chapter has only been an introduction to both database concepts and the database tools available in JBuilder. I strongly recommend that if this material is new to you, you allocate some time in the near future to more thoroughly explore database programming in Java and with JBuilder.

Terms

Record – A collection of fields or columns that represent one coherent entry in the database.

Field – A single item in a record. In SQL Server, this is called a column.

Table – A collection of records that are logically grouped together.

SQL – Structured Query Language. This is the language used by relational databases.

RDBMS – Relational Database Management System. This is a software package used to create and manage relational databases, often with a GUI interface.

ODBC – Open Database Connectivity. These are database drivers.

JDBC – Java Database Connectivity. These are Java classes that act as wrappers around the ODBC drivers.

Review Questions

1. What is JDBC?

2. What is a group of related fields called?

3. What is the purpose of the DriverManager class?

4. Who invented SQL?

5. List three classes found in the java.sql package.

6. What does the ORDER BY SQL statement do?

7. What is ODBC?

8. Is it possible to search for items in a database that are only similar to a given criteria?

9. After successfully getting a resultset returned to you from a statement object, what must you do before attempting to work with that resultset object?

10. What is the purpose of the connection object?

Chapter 10

Entity Beans

Introduction

So far, I have discussed only session Enterprise JavaBeans. Recall that session beans represent a given session with a client. A session bean can be either stateful or stateless. Now it is time for us to move on to entity beans. An entity bean represents some data object, rather than some business process. Usually, the data is stored in some type of relational database. The entity bean maps directly to a row or rows within a table in a relational database. It can also map to one or more rows across multiple tables. Obviously, before you dive too deeply into entity beans, it is assumed that you have a basic understanding of databases. For those of you who lack such a background, I will refer you back to Chapter 9.

In a database, a primary key uniquely identifies a particular row in a table. Since entity beans represent data storage objects, it should be no surprise to you that a primary key also identifies a specific entity bean instance. Each column (or field) in the relational database table is mapped to a particular instance variable in the entity bean. Therefore, each instance variable is actually a representation of an underlying column/field. Because an entity bean represents an underlying data source, its life cycle is somewhat different than the life cycle of session beans. Essentially, the bean's life cycle lasts for as long as the data source is present and accessible. This means that no matter how long an entity bean remains in an inactive state, the container doesn't remove it from persistent storage. The only way to remove an entity bean is to explicitly do so. An entity bean is removed by calling its remove() method, which also removes the underlying data from the database.

Persistence

All entity enterprise beans are, by their very nature, persistent. An entity bean could not represent a data object if it did not persist the data. For this reason, all entity beans support some form of persistence. However, you can choose how your entity bean's persistence is implemented. You can implement the bean's persistence directly in the entity bean class. This means that the bean itself is responsible for maintaining its persistence. This is referred to as bean-managed persistence. Bean-managed persistence gives you more control over exactly how and when your bean will persist its data and how that data will be retrieved. You can also choose to let the container take care of the handling of the entity bean's persistence. This is referred to as container-managed persistence. Container-managed persistence can be much easier for the programmer, since he or she does not have to write the code to handle persisting the data.

An entity bean that implements bean-managed persistence contains the code to access and update a database. The programmer who creates the bean must write database access code directly in the entity bean or in one of its associated classes. The database access calls can appear in the entity bean's business methods or in one of the entity bean interface methods.

It can be more difficult to write an entity bean with bean-managed persistence because you must directly write all the data access code yourself. It can also be quite difficult to alter the entity bean to work with a different data source. If you choose to use bean-managed persistence, I strongly recommend that you create a separate helper class to handle all the data access. This allows you to alter or replace that single class with relative ease should your data source or data access methodologies change.

If you choose to use container-managed persistence, you don't have to write code that handles database access; the container will handle it for you. Container-managed persistence has certain clear advantages compared to bean-managed persistence. Container-managed beans are obviously easier to code. Since you, the programmer, don't have to write any data access code, your job is simplified. With container-managed entity beans, the persistence details can be changed without modifying and recompiling the bean. All that is required, if the data source changes, is the deployer or application assembler can modify the deployment descriptor. This allows you, the programmer, to focus on the business logic and business methods of the bean and not on the underlying system issues. However, using container-managed persistence is not an entity bean programming panacea; it does have some limitations. One such limitation is that the container might load the entire state of the entity object into the bean instance's fields before it calls the ejbLoad() method. This can cause some significant performance problems if the entity bean has many fields.

Remember that entity beans are representations of an underlying data source. This means that each entity bean instance needs to have a primary key, just as the underlying data source should have a primary key. Recall that a primary key is a value that uniquely identifies the instance. For more information about primary keys, refer to Chapter 9. For example, a database table that contains employee records could use an employee's social security number for its primary key. The entity bean modeling this employee table would also use the social security number for its primary key. For enterprise beans, the primary key is usually represented by a string or integer type. However, it can be represented by a Java class containing the unique data. This primary key class can be any class, as long as that class is a legal value type in RMI_IIOP. This, of course, means the class must extend the java.io.Serializable interface. The primary key class can be specific to a particular entity bean class. That is, each entity bean can define its own primary key class. You can also use a single key class and have multiple entity beans share the same primary key class.

To create an entity bean class, you have to create a class that implements the javax.ejb.EntityBean interface. As you should know by now, all Enterprise JavaBeans implement specific interfaces from the javax.ejb package in order to give them the specific characteristics of the type of EJB that you are trying to create. Of course, it must implement one or more ejbCreate() methods. Like session beans, it will have to have a home interface for the bean. The entity bean must have an ejbCreate() method with the same signature for each create() method in the home interface. You will also need a remote interface. Finally, you will need to define and implement the business methods you want your bean to have. You can see that the essentials of bean creation (i.e., home interface, remote interface, implementing a serializable interface, etc.) are common to all types of EJBs.

For entity beans with bean-managed persistence, you will need to implement finder methods. These methods are, in essence, methods that find the data for you. As you will see later in this chapter, JBuilder's Enterprise JavaBean Wizard can accomplish many of these tasks for you. It creates a class that extends the EntityBean interface and writes empty implementations of the entity bean methods. Then, you simply fill in the particular business implementations if your bean requires it.

The EntityBean Interface

This interface is the heart and soul of entity beans, so it warrants a closer look before we begin writing entity beans. The EntityBean interface defines the methods all entity beans must implement. It extends the EnterpriseBean interface.

```
public void EntityBean extends EnterpriseBean
{
    public void setEntityContext(EntityContext ctx) throws EJBException,
      RemoteException;
    public void unsetEntitycontext() throws EJBException, RemoteException;
    void ejbRemove() throws RemoveException, EJBException, RemoteException;
    void ejbActivate() throws EJBException, RemoteException;
    void ejbPassivate() throws EJBException, RemoteException;
    void ejbLoad() throws EJBException, RemoteException;
```

```
    public void ejbStore() throws EJBException, RemoteException;
}
```

The methods of the EntityBean interface are closely associated with the life cycle of an entity bean. The following table summarizes their purpose:

Method	Description
EntityContext()	This method sets the context of an entity bean. The container uses this method to pass a reference to the EntityContext interface to the bean instance. This context is then stored in an instance variable.
unsetEntityContext()	This method is used to free the resources that were allocated during the setEntityContext() method call. The container calls this method before it terminates the current instance of the entity bean.
ejbRemove()	This method is utilized to remove the database entry or entries associated with this particular entity bean. The container calls this method when a client invokes a remove() method.
ejbActivate()	This method is used to notify an entity bean that it has been activated. The container invokes this method on the instance of the entity bean that has been activated.
ejbPassivate()	This method notifies an entity bean that it is about to be deactivated.
ejbLoad()	This method refreshes the data that the entity object represents from the database.
ejbStore()	This method is called in order to store the data that the entity object represents in the database.

Entity Bean Methods

Entity beans can have three different types of methods. These are create methods, finder methods, and business methods.

Create Methods

If you use the Enterprise JavaBean Wizard to begin your enterprise bean, you'll see that the wizard creates for you an ejbCreate() method and an ejbPostCreate() method to the bean class that takes no parameters. You can write additional create methods if your bean requires them. You should remember that calling a create method of an entity bean inserts new data in the database. You can have entity beans without create methods if new instances of entity objects should be added to the database only through DBMS updates or through a legacy application.

If you choose to add additional ejbCreate() methods that include parameters, remember the following few rules:

- All ejbCreate() methods must have an access modifier of public.

- If your entity bean uses container-managed persistence, the ejbCreate() method must return null.

- If your entity bean uses bean-managed persistence, the ejbCreate() method must return an instance of the primary key class for the new entity object. The container uses this primary key to create the actual entity reference.

- The parameters of an ejbCreate() method have the same signature as the corresponding create() method. This means that they must be of the same number and type as those in the corresponding create() method in the bean's remote interface.

- All ejbCreate() methods must have a corresponding ejbPostCreate() method.

- The signature for an ejbCreate() method is the same, regardless of whether the bean uses container-managed or bean-managed persistence.

This is the signature for all ejbCreate() methods of an entity bean:

```java
public PrimaryKeyClass ejbCreate(parameters)
{
// implementation code goes here
}
```

When the client application makes a call to the create() method, the container then executes the ejbCreate() method and inserts a record representing the entity object into the database. The ejbCreate() methods usually initialize some entity state. For this reason, they frequently have one or more parameters and include code that sets the entity state to the parameter values. For example, consider a bank that has a checking account entity bean whose ejbCreate() method takes two parameters: a string and a float value. The method initializes the name of the account to the string value and the account balance to the float value:

```java
public Checking ejbCreate(String customername, float balance)
{
    this.customername = customername;
    this.balance = balance;
}
```

When the ejbCreate() method finishes executing, the container then calls the matching ejbPostCreate() method to allow the instance to complete its initialization. Recall that the ejbPostCreate() matches the ejbCreate() method in its parameters, but it returns void:

```java
public void ejbPostCreate(parameters)
{
    // implementation code goes here
}
```

Follow these rules when defining an ejbPostCreate():

- It must be declared as having an access modifier of public.

- It cannot be declared as final or static.

- It must have a return type of void.

- Its parameter list must match that of the corresponding ejbCreate() method.

You should use ejbPostCreate() to perform any special processing that your bean needs to do before it becomes available to the client. If your bean doesn't need to perform any particular processing, you can simply leave the method body empty.

Finder Methods

Every entity bean must have one or more finder methods. Finder methods are used by clients to locate entity beans. Each bean-managed entity bean must have an ejbFindByPrimaryKey() method that has a corresponding findByPrimaryKey() in the bean's home interface. This is the ejbFindByPrimaryKey() method's signature:

```
public PrimaryKeyClass ejbFindByPrimaryKey(<PrimaryKeyClass primaryKey>)
{
    // implementation code goes here
}
```

Of course, you can define additional finder methods for your bean. For example, you might have an ejbFindByLastName() method. Each finder method must follow certain rules:

- It must have an access modifier that is public.

- Its name must start with the prefix ejbFind.

- It cannot be declared as static or final.

- It must return either a primary key, a collection of primary keys, or an enumeration of primary keys.

- The parameters and return type of the method must be valid Java RMI types.

- For entity beans with bean-managed persistence, each finder method declared in the bean class must have a corresponding finder method in the bean's home interface that has the same parameters but returns the entity bean's remote interface. The client locates the entity bean it wants by calling the finder method of the home interface, and the container then invokes the corresponding finder method in the bean class.

Business Methods

Once you have created an entity bean, chosen what type of persistence to use, and addressed all the basic code, you still need to make the bean do something of practical value. It needs to have methods that execute some business function. This is the whole purpose for creating an entity bean in the first place. These are your business methods. To make these methods available to a client, you will need to declare them in the bean's remote interface using exactly the same signature. Other than this requirement, these business methods are just standard Java methods that perform some desired task and either return some desired value or a void.

Of course, you can use JBuilder's Enterprise JavaBeans Wizard to quickly start the creation of an entity bean. If you have existing database tables you want to use to create enterprise beans from, start with JBuilder's EJB Entity Modeler. If you have an existing entity bean but don't have its home and remote interfaces, use the EJB Interfaces Wizard to create them. You can then modify the code in JBuilder using the code editor and the bean designer. Edit deployment descriptors with JBuilder's Deployment Descriptor editor. Create a test client application with the EJB Test Client Application Wizard to test your new enterprise beans. Later in this chapter, we will create an entire entity bean using the JBuilder tools that are available to you with the Enterprise edition of JBuilder 5.0 and beyond.

Entity Bean Life Cycle

There are three states in the life cycle of an entity enterprise bean:

- Nonexistent
- Pooled
- Ready

The following table summarizes the features of each of these states.

State	Description
Nonexistent	At first, the entity bean instance does not exist. The EJB container creates an instance of an entity bean, and then it calls the setEntityContext() method on the entity bean to pass the instance a reference to its context (that is, a reference to the EntityContext interface). The entity bean is then in the pooled state.
Pooled	Each type of entity bean has its own pool. None of the instances in the pool are associated with data. Because none of their instance variables have been set, the instances have no identity, and they are all equivalent. The container is free to assign any instance to a client that requests such an entity bean. When a client application calls one of the entity bean's finder methods, the container executes the corresponding ejbFind() method on an arbitrary instance in the pool. The instance remains in the pooled state during the execution of a finder method. When the container selects an instance to service a client's requests to an entity object, that instance moves from the pooled to the ready state. There are two ways that an entity instance moves from the pooled state to the ready state: through the ejbCreate() and ejbPostCreate() methods.
Ready	Through the ejbActivate() method, the container selects the instance to handle a client's create() request on the bean's home interface. In response to the create() call, the container creates an entity object and calls the ejbCreate() and ejbPostCreate() methods when the instance is assigned to the entity object. When the instance is in the ready state, it is associated with a specific primary key.

The ready state is where the real action takes place. It is in this state that clients can call the business methods on the entity bean. The container calls the ejbLoad() and ejbStore() methods to tell the bean to load and store its data. These methods also enable the bean instance to synchronize its state with that of the underlying data entity.

When an entity bean instance moves back to the pooled state, the instance is decoupled from the data represented by the entity. The container can now assign the instance of any entity object within the same entity bean home. There are two ways that an entity bean instance moves from the ready state back to the pooled state: The container calls the ejbPassivate() method to dissociate the instance from its primary key without removing the underlying entity object. The container calls the ejbRemove() method to remove the entity object. It calls ejbRemove() when the client application calls the bean's home or remote remove() method. To remove an unassociated instance from the pool, the container calls the instance's unsetEntity-Context() method.

Building an Entity Bean with JBuilder

I have spent several pages discussing the structure and use of entity beans. It seems that it is time to give you a practical example. One of the most ubiquitous examples used for entity beans is the bank account example. The reason for this is that a bank account is an ideal candidate for an entity bean. This example will show you all the particulars of developing an entity bean.

If you follow along with these steps using JBuilder Enterprise, you will be able to create the necessary beans. If you do not have JBuilder, then simply look at the code at the end of the example, enter it in your favorite text editor, and use the Sun Java compiler to compile it.

Step 1:

Start JBuilder Enterprise edition. Start a new project. Then select File ▶ New. You will see this screen:

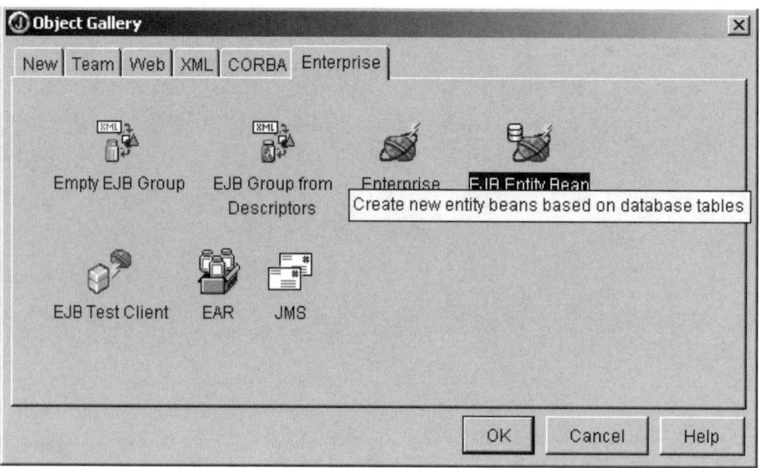

Choose EJB Entity Bean Modeler.

Step 2:

A wizard will launch that walks you through the steps to create the basic code for your entity bean. Use the following guidelines to work your way through the wizard.

On step 1 of 7, select New. You will see a screen like this one, where you can assign a name to your entity bean:

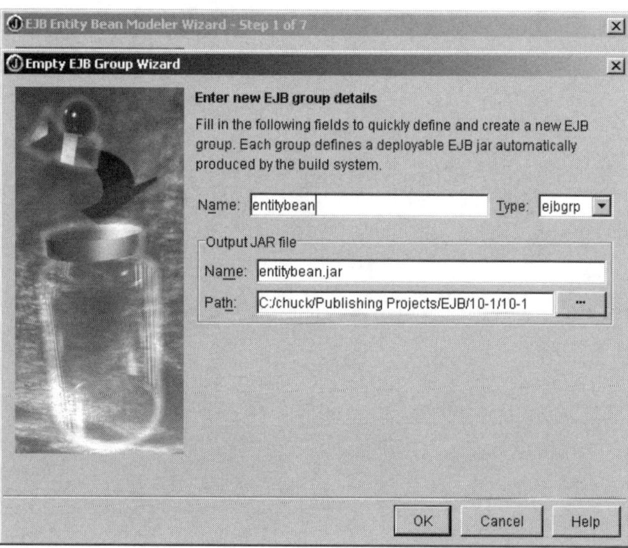

On step 2 of 7, you can choose a data source. You should probably have some existing database on your PC. If you don't have one, simply create a database in your favorite relational database management system (MS Access, Oracle, SQL Server, DB2, etc.). If you like, you can use the bank.mdb MS Access database in the downloadable files. On my machine, I made my task easier by creating a data source to use.

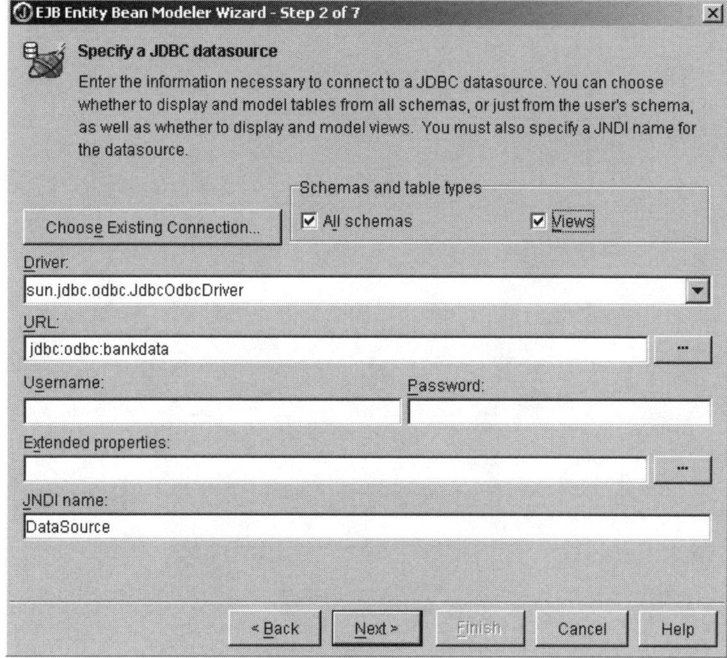

During step 3 of 7, you will select which tables from the database you need to model. If you used my sample database, there are two tables, one for checking and one for savings. I am using both tables.

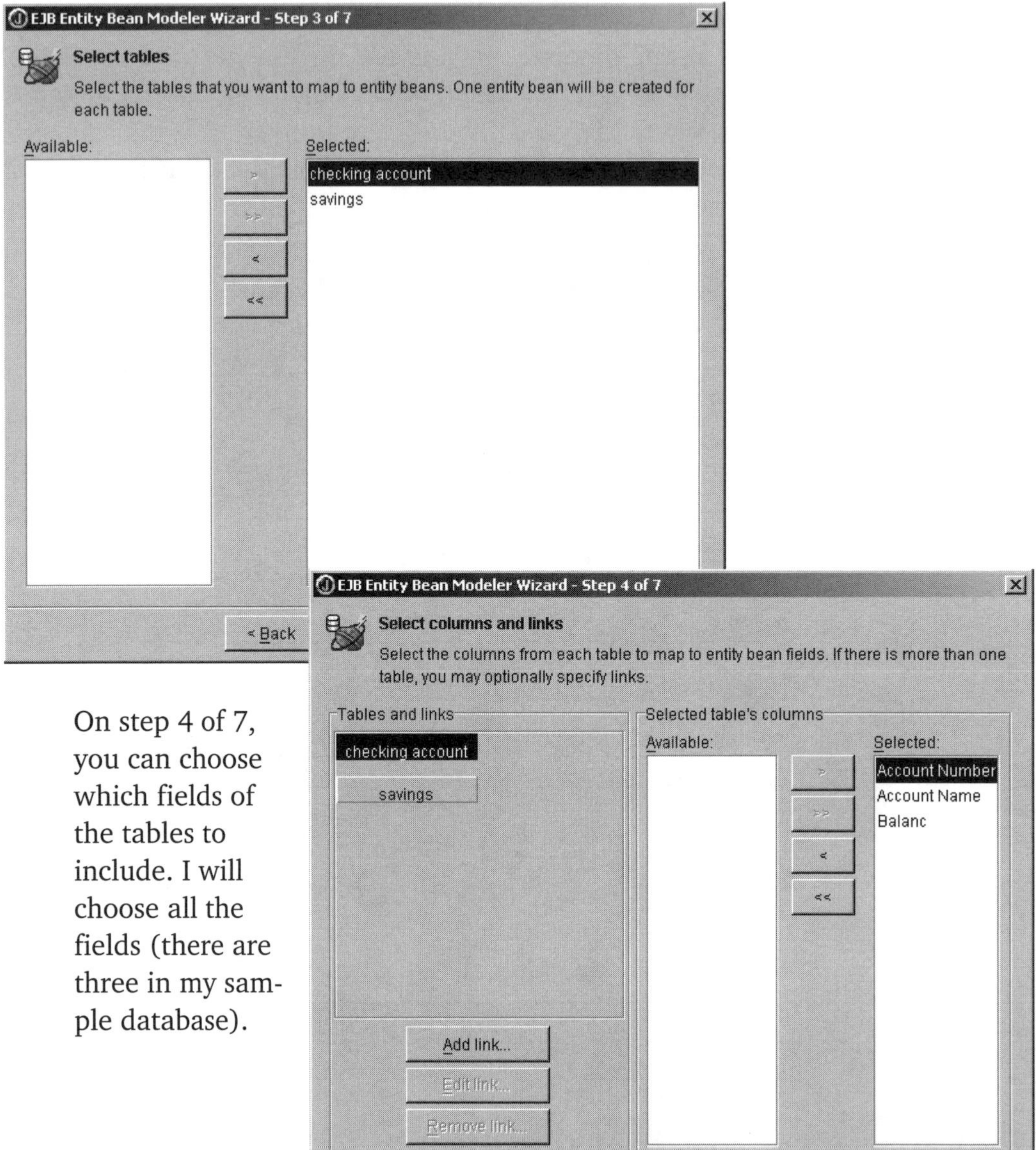

On step 4 of 7, you can choose which fields of the tables to include. I will choose all the fields (there are three in my sample database).

Step 5 of 7 allows you to decide which field in the database table will be the primary key in the entity bean. Obviously, you should use the same field that is the primary key in the database table.

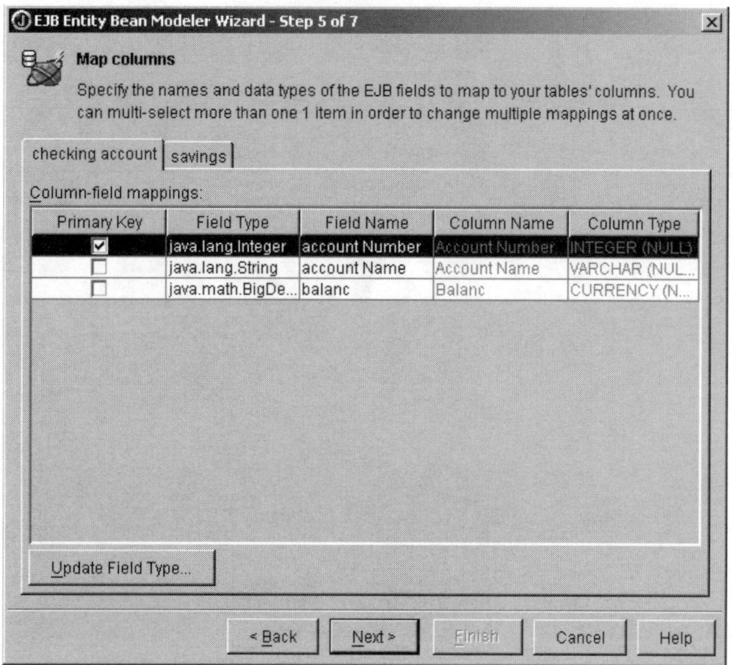

Primary Key	Field Type	Field Name	Column Name	Column Type
☑	java.lang.Integer	account Number	Account Number	INTEGER (NULL)
☐	java.lang.String	account Name	Account Name	VARCHAR (NUL...
☐	java.math.BigDe...	balanc	Balanc	CURRENCY (N...

Note: You will have to use a one-word field name for the bean, for the obvious reason that you will be creating methods with these names.

Step 6 of 7 simply allows you to give names to your EJB package.

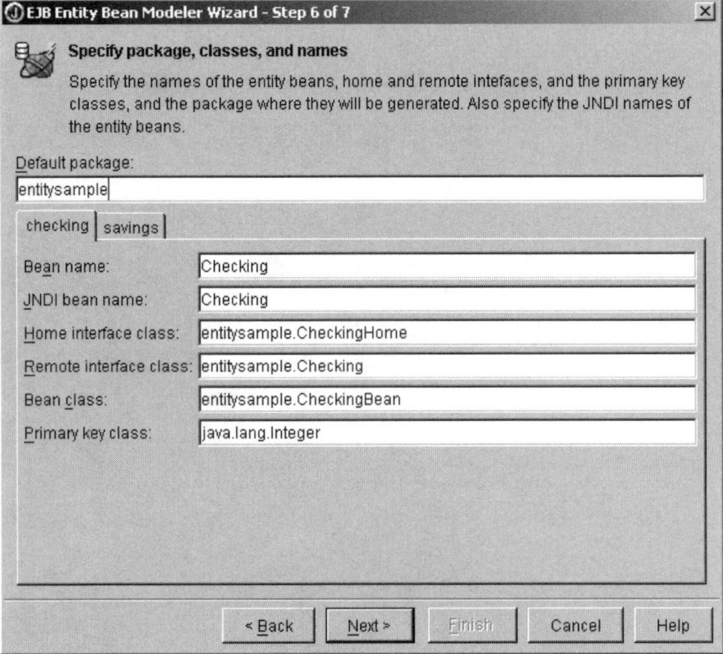

The final step of the wizard allows you to choose what type of persistence you wish to use. For this first example, I will use container-managed persistence. In Chapter 11, I will discuss bean managed persistence at some length.

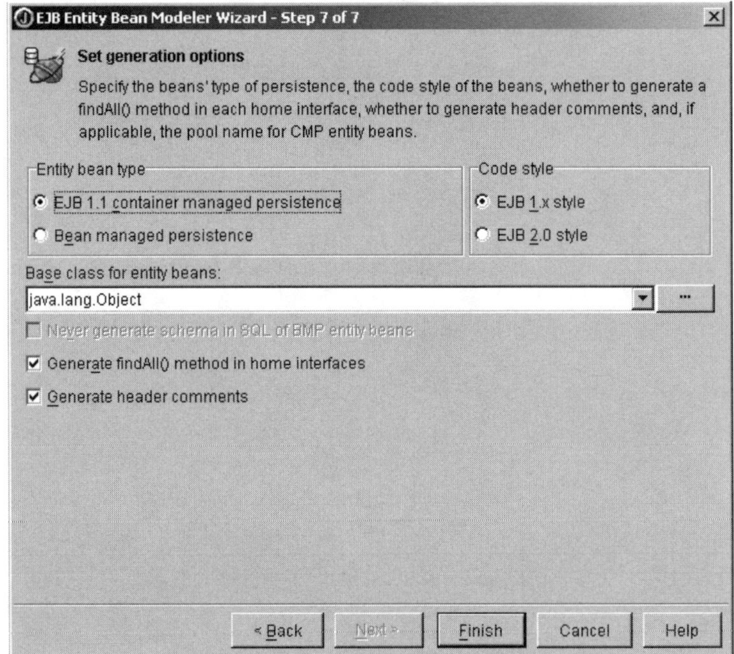

Step 3:

Now if you look at the source code that JBuilder has generated for you, you will see just how useful JBuilder's wizards can be.

> **Note:** The following code segments are rather long, but it is necessary so that those readers who are doing the code manually can see what to enter.

First the checking.java file:

```java
package entitysample;
import java.rmi.*;
import javax.ejb.*;
import java.math.*;
public interface Checking extends EJBObject
   {
   public Integer getAccountNumber() throws RemoteException;
   public String getAccountName() throws RemoteException;
   public void setAccountName(String accountName) throws RemoteException;
   public BigDecimal getBalanc() throws RemoteException;
   public void setBalanc(BigDecimal balanc) throws RemoteException;
}
```

Next we have checkingbean.java:

```java
package entitysample;
import java.rmi.*;
import javax.ejb.*;
import java.math.*;
public class CheckingBean implements EntityBean
   {
   EntityContext entityContext;
   public Integer accountNumber;
   public String accountName;
   public BigDecimal balanc;
   public Integer ejbCreate(Integer accountNumber, String accountName,
        BigDecimal balanc) throws CreateException, RemoteException
```

```java
{
  this.accountNumber = accountNumber;
  this.accountName = accountName;
  this.balanc = balanc;
  return null;
}
public Integer ejbCreate(Integer accountNumber) throws RemoteException,
    CreateException, RemoteException
{
  return ejbCreate(accountNumber, null, null);
}
public void ejbPostCreate(Integer accountNumber, String accountName,
    BigDecimal balanc) throws CreateException, RemoteException
{
}
public void ejbPostCreate(Integer accountNumber) throws CreateException,
    RemoteException
{
  ejbPostCreate(accountNumber, null, null);
}
public void ejbLoad() throws RemoteException
{
}
public void ejbStore() throws RemoteException
{
}
public void ejbRemove() throws RemoveException, RemoteException
{
}
public void ejbActivate() throws RemoteException
{
}
public void ejbPassivate() throws RemoteException
{
}
public void setEntityContext(EntityContext entityContext) throws
  RemoteException
{
  this.entityContext = entityContext;
}
```

```java
      public void unsetEntityContext() throws RemoteException
      {
        entityContext = null;
      }
      public Integer getAccountNumber()
      {
        return accountNumber;
      }
      public String getAccountName()
      {
        return accountName;
      }
      public void setAccountName(String accountName)
      {
        this.accountName = accountName;
      }
      public BigDecimal getBalanc()
      {
        return balanc;
      }
      public void setBalanc(BigDecimal balanc)
      {
        this.balanc = balanc;
      }
    }
```

Then checkinghome.java:

```java
    package entitysample;
    import java.rmi.*;
    import javax.ejb.*;
    import java.util.Collection;
    import java.math.*;
    public interface CheckingHome extends EJBHome
    {
      public Checking create(Integer accountNumber, String accountName,
          BigDecimal balanc) throws CreateException, RemoteException;
      public Checking create(Integer accountNumber) throws RemoteException,
          CreateException;
      public Checking findByPrimaryKey(Integer primaryKey) throws
          RemoteException, FinderException;
```

```
      public Collection findAll() throws RemoteException, FinderException;
    }
```

And of course savingsaccount.java:

```
package entitysample;
import java.rmi.*;
import javax.ejb.*;
import java.math.*;
public interface Savings extends EJBObject
  {
  public Integer getAccountNumber() throws RemoteException;
  public String getAccountName() throws RemoteException;
  public void setAccountName(String accountName) throws RemoteException;
  public BigDecimal getBalance() throws RemoteException;
  public void setBalance(BigDecimal balance) throws RemoteException;
}
```

Then next is savingbean.java:

```
package entitysample;
import java.rmi.*;
import javax.ejb.*;
import java.math.*;
public class SavingsBean implements EntityBean {
  EntityContext entityContext;
  public Integer accountNumber;
  public String accountName;
  public BigDecimal balance;
  public Integer ejbCreate(Integer accountNumber, String accountName,
      BigDecimal balance) throws CreateException, RemoteException
  {
    this.accountNumber = accountNumber;
    this.accountName = accountName;
    this.balance = balance;
    return null;
  }
  public Integer ejbCreate(Integer accountNumber) throws RemoteException,
      CreateException, RemoteException
  {
    return ejbCreate(accountNumber, null, null);
  }
```

```java
    public void ejbPostCreate(Integer accountNumber, String accountName,
        BigDecimal balance) throws CreateException, RemoteException
{
  }
  public void ejbPostCreate(Integer accountNumber) throws CreateException,
      RemoteException
  {
    ejbPostCreate(accountNumber, null, null);
  }
  public void ejbLoad() throws RemoteException
  {
  }
  public void ejbStore() throws RemoteException
  {
  }
  public void ejbRemove() throws RemoveException, RemoteException
  {
  }
  public void ejbActivate() throws RemoteException
  {
  }
  public void ejbPassivate() throws RemoteException
  {
  }
  public void setEntityContext(EntityContext entityContext) throws
      RemoteException
  {
    this.entityContext = entityContext;
  }
  public void unsetEntityContext() throws RemoteException
  {
    entityContext = null;
  }
  public Integer getAccountNumber()
  {
    return accountNumber;
  }
  public String getAccountName()
  {
    return accountName;
```

```
      }
    public void setAccountName(String accountName)
    {
      this.accountName = accountName;
    }
    public BigDecimal getBalance()
    {
      return balance;
    }
    public void setBalance(BigDecimal balance)
    {
      this.balance = balance;
    }
  }
```

And finally savingshome.java:

```
package entitysample;
import java.rmi.*;
import javax.ejb.*;
import java.util.Collection;
import java.math.*;

public interface SavingsHome extends EJBHome
  {
  public Savings create(Integer accountNumber, String accountName,
      BigDecimal balance) throws CreateException, RemoteException;
  public Savings create(Integer accountNumber) throws RemoteException,
      CreateException;
  public Savings findByPrimaryKey(Integer primaryKey) throws
      RemoteException, FinderException;
  public Collection findAll() throws RemoteException, FinderException;
  }
```

Now that is a lot of code to read through, and I apologize to the readers who
found it tedious. However, many readers find it helpful to have the entire
code printed out for their review. Those readers without JBuilder need the
entire code so that they can enter it in a text editor and compile it. I would
like you to notice several things about this code that are of particular interest. Note that in addition to the required entity bean material, JBuilder also
created all the required get and set methods for the instance variables. This

means that all you need to create are the particular business methods that your entity bean needs to implement. Now is the time to ask yourself what those methods might be. For a real bank system, you could have dozens of methods. However, for our example, we just want to add a credit and debit method to both the savings account and the checking account. You will add these methods to the checkingbean and JavaBean classes. Both classes will have identical credit and debit methods.

```
  public void debit(float amount)
{
    balance = balance - amount;
}
public void credit(float amount)
{
  balance = balance + amount;
}
```

Of course, you might wish to expand these classes with methods to transfer money, computer fees, or interest or simply to check to see that the account is not overdrawn when a debit method is invoked. All of that is done with standard Java code.

Summary

In this chapter, you were introduced to the basic concepts, structure, and requirements of entity JavaBeans. The required interface and methods were explained, and you were shown a complete example of a fully functional entity bean. After reading this chapter, you should be able to create basic entity beans that implement container-managed persistence. The next chapter will introduce you to bean-managed persistence.

Terms

PrimaryKeyClass – The class that corresponds to the primary key in the database

Finder Methods – Finder methods are used by clients to locate entity beans.

Pooled State – A state where the entity bean is simply in stasis and not ready for use

Ready State – In this state, the entity bean has been pulled from the pool and is ready to use.

Review Questions

1. What interface must all entity beans implement?
2. What two types of persistence are there?
3. What three states are there for an entity bean?
4. List any three methods of the EntityBean interface.
5. All ejbCreate() methods must have what type of access modifier?
6. All container-managed entity bean create methods must return what?
7. All bean-managed entity bean create methods must return what?
8. All finder methods must have what in their name?
9. Can a finder method be static?
10. All ejbCreate() methods must have what corresponding method?

Chapter 11

Bean-Managed Entity Bean Persistence

Introduction

In Chapter 10, we saw how to create entity beans using container-managed persistence. Clearly, container-managed persistence can be much easier to implement. However, there are cases where you, as the programmer, will wish to have direct and total control of the persistence mechanisms. One such case would be if you wish to persist only selected data, based on some criteria. Container-managed persistence can also be useful if your application requires some complex data validation prior to saving the data. In these and other circumstances, it may be advantageous for you to use bean-managed persistence. An entity bean that utilizes bean-managed persistence contains the required code to access and update a database. This means that the programmer is required to write database access calls directly in the entity bean or in one of its associated classes. The database access calls can appear in the entity bean's business methods or in one of the entity bean interface methods.

Entity beans with bean-managed persistence can be significantly more difficult to write. This is simply because you must write all of the required data access code. This can also make it more difficult to adapt the entity bean to different databases. You don't have to write code that accesses and updates databases for entity beans with container-managed persistence.

Many facets of entity beans are common to all entity beans, regardless of whether they use container-managed persistence or bean-managed persistence. Recall that every entity bean instance must have a primary key. Also, recall that for enterprise beans, the primary key is usually represented by a String or Integer type, but it can be represented by a Java class containing the unique data. This primary key class can be any class, as long as that class is a legal value type in RMI_IIOP. This means that the class must extend the java.io.Serializable interface, and it must implement the Object.equals(Other other) and Object.hashCode() methods, which all Java classes inherit. The primary key class can be specific to a particular entity bean class, or multiple entity beans can share the same primary key class. All of these rules apply, whether the entity bean in question uses container-managed persistence or bean-managed persistence.

As you can see, there are a number of similarities between a bean with bean-managed persistence and one with container-managed persistence. However, some elements of the entity bean are unique to beans using bean-managed persistence. An entity bean with bean-managed persistence must implement an ejbRemove() method. It must implement this method so that it can remove the entity object from the database. A bean with container-managed persistence will not require the implementation of this method, since the container is responsible for the database management. When building an entity bean with bean-managed persistence, remember that methods that access the underlying database object must include the correct database access code. These methods are ejbStore, ejbLoad(), ejbCreate(), ejbRemove(), ejbFindByPrimaryKey(), and all other finder methods. Any business method that accesses the underlying database will also need to have appropriate database access code written into it. Each method needs to contain code to connect to the database. These methods will also require code to build and then execute SQL statements that accomplish the functionality of the method. After an SQL statement completes, the method should close the database connection before returning.

The following example shows the required code for a bean-managed entity bean called Bank_Accounts. The example removes the code that is merely the empty implementations of the EntityBean interface methods, such as ejbActivate() and ejbPassivate(). They are, however, listed in a comment in the code so that you will know to type in those empty methods. If you use JBuilder to create your bean, all the required entity bean methods will be created for you, and you will simply have to enter in the implementation code for certain methods.

As you examine that example, be certain to look at the ejbLoad() method, which accesses the database entity object. This is a good illustration of how a bean with bean-managed persistence implements database access. Notice that all of the methods implemented in the Bank_Accounts class follow the same approach as ejbLoad() uses. The ejbLoad() method begins by establishing a connection to the database. It calls the internal getConnection() method, which uses a data source to obtain a JDBC connection to the database from a JDBC connection pool. After the connection has been established, ejbLoad() then creates a PreparedStatement object and builds its SQL database access statement. It would be possible to implement the connections in a separate method to call, or perhaps even create a database helper class that each of these methods used. In fact, in the second example in this chapter, that's exactly what I will do.

Because ejbLoad() reads the entity object values into the entity bean's instance variables, it builds an SQL SELECT statement for a query that selects the balance value for the savings account whose name matches a pattern. The method then executes the query. If the query returns a result, it extracts the balance amount. The ejbLoad() method finishes by closing the PreparedStatement objects and then closing the database connection. Note that the ejbLoad() method doesn't actually close the connection. Instead, it simply returns the connection to the connection pool.

The following code is for a generic Bank_Accounts class, which is suitable for any type of bank account. The code is rather lengthy, so I omitted empty methods. They are, however, mentioned in a comment so you know what they are. If you are using JBuilder, you can search the help files for "persistence, bean-managed," and you will see an even longer example that has separate classes for checking and savings accounts.

```java
pool. import.java.sql.*;
import java.util.*;
import javax.ejb.*;
import java.rmi.RemoteException;
public class BankAccount implements EntityBean
{
  private EntityContext beancontext;
  private String sz_name;
  private float f_balance;
  public float getBalance()
{

   return f_balance;
  }
public void withdraw(float amount)
{

   if(amount > f_balance)
   {
     // mark the current transaction for rollback...
     beancontext.setRollbackOnly();
   }
  else
   {
      f_balance = f_balance - amount;
   }
 }
  public void deposit(float amount)
{

  f_balance = f_balance + amount;
 }
 // setEntitycontext(), unsetEntityContext(), ejbActivate(),
    ejbPassivate(),
 // ejbPostCreate()implementations are not shown here because those
    functions
 // are empty in this bean
 public PK_Account ejbCreate(String name, float balance)
     throws RemoteException, CreateException
{
```

```
      sz_name = name;
      f_balance = balance;
      try
  {

      Connection connection = getConnection();
      PreparedStatement statement = connection.prepareStatement
        ("INSERT INTO Bank_Accounts (name, balance) VALUES (?,?)*);
      statement.setString(1, sz_name);
      statement.setFloat(2, f_balance);
      if(statement.executeUpdate() != 1)
      {

        throw new CreateException("Could not create: " + name);

      }

      statement.close();
      connection.close();
      return new PK_Account(name);

      }
    catch(SQLException e)
    {

        throw new RemoteException("Could not create: " + name, 3);

    }

  }
  public void ejbRemove() throws RemoveException, RemoveException
  {

    try

    {

      Connection connection = getConnection();
      PreparedStatement statement = connection.prepareStatement
        ("DELETE FROM Bank_Accounts WHERE name = ?");
      statement.setString(1, sz_name);
      if(statement.executeUpdate() != 1)
        {
        throw new RemoteException("Could not remove: " + _name, e);
      }
      statement.close();
      connection.close();
    }
    catch(SQLException e)
      {
      throw new RemoteException("Could not remove: " + _name, e);
```

```
    }
}
public PK_Account ejbFindByPrimaryKey(PK_Account key) throws
    RemoteException,
    FinderException
    {
  try
{
  Connection connection = getConnection();
  PreparedStatement statement = connection.prepareStatement
    ("SELECT name FROM Bank_Accounts WHERE name = ?");
  statement.setString(1, key.name);
  ResultSet resultSet = statement.executeQuery();
  if(!resultSet.next())
{
    throw new FinderException("Could not find: " + key, e);
  statement.close();
  connection.close();
  return key;
}
catch(SQLException e)
{
    throw new RemoteException("Could not find: " + key, e);
}
}
public java.util.Enumeration ejbFindAccountsLargerThan(float balance)
    throws RemoteException, FinderException
{
  try
{
  Connection connection = getConnection();
  PreparedStatement statement = connection.prepareStatement
    ("SELECT name FROM Bank_Accounts WHERE balance > ?");
  statement.setFloat(1, balance);
  ResultSet resultSet = statement.executeQuery();
  Vector keys = new Vector();
  while(resultSet.next())
{
    String name = resultSet.getString(1);
    keys.addElement(new PK_Account(name));
```

```java
      }
        statement.close();
        connection.close();
        return keys.elements();
      }
    catch(SQLException 3)
  {
      throw new RemoteException("Could not find any Accounts LargerThan: "
          + balance, e);
    }
  }


    public void ejbLoad() throws RemoteException
    {
      // retrieve the name from the primary key
      sz_name = (PK_Account) beancontext.getPrimaryKey()).name;
      try
    {

        Connection connection = getConnection();
        PreparedStatement statement = connection.prepareStatement
          ("SELECT balance FROM Bank_Accounts WHERE name = ?");
        statement.setString(1, _name);
        ResultSet resultSet = statement.executeQuery();
        if(!resultSet.next())
      {

          throw new RemoteException("Account not found: " + sz_name);
      }
        f_balance = resultSet.getFloat(1);
        statement.close();
        connection.close();
      }
  catch(SQLException e)
      {
          throw new RemoteException("Could not load: " + sz_name, e):
      }
    }
  public void ejbStore() throw RemoteException
  {
      try
      {
```

```java
      Connection connection = getConnection();
      PreparedStatement statement = connection.prepareStatement
        ("UPDATE Bank_Accounts SET balance = ? WHERE name = ?");
      statement.setFloat(1, f_balance);
      statement.setString(2, sz_name);
      statement.executeUpdate();
      statement.close();
      connection.close();
    }
    catch(SQLException e)
    {
      throw new RemoteException("Could not store: " + sz_name, e);
    }
  }


  private connection getConnection() throws SQLException
  {
    Properties properties = beancontext.getEnvironment();
    String url = properties.getProperty("db.url");
    String username = properties.getProperty("db.username");
    String password = properties.getProperty("db.password");
    if(username != null)
  {
      return DriverManager.getConnection(url, username, password);
    }
  else
{
      return DriverManager.getConnection(url);
    }
  }
  public String toString()
{
    return "Bank Account[name=" + sz_name + ",balance=" + f_balance +"]";
  }
}
```

Notice that the Bank_Accounts class uses a primary key class to uniquely
identify a particular account record. You will recall that entity beans can use
strings, integers, or classes for their primary keys. The primary key class is
defined as PK_Account. Here is the source code for that primary key class:

```
public class PK_Account implements java.io.Serializable
  {
  public String name;
  public PK_Account()
{
  // empty no - arguments constructor
}
  public PK_Account(String name)
{
    this.name = name;
  }
}
```

There are several items in this code that I would like to draw your attention to, as they illustrate key concepts in bean-managed entity beans. This bean has three primary business methods. Those methods are getBalance, deposit, and withdraw. None of these methods communicate with the underlying database. The data is simply stored in, or retrieved from, one of the bean's member variables. You should notice that the ejbCreate() and ejbLoad() methods retrieve data from the database or place data in the database. However, ejbRemove deletes the underlying data. The ejbStore() method has the required code to store the data in the underlying database. The real key to understanding bean-managed persistence is to understand the role of each of the bean's methods and simply place the correct database code in that method. The actual database code is fairly standard data access code that should be familiar to anyone who has ever worked with JDBC. There are no special or exotic database calls required simply because you are accessing the data from an Enterprise JavaBean.

The Deployment Descriptor

The deployment descriptor for the bank account example deploys two kinds of beans: the teller session bean and the Bank_Accounts entity bean with bean-managed persistence. You use properties in the deployment descriptor to specify information about the entity bean's interfaces, transaction attributes, and so on, just as you do for session beans. The bean-managed XML code sample shows typical deployment descriptor property tags for any entity bean with bean-managed persistence. The bean's deployment descriptor type is set to <entity>. All EJBs specify their home interface using the <home> tag, its remote interface using the <remote> tag, and its implementation class name using the <ejb-class> tag.

```
<enterprise-beans>
<entity>
  <description>This entity bean is an example of bean-managed
     persistence</description>
  <ejb-name>Bank</ejb-name>
  <home>AccountHome</home>
  <remote>Account</remote>
  <ejb-class>Bank_Accounts</ejb-class>
  <persistence-type>Bean</persistence-type>
  <prim-key-class>PK_Account</prim-key-class>
  <reentrant>False</reentrant>
</entity>
</enterprise-beans>
<assembly-descriptor>
  <container-transaction>
    <method>
      <ejb-name>Bank</ejb-name>
      <method-name>*</method-name>
    </method>
    <trans-attribute>Required</trans-attribute>
  </container-transaction>
</assembly-descriptor>
```

This example showed you all the key points of a bean-managed entity bean. It has a few business methods and data access methods, and follows all of the requirements for a bean-managed entity bean. You should spend some time carefully studying this example and perhaps making some minor modifications. By manipulating sample code, you will get a better feel for how bean-managed entity beans work.

Now that we have seen how to create a basic bean-managed entity bean, let's do a second one, this time using JBuilder. In addition, this particular bean will use a single helper class to handle all of its data access. This exercise should help you master the concepts of bean-managed persistence.

Since we will need to use the package that our data helper class is in for all our beans, I am also putting the primary key class in that same package.

Step 1:

The first step, which you should be very used to by now, is to start a new JBuilder project. Once your project is loaded, you will go to File ▸ New and add a new entity bean modeler, as you see here:

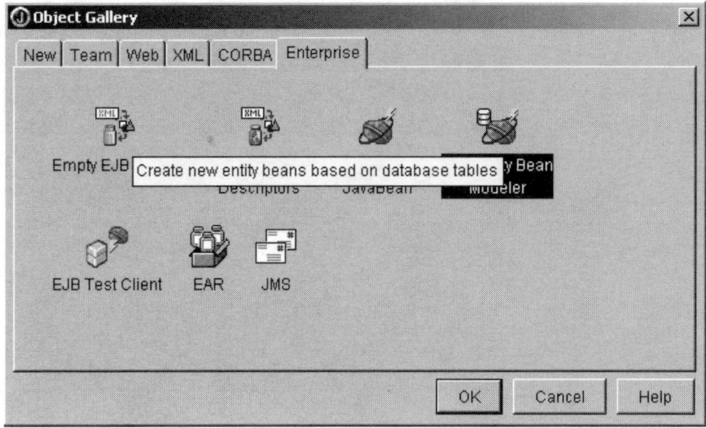

Step 2:

Create a new EJB group called "helper" (since this bean is implementing a helper class).

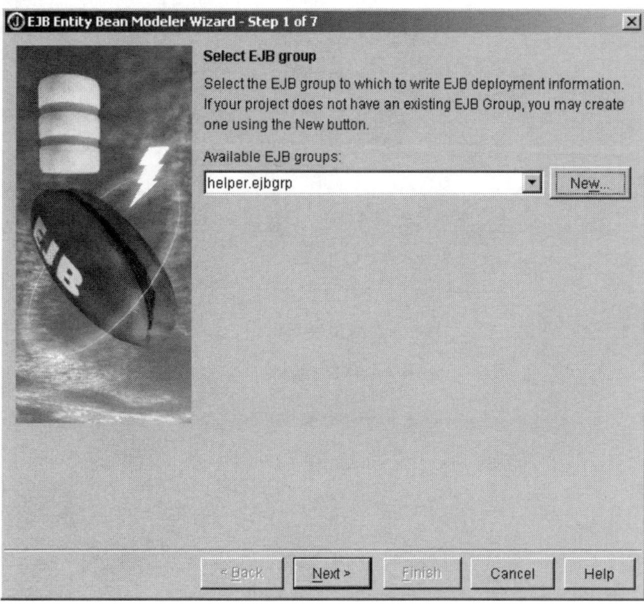

On the data source screen of the wizard, simply choose a generic ODBC driver and the bank data DSN from Chapter 10.

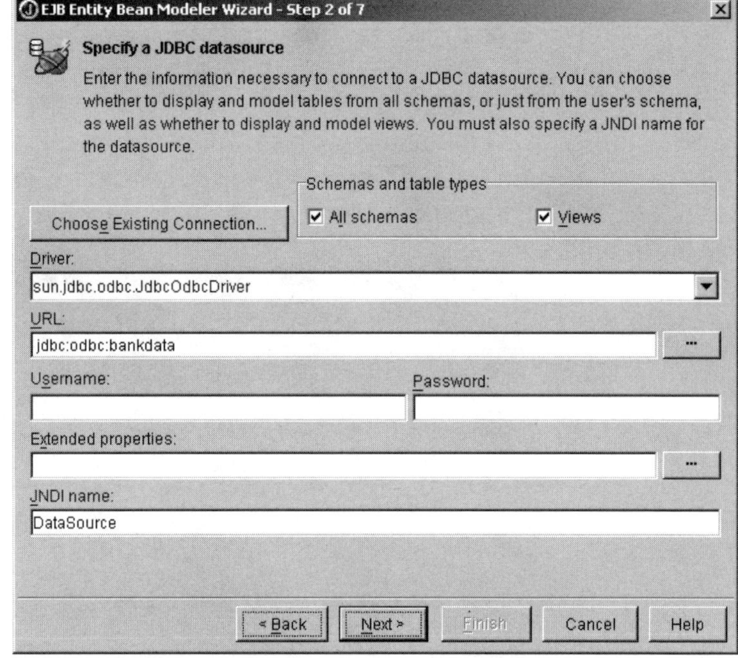

Step 3:

Follow the wizard as you did in Chapter 10 until you get to step 7 of 7, where you should choose the Bean-managed persistence option.

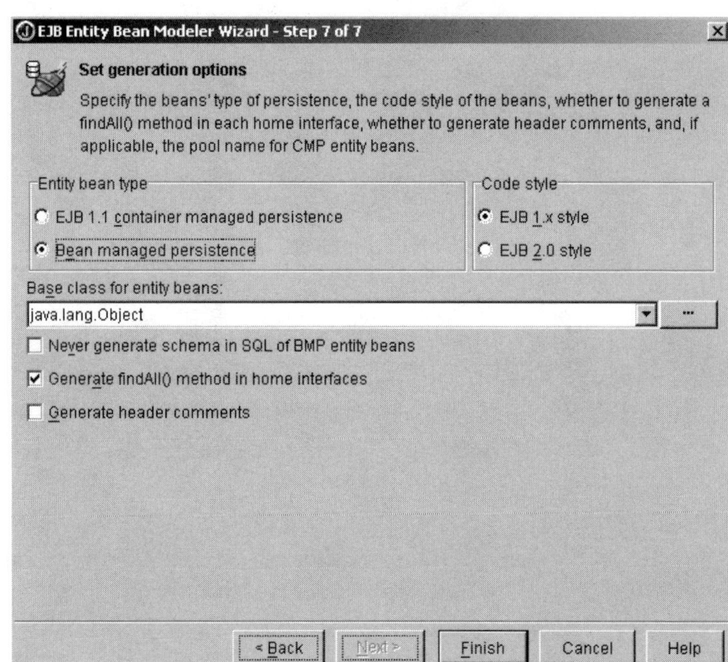

All the basic source code will be created for you. What we are left to do now is to create the data access helper class, and then use it from within the data access methods of checking and savings classes.

Step 4:

Choose File ▸ New Class to add a class to your project. Name that class DataHelper:

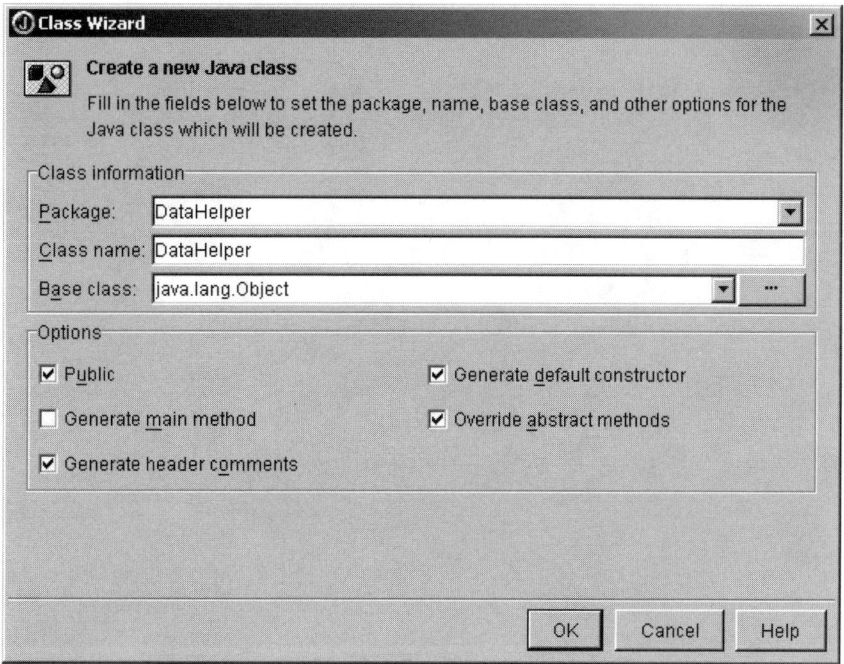

All that will be generated for us is the basic class body and the constructor method. Now we will add the database methods. The entire code would be onerous to present here and would simply duplicate items you have seen before. The primary key class and the business methods have not changed at all. So I will produce for you here the database helper class and a few of the ejb methods using the helper class.

```
package DataHelper;
import java.sql.*;
import java.util.*;
import javax.ejb.*;
```

```java
import java.rmi.RemoteException;
class PK_Account implements java.io.Serializable
  {
  public String name;
  public PK_Account()
  {
    // empty no - arguments constructor
  }
  public PK_Account(String name)
  {
    this.name = name;
  }
}


public class DataHelper
{
  private Connection connection;
  private PreparedStatement statement;
  private EntityContext beancontext;
  private String name;
  private float balance;
  public DataHelper()
  {

  }
  private Connection getConnection() throws SQLException
  {
    Properties properties = beancontext.getEnvironment();
    String url = properties.getProperty("db.url");
    String username = properties.getProperty("db.username");
    String password = properties.getProperty("db.password");
    if(username != null)
    {
      return DriverManager.getConnection(url, username, password);
    }
    else
    {
     return DriverManager.getConnection(url);
    }
  }
```

```java
public boolean insert(String sz_name, float f_balance) throws Exception
{
  connection = getConnection();
  statement = connection.prepareStatement
    ("INSERT INTO Bank_Accounts (name, balance) VALUES (?,?)*");
  statement.setString(1, sz_name);
  statement.setFloat(2, f_balance);
  if(statement.executeUpdate() != 1)
  {
    throw new Exception();
  }
  statement.close();
  connection.close();
  //return new PK_Account(name);
  return true;
}
public boolean delete(String sz_name)
{
    try
    {
    PreparedStatement statement = connection.prepareStatement
      ("DELETE FROM Bank_Accounts WHERE name = ?");
        statement.setString(1, sz_name);
    }
    catch (SQLException s)
    {
      s.toString();
    }
    return true;
}

public PK_Account findbykey(PK_Account key)throws Exception
{
  Connection connection = getConnection();
  PreparedStatement statement = connection.prepareStatement
    ("SELECT name FROM Bank_Accounts WHERE name = ?");
  statement.setString(1, key.name);
  ResultSet resultSet = statement.executeQuery();
  if(!resultSet.next())
      throw new Exception("could not open recordset");
```

```java
        statement.close();
        connection.close();
      return key;
  }


  public void load() throws RemoteException
  {
    // retrieve the name from the primary key
    name =  beancontext.getPrimaryKey().toString();
    try
    {
      Connection connection = getConnection();
      PreparedStatement statement = connection.prepareStatement
        ("SELECT balance FROM Bank_Accounts WHERE name = ?");
      statement.setString(1, name);
      ResultSet resultSet = statement.executeQuery();
      if(!resultSet.next())
        throw new RemoteException("Account not found: " + name);

      balance = resultSet.getFloat(1);
      statement.close();
      connection.close();
    }
    catch(SQLException e)
    {
      throw new RemoteException(e.toString() + "could not load");
    }
  }
  public void save(String sz_name, float f_balance) throws RemoteException
  {
    try
    {
      Connection connection = getConnection();
      PreparedStatement statement = connection.prepareStatement
        ("UPDATE Bank_Accounts SET balance = ? WHERE name = ?");
      statement.setFloat(1, f_balance);
      statement.setString(2, sz_name);
      statement.executeUpdate();
      statement.close();
      connection.close();
```

```
      }
    catch(SQLException e)
    {
      throw new RemoteException("Could not store: " + sz_name, e);
    }
  }
}
```

The methods of this database helper class have essentially the same code as the ejb methods in the first example. However, in this case, since all data access is in a single class, it would be relatively easy to alter the class to access a different data source or to return different data, if the need arises. This is the primary advantage of placing the data access code into a separate helper class. Now, let's take a look at one or two of the ejb methods calling these helper classes.

First, in any class that wishes to use the data helper class, you would have to instantiate that class. So if you wished to use it in a checking account class, you would declare it at the beginning of the class.

```
DataHelper myhelper = new DataHelper();
public void ejbStore() throw RemoteException
{
  myhelper.save(sz_name); //where name is the name on the account you want
                          //to save.
}
  public void ejbRemove() throws RemoveException, RemoveException
{
  myhelper.delete(sz_name);//where sz_name is the name on the account you
                           //wish to delete.
}
```

That's all you would have to do to use this helper class. Simply instantiate it and call its methods, just as you would with any other standard Java class. In my opinion, encapsulating all the data access code into a single helper class makes your entity bean more flexible and scalable.

Summary

In this chapter, you have explored the various facets and uses of bean-managed persistence. We looked at how to implement the data access methods directly in the entity bean's methods, as well as how to use a helper class. This chapter took the database access methods of Chapter 9 and the entity bean concepts of Chapter 10 and blended them to show you how to create bean-managed persistent entity beans. You were shown examples in both plain Java code and using the JBuilder tools.

Terms

EjbRemove() – A method used by entity beans with bean-managed persistence to remove the entity bean.

Helper Class – A class that is used to provide some needed functionality to the main class.

Review Questions:

1. List a circumstance where bean-managed persistence would be preferable to container-managed persistence.

2. How do all EJBs specify their home interface?

3. What are the three data types that can be used for a primary key?

4. What method must an entity bean with bean-managed persistence implement?

5. What methods access the underlying database object?

6. After an SQL statement completes, what should the method do before returning?

7. Does the ejbLoad() method close the connection?

8. Can a primary key class be shared by multiple entity bean classes?

9. Are there many similarities between bean-managed and container-managed entity beans?

10. Must all database code be written directly in the methods that use it?

Chapter 12

Message-Driven Beans

Introduction

So far, I have shown you how to use session beans and entity beans. I discussed these first because they are the most commonly used types of beans. This chapter will introduce you to a lesser known but equally important type of Enterprise JavaBean, the message-driven bean. A simple definition of a message bean would be that it is a bean designed to respond to messages. That may seem a bit too obvious, but it is an accurate description of what a message-driven bean does. These messages are received via the Java Message Service (JMS).

A more technical definition of a message-driven bean would be that it is a stateless, server-side, transaction-aware component that is driven by a Java message (javax.jms.message). Message beans are invoked by the Enterprise JavaBean container when a message is received from a JMS queue or topic. Essentially, a message-driven bean is a message listener. Earlier in this text, you were introduced to the use of event listeners, and it is likely that many readers have worked with event listeners in the past. The message-driven bean is quite similar to a standard event listener, except that it responds to messages rather than events. The basic structure and functionality of event listeners and message listeners are remarkably similar.

A message may originate from a variety of sources. Potential message originators include Java clients, enterprise beans, or Java Server Page (JSP) components. Any of these components are capable of sending a message. It is even possible that a message might come from a non-Java application. Whatever the source of the message, the message-driven bean (MDB) is there to respond to that message and take appropriate action. The client sending the message does not even need to be aware of the MDB deployed in the EJB container. As long as the message conforms to the predefined specifications, the process will function and the message will be propagated to the MDB.

In short, some external source generates a message. That message is then received by the application server. The server, recognizing this as a JMS compliant message, forwards the message to a message bean for processing. While the message may originate from a variety of sources, the application server itself is the actual client for the message-driven bean. This is one reason why the originating component is somewhat irrelevant, at least from the perspective of the message-driven bean. Regardless of what application or component originally generates the message, the MDB will actually receive the message from the EJB container. This makes the creation and management of message-driven beans significantly more straightforward. You will only need to concern yourself with handling messages that come in a consistent format from the EJB container.

Messages and JMS

Before I dive too deeply into message-driven beans, it seems prudent to first give some explanation of a message. As you probably suspect, a *message* is simply a definition of information or data sent from a source to a receiver. Messages, in Java, are handled by the Java Message Service. Message systems allow separate applications to communicate asynchronously. This means that the communication need not occur in real time. A message source can send a message to a receiver, and the receiver can respond at a later time. The Java Message Service, which is part of Java 2 Enterprise Edition (J2EE), supplies you, the developer, with the necessary APIs you will need to create applications that utilize the enterprise message system.

Asynchronous communication can have several advantages over synchronous communication. The first advantage is that there are many items that simply don't require real-time processing. For example, if I make a deposit in my checking account, the deposit need not be processed at that exact second in time. This is just one example in which the processing can actually be done several hours after the action. However, in any case where the processing can be done even several seconds after the initiating activity, then asynchronous communication can be used.

Asynchronous communication is less demanding on the system in question. If there are insufficient resources available to process the data at this instant, then the message can be queued and processed later when the resources are available. This also helps avoid CPU bottlenecks. You can see that there are many situations in which asynchronous communication is desirable over synchronous communication.

Prior to the introduction of message-driven beans, Java Message Service used a somewhat different approach to implement asynchronous method invocation. The approach used an external Java program that acted as the listener and, on receiving a message, invoked a session bean method. In other words, a session bean was the ultimate receiver of the message, but an intermediate Java program was required to listen for the incoming message and then invoke the appropriate session bean. This approach was problematic. The most serious problem was that since the message was received outside the application server, it was not part of a transaction in the EJB server. This put the message process outside the scope and control of the application server. Also, using an external listener for messages made for a cumbersome system that was difficult to work with. Message beans alleviate these problems and allow the entire process to be handled within the scope of the application server.

Message-Driven Bean Structure

I have already explained to you that a message-driven bean is, in some ways, similar to a standard event listener. It is also true that a message-driven bean shares certain key characteristics with all Enterprise JavaBeans. However, it is important to know exactly what differentiates a message-driven bean from standard event listeners and other Enterprise JavaBeans. There are certain defining characteristics of message-driven beans that distinguish them from session beans and entity beans. The most critical of these characteristics are listed here:

- Message-driven beans do not have a home interface.

- Message-driven beans do not have a remote interface.

- Message-driven beans are stateless. This means that they are short-lived instances and do not retain state for a client.

- The EJB 2.0 container sets itself up as a listener for asynchronous invocation and directly invokes the bean. This is why message-driven beans have no interfaces. The EJB container is their client.

- All instances of a particular MDB type are equivalent, as they are not directly visible to the client and maintain no conversational state.

These key features are what differentiate a message-driven bean from other types of Enterprise JavaBeans. You should notice that several of these characteristics of MDBs are dependent upon other features of message-driven beans. To begin with, the fact that message-driven beans do not have remote or home interfaces is dependent upon the fact that they are invoked directly by the EJB container. Home and remote interfaces are used by client applications to remotely invoke Enterprise JavaBeans. With message-driven beans, the application server is the client, and it is located with the Enterprise JavaBeans. Therefore, there are no home or remote interfaces required for clients to invoke.

Also note that all message-driven beans of a particular type are equivalent. The reason for this is that message-driven beans, in some ways, behave like stateless session beans. These beans are invoked to handle a message, and when that message handling is complete, the bean is released back to the MDB pool. They do not retain any conversational state with the client. Therefore, one message-driven bean is much the same as another, at least from the perspective of the client. As long as it's the correct type of message-driven bean, it does not matter which specific MDB is invoked.

A Message-Driven Bean Life Cycle

As with all Enterprise JavaBeans, the message-driven bean has a particular life cycle. Effective use of any EJB is dependent upon understanding its life cycle. The EJB container directly manages the life cycle of a message-driven bean. At the beginning of the life cycle of the MDB, several tasks are performed by the EJB:

- A message consumer is created to receive the messages. This consumer is either a QueueReceiver or TopicSubscriber.

- The EJB associates the bean with a destination and connection factory.

- The message listener and the message acknowledgement mode are registered.

Again, if you consider the nature of a message-driven bean, these steps are perfectly logical. The Enterprise JavaBean container has to set up the message-driven bean to "catch" incoming messages. Particular types of messages are associated with specific MDBs.

As you probably guessed, the end of the MDB's life cycle is also managed by the EJB container. This is accomplished by calling the ejbRemove() method, which removes the bean from the pool of available message beans. Since the message-driven bean is managed by the EJB container and not by clients, it is the EJB container itself that will call the ejbRemove() method of a message-driven bean.

The MDB Class

As with all EJBs, there are some specific items that a message-driven bean must adhere to. These specifications are what make a message-driven bean. The first thing to keep in mind is that there are certain interfaces message-driven beans must implement. This is much like all EJBs and, in fact, many other types of classes in Java programming. A message-driven bean has two interfaces that it must implement:

- javax.ejb.MessageDrivenBean

- javax.jms.MessageListener

It should be clear that the javax.ejb.MessageDrivenBean interface is responsible for identifying this class as a message-driven bean. Like most Enterprise JavaBeans, the message-driven bean invokes a specific interface in order to provide itself with the features of its EJB type. The javax.jms.Message-Listener interface is needed to allow the bean to be a message listener. This interface provides the requisite functionality to listen for messages and to receive those messages.

I would like to pause for a moment to take a closer look at those interfaces. This is one of those details that is possible to skip, but I think most programmers like to have a thorough understanding of why things work, not just <u>how</u> they work.

The MessageDrivenBean interface is required for all message-driven beans. It defines two methods that all MDBs must implement. It extends the EnterpriseBean interface:

```
package javax.ejb;
public interface MessageDrivenBean extends javax.ejb.EnterpriseBean
  {
    public void setMessageDrivenContext(MessageDrivenContext context)
        throws EJBException;
    public void ejbRemove() throws EJBException;
  }
```

Notice the two methods that are defined within this interface. The methods of the MessageDrivenBean interface are connected with the bean's life cycle. The container calls setMessageDrivenContext() to provide the message-driven bean instance with a reference to its MessageDrivenContext. The container calls this method at the beginning of the bean's life cycle. The ejbRemove() method is called by the container at the end of the bean's life cycle. You can use this method to free any resources allocated in the ejbCreate() method.

The second interface of concern to message-driven beans is the MessageListener interface. Only message-driven beans implement the MessageListener interface. Therefore, if you see this method in the source code for any EJB, it is a tell-tale sign that the bean must be an MDB. This interface defines only a single method, onMessage():

```java
package javax.jms;
public interface MessageListener
  {
      public void onMessage(Message message);
  }
```

By examining the code for these interfaces, you should be able to get a better idea of what is going on behind the scenes with message-driven beans.

Like all Enterprise JavaBeans, the message-driven bean class is defined as public. It also cannot be defined as either abstract or final. The primary issues you need to immediately concern yourself with are making sure that your message-driven bean class implements the proper interfaces, is public, and is neither final nor abstract. All of this would probably be much clearer if I simply showed you an example of an MDB.

```java
public class SampleMDB implements MessageDrivenBean, MessageListener
  {
      private MessageDrivenContext mdbContext;
  }
```

This is merely the basic framework for the class and has no methods. We will discuss methods, including constructors, momentarily. You should note the private instance of the MessageDrivenContext class. This mdbContext object is used to access the context within which the MDB is functioning. This would be the particular EJB container that is hosting the MDB.

There are a few other items to consider once you have created the basic framework of the MDB class. These are:

- An MDB must have a no-arguments constructor.

- It must have a no-arguments ejbCreate() method that returns a void.

- It must support an ejbRemove() method that returns a void.

- It must have a single onMessage() method.

- It must be declared like this: public void setMessageDriven-Context(MessageDrivenContext mdc).

There is, of course, a logical reason for each of these requirements. Let me summarize those reasons for you here. The constructor must have no arguments because it is called by the EJB container and will have no arguments passed to it. The ejbCreate() method returns a void because there is no remote client to return anything to. With other types of EJBs, the ejbCreate() method returns an object. The bean is invoked within the context of the application server, thus requiring no return object. The setMessageDriven-Context method is called by the EJB container after the creation of the instance without any transaction context. The ejbRemove() method does any required cleanup. Finally, we have the onMessage() method, which will be discussed in detail later in this chapter.

Remember that when you create message-driven beans, you only need to create the bean class. You do not create any interface classes. This makes the task of writing a message-driven bean much more simplified because you create a bean class only. Recall that message-driven beans don't have home or remote interfaces. To create your own message-driven bean, you need to follow these steps:

1. Create a class that implements the javax.ejb.MessageDrivenBean interface.

2. Define the class as public, not final or abstract.

3. In the bean class, implement the javax.jms.MessageListener interface.

4. Include a public constructor that takes no arguments.

5. Implement the ejbCreate() method that takes no arguments. Remember that this method must be declared as public, and it cannot be final or static. Its return type must be void, and it must not define any application exceptions.

These basic steps allow you to create message-driven beans. Since these beans do not have home or remote interfaces, their creation is actually simpler than other types of Enterprise JavaBeans.

The ejbCreate method

The ejbCreate() method is quite important, and it is the first method that the EJB container will call. This method is called at the time of bean instantiation. Its function is to allocate resources such as connection factories if the bean sends messages. It can also be used to allocate data sources if the bean requires database access.

Let's look at a sample ejbCreate() method:

```
public void ejbCreate () throws CreateException
{
}
```

This is the basic structure of all ejbCreate methods used with message-driven beans. Like all ejbCreate methods for all types of Enterprise JavaBeans, this method throws a CreateException, and unlike all other types of Enterprise JavaBeans, it returns a void.

The Transactional Management Methods

Since the message-driven bean participates in transactions with the EJB container, it is necessary to have a method or methods to handle the management of transactions. The setMessageDrivenContext provides the methods for transaction management. The SampleMDB implements setMessageDrivenContext. This method is called by the EJB container to associate the SampleMDB instance. The context is maintained by the container.

There is only a single input parameter for setMessageDrivenContext. It is an instance of the MessageDrivenContext interface. This gives the MDB access to information about the run-time environment. As you might suppose, this can be rather critical information for the MDB, depending on what functionality you may wish to implement within the bean itself.

The ejbRemove Method

The ejbRemove() method is responsible for conducting any "cleanup" when the bean is being removed. This method is invoked when an MDB is being removed from the pool of available beans. Different application server vendors may implement various methods for deciding when to remove the MDB instances from the pool. For this reason, you cannot be certain when the bean will be removed, but you can have control over what happens when this method is invoked.

Here is a sample ejbRemove() method:

```
public void ejbRemove()
{
    //Removes the bean from the pool
}
```

The specific code that you place in ejbCreate() and ejbRemove() will depend entirely upon your situation and the needs of your specific application.

The Business Methods

All of the structures and methods discussed so far have been concerned with managing the message-driven bean and its communication with the EJB container. However, all of this work is for naught if the bean does not accomplish some useful task. The business logic for the EJB is triggered by the onMessage() method of the MDB. The onMessage() method is called by the container when the JMS queue receives a message. This method does not return any value and only has one argument. The full JMS message object is passed as an argument. This means that the method received a message object and can then access that object's properties and methods in order to get information about a specific message.

The signature for the method is:

```java
public void onMessage(Message msg)
{
  try
  {
    // business logic goes here
  }
  catch(JMSException ex)
  {
  ex.printStackTrace();
}
}
```

Acknowledging Messages

Obviously, when a message is received, it is important for the sender to be notified that the message was received and is being processed. For MDBs that use container-managed transactions, the container will automatically acknowledge a message as soon as the EJB transaction commits. If the EJB uses bean-managed transactions, both the receipt and the acknowledgement of a message occur outside the EJB transaction context.

Some situations may require responding to the sender of the message. To register the "reply to" destination of the sender, the client can use the getJMSReplyTo method of the message object. This is just one of the many things that the message object provides you with. The JMSReplyTo is the destination where a "reply to the message" may be sent. Messages sent with a JMSReply value usually do so because they expect some type of response.

The code to use the JMSReplyTo header looks like this:

```java
public void onMessage(Message msg)
{
  try
  {
      destination d = msg.getJMSReplyTo()
  }
```

```
      catch(JMSException jmse)
      {
      }
}
```

Deploying the MDB

As with all EJBs, once you have created your bean, you will need to deploy it. The destination for an MDB is specified in the deployment descriptor of the MDB in the ejb-jar.xml file. A destination is a JMS-administered object accessible via JNDI.

Here is a sample destination entry in the deployment descriptor:

```
<message-driven-destination>
<destination-type>javax.jms.Topic</destination-type>
<subscription-durability>NonDurable</subscription-durability>
</message-driven-destination>
```

You may notice that there are items in this deployment descriptor that you have not seen in previous descriptors. The description of an MDB in the EJB 2.0 deployment descriptor contains the following elements specific to MDBs:

- A message-driven-destination, which contains the destination type (Queue or Topic).

- The JMS acknowledgement mode. This can be either auto-acknowledge or dups-ok-acknowledge.

- A JMS message selector. This is a JMS concept which allows the filtering of the messages sent to the destination.

The MDB deployment descriptor specifies whether the bean is meant for a topic or a queue. A bean set for a topic can act as a durable subscriber, guaranteeing that the listener receives all messages even if the listener is unavailable for a significant period of time. The deployment descriptor also sets transaction demarcation and security.

If the transaction type is Container, the transactional behavior of MDB methods is defined the same as other enterprise beans in the deployment descriptor.

Here is the entry for the transaction type in the deployment descriptor:

```
<transaction-type>Container</transaction-type>
<acknowledge-mode>Auto-acknowledge</acknowledge-mode>
```

You should notice that the deployment descriptor contains all the information except the destination name required to deploy a message-driven bean. The destination name is set in an application server's vendor-specific configuration file or as a system property.

A JBuilder MDB Example

After all this discussion about message-driven beans, it seems like it's time to actually look at an example. In this section, I will walk you step by step through the process of creating a message-driven bean using JBuilder.

As always, this project will begin by launching JBuilder, and then starting a new project. After that, however, things are a little bit different for message-driven beans. JBuilder does not directly provide a wizard for message-driven beans, so you have to be a little creative. What I am going to show you is how to use the wizard to create a stateless session bean (the one closest to a message-driven bean) that we will customize to meet our needs.

Step 1:

Choose File ▸ New to add a new EJB to your project.

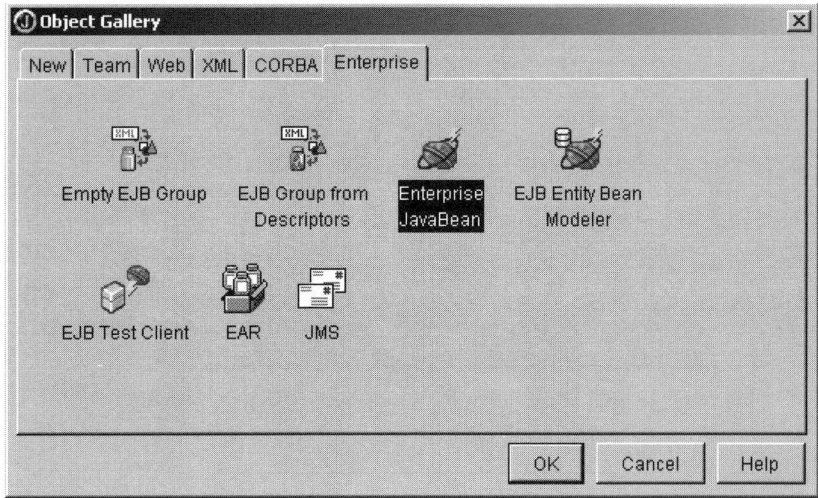

Step 2:

Much of the steps taken through the EJB Wizard will be exactly like they have been before. Simply follow our normal routine as if you were creating a stateless session bean. When the wizard is done, you should be looking at something like this:

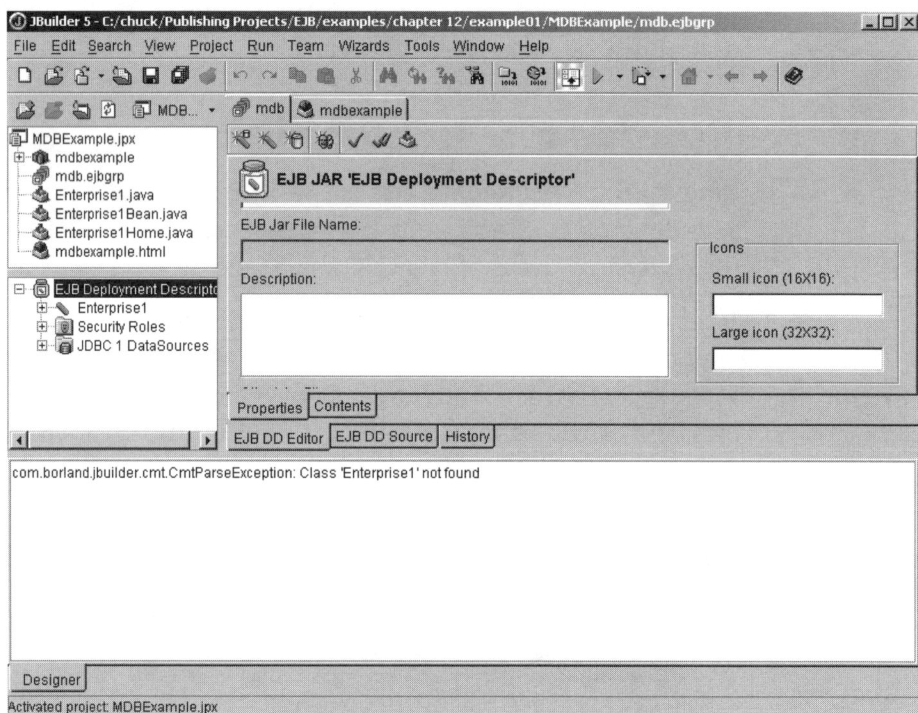

Step 3:

Now you will need to delete a few unnecessary items that were created for you. The first thing you will need to delete is the home interface code. Recall that message-driven beans have neither home nor remote interfaces.

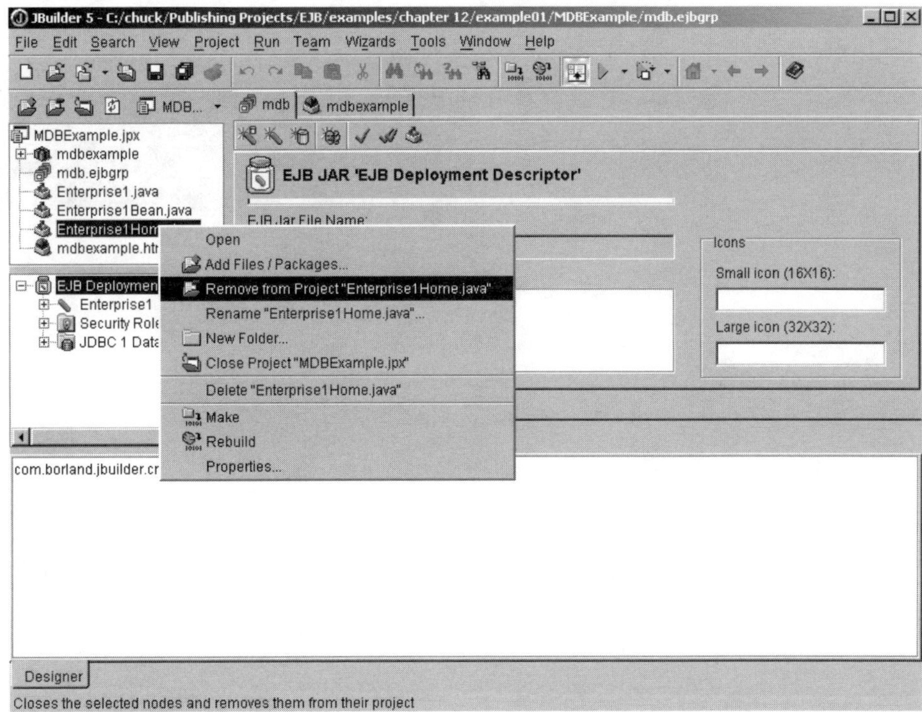

Then in the source code, you will need to remove the passivate, activate, and setSessionContext methods.

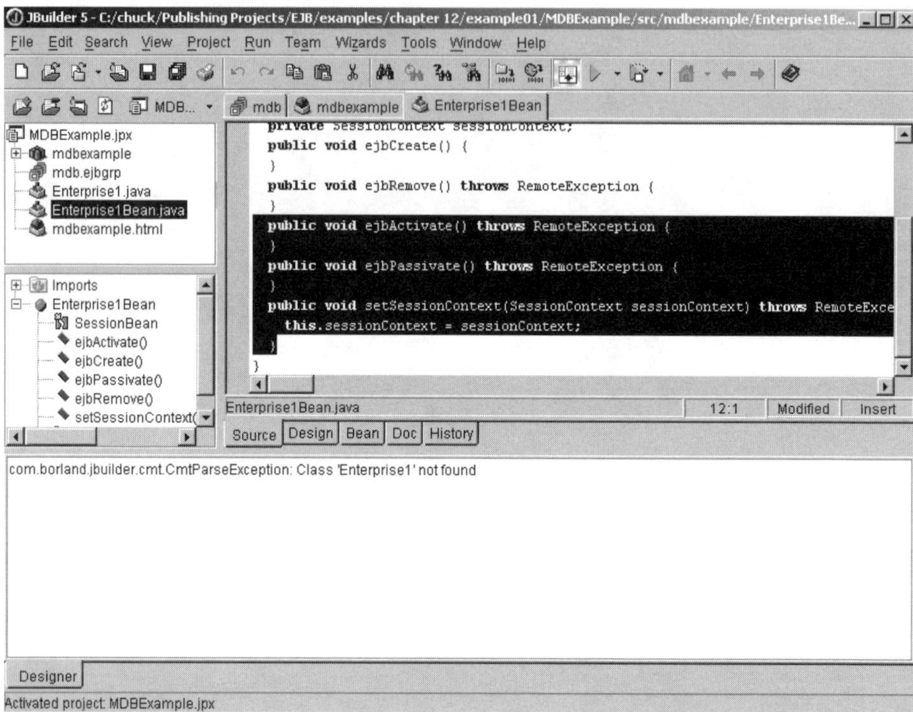

Step 4:

Now we add a few things and modify a few minor things. You will change the interfaces the main class implements and add the required methods for a message-driven bean. When you are done, your class should look like this:

```
package mdbexample;
import java.rmi.*;
import javax.ejb.*;
public class Enterprise1Bean implements MessageDrivenBean,
MessageListener
{
  private MessageDrivenContext mdbContext;
  public void ejbCreate()throws CreateException
```

```
      {
      }
      public void ejbRemove()
      {
      }
    public void onMessage(Message msg)
    {
      try
      {
        // business logic goes here
      }
      catch(JMSException ex)
      {
      ex.printStackTrace();
    }
    }
```

You should notice that the code is not that different from the code for a stateless session bean. Like all Enterprise JavaBeans, this code imports the java.rmi and javax.ejb packages. There are a few differences, listed here:

- The addition of the onMessage() method

- The change in the interfaces the class implements

- The ejbCreate() method in an MDB throws an exception, and in a stateless session bean, it does not.

- The ejbRemove() method in an MDB does not throw an exception, and in a stateless session bean it does.

- The MDB uses an instance of the MessageContext class, whereas the stateless session bean uses an instance of the SessionContext class.

Remember that your business logic should be contained within the onMessage() method. However, there is nothing at all preventing you from having that method call other methods or even implement helper classes. You could have additional classes that are invoked in the onMessage() method in order to accomplish the goals of your business logic.

Summary

This chapter introduced you to a new kind of Enterprise JavaBean: the message-driven bean. MDBs overcome the limitations of synchronous messaging using session and entity beans in the EJB 1.1 container. I have shown you the basic requirements of a message-driven bean and given you a view of how the message bean interacts with the container. Finally, the chapter showed you how to create your own message-driven beans using Borland's JBuilder development environment.

Terms

JMS – Java Message Service

MessageContext – A class, similar to the SessionContext class, that gives information about the context of the message

MessageListener – An interface that allows the bean class to receive JMS messages

Review Questions

1. What is a message-driven bean?
2. What interface(s) must a message-driven bean implement?
3. What are the requirements for a message-driven bean's home interface?
4. What are the requirements for a message-driven bean's remote interface?
5. What is passed to the onMessage() method as an argument?
6. Where is the business logic placed in a message-driven bean?
7. How does a message-driven bean maintain its state?
8. What arguments must be passed to a message-driven bean's constructor?
9. How is a message-driven bean's life cycle managed?
10. What objects can be message consumers?

Chapter 13

Java Server Pages

Introduction

Looking at the title to this chapter, you may ask what Java Server Pages has to do with Enterprise JavaBeans. The answer is that Java Server Pages (JSP) are frequently used in conjunction with Enterprise JavaBeans. Java Server Pages are a web development technology used to dynamically configure the visual interface. You see, with Java Server Pages, the user interface is separated from content generation. This essentially means that the actual user interface does not contain the code that has the business logic. That is where EJBs come in. They are excellent candidates for containing the actual business logic. The JSP page then acts as a client for the Enterprise JavaBeans. This makes Enterprise JavaBeans and Java Server Pages natural partners. In fact, both standard JavaBeans and EJBs can be, and frequently are, effectively integrated with Java Server Pages.

In an *n*-tier architecture, the various layers of the application handle different aspects of the operation. Too often, developers use the same tool to develop all the various components of the application. Since each component has a very different function, it seems a bit inappropriate to use the same tool for developing these various components. This is where the combination of JSP and EJB comes into play. JSP is a perfect tool for the user layer, whereas Enterprise JavaBeans is an ideal solution for the middle layers of the *n*-tier architecture. This combination of tools is ideal for *n*-tier architecture.

This chapter will give you an introduction to Java Server Pages. Chapter 14 will illustrate how to integrate these pages with Enterprise JavaBeans. It should come as no surprise to you that JBuilder also provides some very good tools for creating Java Server Pages. I will introduce you to those later in this chapter.

The Basics of JSP

I would like to start by giving you a basic overview of JSP technology. Java Server Pages use XML-like (Extensible Markup Language) tags and scripts written in the Java programming language to generate the content for the page. Any formatting tags, such as HTML and XML, are passed directly back to the response page. Essentially, Java Server Pages are Java code embedded into HTML documents. This allows you to leverage your Java programming skills into HTML skills. The one caveat is that your web server must support Java Server Pages in order for you to be able to use this technology. Fortunately, most of them do. Recall this when working with the examples in this chapter. If your web server does not support Java Server Pages, the examples in this chapter (and the next) will not work properly.

Java Server Pages are really just an extension of the Java servlet technology. For some of you, this may just lead to the question, what are servlets? *Servlets* are essentially platform-independent, server-side modules that fit into a web server framework. This is in contrast to applets, which are client-side modules embedded in HTML documents. Servlets can be used to extend the capabilities of a web server. Basically, an applet works with the browser displaying the HTML document that it is embedded in. Conversely, a servlet works with the web server that is hosting the HTML document. Unlike other scripting languages, servlets involve no platform-specific modifications. Servlets are Java application components that are downloaded, when needed, to the part of the system that requires them. This makes them a very flexible, platform-independent technology.

As with all things Java, Java Server Pages are created in accordance with a particular specification, defined primarily by Sun Microsystems. However, Sun does get a lot of input from the software development industry when creating any of its specifications, and the JSP specification is no different. There are some key components to the Java Server Page specification that you will need to keep in mind, and these will be covered later in this chapter.

Java Server Pages is a technology that allows you to mix static HTML with dynamically generated HTML into a single HTML document. Some readers may be asking: Doesn't CGI already do that? Why do I need Java Server Pages? It is true that Common Gateway Interface (CGI) attempts to provide similar functionality but is much more limited. Most web pages that are built with CGI programs are mostly static HTML, with the dynamic part limited to a few small portions of the page. Unfortunately, most CGI variations force you to generate the entire page via your code, even though only a small portion is actually being generated dynamically. JSP allows you to create the two parts separately.

This chapter will walk you through the fundamentals of Java Server Pages. I intend to use several examples to clarify the basics of this technology. After you have mastered the basic JSP skills presented in the beginning of this chapter, you will then be able to move to the last section where I will show you how to use JavaBeans with Java Server Pages. If you already have a basic working knowledge of JSP and are just trying to find out how to integrate Enterprise JavaBeans into Java Server Pages, then you should feel free to skip on to the "JSP and JavaBeans" section of this chapter.

How to Build a JSP

I have now spent several paragraphs giving you a brief overview of Java Server Pages. It would seem that now is the time to show you a sample Java Server Page. This page is rather simple; it does not perform an astounding task, but it does illustrate the basics of JSP.

```
<HTML>
<HEAD>
    <TITLE>Example 13-01</TITLE>
</HEAD>
<BODY BGCOLOR = white>
<FORM METHOD ="post" action = "Howdy.jsp">
<br>
<br>
Please Enter Your Name
<br>
<input name = "username" type = "text">
<input type = "submit" name = "submit" value = "Enter">
<br>
<br>
</BODY>
</HTML>
```

This first document is a standard HTML document.

> **Note:** If you are rusty on your HTML, please examine Appendix E for a review of basic HTML.

If you examine this HTML document, you should notice that it is, for the most part, standard HTML that you have probably seen quite a few times. There is only one line of HTML code that might seem new or different to you:

```
<FORM METHOD ="post" action = "Howdy.jsp">
```

You have probably seen FORM METHODs before. In this case, however, the object of the Action tag is a Java Server Page. Many HTML programmers are used to using Java scripts or VB scripts as the targets of form actions, but in this case, the object is a separate document, a Java Server Page document. That means that the content of the HTML form segment of the HTML page will be directed to our Java Server Page, as input to that JSP.

Our example depends on two documents, the HTML document and the JSP document. You have just seen the HTML document and had its contents carefully explained to you. It is, for the most part, a rather simple, standard HTML page. Now I would like to direct your attention to the Java Server Page document. The JSP document can be written in any standard text editor. Windows users will probably wish to use the Notepad or WordPad text editors, while Linux users with the KDE interface might choose the Advanced Text Editor. Regardless of the text editor you use, you should save your Java Server Page with the extension ".jsp."

The actual JSP will appear much like standard HTML documents, with a few new lines added to it.

Note: You won't see this work without a JSP-compatible web server. In fact, none of the examples in this chapter will work if your web server is not Java Server Page compatible. Check the documentation of your web server to see if it is JSP compatible.

Below is the actual code for howdy.jsp.

```
<html>
<head>
<Title> Who am I and what time is it?<title>
<Body>
Howdy,
<% = request.getParameter("username") %>
<br>
The current time is
<% = new java.util.Date() %>
</body>
<html>
```

As I told you earlier in this chapter, much of this is just standard HTML. However, two lines should stand out to you as clearly not being basic HTML code. These lines are:

```
<% = request.getParameter("username") %>
<% = new java.util.Date() %>
```

Note that both of these lines start with a <% symbol and end with a %> symbol. Any code placed between these two symbols is basically Java code embedded into an HTML document. In other words, it is Java Server Page code. So a good basic definition of Java Server Pages would be that they are Java code embedded in an HTML document.

The first line of JSP code simply retrieves the "username" value that was submitted from the HTML form. That value is displayed along with the word "Howdy." The second line of Java Server Page code retrieves the current date/time using the familiar Java data object found in the utility package. If you launch the first code on a machine running a JSP-compatible browser, you will be able to view the following sequence:

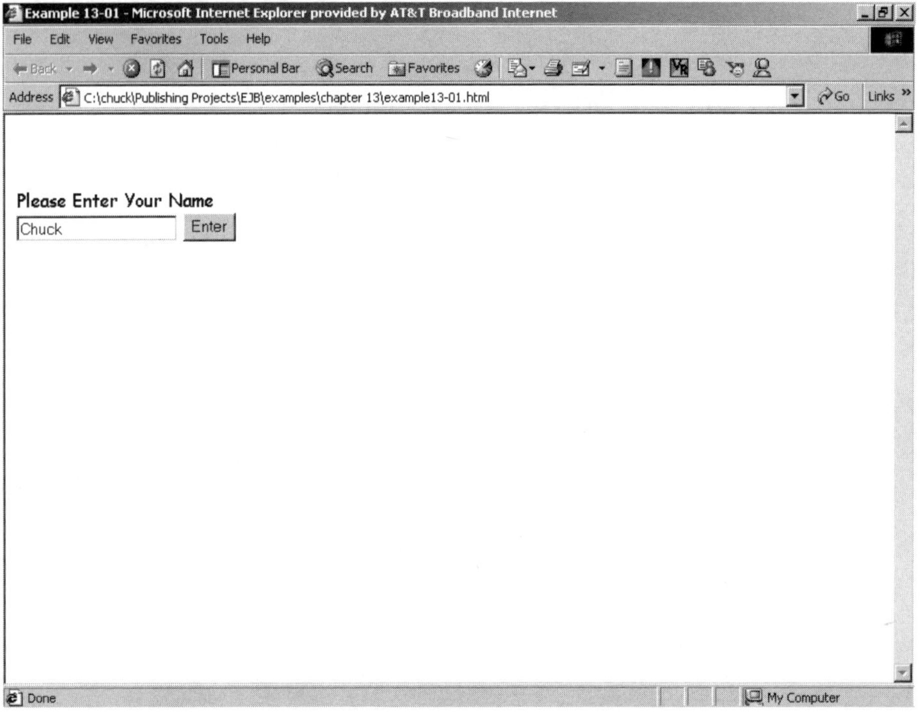

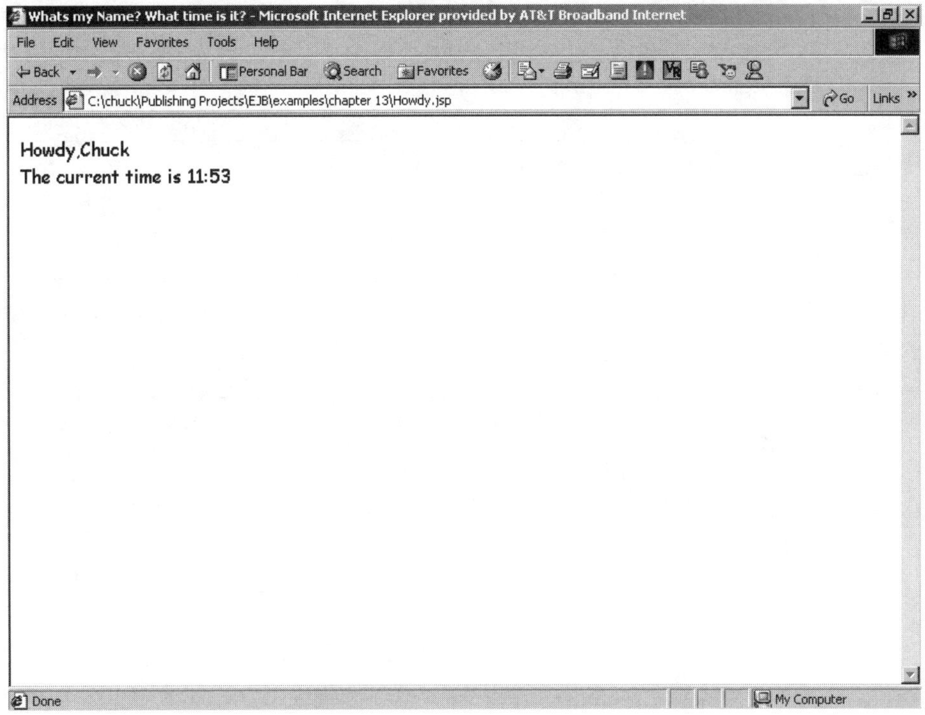

Most of the JSP code utilizes Java commands (thus the name Java Server Pages). You should keep this in mind as you develop Java Server Pages. Most standard Java code is available to you within JSP documents. This is one of the most useful features of Java Server Pages. In addition to the Java code, there are some other objects implicitly available to all Java Server Pages. One such object is the request object used in the preceding example. That object allowed you to gain information about the request that had been sent to the JSP. It also allows you to gain information about the generator of that request. The following table summarizes the objects you have implicitly available to you and what they are used for.

Object	Type	What the Object Represents
request	This is a subtype of the javax.servlet.ServletRequest.	The request that triggered this JSP
response	This is a subtype of javax.servlet.ServletResponse.	The response to the request that invoked this JSP

Object	Type	What the Object Represents
session	java.servlet.HttpSession	The session created for the requesting client
application	java.servlet.ServletContext	The context that was obtained from the servlet configuration object
out	javax.servlet.ServletConfig	This is an object that writes to the output stream. It is very similar to the system.out object.
page	java.lang.Object	This is an instance of this page implementation class.
pageContext	javax.servlet.PageContext	This is the servlet context retrieved from the servlet configuration object.

Each of the objects you see in this table can be very useful to you when developing Java Server Pages. You will see several of them used in examples throughout this chapter. It is not necessary for the purposes of this book to have an in-depth discussion of the nuances of each of these objects. You merely need to be aware of what they are and their general purpose. However, if you are looking for a more in-depth discussion of these Java Server Page objects, I suggest you consult Appendix A at the end of this book for other resources that give that topic a more thorough treatment.

The preceding example does illustrate the basics of Java Server Pages, but it simply does not go far enough. For example, what happens if the person clicks the submit button without first entering a name? What if you wish to do other things with that username? Would these issues be better addressed if the name was stored in some variable? Let me show you an example that addresses all of these issues.

In this example, the original HTML document will not be changed, just the Java Server Page document. I will not show you the HTML document again, but rather just the JSP document. Let's take a look at that document here:

```
<html>
<head>
```

```
<Title> Howdy Part 2</title>
<Body>
Howdy,
<%
  String s_name= request.getParameter("username")
  if(s_name.length() == 0)
  {
        %>
            You did not enter a name!
        <%
  }
  else
  {
      %>
      <% "Howdy there " + s_name %>
  }
%>
<br>
The current time is
<% = new java.util.Date() %>
</body>
<html>
```

There are a number of simple but interesting differences between this JSP
and our first JSP. You can see that several items have been changed. The first
thing that you should notice is that I created a string variable called s_name,
and it holds the name that is passed from the HTML document. This is
important because it illustrates that I can declare and use variables in much
the same way that I might in a normal Java application. It is yet another
example of how you can integrate Java code into a web page through the
use of Java Server Pages.

Next, I would like to direct your attention to the if-else statements. The first
thing about this that you should note is that the statements are structured
exactly as they are in Java. This is yet another example of how you can use
Java code in JSP. In this particular if statement, I check the length of the
string variable. Recall that the string object, in Java, has a number of properties, including length. This demonstrates that not only can you create object
variables in JSP, but they have much the same properties and methods that
you have been accustomed to in your previous Java programming

experience. The only other item to note is that in the if-else statement there are portions where I close the JSP code with a %> and then reopen it with a <%. This allows me to easily intersperse standard HTML code within my Java Server Page code.

While this example is not much more complicated than the first one, it should illustrate to you a number of important aspects of Java Server Pages, the first being that you can use standard Java code in JSP. In fact, that is the whole point of JSP. The second thing to note is that you can mix HTML and Java code in a Java Server Page document. Perhaps the most compelling reason for a Java programmer to utilize Java Server Pages is because it allows you to leverage your existing Java programming skills into a server-side web development technology.

Using the Inherent Objects

As I previously mentioned, there are several objects you have access to inherently. Those particular objects were outlined for you in the previous table. It may not be immediately apparent to you just how useful those objects can be to you. Each of these inherent objects offers you a wealth of information and functionality. Perhaps the best way to illustrate this fact is with another example.

I call this example "snoop." The reason is that it sort of "snoops" around and gives you some information about the server that the JSP is running on. You will find the source code for this example in the downloadable files under examples/chapter 13/snoop.jsp. The purpose of this code is to show you how you can use the request object to retrieve information about the user who is requesting the page. The request object has a number of properties that tell you quite a bit about the server that is hosting the page and making requests to JSP.

```
<html>
<head>
<title> Snoop </title>
</head>
<body bgcolor = white>
<br>
<br>
```

```
<center>Here is some information about your request </center>
<br>
<br>
The Server Name is:
<% = request.getServerName() %><br>
The protocol used is:
<% = request.getProtocol() %><br>
The Port used is:
<% = request.getServerPort() %><br>
The HTTP Method used is:
<% = request.getMethod() %> <br>
</body>
</html>
```

If you run this code inside a web server that supports JSP, you should see the following image (of course, the actual information retrieved will be different on your server than on mine).

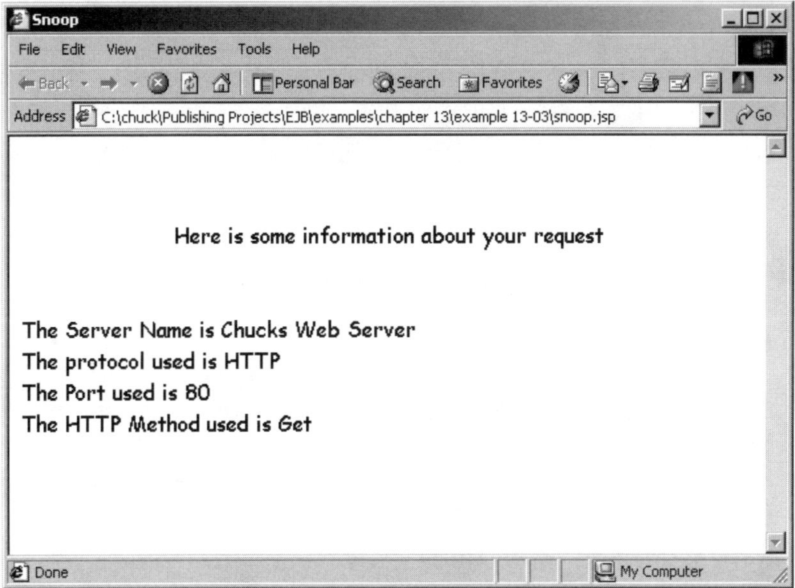

You should notice the wide variety of information you can get from the request object. Each of the objects you have access to in Java Server Pages has an equally rich array of information for you. If you consider the usefulness of these inherent objects, combined with the standard Java programming objects, you can immediately see why Java Server Pages are such an exciting web development tool.

Advantages of JSP

As you are probably already aware, Java Server Pages are not the only way to accomplish the tasks you have been shown. There are a number of web development technologies available, each with its own advantages and disadvantages. In this section, I compare and contrast Java Server Pages with other web technologies. However, I must admit before we begin this comparison that I do have a fondness for all things related to Java, including JSP, so I cannot guarantee that my analysis is completely unbiased. Since I cannot guarantee this, I will certainly endeavor to at least be accurate!

The following sections should help you understand why Java Server Pages are so popular. In short, it tries to answer the question: Why should I use Java Server Pages?

JSP vs. JavaScript

This is a difficult comparison for me since I am an avid fan of both Java Server Pages and JavaScript. JavaScript can generate HTML dynamically on the client. However, it is a client-side technology. It can interact with the client (i.e., the browser), but it cannot interact with the server. This is a major hurdle for e-commerce solutions. With the exception of cookies, HTTP and form submission data is not available to JavaScript. I still feel that JavaScript is the best client-side solution, and it is simply fantastic for various image effects and browser manipulations. However, it simply is not capable of handling server-side functionality.

JSP vs. Static HTML

Since JSP is embedded into standard HTML, it should be obvious that Java Server Pages encompass all the functionality of HTML, plus the functionality of JSP. That fact alone makes JSP a superior choice to standard HTML. Standard HTML, of course, cannot contain dynamic information.

JSP vs. Active Server Pages (ASP)

Active Server Pages is a technology similar to Java Server Pages. ASP is only available from Microsoft. The biggest advantage that Java Server Pages has over ASP is platform independence. Active Server Pages only works on Microsoft's web server, Internet Information Server (IIS).

JSP vs. Pure Servlets

You could comment that servlets give you all the functionality that Java Server Pages does, and you would be correct. The primary advantage of Java Server Pages is not in functionality. It is the fact that they can be embedded directly into HTML documents. This makes them very easy to code and equally easy to maintain.

How Does JSP Work?

By this point, you know how easy JSP is to use. You just finished reading about how JSP compares to other web development technologies. The only question left is, exactly how do these JSPs work? You have seen functioning examples, but how, exactly, is all this taking place? Let me take a moment to answer that question for you. The first step is that the Java Server Page code is parsed into a Java source file, which is then compiled into a servlet class. This occurs immediately when the page is first requested. This means that the code you placed between the <% and %> (i.e., the Java Server Page code) is compiled into Java classes on the server side. The Java servlet class file is then accessed from the HTML document.

JSP in JBuilder

Throughout this book, you have seen that almost any task is easier and more efficient if done with JBuilder. With that in mind, it should not surprise you that Java Server Pages are no exception. JBuilder provides you with a set of tools for developing Java Server Page projects. Let me walk you through an example that illustrates this simple fact.

As always, you should start by launching JBuilder and selecting File ▸ New Project. The code for this project is in the downloadable files under examples/chapter 13/example_04.

Step 1:

Select File ▸ New. On the Web tab, you will notice a Java Server Page object.

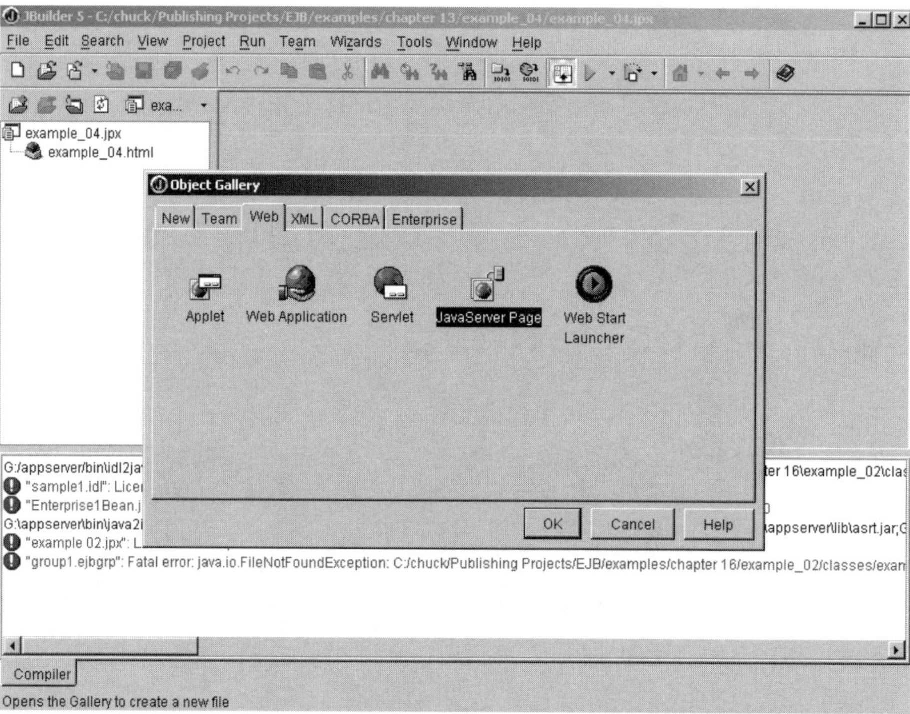

Selecting that option will launch the Java Server Page Wizard. Most of the screens in the wizard are fairly self-explanatory. For the most part, we will simply use the default settings. The wizard only has three screens, and they are shown here:

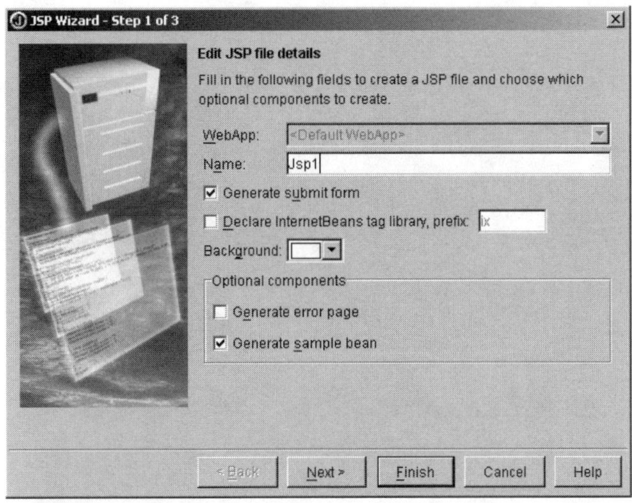

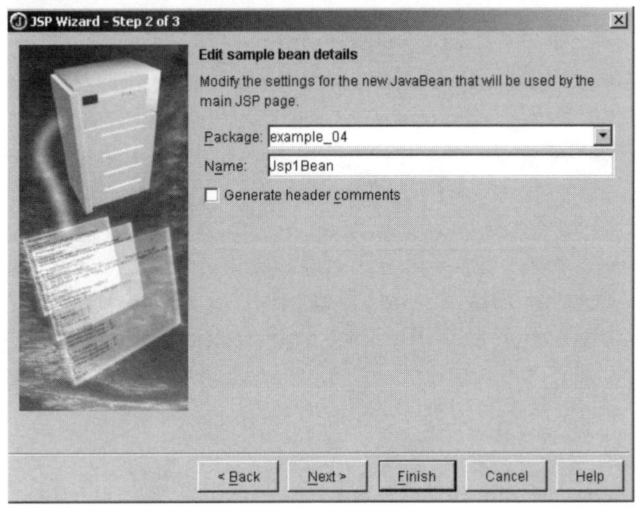

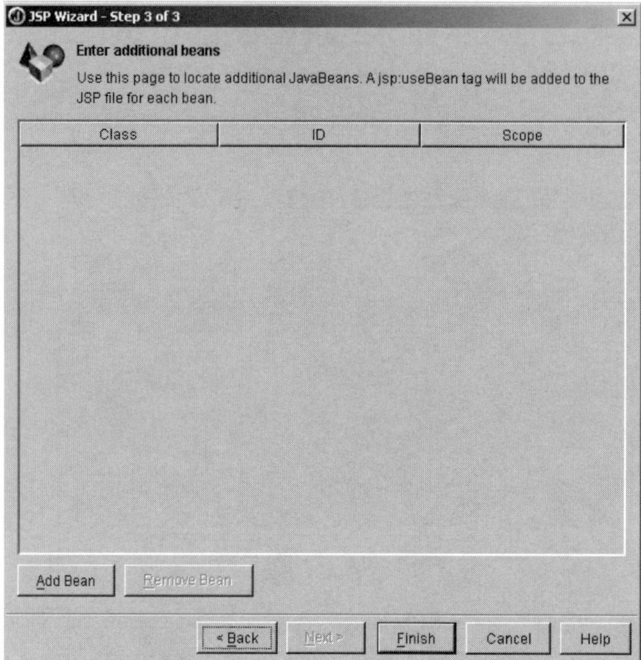

Now I want you to pay particular attention to this last screen. This one will be of particular importance in the next chapter. As you can see, JBuilder allows you to select JavaBeans that you wish to embed in your Java Server Page. I will hold off on that discussion until the section "JSP and JavaBeans," but just keep that in mind.

Step 2:

At this point, JBuilder has generated the basic JSP code for you. You will probably notice that JBuilder does assume that you will be incorporating some JavaBeans into your JSP. Here is the code that JBuilder will generate for you:

```
<html>
<head>
<title>
Jsp1
</title>
</head>
```

```
<jsp:useBean id="Jsp1BeanId" scope="session"
    class="example_04.Jsp1Bean" />
<jsp:setProperty name="Jsp1BeanId" property="*" />
<body>
<h1>
JBuilder Generated JSP
</h1>
<form method="post">
<br>Enter new value  : <input name="sample"><br>
<br><br>
<input type="submit" name="Submit" value="Submit">
<input type="reset" value="Reset">
<br>
Value of bean property is :<jsp:getProperty name="Jsp1BeanId"
    property="sample" />
</form>
</body>
</html>
```

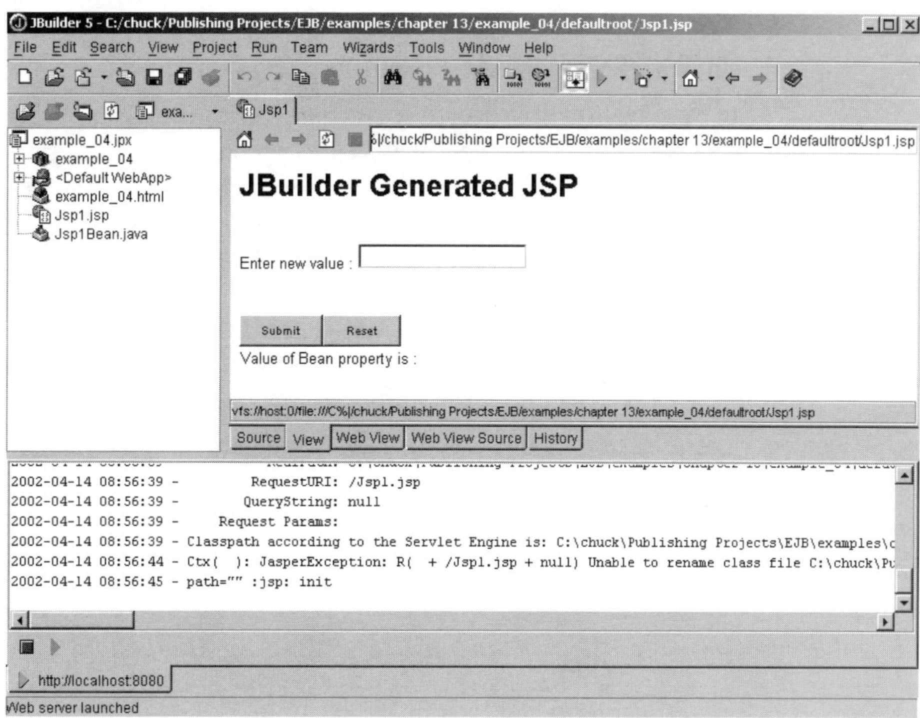

That is it; just a few simple steps with a wizard and the basic JBuilder code is done for you. You can now alter that code in any way that you see fit. What is really interesting is the various options JBuilder gives you for viewing the Java Server Page you have created. For example, the View tab in the previous figure will show you what this page would look like.

As you can see, JBuilder can be a very useful tool in creating Java Server Pages. It makes the creation and management of these pages much easier and faster.

Directives and Attributes

So far, I have only touched on a few basics of Java Server Pages, and a thorough coverage of JSP is beyond the scope of this book. However, I would like to show you a few more features of JSP that you may find useful. Since these items are so useful and still quite easy to master, it seems proper to give them at least cursory coverage.

Let me begin with directives and attributes. There are a number of directives you can use in Java Server Pages to accomplish a variety of programming goals. *Directives* are simply messages to the JSP container, directing that container to do something. Each of these directives has attributes you can utilize to derive important information. Let's look at a few of the directives and their attributes.

The Page Directive

This directive is one that is used quite frequently. It has a number of attributes that can be quite useful to you. The attributes of the page directive are listed here. The more commonly used attributes will be explained with sample code.

- Language
- Extends
- Import
- Session

- Buffer

- Autoflush

- IsThreadSafe

- Info

- ErrorPage

- IsErrorPage

- ContentType

Let's first look at the session attribute. This is a very useful attribute that will give you a great deal of information regarding the current session between the client and the web server. The following example illustrates the usefulness of this attribute.

```
<html>
<head>
  <title> Session Attribute Example</title>
</head>
<body bgcolor = white>
<br>
<br>
Session ID is:
  <% session.getId() %>
<br>
<br>
Session Creation Time is:
  <% session.getCreationTime() %>
<br>
<br>
Session was last accessed at:
  <% session.getLastAccessedTime() %>
<br>
<br>
</body>
</html>
```

You can see that the session attribute has several properties that you can access in order to get information about the client-web server session.

Some of the other attributes of the page directive are summarized in this table:

Attribute	Purpose
buffer	This specifies how the initial "out" JSP object will handle content.
isThreadSafe	This provides the JSP container with information about how to handle requests for this page.
errorPage	This attribute defines a separate error page to display errors.
autoFlush	This defines whether or not the buffer used with the "out" object will be automatically flushed when it becomes full.

The Import Directive

Another very important directive is the import directive. This directive does not have a host of attributes for you to use, but it does allow you to do something very useful. It allows you to import other files. You can import standard Java packages (any Java package, in fact), URLs, or even other JSP files. You will find this directive quite useful. Here is an example:

```
<%@ page import = "java.util.*" %>
<html>
<head>
  <title> Importing the java.util example </title>
</head>
<body bgcolor = white>
  <br>
  <br>
    The time is now
  <% new Date() %>
</body>
</html>
```

Notice that the import statement works exactly the same way as it does in your standard Java applications. This will be very useful to you.

JSP and JavaBeans

So far, this chapter has given you a brief but adequate introduction to the structure and utilization of Java Server Pages. The rest of this chapter will take that knowledge a step further by showing you how to integrate JavaBeans into Java Server Pages. It is imperative that you have a firm grasp of the information in the preceding sections before continuing. Without a firm understanding of the basics of Java Server Pages, you will be unable to complete the material in the rest of this chapter.

One question I would like to address before we dive in is, why is incorporating JavaBeans and JSP so important? The answer is e-commerce. You already know that JavaBeans are a very useful and versatile component architecture. You also know that Enterprise JavaBeans are excellent candidates for the business layer of an *n*-tier architecture. After reading this chapter, you now realize that Java Server Pages are a very versatile way to develop server-side web solutions.

Since e-commerce involves the use of web pages as the client layer of an *n*-tiered system, the collaboration of Java Server Pages to handle the presentation layer details, with JavaBeans to encapsulate the business logic, is a natural step to take. Fortunately for Java programmers, it's also a rather simple step to take (particularly if you utilize JBuilder). This chapter, unlike most of the other chapters in this book, will use only JBuilder for the various examples. The reason is twofold. The first reason is that it is simply much easier to do with JBuilder. The second reason is that once I present you with the code generated by JBuilder, you can easily reproduce the same or similar code in any text editor, thus embedding beans into your Java Server Pages without using JBuilder.

I am going to show you, step by step, how to create a combination Java Server Page/JavaBean project using JBuilder. This JSP functionality is somewhat limited, but it does illustrate the points that I am trying to communicate. The JSP will allow text input, and when the Submit button is pressed, it will display the text output. In this example, the JavaBean is used to count the number of times the web page is visited. For our first example, I will show you how to do this using the JSP Wizard. This wizard is an excellent starting point for developing JSPs. Unfortunately, the wizard will not generate a complete application, but it will take care of all the details required to get your application up and running. You will be left with very little code to add.

Step 1:

Of course, the first step is to start a new JBuilder project. This is, obviously, the first step with any of the JBuilder examples in this book.

Step 2:

Now you will use the JSP Wizard. To launch this wizard, select File ▸ New. You will see a screen much like the one in the image below. Choose the Java Server Page option from the Web tab.

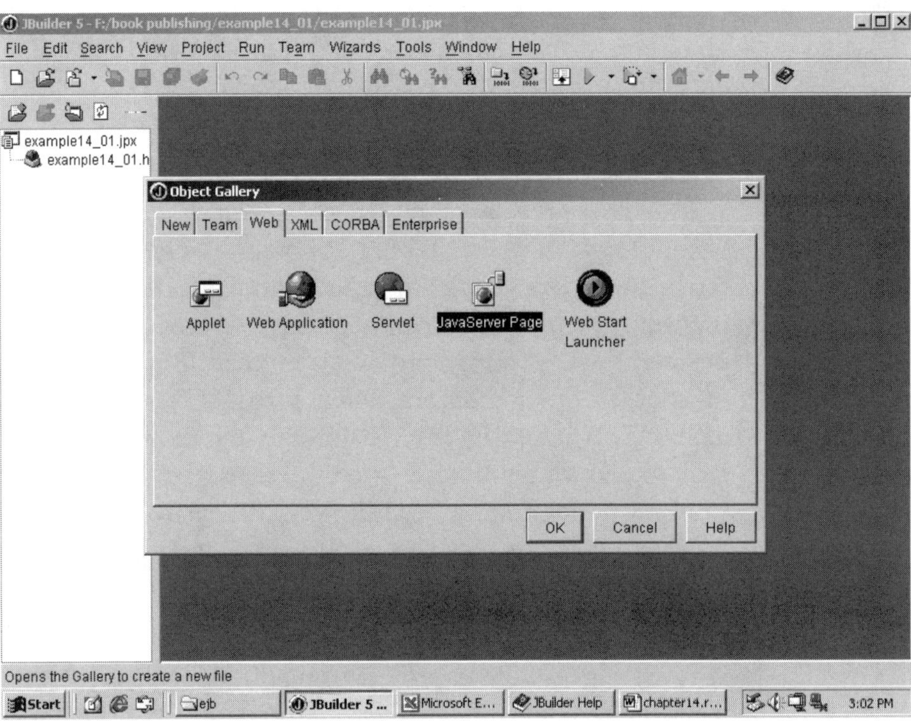

Go through the JSP Wizard, keeping just the default values as I asked you to do earlier in this chapter.

When the wizard is done, take a look in the project explorer in the upper left-hand side of the screen, and notice that there is a bean included. Beans are so commonly used with JSP that the JSP Wizard will create an empty JavaBean for you when you create your Java Server Page. This is very convenient for us, given that our purpose is to integrate the two technologies into a single project.

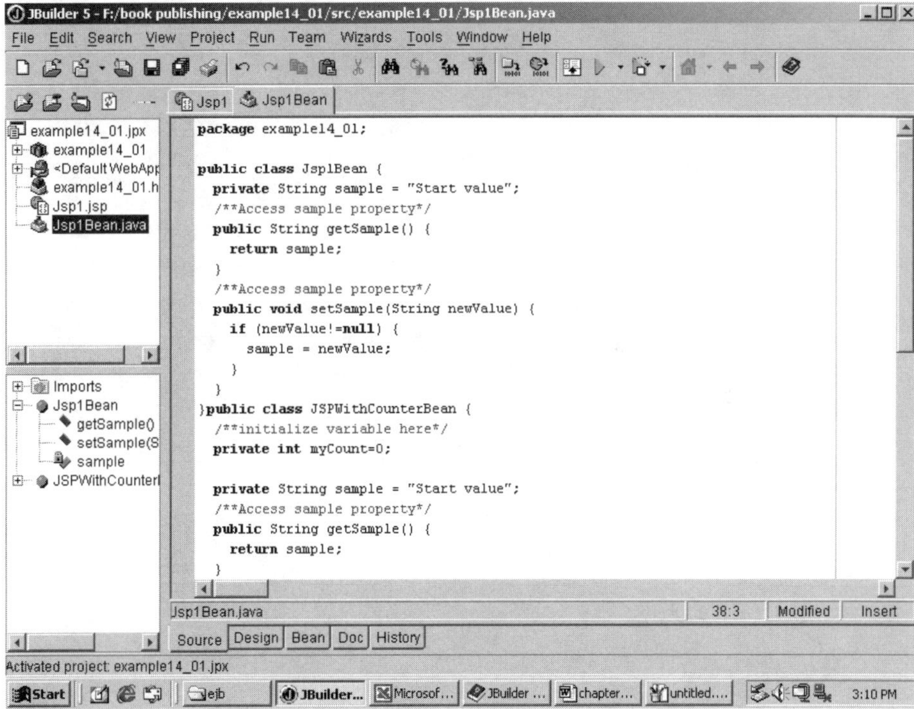

However, this sample bean does not quite have the functionality we are looking for. For this reason, I am going to replace that bean code (simply highlight it, delete it, and type in the new code) with the JavaBean code in the next step.

Step 3:

Replace the sample bean code with this code:

```java
package example13_07;
public class CounterBean
{
  private int count=0;
  public int getCount()
  {
    return count;
  }
  public void increaseCount()
  {
    count++;
  }
}
```

Now we have a JavaBean that acts as a page hit counter, but we still need to tie it into the Java Server Page in order to make it work. We will now need to change our JSP code. You can replace the default code that Borland JBuilder created for you with the code you see here:

```html
<<html>
<head>
<jsp:useBean id="CounterBean" scope="session"
  class="jsptutorial.CounterBean" />
<jsp:setProperty name="CounterBean" property="*" />
<title>
JSP using a JavaBean as a counter:
</title>
</head>
<body>
<h1>
JBuilder Generated JSP:
</h1>
<form method="post">
<br>Enter new value: <input name="sample">
<br>
<br>
<input type="submit" name="Submit" value="Submit">
<input type="reset" value="Reset">
<br>
```

```
<p>This page has been visited :<%= CounterBean.count() %> times.</p>
</form>
</body>
</html>
```

You can see that this code is not particularly complicated, but it does demonstrate the basics of implementing a JavaBean inside of Java Server Pages. Next I want to direct your attention to a few specific lines of this code. These particular lines of code show you precisely how to implement a JavaBean into your Java Server Page.

```
<jsp:useBean id="CounterBean" scope="session"
 class="jsptutorial.CounterBean" />
```

This line of code simply says for Java Server Pages to use a particular bean. The portion gives the bean an ID and scope to use. Finally, the code identifies the class that the bean is from. You could actually implement any JavaBean in this manner.

Finally, toward the bottom of the page, there is code that actually accesses one of the properties of our JavaBean.

```
This page has been visited :<%= CounterBean.count() %> times
```

You could access any public method or property of the JavaBean you have connected to your Java Server Page. Simply use the bean name and the property name or method.

Summary

This chapter introduced you to the basics of Java Server Pages. You saw how JSP embeds into HTML documents. I also showed you how JSP combines traditional Java code with various inherent JSP objects. Several examples using Java Server Pages were shown in their entirety and explained.

In this chapter, you were also given a comparison between Java Server Pages and other web development technologies. This is important information for you to know. Finally, I showed you how to use JBuilder to create Java Server Pages. This chapter was not designed to make you a JSP expert. Its purpose was to give you an introduction to Java Server Pages.

Terms

JSP – Java Server Pages. A server-side technology that embeds Java code into HTML documents.

CGI – Common Gateway Interface. Another server-side web technology.

ASP – Active Server Pages. A Microsoft-specific server-side web technology.

Directives – These are simply messages to the JSP container.

XML – Extensible Markup Language. This is a markup language, similar to HTML, that allows the developer to create her own tags.

Review Questions

1. Give a simple definition of Java Server Pages.

2. What code in an HTML document is used to embed JSP code?

3. What inherent JSP object is used to send output to the screen?

4. List five inherent JSP objects.

5. What is the primary advantage of JSP over ASP?

6. What type of platform will Java Server Pages execute on?

7. What inherent JSP object is used to get information submitted from an HTML form?

8. What types of Java variables can you use in JSP?

9. What is the primary advantage of JSP over JavaScript?

10. Can Enterprise JavaBeans be used in conjunction with JSP?

Chapter 14

Distributed Computing

Introduction

This book has dealt primarily with the topics of Enterprise JavaBeans and JBuilder. It is important for you to realize that EJBs are just one approach, among many, to distributed computing. This means that the field of distributed computing is broader and more diverse than simply EJBs. I certainly feel that Enterprise JavaBeans is one of the best approaches to enterprise computing, but it is not the only one. You should also be aware that JBuilder Enterprise edition ships with a number of tools specifically designed for enterprise computing. This chapter has two goals. The first goal is to give you a broad-based understanding of distributed computing. In Chapter 5, you were given a brief introduction to this topic, and this chapter will take the topic further. I believe that you will be a much better developer if you have a fundamental understanding of the technologies underlying the programming techniques that you utilize in your code. The second goal of this chapter is to give you a brief introduction to other distributed computing tools available to you in JBuilder.

Chapter 5 provided a brief introduction to distributed computing, just enough to get you started. For those of you who either skipped that portion or don't recall it, the essentials of it are presented here and expanded upon in the next section. The rest of the chapter goes on to expound upon the topic of distributed computing and the tools available to you in JBuilder. Chapter 15 goes into some depth on the topic of CORBA, a very popular distributed approach.

Basics of Distributed Computing

In the early days of computers, all applications were single-component monolithic applications. This strategy continued well into the era of personal computers. All applications, from mainframe applications written in COBOL to desktop applications written in C, were formed from a single component. This single-component architecture had a few serious drawbacks. If any portion of the process changed, the entire application had to be recompiled and redistributed. This single-layer approach also seriously inhibited scalability. If a business grew, as all businesses wish to do, single-unit software could not easily be scaled to handle increased demand. There was no way to distribute the workload across multiple machines. This type of architectural design is now referred to as a single-tiered architecture.

Eventually, the concept of client-server applications became prominent in the world of personal computers. In a client-server architecture, there is a centralized server component where the data is stored. Business rules may also be implemented at this layer, or they can be implemented in the client. The client layer is located on individual machines and provides the interface for users to interact with the system. This interface is often graphical in nature. When you use a web page, you are interacting with a client-server system. Your web browser is the client, and the web server you are connecting to is the server. The figure on the following page provides a graphical overview of how the client-server, or two-tiered, architecture works.

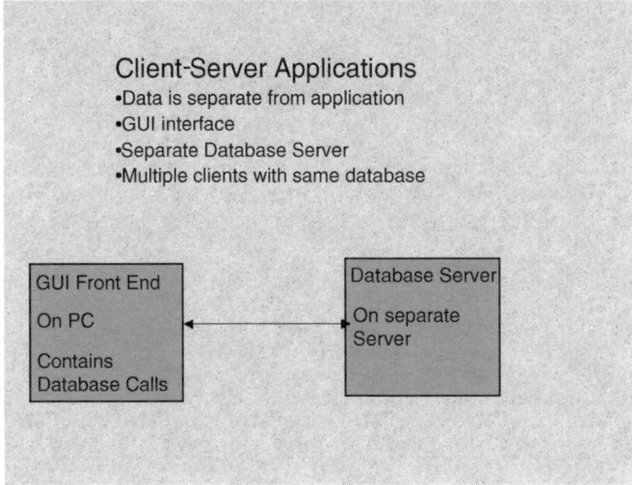

While this architecture is a significant improvement over single-unit applications, it still has some serious limitations. Scalability is difficult to implement. The workload is still focused on specific locations, and you cannot easily distribute the workload across more machines. A problem also arises if you have multiple types of clients, such as a desktop application client and a web interface client. However, this type of architecture is distributed and is an improvement over the single-tiered architecture. Another term for client-server architecture is two-tiered architecture.

The next stage in the development of distributed architectures is the *n*-tiered architecture. The *n* simply stands for some number, usually greater than 2. Three-and four-tiered architectures are quite common. In this system, additional layers are interposed between the client and the database. You might find a business layer that handles all the business rules of an organization. You might also find a database layer that handles all the actual communication with the database. The image on the following page shows how an *n*-tiered application is designed graphically.

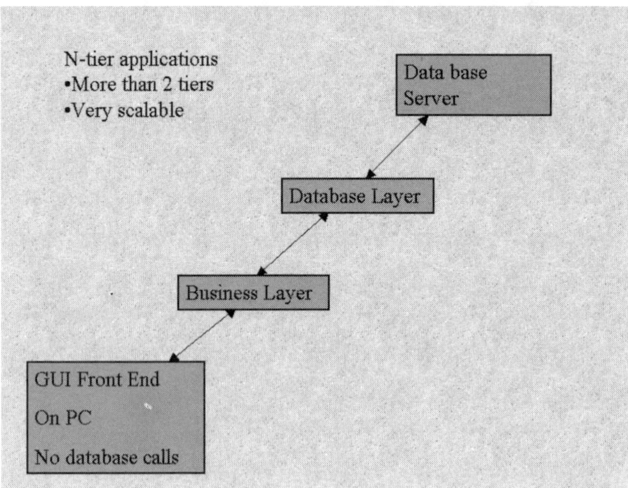

N-tiered architectures lend themselves to scalability and maintainability. If a particular portion of the system becomes a bottleneck for performance, then that layer can be redefined in multiple components and distributed to multiple servers or simply moved to a more powerful server. Either method can be completely transparent to the client applications. The location and distribution of the other layers is irrelevant to the client. Furthermore, the client's applications themselves need only handle the presentation of the interface to the user and the communication with the next tier. This means that you can create very lightweight clients.

This type of architecture has become quite popular since the advent of the Internet and corporate intranets. Using an *n*-tiered approach, you can develop an application that uses a web page as the client (recall Chapter 13 and Java Server Pages). If one of the middle layers, or even the database layer, is changed, the change is transparent to the clients. Whether the clients are web-based or traditional desktop applications, there is no need to alter the client in any way and thus no need to redistribute it.

Enterprise JavaBeans are particularly well suited to *n*-tiered architecture. They are most often used to create the business layer, but they can also create the database layer. In fact, they are appropriate for any tier other than the actual user interface. The entire purpose of EJB is to provide you with the middle layer in a multi-tiered architecture.

You may wonder how these various architectures communicate. Essentially, regardless of the specific distributed architecture, they must find some way to gather the methods they wish to expose, expose those methods, and then allow the client application to interact with the methods. The process of a client gathering information and sending it to the parameters of a remote method is called *marshalling*. Using any procedure that exists in another component is referred to as a Remote Procedure Call, or RPC.

There are various ways to allow a client to be aware of a remote component's methods and the method signature. In this book, you have already seen how Enterprise JavaBeans uses remote interfaces and home interfaces to accomplish this goal. Many distributed component architectures, including CORBA, COM, and DCOM, utilize a specialized language to define the public interface. This is usually referred to as an Interface Definition Language (IDL). Interface Definition Language is code that describes the exposed methods. It is independent of the implementation code used in the component. This figure should give you a graphical overview of how this is done:

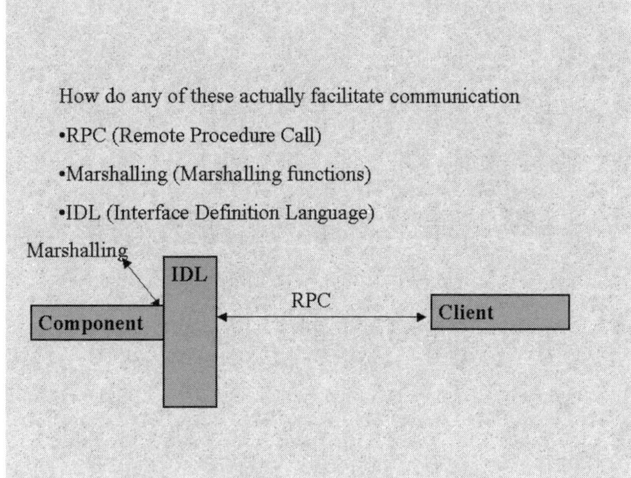

This section should provide you with a basic overview of how distributed computing developed and what the different distributed architectures are. The rest of this chapter will deal with introducing you to three things. The first is the use of design tools within Java, specifically using UML. The second thing is how to use other component technologies and code with Java. Finally, I will provide you with a brief introduction to some non-EJB component technologies, namely COM and DCOM. Chapter 15 will give you an introduction to CORBA.

Java and UML

UML, or Unified Modeling Language, has quickly become the preeminent method for designing object-oriented programming. This particular tool is now the de facto industry standard for software design.

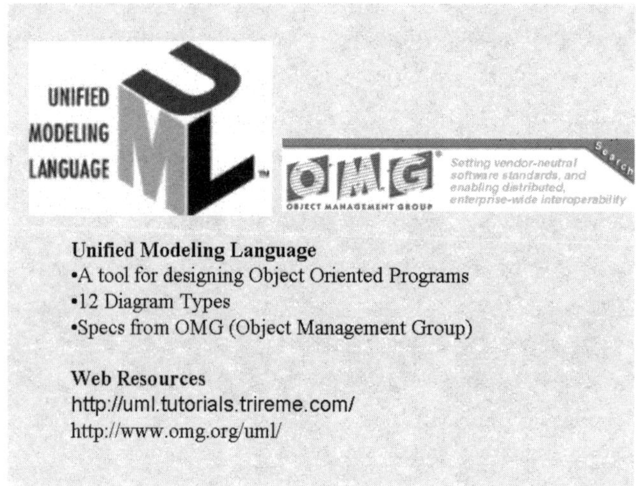

Clearly, there are several different approaches to designing distributed systems. Virtually all of them depend on object-oriented programming. Distributed programs are also somewhat complex. This means that it is imperative that you spend some time in planning and design prior to writing the actual code. In fact, you would be well advised to spend some time planning before you write any code.

As I previously mentioned, the foremost object-oriented design methodology available today is Unified Modeling Language. UML is a standard notation for modeling object-oriented systems. It is essentially a design tool that graphically describes a set of elements. UML is not a programming language; it is a design language. You can use UML to design any object-oriented program, regardless of what programming language the application is written in. Since UML is for object-oriented programming, its importance to Java cannot be overestimated. Unlike other programming languages such as C++, Java is purely object oriented. As you already know, it is simply not possible to write Java programs without using object orientation. For this reason alone, the study of UML is important to any Java programmer. However, it is even more important that we utilize an effective design language such as UML when dealing with complex distributed architectures such as EJB or CORBA (you will see more about this in Chapter 15).

UML is essentially a blueprint for object-oriented programs. UML provides a graphical representation of a system design. Having a standardized method for representing the portions of a system can be essential for communication among team members. The Unified Modeling Language standard defines 12 different diagrams that can be used to model different aspects of any given software system. Each of these diagrams has a different purpose. The following table summarizes the various diagram types.

Type	Diagram
Structural	Class
	Object
	Component
	Deployment
Behavior	Use-Case
	Sequence
	Activity
	Collaboration
	State Chart
Model Management	Packages
	Subsystems
	Models

As you can see, there are several different diagram types, each with its own purpose. These 12 diagrams can be grouped into three different categories based on their functionality. One does not need to employ all 12 diagrams on every project. However, some diagram types are more commonly used then others. I would like to take a moment to review the most commonly used UML diagrams.

The class diagram is a ubiquitous diagram. Virtually any software designed with UML will include a class diagram. Given that UML is a tool for designing object-oriented programs, it makes sense that class diagrams would show up in almost every UML project. These diagrams define the framework of the code for a class. The class diagram is divided into sections, each defining a portion of the class. The following image shows the parts of a class diagram:

Class Diagram

Class Name
Member Variables
Member functions

+ denotes public

-denotes private

-# denotes protected

———◆ Connects classes

The next type of diagram that is seen very frequently in UML projects is the use-case diagram. The purpose of this diagram is to provide a general overview of the actors who might interact with a system and how they would interact. An actor might be a human user of the system or another system that works with this system (either by inputting data or by consuming data). Actors are essentially any entity that might interact with the system. The following image shows a use-case diagram:

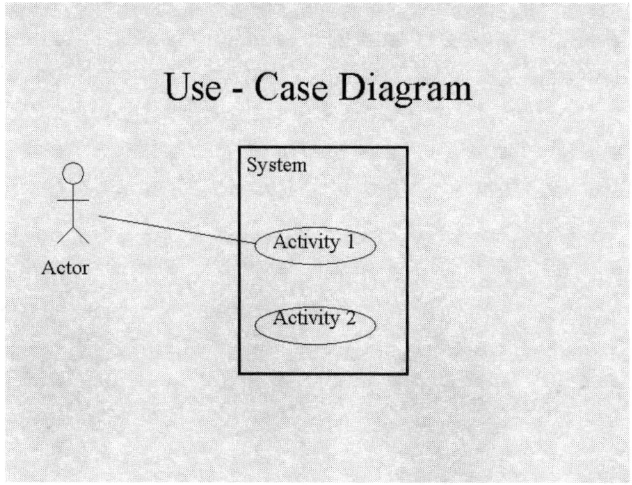

Another diagram that is also used quite often, though not quite as commonly as the preceding two, is the sequence diagram. As the name suggests, the sequence diagram is used to describe the sequence of events that occur during the execution of the program. Each event that can occur may in turn trigger another event. This sequence is graphically illustrated in the sequence diagram. Take a look at this example:

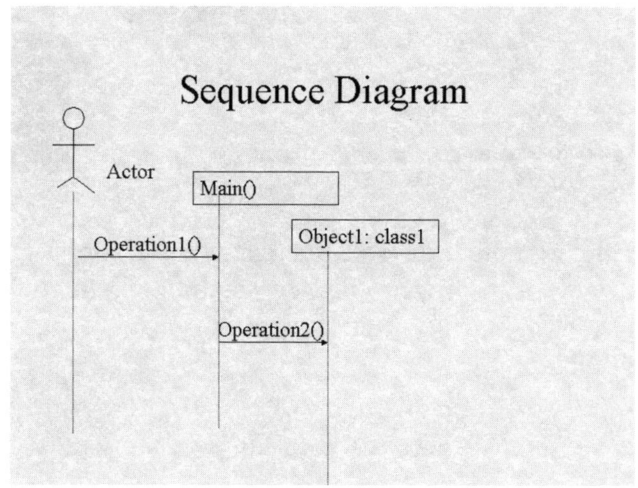

Some other widely used diagrams include the component diagram, which shows the objects created from classes, and the deployment diagram, which graphically illustrates the actual deployment of those objects. The state chart diagram graphically demonstrates changes in the system's state. Since changes in state are related to actions, the state chart diagram and the sequence diagram are closely related.

Each diagram in UML has a specific purpose. Some diagrams, such as the use-case diagram, provide an overreaching, strategic view of the general flow of the program. Other diagrams, such as the class diagram, illustrate the framework of the specific code that will be written to implement the system.

UML is designed to describe a wide range of different scenarios. For that reason, it uses broad terms to describe different relationships. UML specifications have to be general enough to be applicable to a range of programming situations.

Clearly, a complete examination of Unified Modeling Language is not possible in the space of a single chapter. Moreover, such an undertaking is beyond the scope of this book. I would hope that this section gives you enough information about UML to establish a basis for you to continue studying the topic. Consult Appendix A, where you will find a number of other resources on this topic and others.

JBuilder and UML

JBuilder provides a number of tools that can be used for designing projects with UML. If you look in your drop-down menu under Tools and IDE Options, you have the ability to set some of the visual parameters for using UML within JBuilder.

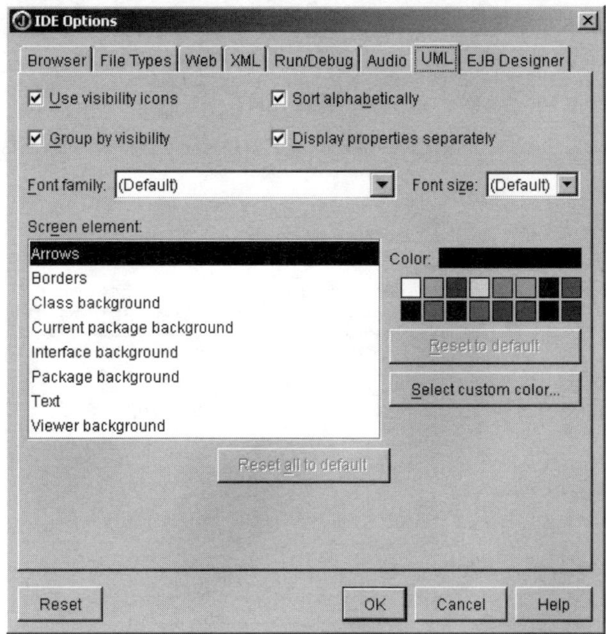

More recent versions of JBuilder (such as 6.0 and 7.0) have a tool called the UML Browser. When you look at any project, you will see a tab at the bottom with the caption "UML." That tab will have class diagrams for your classes done automatically for you. For example, if you go back to the first example in Chapter 11, you see the UML tab.

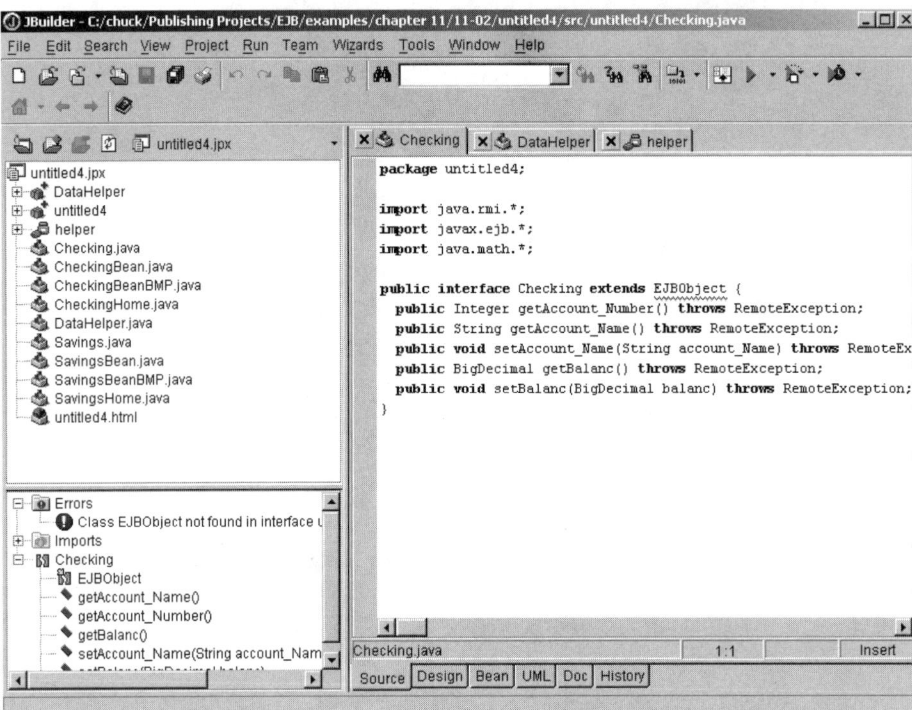

If you select that tab, you will see a class diagram already done for your class.

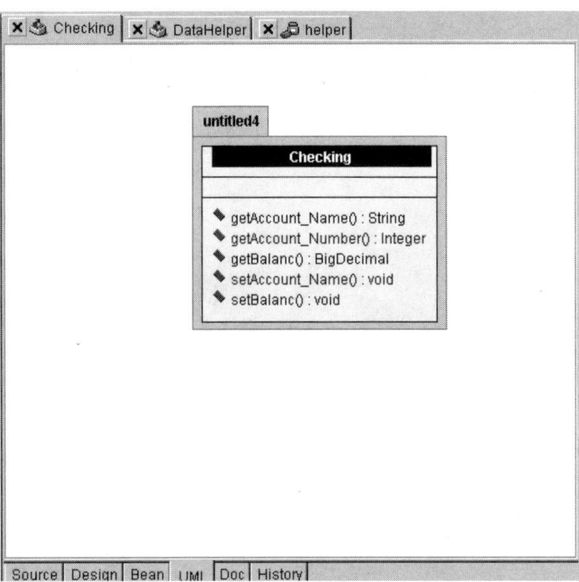

Of course, you should create the UML diagrams and then write the code. However, seeing class diagrams created for you from your classes can be a wonderful way for you to learn about UML diagrams. If you choose to view the UML diagram for a class that has external dependencies, JBuilder will even give you diagrams showing those dependencies.

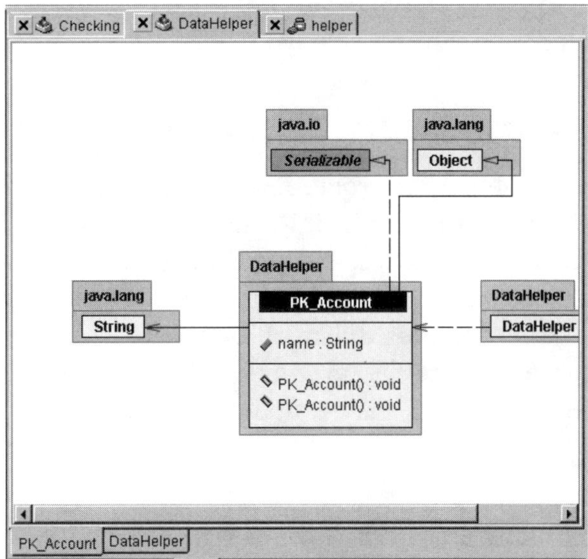

JBuilder's UML Browser provides various features for customizing the diagram display; navigating diagrams and source code; viewing inner classes, source code, and Javadoc; creating and printing images; and refactoring.

Customizing UML Diagrams

Although you can't manipulate the UML diagrams, such as moving or resizing elements, you can customize the UML display in the Project Properties and the IDE Options dialog boxes. For example, you can filter what is displayed in a given diagram on a project basis, as well as include references from project libraries. You can also globally customize the display of your UML diagram by setting the sort order, font, colors, and various other options.

Setting Project Properties

There are several project properties you can set for your UML diagrams in the Project Properties dialog box. Filtering is available on the UML page. Library references are available on the General page. To open the Project Properties dialog box, choose Project ▸ Project Properties or right-click the project file in the project pane and choose Properties.

Filtering Packages and Classes

On the UML page of the Project Properties dialog box, you can exclude packages and classes from your project's UML diagrams, as well as include references from generated sources. Choose the Add button to add any classes or packages to the exclusion list. Any classes or packages in the list are then excluded from the UML diagram. If you choose the Diagram References From Generated Source option, generated source references, such as IIOP files and EJB stubs, are displayed in the UML diagram.

Java Native Interface (JNI)

While many programmers find Java to be their language of choice, not all components you encounter are written in Java. In fact, COM and DCOM components written in a language such as C++ are quite common. There are a number of toolkits available to simplify various programming tasks that are distributed as COM components. This brings us to the issue of how we can get Java to communicate with COM. The answer lies in the Java Native Interface, or JNI. Via this interface, a Java programmer can access COM and DCOM components.

COM components take on increased importance within certain operating systems. For example, the proliferation of COM components for Windows platforms is astounding. Even though Java code is designed to run on multiple platforms, there are certain situations where that might not be adequate. The standard Java class library simply does not support platform-dependent features needed by your application. For this reason, you may wish to access some existing library written in another language. This would give your Java code access to the functionality of this component.

Another situation involving being able to work with code in other languages would be when you need to access low-level routines. Such routines are often written in a language such as assembly, or perhaps C. The Java Native Interface is a standard cross-platform programming interface included in the JDK. This interface allows you to write Java programs that can interact with applications and libraries written in other programming languages, such as C++ or assembly. By utilizing the JNI, you are able to write Java native methods to create, inspect, and update Java objects, call Java methods, catch and throw exceptions, load classes and obtain class information, and perform run-time type checking. By native method, I mean a method written in another language. In other words, it is "native" to that programming language. In addition, you can use the Invocation API to embed the Java Virtual Machine into your native applications, and then use the JNI interface pointer to access JVM features.

How Does JNI Work?

You are probably thinking that all this sounds intriguing, but how does it actually work? The way native methods are accessed from Java applications changed with the advent of the JDK 1.1. The previous methodology permitted a Java class to directly access methods in a native library. With the new method, the JNI acts as an intermediate layer between the Java class and the native library. Instead of having the JVM make direct calls to native methods, the JVM uses a pointer to the JNI to make the actual calls. This method even allows for the use of different Java Virtual Machines. Even if the JVM implementations are different, the layer they use to access the native methods (the JNI) will be consistent.

Fortunately for you, it's not really that difficult to incorporate JNI into your Java application. Using the keyword "native," making Java methods native is very easy. Here is a summary of the steps that need to be taken:

1. Delete the body of the method.

2. Add a semicolon at the end of the method's signature.

3. Add the native keyword at the beginning of the method's signature.

4. Include the method's body in a native library to be loaded at run time.

Of course, an example would be helpful. Assume the following method exists in a Java class.

```
public void nativeMethod ()
{
    //the method's body
  }
```

This is how the method becomes native:

```
public native void nativeMethod ();
```

Once you have declared the method to be native, its actual implementation will be included in a native library. Yes, it is really that simple. The most important thing to remember is the use of the keyword "native." This identified the method as a native method. It is the responsibility of the class to which this method belongs to invoke the library so its implementation becomes globally available. The easiest way to have the class invoke the library is to add the following to the class:

```
static
{
  System.loadLibrary (nameOfLibrary);
}
```

Note the way in which the keyword "static" is used here. You may have never seen it used in this manner before. The reason it is used is that a static code block is always executed when the class is first loaded. You can include almost anything you wish in a static code block. However, loading libraries is the most common use for it.

It is possible, however, that the library does not load properly. If, for any reason, the library fails to load, an UnsatisfiedLineError exception will be thrown once a method from that library is called. The JVM will add the correct extension to its name (.dll in Windows and .so in Unix). This means that you don't have to specify it in the library name.

The Java Development Kit even includes a method for allowing a programmer to produce C header files for Java classes. The JDK supplies a tool called javah, which is used to generate C header files for Java classes. The following is the general syntax for using javah:

```
javah [options] className
```

className represents the name of the class (without the .class extension) for which you want to generate a C header file. You can specify more than one class at the command line. For each class, javah adds a .h file to the class's directory by default. To put the .h files in a different directory, use the -o option. If a class is in a package, you must specify the package along with the class name. For example, to generate a header file for the class myClass in the package myPackage, do the following:

```
javah myPackage.myClass
```

The generated header file will include the package name (myPackage_myClass.h). Below is a list of some of the javah options:

Option	Description
-jni	Creates a JNI header file
-verbose	Displays progress information
-version	Displays the version of javah
-o directoryName	Outputs the .h file in specified directory
-classpath path	Overrides the default class path

The contents of the .h file generated by javah include all the function prototypes for the native methods in the class. The prototypes are modified to allow the Java run-time system to find and invoke the native methods. This modification basically involves changing the name of the method according to a naming convention established for native method invocation. The modified name includes the prefix Java_ to the class and method names. So, if you have a native method called nativeMethod in a class called myClass, the name that appears in the myClass.h file is Java_myClass_nativeMethod.

COM and DCOM

This book's primary concern is to show you how to utilize JavaBeans and Enterprise JavaBeans. Java is a powerful programming tool and EJB is a very good tool for distributed component architectures. However, Java does not exist in a vacuum. You will encounter other distributed architectures. It is even possible that via the Java Native Interface, you may interact with such component architectures within your Java code.

Aside from JavaBeans, the most commonly used component architectures are CORBA, COM, and DCOM. CORBA is quite popular with Java programmers, and therefore, an entire chapter (Chapter 15) is devoted to that topic. COM and DCOM are primarily Microsoft technologies that are popular with Visual Basic and Visual C++ programmers. However, as you have just seen, you can access code written in other languages using the Java Native Interface. This means it is entirely possible to access COM code written in Visual C++ from within a Java program using JNI. Given the proliferation of COM components and the heterogeneous nature of most programming teams, encountering such a situation is not only possible but very probable.

COM stands for Component Object Model. It is a method whereby a component can expose some of its methods to the outside world. Then other components/applications can access those methods. In the Microsoft Windows operating system, the use of COM-based components, via ActiveX, is commonplace. ActiveX is simply an easy-to-use implementation of COM. ActiveX is completely dependent upon classes. In order to expose a method, the method must be a member of a class, and that class must be declared in such a way as to make it potentially accessible to external code.

In many ways, COM works much like CORBA. When an application is written, certain methods are exposed. They are exposed by using an Interface Definition Language (IDL) that defines what methods are to be exposed and what those methods' signatures are to be. The Interface Definition Language is independent of the implementation language. This means that writing your component in C++, Visual Basic, or Delphi makes no difference. The Interface Definition Language is the same for any component written to COM specifications. This is why the application component is not concerned about what programming language a given COM component was written in.

The following image should provide you with a graphical illustration of how COM components are structured:

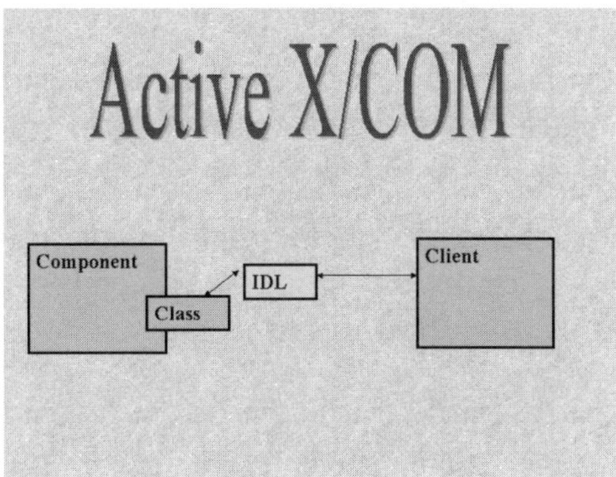

Distributed Component Object Model, or DCOM, is simply an implementation of COM that is remotely accessible. The COM component might be located on a different machine on the local area network or in a different city over the Internet. DCOM allows COM to become truly distributed, even to the extent of using the Internet as the communication medium for the components in question. Together, COM and DCOM are the cornerstones of Microsoft's component strategy. I do realize that some Java programmers are somewhat uncomfortable utilizing Microsoft technologies; however, the fact remains that you <u>will</u> encounter them. If you are armed with a basic understanding of how COM and DCOM work and a working knowledge of the Java Native Interface, you will be able to utilize those components in your Java environment. Interestingly enough, while Java provides a relatively pain-free method for accessing COM and DCOM, as of publication the reverse is not true. Microsoft has not yet provided a method for accessing Java components from within Microsoft development tools. This fact simply confirms that Java is a very powerful <u>and</u> flexible development tool.

Summary

This chapter was designed to give you a solid understanding of distributed computing from the perspective of a Java programmer. I introduced you to the general concepts of distributed programming. You were also shown the specifics of using the Java Native Interface to access COM components. Unified Modeling Language was introduced to you as well.

You were also shown how to use the rich array of tools provided by JBuilder to facilitate your distributed computing. JBuilder can be helpful in creating JNI applications, as well as using UML design.

Terms

UML – Unified Modeling Language. UML is a tool for designing object-oriented programs.

JNI – Java Native Interface. This is an interface for accessing code written in other programming languages.

ActiveX – An easy-to-use implementation of COM.

Static Block – A block of code declared as static. It will execute as soon as the class loads.

Review Questions

1. What are the three categories of UML diagrams?

2. Which UML diagram is used to show the basic code for classes?

3. What diagram shows the various entities/actors that might operate on a system?

4. What keyword is used to denote a method that is written for another language's library?

5. In what type of code block are native libraries usually loaded?

6. How many UML diagrams are there?

7. UML standards are defined by __________.

8. What does the # symbol in a class diagram indicate?

9. What is always executed when the class is first loaded?

10. What exception will be thrown if the library fails to load?

Chapter 15

CORBA and EJB

Introduction

Throughout this book, I have focused on the use of Enterprise JavaBeans as a distributed architecture for Java. Considering the title of this tome, that seemed like a logical approach for me to take. However, EJB is not the only mechanism for supporting distributed architectures. Another architecture that is quite popular is CORBA.

CORBA, or Component Object Request Broker Architecture, is a widely used technology that works with multiple languages. Since CORBA is so widely used and does operate with Java and Enterprise JavaBeans, I feel that some coverage of the topic is in order. This chapter will not make you an expert in CORBA; however, it should give you a basic working knowledge of the topic. There are a number of books describing, in quite some detail, the use of CORBA with Java, C++, and other languages. If you are looking for in-depth coverage of CORBA, you should look at the resources I have listed in Appendix A. However, this chapter should be enough to give you a basic knowledge of the topic.

Enterprise JavaBeans are a more recent technology than CORBA and in many ways a much more flexible and versatile technology. Some developers would even say that Enterprise JavaBeans are a replacement for CORBA and that eventually CORBA will be completely supplanted by EJBs. However, the rumors of the death of CORBA have been drastically exaggerated. A more common feeling among experienced developers is that while EJBs will supplant CORBA in many ways, you are more likely to see both the technologies continue to be utilized. Using JBuilder, you can even mix the two technologies (as you will see later in this chapter). So not only is CORBA not supplanted by EJB, but the two can, and frequently do, work in conjunction.

Chapter 14 provided you with an overview of distributed computing with Java and JBuilder. That information should have given you enough of a baseline knowledge to move forward into the subject matter of this chapter. This chapter will give you an introduction to CORBA with Java and JBuilder. It is important that you realize that CORBA can be used separately from Enterprise JavaBeans or in conjunction with them. The ability of EJB and CORBA to work together is another very good reason to study CORBA in a book about Enterprise JavaBeans. The purpose of this chapter is not to make you a CORBA guru. An entire book would not be able to accomplish such an ambitious goal. However, CORBA is used widely enough in distributed Java applications that it is important that you have at least a basic conceptual understanding of the technology.

CORBA Basics

The first step in our journey is to make certain that you have a firm knowledge of the basics of CORBA. The CORBA standards are set by the Object Management Group (OMG). This organization is a vendor — independent group that collaborates on the standards for a variety of object-oriented technologies including CORBA and UML (Unified Modeling Language). This chapter will cover the basic standards and functions for CORBA. If you wish to get more information on this organization, you should start at their web site (www.omg.org). Given the OMG's prominence in the software development community in general, object-oriented programming in particular, it would probably be advisable for you to spend some time at least familiarizing yourself with the organization.

Let us begin with the acronym "CORBA." It stands for Component Object Request Broker Architecture. You can get a basic understanding of what CORBA is by considering what the words in this acronym mean. The term "component" simply refers to software components. Objects are software objects made from classes. CORBA applications are composed of objects. These objects are basically individual units of software that combine functionality and data. These objects are created from classes, just like all the objects you have dealt with in Java. There can be multiple instances of an object of a single type. The word "request" should indicate to you that certain objects request the services of other objects. Next, consider the term "broker." This term indicates that CORBA's purpose is to broker these requests for objects. Finally, we come to the word "Architecture," which refers to a design methodology. So what we come to is a definition for CORBA: A distributed architecture that manages requests for resources in remote objects.

One of CORBA's strong points is that it is a technology that is not language dependent. You can utilize CORBA in conjunction with most modern, commercially available programming languages. However, it seems to have gained most of its popularity among Java and C++ developers. When you use CORBA, the actual language that the object was written in is irrelevant. As long as the object conforms to the CORBA standards, it will be accessible to any other object using CORBA. This means that each object may even be written in a different programming language. Thus, you can even create objects in C++ and use CORBA to access them from Java, and vice versa.

Interface Definition Language

An interface definition language, or IDL, is a language that handles the exposed interface. Since this interface definition language is the same for all CORBA objects, the language the object is written in does not matter. It is the IDL that allows interlanguage interoperability. The concept of using an interface definition language is common to many distributed architectures. Component Object Model (COM) and Distributed Component Object Model (DCOM) also use interface definition languages to create interfaces for components. The concept of an IDL is really fairly simple. It is a very basic, pseudo programming language that conforms to the specifications of a particular distributed programming architecture. Interfaces are written in the interface definition language rather than in a specific programming language. This makes the components that use that particular IDL programming language neutral. They are not concerned with which programming language that the component is written in; they are only concerned with the format of the interface definition language.

In CORBA, the IDL is used to create the interface for the remote object you wish to use. For each object type, you define an interface in IDL. The interface is the part of the contract that the server object offers to the clients that invoke it. Any client that wants to invoke an operation on the object must use this IDL interface to specify the operation it wants to perform and to marshal the arguments that it sends. Recall from Chapter 6 that marshalling is the process of gathering together arguments to send to a remote object. When the method invocation reaches the remote object, the same interface definition is used there to unmarshal the arguments. This allows those arguments to be passed to the method in question, just as if that method had been invoked locally. All this is effected so that the object can perform the requested operation with these arguments and return the appropriate value, if the method returns a value. The interface definition is then used to marshal the results in order to send the return value back to the client and to unmarshal it when it reaches the client.

The IDL interface definition is independent of the programming language used to create the object but maps to many of the popular programming languages via standards established by the Object Management Group (OMG). The OMG has standardized mappings from IDL to C, C++, Java, Lisp, Python, and several other popular programming languages. This means that you have a number of choices when it comes to deciding what particular language you wish to use to create your CORBA objects.

This essentially means that the object and the interface used to access the object are separate entities, each with its own specifications. This separation of interface from implementation, enabled by the IDL, is the real essence of CORBA. Separating the implementation code from the interface code enables interoperability. The interface for each object is defined very strictly according to very specific guidelines. However, the actual implementation code can be done in any manner that the programmer feels is appropriate. Since the actual implementation code is separate from the interface, this means that the implementation code is really irrelevant from the point of view of the interface. Clients access objects only through their advertised interface. The client can only invoke the specific operations that the object exposes through its IDL interface, with only those parameters that are included in the invocation.

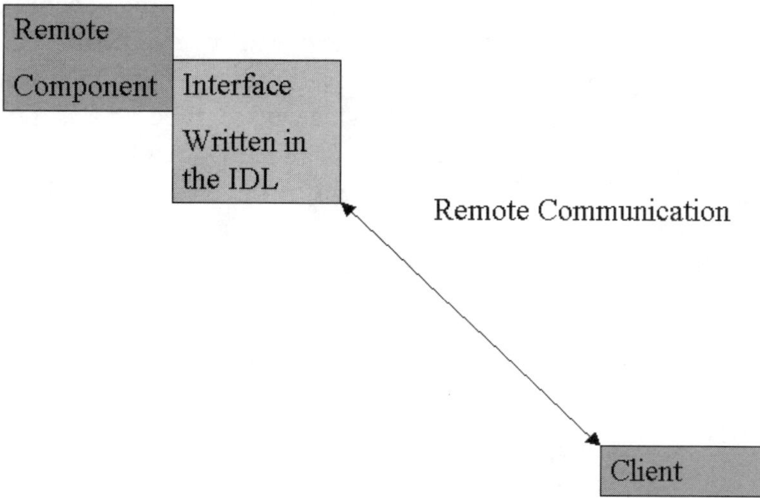

The Specifics of IDL Implementation

Now that I have explained to you the purpose of the interface definition language, you may be curious as to how this is accomplished. In this section, I will endeavor to explain this to you. The primary coding technique used to facilitate IDL is the use of stubs. *Stubs* are code modules that have the method declarations but no body. You compile your IDL into client stubs and object skeletons. These stubs serve as proxies for clients and servers, respectively. Because IDL defines interfaces so strictly, the stub on the client side has no trouble meshing perfectly with the skeleton on the server side, even if the two are compiled into different programming languages. By using stubs, the client will actually have the framework of the server object. It will have access to the signatures of the methods, the parameters required, and the data types returned. This gives the client a rather complete picture of the server object.

Recall that an object is created from a class. This means that even though two or more objects may be created from the same class, they are distinct objects. There must be some method for keeping the identities of these objects straight. This is accomplished via object references. In CORBA, every object instance has its own unique object reference. Clients use the object references to direct their invocations, identifying the specific object instance they wish to invoke to the Object Request Broker (ORB). The client acts as if it's invoking an operation on the object instance, but it's actually invoking a method located on the IDL stub. This stub method acts as a proxy for the real method in the object instance. The method call is passed through the stub on the client side. It is then sent through the Object Request Broker and the skeleton on the implementation side. Finally, the method call arrives at the object where it is executed. The following figure illustrates this process:

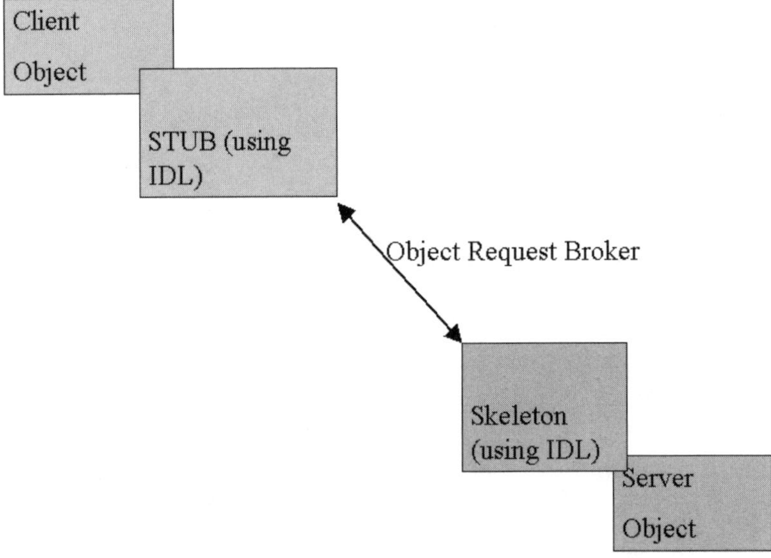

The preceding image gives you a rough overview of how CORBA communication takes place. There are several details that need to be discussed in order to give you a complete picture of CORBA. In order to make the remote invocation, the client uses the same code that it used in the local invocation previously described. However, in this call, it substitutes the object reference for the actual remote instance. The one detail that has been conspicuously absent from this discussion is how the call is routed to the actual remote object. This is where the Object Request Broker comes in. As its name suggests, it brokers requests for objects. When the Object Request Broker examines the object reference, it will realize that the target object is remote. The ORB then routes the invocation to the appropriate remote object's ORB.

The Interface Definition Language standardization allows the client to know all the pertinent information about a remote object. Due to the standardized IDL, the client knows the type of object it's invoking. This is due to the fact that the client stub and object skeleton are generated from the same IDL. That means that the client knows exactly which operations it may invoke, what the parameters are, and what data type is likely to be returned by the method. The second issue regards the methodology of the data transmission between the client's ORB and the server object's ORB. They both must agree on a common protocol. As you might have guessed, the Object Management Group has defined this standard as well. The protocol used is the standard protocol IIOP. It is certainly possible that individual ORBs may use other protocols besides IIOP, but virtually all speak the standard protocol IIOP for reasons of interoperability. It is also required in order to comply with the OMG CORBA standards.

Obviously, the client does not know if the object it is calling is remote or not. The Object Request Broker, however, does know. There is nothing in the object reference token that the client holds and uses at invocation time that identifies the location of the target object. The stub in the IDL does not identify the location of the object that is being invoked. This ensures location transparency. Not only does the client not know where the object is, it does not need to know.

The Object Request Broker

Since CORBA depends on the use of Object Request Brokers (ORBs), it seems prudent to take some time to examine these request brokers and see how they function. CORBA specifies a system that provides interoperability between objects in a heterogeneous, distributed environment that is in a way transparent to the programmer. That may seem like an overly technical definition to you, and I would tend to agree.

Let me explain this in more easily accessible terms. The CORBA system is designed to operate in an environment that is spread across several machines (thus the term "distributed"). This environment may include components written in different languages (thus the term "heterogeneous"). The location of these objects and the underlying communication strategy should not be a concern for the programmer (this is the "transparent" part). Neither CORBA nor any software development process is created in a vacuum. Each new technology is based on other technologies. The CORBA design is no exception; it is based on the OMG Object Model.

The OMG Object Model

The Object Management Group defines an object model used for all object-oriented architectures. The OMG Object Model defines common object semantics for specifying the externally visible characteristics of objects. This method standard is independent of the specific implementation. In the framework of this model, clients request services from server objects through a well-defined interface. The interface is specified in the OMG IDL (Interface Definition Language). Thus, the IDL is essentially the key to the object model in CORBA. A client accesses an object by sending a request to the object. The request is first sent to a proxy stub, and then the Object Request Broker sends it on to the actual remote object. The object reference is an object name that defines an object reliably.

The foundation of CORBA is the Object Request Broker (ORB). It is via the ORB that communication is taken from a proxy stub and sent to an appropriate server object. The ORB encompasses all of the communication infrastructure necessary to identify and locate objects and handle communications. Different vendors can create their own Object Request Brokers, as long as they conform to certain key specifications set forth by the ORB. The ORB core is the most crucial part of the Object Request Broker; it is responsible for communication of requests.

The basic functionality provided by the ORB consists of passing the requests from clients to the appropriate server objects. In order to make a request, the client can communicate with the ORB core through the IDL stub. The stub represents the mapping between the language of implementation of the client and the ORB core. This means that the client can be written in any programming language, as long as the implementation of the ORB supports this mapping. Recall that language independence is a hallmark of CORBA. The ORB core transfers the request to the specific object implementation through an IDL skeleton on the server side.

The Underlying Mechanisms

This section will take you a little deeper into the underlying CORBA structure. First we will discuss how communication between the server object and its ORB work. The communication between the server object and the ORB core is accomplished by the Object Adaptor (OA). It handles a variety of services for the server object, including generation and interpretation of object references. The Object Adaptor is also responsible for method invocation, object and implementation activation and deactivation, mapping references corresponding to object implementations, and registration of implementations. A given ORB system will have multiple Object Adaptors, each handling a different function. It is expected that there will be many different special-purpose object adapters to fulfill the needs of specific objects.

Another issue to address is how object implementation activation is handled. As with everything else in CORBA, the Object Management Group has a set of specifications for this. The OMG specifies four policies in which the OA may handle object implementation activation. The first policy is Shared Server Policy, in which multiple objects may be implemented in the same program. Of course, this implies another policy called Unshared Server Policy, in which multiple objects cannot be implemented in the same program. The third policy is the Server-per-Method Policy. In this policy, a new server is started each time a request is received. The fourth policy is the Persistent Server Policy. In the Persistent Server Policy, the object's implementation is supposed to be constantly active. The following table lists these policies and summarizes their functionality:

Policy	Function
Shared Server	Using this policy, a single ORB can be used for multiple method invocations.
Unshared Server	This policy does not allow a single ORB to be used by different method invocations.
Server-per-Method	With this policy, each time a method is invoked, a separate ORB is instantiated to handle that object.
Persistent Server	Using this policy, an ORB is persistent; it stays loaded into memory. It handles a single method invocation at a time, but when that method invocation is complete, the ORB is not removed from memory.

If a request is invoked under any other policy, the object will be activated by the OA in accordance with that policy's specification. In order to accomplish this task, the OA needs to have access to information about the object's location and operating environment. This information is stored in a special database called Implementation Repository. This repository is a standard component of the CORBA architecture. The information is obtained from there by the OA at the time the object is activated. The Implementation Repository may also contain other information pertaining to the implementation of servers, such as debugging and version and administrative information.

The interfaces to objects can be specified in two ways: either in OMG IDL or they can be added to Interface Repository, another component of the architecture. If the latter method is used, then a Dynamic Invocation Interface is utilized. The Dynamic Invocation Interface allows the client to specify requests to objects whose definition and interface are unknown at the time the client is compiled. In order to use DII, the client has to compose a request that includes the object reference, the method being invoked, and a list of parameters. These specifications are retrieved from the Interface Repository, a database which provides persistent storage of object interface definitions. The Interface Repository also contains information about types of parameters, certain debugging information, etc.

So while the use of Interface Definition Language for static client-side connections to objects via CORBA is more common, there is a dynamic method using the Dynamic Interface Language. As you might guess, there is a similar dynamic method available on the server side. The server-side component that is analogous to DII is the Dynamic Skeleton Interface (DSI). With the use of this interface, the operation is no longer accessed through an operation-specific skeleton generated from an IDL interface specification; instead it is reached through an interface that provides access to the operation name and parameters. Thus, DSI is a way to deliver requests from the ORB to an object implementation that does not have compile-time knowledge of the object it is implementing. Although it seems at first glance that this situation doesn't happen very often, in reality, DSI is an answer to interactive software development tools based on interpreters and debuggers. It can also be used to provide inter-ORB interoperability.

About the OMG

The past several pages have thrown about the term OMG quite a bit. Obviously, it is an organization concerned with standards for object-oriented programming. You may be interested in getting a bit more detail than that. The Object Management Group is a non-profit consortium created for the purpose of promoting theory and practice of object-oriented technology in distributed computing systems. The OMG was formed in 1989 and has become the single most influential force in object-oriented programming. It was originally formed by a consortium of 13 companies. Now OMG membership has grown to over 500 software vendors, developers, and users.

The OMG is a voluntary organization. It has no legal way of enforcing the standards it creates. However, standardization is in the interest of all software developers. When that fact is coupled with the major players in software development all being involved in the OMG, compliance becomes an almost automatic thing. Some of the companies involved in the OMG include Alcatel, Borland, Compaq, Hewlett-Packard, EDS, Oracle, Rational Rose, the Los Alamos National Laboratory, CISCO, and a host of other industry giants. With this array of industry heavy hitters involved in the OMG, the clout of the organization is clearly increased.

From a practical standpoint, OMG realizes its goals through creating standards that allow interoperability and portability of distributed object-oriented applications. The OMG does not produce software, development tools, or implementation guidelines. It only produces specifications, which are put together using the ideas of OMG members who respond to Requests for Information (RFI) and Requests for Proposals (RFP). The format for using RFIs and RFPs to gather input is akin to the Internet Engineering Task Force's (IETF) use of Requests for Comments (RFC). The advantage of this type of collaborative approach to developing standards derives from the fact that most of the major software companies interested in distributed object-oriented development are also OMG members.

The Object Management Architecture (OMA)

CORBA is one distributed software approach espoused by the OMG. The OMG does endorse a variety of distributed software architectures and object-oriented design approaches. There is an over-reaching, object-oriented architecture that provides a framework for CORBA to fit in. This architecture is the Object Management Architecture (OMA). OMA is a high-level vision of a complete distributed environment. Think of OMA as the strategic view and the actual CORBA specifications as the tactical view. OMA consists of four components. These four components can be put roughly into two subcategories: system-oriented components (Object Request Brokers and Object Services) and application-oriented components (Application Objects and Common Facilities).

Of these four parts, the Object Request Broker is the one that constitutes the foundation of OMA. The ORB manages all communication between its components. It allows objects to interact in a heterogeneous, distributed environment, independent of the platforms on which these objects reside and techniques used to implement them (recall earlier that I provided you with an explanation of this "definition"). In performing its task, it relies on Object Services, which are responsible for general object management such as creating objects, access control, keeping track of relocated objects, etc.

Common Facilities and Application Objects are the components closest to the end user, and in their functions, they invoke services of the system components.

Implementations of CORBA

Remember that the OMG does not create software or development tools. It creates standards. This implies that as long as the standards are adhered to, there can be a variety of specific implementations of that standard. This is exactly the case with CORBA. There are many implementations of CORBA currently available; they vary in the degree of CORBA compliance, quality of support, portability, and availability of additional features. Most implementations of CORBA come as part of commercial software packages such as JBuilder and, hence, cost money. Unfortunately, as of publication, there are no fully compliant public domain implementations; ILU from Xerox PARC is probably the closest you will get to a free implementation of CORBA right now.

There are, however, a variety of commercially available implementations of CORBA. Orbix from Iona is a very solid, fully compliant commercial implementation with excellent support. VisiBroker from Visigenic is also 2.0 compliant and offers interoperability with Java. ObjectBroker from Digital is 1.2 compliant. Other implementations include Expersoft's Xshell.

CORBA and JBuilder

As with all things I have shown you in Java, CORBA is a lot easier using JBuilder. In this section, I will show you the various tools JBuilder provides for creating CORBA applications. As you will see, JBuilder takes care of many of the details of implementing CORBA, allowing you to focus on the specific business problems you are trying to solve.

Before you can use the CORBA tools provided to you in JBuilder, you will need to go to Tools ▸ Enterprise Setup. You will be presented with a screen that allows you to configure the various enterprise options for JBuilder. You must use the drop-down box to select one of the CORBA configurations; I chose VisiBroker.

After you have set that option, you can then go to File ▸ New and choose the CORBA tab. You will see an array of choices you have for CORBA objects.

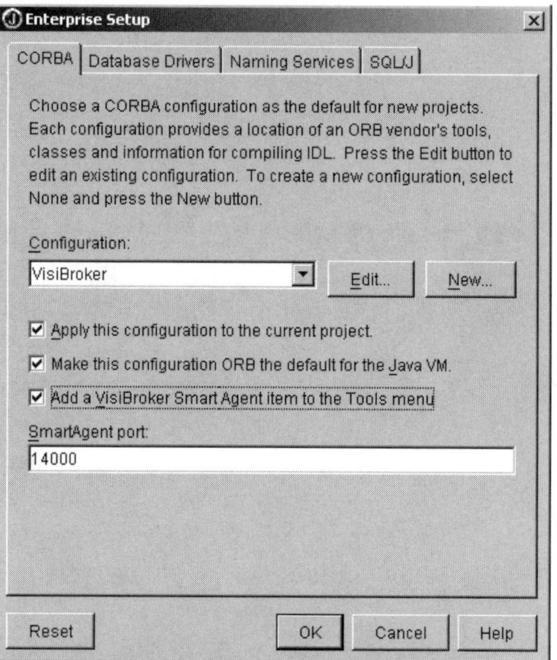

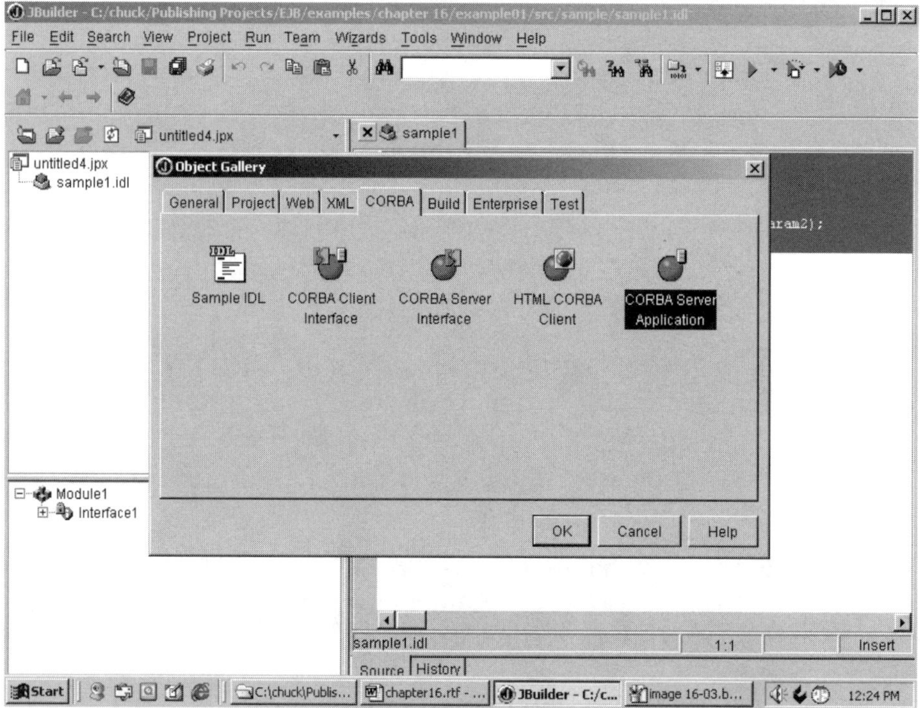

The first thing I will choose is a sample IDL. This will generate code for a sample IDL that you can review in order to get a better idea of how IDLs work. The code is really quite simple:

```
module Module1
{
  interface Interface1
  {
    string operation1(in long param1, in float param2);
  };
};
```

As you can see, the sample IDL is literally a "stub" for an actual method that would exist in a server object. The stub is created as an interface that can be implemented with any Java class.

After you examine that sample IDL, create a CORBA server and a CORBA client object using JBuilder. When you select File ▸ New, you can choose the CORBA tab and the server object.

This will take you to a screen that allows you to set the various configurations for your CORBA server object.

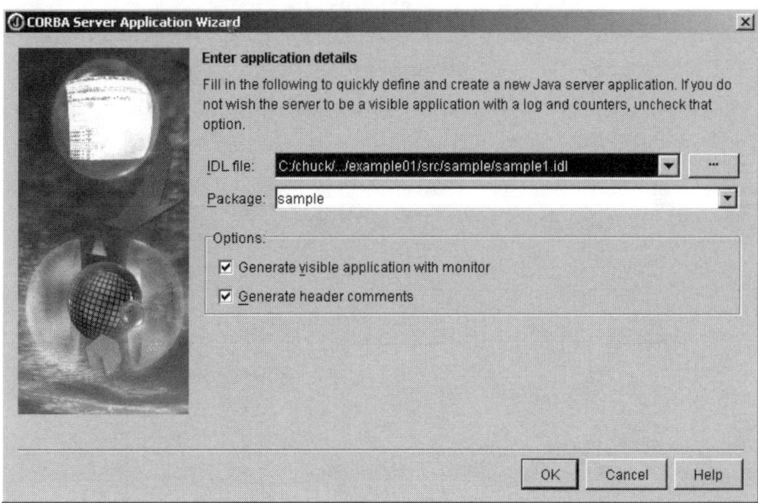

Let us take a moment to examine the source code that JBuilder produced for us and make sure you understand all the nuances of that code.

```java
package sample;
import sample.Module1.server.*;
import javax.swing.UIManager;
import java.awt.*;
import org.omg.PortableServer.*;
public class Module1ServerApp
{
  boolean packFrame = false;

  public Module1ServerApp()
{
    ServerFrame frame = new ServerFrame();

    if (packFrame)
      frame.pack();
    else
      frame.validate();
    Dimension screenSize = Toolkit.getDefaultToolkit().getScreenSize();
    Dimension frameSize = frame.getSize();
    if (frameSize.height > screenSize.height)
        frameSize.height = screenSize.height;
    if (frameSize.width > screenSize.width)
        frameSize.width = screenSize.width;
    frame.setLocation((screenSize.width - frameSize.width) / 2,
        (screenSize.height - frameSize.height) / 2);
    frame.setVisible(true);
  }
  public static void main(String[] args)
{
    try
    {
    UIManager.setLookAndFeel("com.sun.java.swing.plaf.
                            windows.WindowsLookAndFeel");
    }
    catch (Exception ex)
    {
    }
    new Module1ServerApp();
    try
    {
```

```java
      java.util.ResourceBundle res = java.util.ResourceBundle.getBundle
                            ("sample.Module1.server.ServerResources");
      String name;
      if (System.getProperties().get("vbroker.agent.port") == null)
      {
        System.getProperties().put("vbroker.agent.port", "14000");
        }
        if (System.getProperties().get("org.omg.CORBA.ORBClass") == null)
      {
        System.getProperties().put("org.omg.CORBA.ORBClass",
                               "com.inprise.vbroker.orb.ORB");
        }
        if (System.getProperties().get("org.omg.CORBA.ORBSingletonClass") ==
                                    null) {System.getProperties().put
                                    ("org.omg.CORBA.ORBSingletonClass",
                                      "com.inprise.vbroker.orb.ORB");
        }
        org.omg.CORBA.ORB orb = org.omg.CORBA.ORB.init(args, System.
                                                getProperties());
        POA poaRoot = POAHelper.narrow(orb.resolve_initial_references
                                ("RootPOA"));
        name = "Interface1";
        org.omg.CORBA.Policy[] Interface1Policies =
      {
          poaRoot.create_lifespan_policy(LifespanPolicyValue.PERSISTENT)
        };
        POA poaInterface1 = poaRoot.create_POA(name + "_poa",
                                        poaRoot.the_POAManager(),
                                        Interface1Policies);
        poaInterface1.activate_object_with_id(name.getBytes(), new
                                        Interface1Impl());
        ServerMonitor.log(ServerResources.format(res.getString("created"),
                        "Module1ServerApp.java Interface1"));
        poaRoot.the_POAManager().activate();
        ServerMonitor.log(ServerResources.format(res.getString("isReady"),
                        "Module1ServerApp.java Module1"));
        orb.run();
      }
    catch(Exception ex)
    {
```

```
        System.err.println(ex);
      }
    }
  }
```

I realize that there is a lot to digest in this code. It is not important that you examine every single line and have a total understanding of each line. It is only important that you peruse the code and get a feel for certain key portions of it.

The first thing to note is the import statements. Notice that this code imports org.omg.PortableServer. The org.omg package contains a number of classes that encapsulate functionality defined by OMG standards. As we go through the code, you will notice several classes from this package being used.

You probably noticed that this code simply produces some Swing-based GUI elements. Don't worry if you are unfamiliar with Swing. The details of Swing are unimportant for our purposes here. However, if I may make a completely brazen and shameless plug, I suggest that if you wish to learn more about Swing, consider my *JBuilder JFC and Swing Programming* book due out in the fall of 2002.

Most of the code at the beginning is relatively standard Java code, similar to what you have probably seen many times. However, when you get to the try block of the main function, you should notice several items that may not be familiar to you. The first item of note is the fact that there are multiple calls to the system.getProperties method. You should also notice that in this same section of code, there are multiple code segments that utilize classes found in the org.omg package. Thankfully, JBuilder includes code that you can import, which will give you the functionality of Object Request Brokers that you require.

You can also use JBuilder to create the interface for your CORBA server object.

```
package sample;
import org.omg.CORBA.*;
import org.omg.PortableServer.*;
public class Interface1ServerImpl1 extends sample.Module1.Interface1POA
  {
  String _name = "Interface1";
```

```
   public Interface1ServerImpl1(java.lang.String name)
   {

      this._name = name;
   }
   public Interface1ServerImpl1()
   {

   }
   public String operation1(int param1, float param2)
   {

      return "";
   }
}
```

I am certain you noticed that the server interface is far simpler than the server implementation code. This is to be expected. The interface is rather simple code. It simply provides a "rough draft" overview of the contents of the object in question.

You should notice that JBuilder takes care of most of the details of implementing CORBA, thereby allowing the programmer to focus on the actual business problem he or she is attempting to solve.

Using EJB with CORBA

There may be situations where you wish to use both of these distributed technologies within the same project. Fortunately for you, JBuilder makes this a relatively easy undertaking. In this section, I will walk you through the process of incorporating server-side CORBA into an Enterprise JavaBean. This means that the code in this bean can be accessed either in Java as an EJB or through other programming languages via CORBA.

As with all the examples for JBuilder, you should start by launching JBuilder and starting a new project. Make sure you create the project in a folder or directory that you will be able to find later.

Step 1:

Add an EJB to the project.

For the purposes of this example, I am going to use a stateless session bean, as depicted in this image:

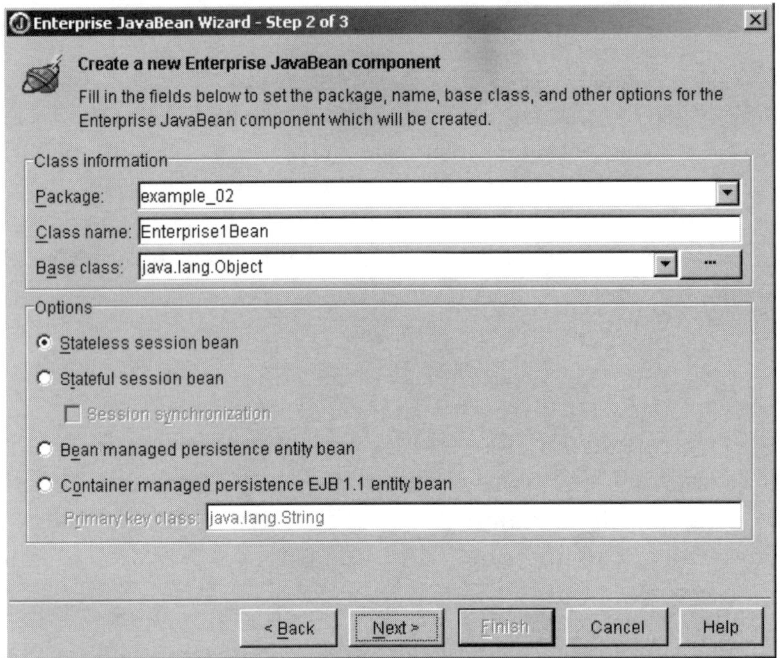

Step 2:

I am now going to add a single method. This method's only purpose is to demonstrate that our project can expose methods via both EJB and CORBA. For this reason, I will continue with the ubiquitous "Hello World" done Texas-style as "Howdy Y'all." With this in mind, I will add this bean's only business method:

```
public string howdy()
{
    return "Howdy Yall";
}
```

Step 3:

Add in a sample interface. This will be used to create your CORBA server interface in Step 4.

Step 4:

Now to add in the CORBA interface, you should be aware that we will be creating the server-side interface. We are creating a single application that acts as both an EJB and a CORBA server.

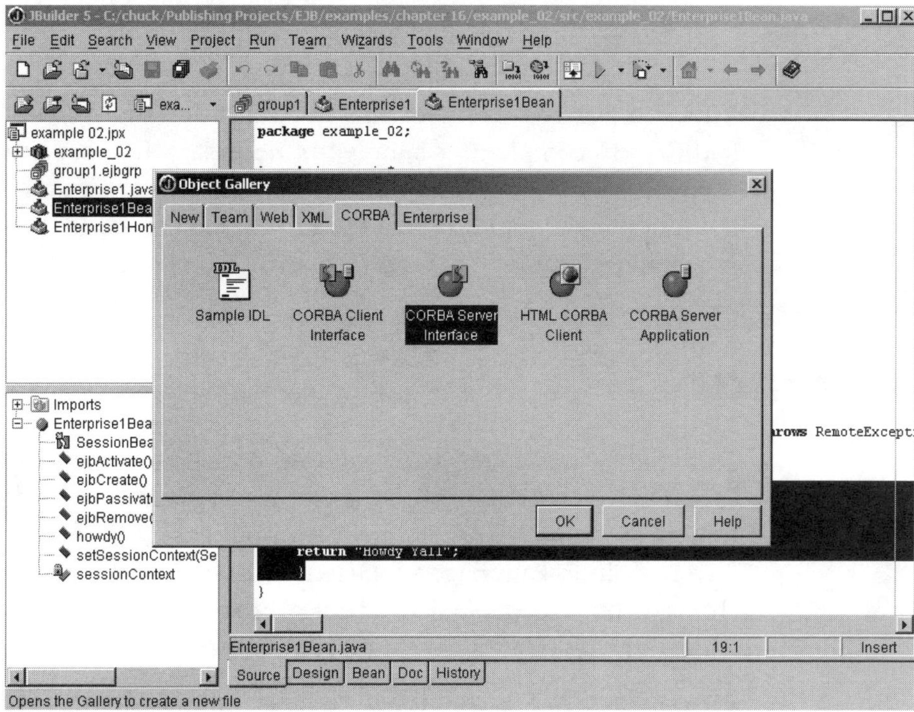

By default, the server interface that JBuilder creates for us has a single sample business method in it:

```java
public String operation1(int param1, float param2)
{
    return "";
}
```

Obviously, this method is not appropriate for our needs, so I will make a few changes. The first thing I will do is import the file that has the code for our Enterprise JavaBean in it.

```java
import example_02.Enterprise1Bean;
```

Now I will change the business method of the CORBA interface so that it calls this class's business method.

```
public String SayHowdy()
{
   Enterprise1Bean localbean = new Enterprise1Bean();
   return localbean.Howdy();
}
```

Now you may feel that creating an application that is both EJB compliant and CORBA compliant is simply not necessary. In most situations, you would probably be correct. However, you may encounter situations where you want the functionality of both architectures to expose a business method. As the preceding example illustrates, this is certainly possible.

Summary

This chapter has given you a solid introduction to the inner workings of CORBA. The majority of the chapter was concerned with making sure you understood the CORBA architecture. You were introduced to how the Interface Definition Language was used to create stubs and skeletons. I also showed you how the Object Request Broker allowed the code executed on stubs to be redirected to the appropriate server object.

Also covered in this chapter were newer, more dynamic methods of facilitating calls to methods in remote objects. These methods depended upon the Dynamic Interface Language and the Dynamic Skeleton Language. Both of these also depend on the repository on the server side to provide the requisite information to successfully make a connection.

Finally, the chapter showed you how to incorporate CORBA with JBuilder. Once again, we saw that CORBA, like most other programming tasks, is much easier using the rich set of tools provided to you by Borland's JBuilder. After studying this chapter, you should have a solid, basic understanding of CORBA, the architecture of CORBA, and how to implement it in Java using JBuilder.

Terms

ORB – Object Request Broker. This is the part of CORBA that makes communication with remote server objects possible.

CORBA – Component Object Request Broker Architecture

IDL – Interface Definition Language. This is the language used to define the interface for the client in a CORBA application.

Stub – This is a copy of the server component's code, but only defining the interfaces. It has no implementation code.

Skeleton – This is the server-side equivalent to the IDL.

Proxy – Code that is "standing in" for other code. The IDL works as a proxy for the server object.

DIL – Dynamic Interface Language. This is a client-side technology used when there is not enough information known about the server object when the client is compiled. It is a substitute for IDL.

DSI – Dynamic Skeleton Interface. This is the dynamic object that is analogous to the skeleton.

Review Questions

1. What part of the CORBA architecture is used on the client side to define the methods in the remote object?

2. What portion of the CORBA architecture is used to manage communication between the client and the remote object?

3. What is OMA?

4. What four policies does OMA define?

5. What protocol is used for communication in CORBA?

6. What is an Object Adaptor?

7. What object in CORBA is responsible for the actual remote method invocation?

8. What is the repository?

9. How many free CORBA implementations are currently available?

10. What allows interlanguage interoperability?

Chapter 16

Exception Handling with EJB

Introduction

In previous chapters of this book, I have shown you examples where exception handling is used. In each place that exception handling was used, either exceptions are caught or they are thrown. However, in these examples, the exception handling was only secondary to the Enterprise JavaBeans technique that was being shown. I have not yet taken the time to give you any thorough explanation of exception handling and how it relates specifically to Enterprise JavaBeans.

It is now time to give you some details about exception handling in Enterprise JavaBeans. Hopefully, this chapter will clear up questions you may have about when you should use certain exception handling strategies. Why are some exceptions trapped and others thrown? Why are certain exception classes used rather than others? It is my goal to answer these questions, and others, in this chapter. After reading this chapter, you should have a basic working knowledge of exception handling in general, and about EJB exception handling in particular.

Exceptions are simply a fact of software development. They can, and do, occur. Being able to handle them appropriately is a vital part of good software development. It is possible to simply mimic the exception handling you see in examples in books like this one. However, if you are going to effectively utilize exception handling, you will need to have at least a cursory knowledge of how and why it works; parroting someone else's exception handling is simply not sufficient. This is especially true in regard to handling exceptions in rather specialized situations, such as with Enterprise JavaBeans.

Basic Exception Handling

Undoubtedly, you have used exception handling in your previous Java coding experience. It is virtually impossible for you to have done any Java programming at all without having used some throws clauses and some try-catch blocks. In fact, some readers may have enough Java experience that they have written a great deal of exception handling code. However, if you are like many programmers, you have not thought much about the structure and mechanisms of exception handling. For this reason, before we dive too deeply into the rather narrow and specialized topic of exception handling in relation to Enterprise JavaBeans, it would be a good idea to review a broader topic that concerns the basics of exception handling in general.

The first question that needs to be answered is, what, precisely, is an exception? Many developers, surprisingly, get this simple question wrong. Often developers equate an exception with an error. An exception is not, contrary to common misconceptions, simply a synonym for an error. An error is essentially anything that goes wrong in a segment of code. An exception is a specific type of error. It is literally an exception to the normal execution of a program. An error is a general catchall term for any type of programming flaw at any level. An exception is a very specific type of error. It is an error that occurs at run time, and it represents an interruption to the normal or planned execution of your application.

As I stated, the term "error" is a rather broad, catchall phrase. However, errors can be divided into certain classifications, depending on the nature and cause of the error. There are essentially three types of programming errors. These error types are common to all software development and are not specific to any particular programming language. These three error categories are syntax error, logic error, and run-time error.

The first error category that I will address is that of *syntax errors*. A syntax error occurs when you attempt to use the programming language in a manner inconsistent with the compiler's standards. This can be something as simple as misspelling a keyword or perhaps not following the rules of a given language. Some common Java examples include forgetting to end a statement with a semicolon or forgetting the closing brace to a given code block. This type of error is the simplest to catch and the easiest to fix, since the compiler will not compile your program and will tell you that there is a syntax error. Many compilers will even let you click (or double-click) on the error message and will then take you directly to the line of code generating the error. Borland's JBuilder does this for you. The Sun Java Development Kit does not do this; however, its compiler error messages do include the line number where the error was generated. Syntax errors are generally only a stumbling block for beginning programmers. Developers with even moderate experience generally have very little trouble tracking down and correcting syntax errors.

The second type of error that I would like to address is the *logic error*. Unlike the syntax error, this error category is quite troublesome for programmers of all skill levels, from novice to expert. A logic error will not be immediately apparent. Even if your program contains a logic error, it will still compile and even execute without any immediate apparent problems. However, if the logic in part of your code is flawed, the data processing is not accurate. The logic error may be a major flaw in some critical algorithm or function. It might also be the most minute piece of a minor formula that is coded improperly. Logic errors are particularly hard to detect and debug, especially if the logic error is subtle. Consider a programming error that miscalculated interest on a savings account, but it only miscalculated it by .005%. This might not become apparent for quite some time, perhaps several months. However, though the error seems small, by the time it is caught it may have caused significant financial damage. This is the type of error generally referred to when the term "debugging" is used. Logic errors are the bane of all programmers, regardless of their level of training or experience.

Finally, we come to the category of *run-time errors*. As the name suggests, these are errors that occur at run time. Essentially, your code attempts to do something at run time that it cannot do. This might include opening a file that does not exist (or the filename is misspelled), attempting to connect to an Internet resource that is unavailable, dividing by zero, or a host of other possible scenarios. This error category is what we call an *exception*. The word literally means an exception to the normal, and planned, execution of your program.

Logic errors must be ferreted out by slow, painstaking debugging. Syntax errors are, by definition, caught and corrected at compile time, usually without much difficulty to all but novice programmers. Run-time errors, or exceptions, cannot actually be debugged or removed. At least, not in many cases. Therefore, these exceptions must be trapped. In most popular commercial programming languages, this is accomplished via the try-catch block (or something very similar). This is the case with Java. An example of a Java try-catch block is shown here:

```
Public void samplefunction(string filename)
{
  try
  {
    // code to open file goes here
  }
  catch(exception e)
  {
    // exception handling code goes here.
  }
}// end of class
```

A try-catch block is literally instructing the Java Virtual Machine to attempt, or "try," the code in the try block. If an exception occurs during that attempt, the code will cease execution at the line where the exception occurred and throw an exception. The catch block literally "catches" the exception that was thrown. What you do with that exception is completely up to you as the programmer. You may give the user some visual indication that an error has occurred (such as a pop-up box). It is also commonplace to simply log the error to a standard text file. You might even attempt to correct the situation that generated the error and then reattempt the code in the try block.

In Java, you have two choices for exception handling within any given method. You can implement try-catch blocks to immediately handle any exception that occurs. Or, you can declare that method with a throws clause, designating that the method throws all exceptions of the specified type. Should an exception occur, it is "thrown" up the call stack until it either meets a method with a try-catch block or ceases executing, which will happen if it gets back to the beginning of the application without encountering such an exception trap.

Recall from our earlier example of a try-catch block, as well as your own Java experience, that catch blocks have a parameter. That parameter is a class of the exception type. Java has defined a number of exception classes, each designed to handle the details of specific types of exceptions. The Exception class is the parent class of them all. This can be used as your catch block's parameters to catch all exceptions, regardless of type. Or, you can have multiple catch blocks, each catching a specific type of exception. This diversity of exception classes, each tailored to handle a specific type of exception, is one of the real strengths of the Java programming language. All of these exception classes inherit from java.lang.exception. The hierarchy of major exception classes in Java is shown in the diagram on the following page.

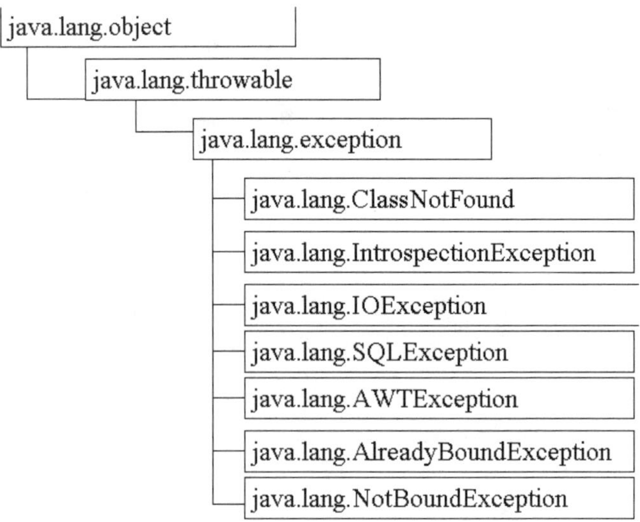

There are, of course, many more exception classes defined within Java. It is beyond the scope of this book to give a thorough treatment of all of these exception classes. The real question to ask now is, when do you trap an exception within the method and when do you throw it? For most programming situations, this is simply a matter of the programmer's personal choice. Do you prefer to have exception handling in each and every method, or do you prefer to have a few centralized locations that trap exceptions? A valid argument can be made for either option. However, this is not the case with Enterprise JavaBean exceptions. The choice is not simply a matter of your own personal preference. In many cases, the Java programming specifications require a specific approach to exception handling. You have already seen several EJB methods that are required by the EJB specifications to throw certain exceptions.

Note: EJB methods are required to throw exceptions, not catch them.

You may have asked yourself why this is. One good reason is that many of these methods are being invoked by a client. If the method is trapped and handled in that method, the client is still connected; thus, it too is locked until the exception handling is complete. When you throw an exception, you don't encounter this situation. Another reason to throw exceptions (one that is applicable to Enterprise JavaBean exceptions) is that the exception is meant to be caught by the EJB container, not by the Enterprise JavaBean class itself. As you have already seen throughout this book, the EJB container handles many of the details of managing Enterprise JavaBeans for you. It should be no surprise that the EJB container also handles some EJB-specific exceptions.

EJB Exceptions

In addition to the plethora of exception classes created to handle every conceivable type of error, there are exception classes specifically for Enterprise JavaBeans and the unique exceptions encountered when developing EJBs. Two such exception classes that you have undoubtedly noticed throughout this book are the ubiquitous EJBException and the equally common RemoteException.

As you probably guessed (at least, I hope you guessed!), the EJBException class is designed specifically to trap those exceptions that are unique to Enterprise JavaBeans. The EJBException exception is thrown by an instance of an enterprise bean. When the exception is thrown, the method is thrown to its container to report that the business method or callback method that was invoked could not be completed due to some unexpected error.

Exception classes, like all classes, have constructors. There are several constructors defined for the EJB exception class. Which constructor is called depends on what parameters are passed to the exception class. This table summarizes the various constructors for the EJBException class:

Constructor	Purpose
public EJBException()	Constructs an EJBException with no detail message
public EJBException(java.lang. String message)	Constructs an EJBException with the specified detail message

Constructor	Purpose
public EJBException(java.lang. Exception ex)	Constructs an EJBException that embeds the originally thrown exception

In addition to several constructors for the EJBException class, the class also has several methods defined that allow it to provide you with a variety of valuable information regarding the exception that occurred.

Method	Purpose
public java.lang.Exception getCausedByException()	Obtains the exception that caused the EJBException being thrown

In addition to the constructors and methods that are unique to the EJException class, this class inherits a number of methods from its own superclass hierarchy.

Methods inherited from class java.lang.Throwable:

- fillInStackTrace
- getLocalizedMessage
- getMessage
- printStackTrace
- toString

Methods inherited from class java.lang.Object:

- clone
- getClass
- finalize
- equals
- hashCode
- notify

- notifyAll

- wait

This rather lengthy list of methods that are available to an instance of the EJBException class should be encouraging to you as an Enterprise JavaBean developer. There is virtually nothing that you might wish to know about an exception that you cannot discover via one of the methods above.

Besides the EJBException class that you have seen throughout this book, you have also encountered the RemoteException class. This exception class is not unique to Enterprise JavaBeans, but it is used for a variety of remote access exceptions. A RemoteException is the common superclass for a number of communication-related exceptions that can occur during the execution of any remote procedure call. Each method of a remote interface must list RemoteException in its throws clause. A remote interface is any interface that extends java.rmi.Remote. Like the EJBException class, this class has several different constructors. The following table summarizes these constructors and their purpose:

Constructor	Purpose
RemoteException()	Constructs a RemoteException with no specified detail message
RemoteException(String s)	Constructs a RemoteException with the specified detail message
RemoteException(String s, Throwable ex)	Constructs a RemoteException with the specified detail message and nested exception

In addition to these constructors, the RemoteException class has a method that is unique to this class.

Method	Purpose
String getMessage()	Returns the detail message, including the message from the nested exception, if there is one
getCausedByException()	Returns the exception that caused the EJBException being thrown

In addition to these methods, the RemoteException class inherits several methods from classes in its hierarchy.

Methods inherited from class java.lang.Object:

- clone
- finalize
- getClass
- equals
- hashCode
- notify
- notifyAll
- wait

Methods inherited from class java.lang.Throwable:

- fillInStackTrace
- getMessage
- getLocalizedMessage
- printStackTrace
- toString

With the RemoteException class, much like the EJBException class, you are provided with a wide array of methods to help you determine the cause of the exception and the state of the system when the exception was generated.

The Java programming language has a number of exception classes, each tailor-made to handle certain types of exceptions. Previously in this chapter, I have shown you the basic hierarchy of exceptions that are associated with Enterprise JavaBeans. However, there have been exception classes, related in one way or another to EJBs, presented to you throughout this book. What I would like to do now is provide you with a summary of those classes and their uses. It seems appropriate to do this now for two reasons. The first reason is that I have just finished giving you a basic coverage of exceptions and how they work. This means that you may now be able to achieve a deeper level of understanding of these exception classes. The second reason is that these classes and their explanations are scattered throughout this book, making them very hard to find. Gathering them all in a single place will make it easier for you to look up information about a particular exception.

Type of Exception	Exception Class	Purpose
RMI Exception	java.rmi.NoSuchObject-Exception	If a client attempts to call a method in a bean object after the ejbRemove() method has been invoked, the container throws the java.rmi.NoSuchObjectException.
	java.rmi.Remote-Exception	A remote method declaration must throw the exception java.rmi. RemoteException
	AccessException	An AccessException is thrown by certain methods of the java.rmi.Naming class as well as methods of the java.rmi.activation. ActivationSystem interface. It is used to indicate that the caller does not have permission to perform the action requested by the method.
IO Exceptions	java.io.NotSerializable-Exception	If you attempt to serialize an object that does not implement this interface, a java.io.NotSerializable Exception is thrown.
	IOException	All methods of the objectOutput-Stream class can throw an IOException.
	ConnectIOException	A ConnectIOException is thrown if an IOException occurs while making a connection to the remote host.
	MarshalException	A MarshalException is thrown if a java.io.IOException occurs while marshalling the remote method call.

Type of Exception	Exception Class	Purpose
Other Exceptions	ServerException	A ServerException is thrown as a result of a remote method call if the execution of the remote method on the server machine throws a RemoteException.
	UnexpectedException	An UnexpectedException is thrown if the client of a remote method call receives a checked exception that is not among the checked exception types declared in the throws clause of the method in the remote interface.
	ServerError	A ServerError is thrown as a result of a remote method call if the execution of the remote method on the server machine throws a java.lang.Error.
	StubNotFoundException	A StubNotFoundException is thrown if a valid stub class could not be found for a remote object when it is exported.
	NotBoundException	A NotBoundException is thrown if an attempt is made to lookup or unbind in the registry a name that is not bound.
	NoSuchObjectException	A NoSuchObjectException is thrown if an attempt is made to invoke a method on an object that does not exist in the remote JVM.
	RemoteException	A RemoteException is the common superclass for a number of communication-related exceptions that may occur during the execution of a remote method call.

Type of Exception	Exception Class	Purpose
	ConnectException	A ConnectException is thrown if a connection is refused to the remote host for a remote method call.
	AlreadyBoundException	An AlreadyBoundException is thrown if an attempt is made to bind an object in the registry to a name that is already bound.

This is, of course, not an exhaustive list of Java exceptions. Such a list would be quite long, indeed. However, it is a summary of those exception classes that are most pertinent to the study of Enterprise JavaBeans and related topics. You do not need to commit this table to memory; however, I do suggest that you review it a few times to ensure that you are familiar with it. If you should need to consult the list again, I trust you will have this book handy as your primary EJB reference!

If you want to dive more deeply into the specifics of each of these exception classes to include seeing their source code, I recommend two sources. The first is your JBuilder help file. It frequently has details on exception classes, including examples of their use and, in many cases, the source code. The next obvious source to consult would be the Sun Microsystems Java page; you can find their web address in Appendix A.

Summary

With any code you write, exceptions can, and probably will, occur. Proper handling of exceptions is just as important as proper implementation of a programming language's syntax. I am certain that you have encountered exceptions in your previous programming experience and are probably familiar with basic exception handling in Java. The goal of this chapter was to introduce you to the conceptual foundations of exception handling in general and provide you with specifics about those exceptions that are specific to Enterprise JavaBeans. Hopefully, after reading this chapter, you have a much firmer understanding of exception handling in general and as it applies to Enterprise JavaBeans.

Terms

Error – Any flaw in your program's execution or compilation

Exception – An unexpected interruption in the normal flow of your program's execution

Syntax Error – An error in the implementation of the programming language

Logic Error – Any error in the logical data processing in your application

Review Questions

1. What two exception classes are specific to Enterprise JavaBeans?

2. Are the terms "error" and "exception" synonomous? Why or why not?

3. What are the three types of errors?

4. What two classes do all exception classes inherit from?

5. How many different constructors are there for the EJBException class?

6. What class does the EJBException class inherit directly from?

7. How many different constructors are there for the RemoteException class?

8. What class does the RemoteException class inherit from?

9. What is the purpose of the printStackTrace() method?

10. Is the RemoteException class used with non-EJB classes?

Chapter 17
EJB Security

Introduction

So far, you have encountered a number of topics. You began your journey into JavaBeans by studying the structure, creation, and use of standard JavaBeans. You then spent several chapters learning about Enterprise JavaBeans. In Chapter 13 you were introduced to Java Server Pages and how to incorporate JavaBeans into JSP. Chapters 14 and 15 introduced you to the fundamental concepts of distributed computing and CORBA. The preceding chapter, Chapter 16, gave you a solid coverage of exception handling with Enterprise JavaBeans. All of this should have provided you with a solid working knowledge of EJB technology.

Up to this point, I have left one question unasked, much less answered. How secure is Enterprise JavaBean communication? I have already mentioned EJB's growing popularity in e-commerce. It seems prudent to inquire about security before using a technology to transfer customer orders, private information, credit card numbers, etc. Fortunately, Enterprise JavaBeans has a built-in security model, so you don't have to concern yourself with the minute details of implementing security. This chapter will endeavor to provide you with an introduction to security in Enterprise JavaBeans.

The EJB Security Model

As with all other things in Java, there is a clearly defined specification for Enterprise JavaBean security. The security model we will examine is the one enacted with the release of Java 1.1, the current version of Java as of the publication of this book. The security model advocated by the EJB version 1.1 specification is a declarative model. The declarative security model does not involve the introduction of any security-oriented code into the business methods of your EJB. This means that the business methods you create will not need to contain any code at all to handle EJB security. In fact, using this security model, you will not be required to write any security code anywhere in your Enterprise JavaBean. This should be quite a relief to you, since we have not been writing any security code in the previous 16 chapters! So you won't need to go back and revise any of the Enterprise JavaBeans you have already created in order to account for security issues. In short, no security code was introduced in the EJB examples you have encountered in this book because security code is not usually written into an Enterprise JavaBean.

To give you the most accurate description of EJB security possible, let me quote directly from Enterprise JavaBeans Specification, v1.1, Section 15.1:

> *The EJB architecture encourages the bean provider to implement the enterprise bean class without hard-coding the security policies and mechanisms into the business methods. In most cases, the enterprise bean's business method should not contain any security-related logic. This allows the deployer to configure the security policies for the application in a way that is most appropriate for the operational environment of the enterprise.*

What this excerpt means, in essence, is that the person who is responsible for deploying the Enterprise JavaBean is also responsible for its security, not the Enterprise JavaBean developer. Though, of course, it is possible, even likely, that you might be responsible for both writing the EJB code and deploying it. If that is the case, then you will be responsible for the EJB's security, but due entirely to your role as deployer, not as developer.

If you give this some thought, considering what you have already learned about Enterprise JavaBeans, this designation of responsibility for security should make perfect sense to you. Remember that one of the first things you learned about Enterprise JavaBeans is that EJBs are hosted by an Enterprise JavaBean container. You should also recall from what you have already learned that the EJB container is responsible for the communication between the client and the Enterprise JavaBean. Since the container is responsible for the communication, it is only logical that it also be responsible for securing that communication.

Now that I have established for you that the container is responsible for EJB security, this leads to another question. How does one go about defining the security parameters one wishes the EJB container to implement? The answer is that they are defined within the JAR file. This again makes good sense within the framework of how EJBs are deployed and managed. Since the JAR file will be used to install the bean, using it to inform the EJB container of what security parameters to establish is quite logical. The security parameters of a specific Enterprise JavaBean are defined inside the JAR file that is used to distribute that bean. Recall that a JAR file has a descriptor file that describes the contents of that JAR. Certain elements of this descriptor file are also used to define security parameters for EJBs. Recall that I stated earlier in this chapter that Enterprise JavaBeans utilize a declarative security model. That literally means that you declare the various security parameters in the JAR file.

Declarative Security Setup

Now that we have answered the question of who is responsible for security, perhaps it's time to address the question of exactly how they should implement that security. The EJB1.1 declarative security model is specified using the ejb-JAR security-role and method-permission elements. What this means in plain English is that the security specifications are set within the JAR archive file. When that file is used to install the Enterprise JavaBean, the bean container will read its security specifications and adhere to them if possible. There are two specific elements in the JAR file that define the security attributes for the EJB that is being installed. They are the ejb-JAR security-role and method-permission elements. The ejb-JAR security role element defines the security roles for specific user groups. The method-permission element determines what roles will have permission to invoke specific methods of the Enterprise JavaBean in question. This means that by using this declarative security model, you have control of access to your Enterprise JavaBean at a very granular level. Not only are you able to define access permissions to your bean on a group-by-group basis, but you can also specify that access to specific methods of that bean. You might have a group that can access one method of an EJB but is unable to access another.

The application assembler defines the required method permissions for each security role. By looking at the role of the Enterprise JavaBean, the method-permissions logically follow. Here is another way to look at the implementation of the declarative security model: A method permission is a permission to invoke a specific method or a group of methods of the Enterprise JavaBeans' home and/or remote interfaces. A security role is a semantic grouping of method permissions. A user must have at least one security role associated with a method or have permission to invoke the method. You can see that security roles and method permissions work in conjunction to handle EJB security. You should also note the fact that you are given a very high degree of control over the access to your Enterprise JavaBeans. You can carefully fine-tune access, down to the method level. This gives EJBs a very high level of security. That also happens to be one reason why they are so popular with e-commerce developers.

Now it is time to examine some specifics of the declarative security model. Consider the simple fact that the application assembler has no knowledge of the actual security environment that the Enterprise JavaBean will be functioning in. In other words, when the EJB is being assembled and prepared for distribution and installation, the person that is accomplishing this task may not know the specifics of the environment that the EJB will be installed and executed in. He or she won't know the application server, network infrastructure, or even the operating system. This means that specific users cannot be assigned specific rights during installation. Because of this fact, the security roles are meant to be logical roles, each representing a type of user that should have the same access rights to the grouping of methods. This means that security roles are assigned to user types, not to individual users.

Security Roles

We can see that security roles are assigned to types of users, not specific users. However, this does not answer the more fundamental question of, what, exactly, is a role? Let me give you the most exact definition of a security role that I can by quoting directly from the Enterprise JavaBeans Specification, v1.1, Section 15.3:

> *It is important to keep in mind that the security roles are used to define the logical security view of an application. They should not be confused with the user groups, users, principals, and other concepts that exist in the target enterprise's operational environment.*

In simpler terms, this excerpt is saying that a role is simply a predefined view of an application. This view is based on the level of security you wish that role to have. Roles are not user groups or users. Roles are assigned to user groups to define the permissions of those groups. You may indeed assign security roles to specific groups, but do not let this confuse you. A role can be assigned to a group, and it can, in essence, be a property of a group, but it is not a group. That is an important distinction for you to understand.

Now that we know what a security role is, it is important to understand how a role is defined. Recall that security roles are established in the ejb-JAR. There are specific elements in the ejb-JAR file that are used to describe a security role. A security role is defined using the following ejb-JAR elements:

Element	Description
security-role	This element contains the definition of a security role.
role-name	The role-name element contains the name of a security role.
description	An optional description of the security role.

NOTE: While the description element is optional, it is highly recommended that you use it.

You can see that there are primarily three elements in the ejb-JAR that are used to define security roles. While you may or may not wish to devote the time to simply memorize these three elements, with a little experience developing Enterprise JavaBeans, you will find that these elements, as well as other specifics about the ejb-JAR file, become committed to your memory.

Now that you know the basics of security roles, let's look at an example. This example illustrates a security role definition in a deployment descriptor.

```
<assembly-descriptor>
  <security-role>
  <description>
  This role includes only the management personnel at Acme Widgets.
  </description>
  <role-name>management</role-name>
  </security-role>
  <security-role>
  <description>
  This role includes the employees of the human resources department. The
      role is allowed to view and update all employee records.
      </description>
      <role-name>human-resources</role-name>
  </security-role>
```

Take some time to examine this example carefully. You can see that it is relatively simple and easy to follow. This is the format of all security role declarations that you will encounter. Once the application assembler has defined security roles for the enterprise beans in the ejb-JAR file, it can also specify the methods of the remote and home interface that each security role is allowed to invoke. It is logical that the assembler would define both the security roles and the method permissions. The assembler defines the method permissions in the deployment descriptor using the method-permission elements as follows:

- Every method-permission element must include a list of one or more security roles and a list of one or more methods. All the listed security roles are allowed to invoke all the listed methods.

- Every security role in the list is identified by the role-name element.

- Each method (or a set of methods, as described below) is identified by the method element.

- An optional description can be associated with a method-permission element using the description element. Again, while this description is optional, it is not advisable to omit it. Descriptions can be key to maintaining code.

- A security role or a method may appear in multiple method-permission elements.

If you follow these rules, setting up security roles and method permissions will be quite easy. You might notice some similarities between the appearance of this file and the appearance of HTML code. Much like HTML code, the code in the ejb-JAR file has tags that are opened and closed. The content of these tags are what define the security of that EJB, just as the content of HTML tags defines a web page.

Not all methods will necessarily be assigned to security roles. It is entirely possible that some methods are not assigned to any security roles. This means that none of the security roles defined by the application assembler need access to the methods. You may do this if you have a method in an Enterprise JavaBean that you do not wish to expose in this particular deployment. The fact that you can choose to provide or deny access to individual methods allows you a great deal more flexibility in creating and deploying EJBs. Rather than create multiple copies of an EJB for various security situations, you can simply create a single Enterprise JavaBean. Then you can use the ejb-JAR file to define permissions that are appropriate for a particular security setting.

The method element uses the ejb-name, method-name, and method-params elements to denote one or more methods of an enterprise bean's home and remote interfaces. Like many things in programming, there is not a single correct way to compose a method element. In fact, there are three legal styles for composing the method element. These styles are summarized in the following table:

Style	Example

Style 1	`<method>`
	`<ejb-name> SAMPLENAME</ejb-name>`
	`<method-name>*</methodname>`
	`</method`

Style 2	`<method>`
	`<ejb-name> SAMPLENAME </ejb-name>`
	`<method-name>Method</method-name>`
	`</method>`

Style 3	`<method>`
	`<ejb-name>SAMPLENAME</ejb-name>`
	`<method-name>Method </method-name>`
	`<method-params>`
	`<method-param>Parameter 1 </method-param>`
	`<method-param>Parameter 2 </method-param>`
	`</method-params>`
	`</method>`

You can use any method you like. They are all "legal" and will be accepted by the container in which you install the Enterprise JavaBean. However, I personally prefer more detail to less, so I would recommend style three or style two. Style one seems to not give enough information, but I stress that this is just my personal preference and is no way a reflection of Java standards or even industry common practices.

The following example illustrates the use of method elements using each of the three styles:

```
<method-permission>
  <role-name>manager</role-name>
  <method>
    <ejb-name>ManagerBean</ejb-name>
```

```
        <method-name>*</method-name>
      </method>
    </method-permission>
    <method-permission>
      <role-name>Human Resources</role-name>
      <method>
        <ejb-name>AcmeWidgetPayroll</ejb-name>
        <method-name>findByPrimaryKey</method-name>
      </method>
      <method>
        <ejb-name>AcmeWidgetPayroll</ejb-name>
        <method-name>getEmployeeSalary</method-name>
      </method>
      <method>
        <ejb-name>AcemeWidgetPayroll</ejb-name>
        <method-name>changeSalary</method-name>
      </method>
    </method-permission>
```

Notice how you can define access to each individual method of a JavaBean. You can see how the method access privileges are mapped to specific security roles. Hopefully, the correlation between method permissions and security roles is becoming more clear to you with these examples.

EJB Custom Security

For most purposes, the basic declarative security model is adequate. However, there may be situations where you wish to have even greater control over the specifics of security access. In these cases, you can utilize custom EJB security.

You probably already guessed that there is a specification for how to go about using custom EJB security. The EJB 1.1 specification defines a mechanism by which custom security can be implemented by the bean provider. However, doing this will require the introduction of security logic into the EJB's business methods. Let me quote the Enterprise JavaBeans Specification, v1.1, Section 15.2.5, which states:

Note: In general, security management should be enforced by the container in a manner that is transparent to the enterprise bean business methods. The security API described in this section should be used only in the less frequent situations in which the enterprise bean business methods need to access the security context information.

Even though this is "custom" EJB security, the Enterprise JavaBean specifications define some standards for this. In fact, it defines an entire API just for this purpose. The EJB 1.1 custom security API consists of the following two javax.ejb.EJBContext interface methods:

- java.security.Principal getCallerPrincipal()

- boolean isCallerInRole(java.lang.String roleName)

By implementing these methods, along with some custom code of your own, you can add any type of security validation you want to your EJB. When using isCallerInRole, there must be a security-role-ref element in the ejb-JAR deployment descriptor for all the security role names used in the enterprise bean code. Declaring the security role's references in the code allows the application assembler or deployer to link the names of the security roles used in the code to the security roles defined for an assembled application through the security-role elements. A role-link element must be used, even if the value of role-name is the same as the value of the role-link reference. Examine the following deployment descriptor for an example of this:

```
<enterprise-beans>
<entity>
<ejb-name>AcmeWidgetsPayroll</ejb-name>
<ejb-class>com.acme.payroll.PayrollBean</ejb-class>
  <security-role-ref>
  <description>
  This role should be only assigned to the employees of the payroll
      department.
  Members of this role have access to all payroll records.
  The role has been linked to the payroll-department role.
    </description>
    <role-name>payroll</role-name>
    <role-link>payroll-department</role-link>
  </security-role-ref>
  </entity>
```

```
</enterprise-beans>
```

As you can see, you have several options when it comes to Enterprise JavaBeans security. You may find occasions where you need to implement custom security. However, I recommend against it, unless you find it absolutely 100 percent necessary. There are several reasons that I recommend against it:

- Placing security code into business methods makes the code less readable.

- Having security code spread throughout your bean makes maintenance more difficult.

- Handling security yourself leaves open the possibility that you will miss some critical portion of the security and leave a significant security hole in your application.

In addition to these technical reasons for recommending against custom EJB security, there is the practical reason that custom security adds a layer of difficulty to your programming that is probably not needed in most cases.

Summary

In this chapter, I showed you how Enterprise JavaBeans security is implemented. The most common way is to specify security roles and method permissions within the JAR descriptor. So when the EJB is installed, the container will know what security roles and permissions to use.

It is also possible to create custom EJB security solutions. This gives you a great deal more control over the security and access to your Enterprise JavaBean; however, it also introduces a lot more complexity to your coding. This chapter should have provided you with a basic working knowledge of EJB security and should allow you to understand and appreciate how security is handled with Enterprise JavaBeans.

> ## Terms
>
> *Security Role* – A role that defines the security for a given set of elements
>
> *Method Permission* – Specific permissions to a given method that are assigned to a security role

Review Questions

1. What model is used for EJB security?

2. In this model, who is responsible for EJB security?

3. Where are these security parameters established?

4. What two methods are defined in the custom security API?

5. What three elements does the method element use to define method permissions?

6. How many styles of method element declarations are permitted?

7. Every security role is identified by what?

8. May a given security role appear in multiple method-permission elements?

9. Is there any case where you might place security logic within a business method?

10. Give one reason why custom security may not be desirable.

Chapter 18

EJB and Transactions

Introduction

By this point in the book, you should have a very solid grasp of Enterprise JavaBeans. You should be comfortable with the basic structure, creation, and use of EJBs. Chapters 13 and 17 should have highlighted the importance of EJBs for e-commerce. Enterprise JavaBeans are an excellent choice for the non-presentation layers in any *n*-tiered e-commerce system. Given the importance of EJBs to e-commerce development and the fact that e-commerce (as well as database programming in general) involves transactions, it seems wise to devote some portion of this book to the study of transactions and how they relate to Enterprise JavaBeans. This chapter will focus on defining transactions, understanding transactions, and utilizing transactions with EJBs.

Transaction Basics

I think most readers have a basic idea of what a transaction is but may lack a clear, formal definition. So let's begin our study of transactions by examining exactly what they are. In your day-to-day life, a transaction usually refers to some business deal. You exchange a quantity of money in return for goods or services. Any purchase you make is a transaction. However, such a transaction is usually composed of several smaller steps. Let us consider a simple example, like purchasing a movie ticket. This simple transaction actually involves several small steps, all of which culminate in the purchase of a movie ticket.

1. You request a ticket from the ticket clerk.

2. The clerk informs you of the price.

3. You hand the clerk an appropriate amount of money.

4. The clerk (usually with the aid of a computer) produces one or more tickets for the movie you wish to see.

5. The clerk gives you the ticket.

6. If required, the clerk also gives you the appropriate amount of change.

You can see that this rather simple task actually involved six separate steps. Now the question arises: Is each step a single transaction? Or is the combination of these steps a transaction? In fact, you might wonder if these steps, in addition to others that we did not consider, constitute a transaction. For example, would the drive to the movie theater be part of the transaction? Perhaps even the process of selecting which film you wish to see is part of the transaction. In this case, it is the culmination of all the steps presented in our original list that produces a transaction, a fact you probably guessed. The additional steps mentioned do not constitute part of the transaction and neither would a single step by itself constitute a transaction. In this situation, it is relatively obvious what the actual transaction was; however, not all situations will be quite so straightforward. What is needed is a quantifiable way to determine what is, and what is not, a transaction. Fortunately, such a method exists; it is called the ACID test. Transactions must satisfy the ACID properties, which are Atomicity, Consistency, Isolation, and Durability.

What do each of these terms in the ACID test mean? How do they help us determine what is and what is not a transaction? Let's look at each term to see what it means. In order to consider something a transaction, an item must fit all of these criteria.

- *Atomicity* – In a transaction involving two or more discrete pieces of information, either all of the pieces are committed or none are.

- *Consistency* – A transaction either creates a new and valid state of data or, if any failure occurs, returns all data to its state before the transaction was started.

- *Isolation* – A transaction in process and not yet committed must remain isolated from any other transaction.

- *Durability* – Committed data is saved by the system so that even in the event of a failure and system restart, the data is available in its correct state.

As you can see by examining the features of the ACID test, the individual steps in purchasing a ticket do not qualify as transactions. To begin with, each item cannot be executed in isolation. Each of those steps only has meaning in relationship to the other steps. Those individual steps also fail the durability test; data is not saved unless all the steps are completed. However, if you consider all the steps taken as a whole unit, then they do fit the criteria. Beginning with atomicity, all the steps are either committed or none are. All the steps together also pass the durability and isolation criteria. So all of the steps, in conjunction, constitute a transaction. You can also readily see that the additional steps I mentioned to you are not part of the transaction. To begin with, none of those steps have the property of durability. Furthermore, the additional steps lack the properties of isolation and consistency. However, the most important reason why they are not part of the transaction is atomicity. The original steps listed have atomicity: They either all work or none do. This is not the case with the additional steps of selecting a film and driving to a theater.

Now you have been given a thorough explanation of what constitutes a transaction and an example of a transaction, as well as a reliable test to see if a particular item or items is indeed a transaction. What is needed now is a clear and concise definition of a transaction. Let me give you one possible definition. (If you consult ten different computer programming books, you will probably find ten slightly different definitions of a transaction; however, they should all, essentially, mean the same thing.)

A *transaction* is an action or series of actions that must all be executed in order for a given process to be completed.

Even though a given transaction can be thought of as a single, coherent unit of operation, transactions do take place within some broader context. A transaction context consists of all the participating components that uniquely identify a transaction. This definition may still not clarify the concept of a transaction context for you, so let's look at a concrete example. Recall our previous example using the transaction of purchasing a movie ticket. The transaction context for a transaction initiated with a human clerk at the movie theater will be different than the transaction context of a ticket purchased online. The transaction context is essentially the environment in which the transaction takes place. In e-commerce situations, this context can significantly impact the way the code is written or executed. In our movie ticket example, while the ultimate goal is the same, there are significant differences between purchasing a ticket online and purchasing one at the movie theater.

Recall from the ACID test that another criteria of a transaction is isolation. The movie theater probably has more than one ticket window and perhaps a web site that allows ticket purchasing. This means that there are likely to be several transactions occurring simultaneously. These transactions may even be virtually identical. For example, there are undoubtedly several transactions occurring simultaneously involving the purchase of exactly two tickets to the latest blockbuster movie. These transactions must each be a completely isolated unit. Each transaction should have no direct effect on any other transaction. Obviously, in our example, each transaction has an indirect effect on the other transactions. Each transaction reduces the total number of movie tickets available, thus affecting the other transactions in an indirect way. However, this does not involve any direct interaction between transactions. It is simply that the various concurrent transactions are all interacting with the same database, but they are not interacting with each other. Multiple transactions of this type can be handled simultaneously.

However, in some situations, multiple transactions cannot be handled simultaneously. Each transaction must be queued and handled one at a time. This means that the atomicity criteria of the ACID test is even more important for these transactions. We have to isolate each transaction so that each one executes as a single atomic unit. Once a particular transaction is complete, you must have consistent data that has been made durable. Committing the transaction to some durable state is usually accomplished by saving it to some permanent storage, such as a relational database. To achieve this, the container may execute different transactions in separate threads and manage all these threads in such a way that the ACID properties of each transaction are carefully maintained. The most important point to recall from this section is that transaction isolation is essential for any operation that involves modification of an underlying database.

EJB and Transactions

This brings us to the subject of Enterprise JavaBeans and their relationship to transactions. A need to keep transactions atomized and in separate threads is one of the reasons why EJBs should not initiate or manage their own threads. Such threads may interfere with the container's thread management and can cause unpredictable results. All threads used with Enterprise JavaBeans should be initiated and managed by the EJB container. You may have wondered why this book does not examine multi-threading with Enterprise JavaBeans. You can now see that the answer is simple: EJBs do not handle multi-threading; the EJB container does. Its thread handling is transparent to the EJB developer.

With Enterprise JavaBeans, every method invoked on any EJB by any client initiates a transaction. From the point when the client requests a service to the point when a result is returned to the client constitutes a single transaction. Depending upon the requested service, a transaction context may or may not need to be propagated. If transaction context needs to be maintained, transaction isolation is also required. What this means is that if a service requires multiple method calls, as you frequently see with stateful session beans, a transaction context will need to be maintained.

This information about transactions should not be completely new information to you. The error handling you have used throughout this book (and which you examined closely in Chapter 17) is, in part, designed to "roll back" one of these transactions should some error occur. All the EJB method invocations you have used have passed the ACID test. Each invocation is atomized, consistent, and isolated. Not all EJB transactions are durable, since they are not all saved to a database. Of course, entity beans are all durable, and session beans are not.

Don't let the addition of transactions concern you. It really is not an addition at all. You have been using transactions with all of the Enterprise JavaBeans you have created in this book. With EJBs, the details of handling a given transaction are managed, for the most part, by the EJB container. The Enterprise JavaBean specification requires that EJB containers provide transaction support to all Enterprise JavaBeans participating in a transaction. This means that regardless of which particular vendor's EJB container you use, you can be assured that the container supports transactions. This is normally done declaratively in the ejb-JAR file for the bean. Recall from Chapter 17 that security parameters are also defined in the ejb-JAR file. From your previous study of the various types of EJBs, you should realize that all stateful session beans and entity beans will require some kind of transaction support. On the other hand, stateless session beans may or may not require transaction support. How the container manages an EJB's transactional requirements are specified using transaction attributes. These attributes, as defined by the EJB 1.1 specification, are listed below.

1. Not supported

2. Supports

3. Required

4. Requires new

5. Mandatory

6. Never

This list on its own is probably not very meaningful without seeing it in some context. The following list shows these specifications as they would appear in an ejb-JAR file.

1. <![endif]>NotSupported

2. <![endif]>Supports

3. <![endif]>Required

4. <![endif]>RequiresNew

5. <![endif]>Mandatory

6. <![endif]>Never

These various attributes provide instructions to the container that tell the container how it should manage transactions for a particular bean. The meanings of the above attributes are listed in this table.

Attribute	Meaning
Not Supported	This attribute means that the bean does not need any transaction support from the container. The container will not propagate any transaction context associated with a client to this bean or to the beans that this bean calls. Once the method on this bean returns, the original transaction context of the client is resumed.
Supports	This is simply the opposite of Not Supported. The transaction context is propagated to the bean and all the beans that this bean contacts. If the client of this bean is part of a transaction, this bean and all the beans that this bean calls become part of the original transaction.
Required	This means that the bean in question must have a transaction context. A bean with a Required attribute cannot operate without a transaction context associated with it. If a client that is not part of a transaction calls this bean, the container starts a new transaction. Once the method invoked on the Required bean returns, the new transaction initiated by the Required bean ends. If, however, the client is part of a transaction scope, the Required bean is automatically included in that transaction scope.

Attribute	Meaning
Requires New	This transaction attribute always starts a new transaction, whether the client that called a method on this bean is part of a transaction or not. If the client of this bean is already part of a transaction, then that transaction is suspended until the new transaction completes, and the old transaction is then resumed.
Mandatory	A bean with this attribute requires that it is always part of a transaction. If the client calling this bean is not part of a transaction, the bean will throw a TransactionRequired-Exception.
Never	This attribute is just the opposite of Mandatory. If this attribute is set, the bean can never be part of a transaction. If the client invoking a method on this bean is part of a transaction, this bean will throw a RemoteException.

Specifying Transaction Support Declaratively

Recall from Chapter 17 that the preferred security model for Enterprise JavaBeans is the declarative model. You will be glad to know that Java is a very consistent language. If a methodology works in one context, it is often a good idea to apply it within another context. With this in mind, you should not be surprised to learn that the preferred method for specifying transaction support is also declarative. What this means is that transaction attributes are specified in the assembly-descriptor portion of the ejb-JAR file, in much the same way as security roles and method permissions. The element used is container-transaction which contains another element method. Generally, all methods of a bean are provided the same transaction attribute. A sample assembly-descriptor would look like the one you see here:

```
<assembly-descriptor>
  <method>
    <ejb-name>Your Beans Name goes here</ejb-name>
    <method-name>*</method-name>
  </method>
  <transaction-attribute> Supports </transaction-attribute>
</assembly-descriptor>
```

You can see that this is very similar to the declarative security used in Chapter 17. You should also develop an appreciation for just how important and useful the ejb-JAR file is. You may have previously thought that it simply lists files that are archived and allows for their extraction. You can now see that the JAR file itself is responsible for setting up security and transactions for your Enterprise JavaBeans.

Transaction Isolation

According to the ACID test, a transaction must be isolated. This means that its actions must not interlope with the actions of any other transaction, and vice versa. This isolation is a key feature of transactions. When multiple Enterprise JavaBeans are concurrently accessing a database table, it becomes important to carefully manage transactions and the order in which they access the database. Transaction isolation defines the characteristics and behavior of concurrent transactions. For example, while an inventory database table is being updated, you probably do not want any other transaction to read these tables until the transaction is complete. This level is called TRANSACTION_READ_COMMITTED. There are five levels of transaction isolation defined by the EJB standard. These levels are summarized in the following table:

Isolation Level	Description
TRANSACTION_READ_COMMITTED	This level means that another transaction can read the table only after the first transaction either commits or performs a rollback.
TRANSACTION_NONE	This level indicates that there is no transaction isolation.
TRANSACTION_READ_UNCOMMITTED	This isolation level allows uncommitted reads on tables.

Isolation Level	Description
TRANSACTION_SERIALIZABLE	This level of isolation does not allow a transaction to read a collection of rows satisfying a WHERE clause more than once. Also, it prevents a transaction from reading a new row inserted by another transaction satisfying the WHERE clause after it has read the set of rows.
TRANSACTION_REPEATABLE_READ	With this level of transaction isolation, if one transaction reads a row and then another transaction updates the same row, the changes to the row made by the second transaction are not visible to the first transaction until the first transaction commits and then reads the table again.

When you utilize the java.sql package to perform transactions, a java.sql.Connection object sets the transaction isolation level by calling setTransactionIsolation(int). The argument specifies that the transaction isolation levels are defined as public static final int in the connection interface. Their values are listed here:

```
TRANSACTION_NONE = 0
TRANSACTION_READ_UNCOMMITTED = 1
TRANSACTION_READ_COMMITTED = 2
TRANSACTION_REPEATABLE_READ = 3
TRANSACTION_SERIALIZABLE = 4
```

You can see that setTransactionIsolation allows you to programmatically set the level of transaction isolation. The getTransactionIsolationLevel() method returns the isolation level of transactions using a particular connection.

This example from java.sql was given to show you other ways to set transaction isolation levels. When developing Enterprise JavaBeans, you will never set transaction isolation levels in this manner. This work is done by the container developer. The container developer may, in turn, delegate this work to the database implementation. The method chosen is vendor specific.

Non-Transactional Beans

This information is very valuable when developing Enterprise JavaBeans that participate in transactions. However, there are EJBs that do not participate in transactions. These are non-transactional beans. Most stateless session beans are non-transactional.

Client-Demarcated Transactions

In most cases, you will simply let the container manage your transactions. However, it is possible for a client to manage the transactions. J2EE provides the javax.transaction package to do this. Specifically, you use the javax.transaction.UserTransaction interface. This interface provides methods to begin and end a transaction, mark a transaction for rollback, set a transaction's time out parameter, etc. The client can either be an external client or another EJB. In EJB 1.1 specification, the entity beans may only have container-managed transactions. However, session beans can demarcate transactions. The process involves creating a UserTransaction object and invoking all methods between a begin and commit or rollback method.

If the client is another bean, the transaction-type element in the ejb-JAR file should have a value bean as given below:

```
<ejb-jar>
  <enterprise-bean>
    <session>
      <transaction-type>bean</transaction-type>
```

There are some things you must keep in mind when using client-directed transactions. When a client explicitly initiates a transaction, any application exception thrown does not automatically cause a rollback. It is the client's responsibility to determine whether the transaction can be committed or rolled back. This is true even if the client invokes methods on a bean that has its transactional attribute set as Required or Supports. If a system is thrown from a method, the transaction is rolled back and the client receives a TransactionRollBackException.

Summary

This chapter has given you a basic working knowledge of transactions and their use in Enterprise JavaBeans. You have seen that transactions usually use a declarative model, quite similar to the security declarative model used in Chapter 17. I have shown you the various standards for defining a transaction, as well as the levels of transaction isolation you can use. While not recommended for beginners, I have given you a brief glimpse of client-managed transactions.

Terms

Transaction – An action or series of actions that must all be executed in order for a given process to be completed

ACID test – A test for determining if a given action or series of actions constitutes a transaction

Review Questions

1. What are the four parts to the ACID test?

2. What is a transaction context?

3. Transaction isolation is essential for any operation that ______________.

4. What is atomicity?

5. Should Enterprise JavaBeans handle thread management?

6. What are the six transactional attributes?

7. Which transaction attribute prevents a bean from participating in a transaction?

8. What does the TransactionRequiredException exception indicate?

9. What does the Requires New attribute do?

10. What is the preferred method for defining transaction support?

Appendix A

Resources

This appendix is provided to allow you to continue to study any of the topics presented in this book. Obviously, one book cannot cover it all, so each of the resources provided is an excellent place to further your knowledge of a given area. This list is not as large as it could be because I have only listed those resources that I would personally recommend to a student or colleague.

Products:

Borland JBuilder	*http://www.inprise.com/jbuilder/*
JBuilder downloads	*http://www.borland.com/jbuilder/offers/*
Sun Microsystems JavaBean page	*http://java.sun.com/products/javabeans/*
Sun Java BDK	*http://java.sun.com/products/javabeans/software/*
Sun Java SDK	*http://java.sun.com/products/jdk/1.1/index.html*

Online Java Tutorials:

Sun Microsystems EJB tutorial	*http://developer.java.sun.com/developer/ onlineTraining/Beans/EJBTutorial/*
EJB tutorial	*http://www.ejbtut.com/*
Another EJB tutorial	*http://www.execpc.com/~gopalan/java/ejb.html*
Java Cabana	*http://www.javacabana.com/*
Sun Microsystems JavaBean tutorial	*http://developer.java.sun.com/developer/ onlineTraining/Beans/Beans1/*
JGuru.com	*http://www.jguru.com/*
Free Java help	*http://www.freejavahelp.com/*
Java Developer's List	*http://www.jfind.com/*
Sun Microsystems Java inner class page	*http://tns-www.lcs.mit.edu/manuals/ java-api-1.1beta2/guide/innerclasses/*
Java World inner classes	*http://www.idg.net/english/crd_class_756221.html*

Java Magazines:

Java Developer's Journal	*http://www.javadevelopersjournal.com/java/*
Java Report online	*http://www.adtmag.com/java/index.asp*
Java Pro	*http://www.fawcette.com/javapro/*
Java World	*http://www.javaworld.com/*

Other Online Tutorials and Guides:

A gentle introduction to SQL	*http://www.dcs.napier.ac.uk/~andrew/sql/*
SQL interpreter and tutorial	*http://www.sqlcourse.com/*
Java server pages	*http://java.sun.com/products/jsp/*
A tutorial on Java server pages and servlets	*http://www.apl.jhu.edu/~hall/java/Servlet-Tutorial/*
The official CORBA site	*http://www.corba.org/*
Distributed object computing with CORBA	*http://www.cs.wustl.edu/~schmidt/corba.html*
UML resource page	*http://www.omg.org/uml/*
UML tutorial	*http://uml.tutorials.trireme.com/*
Unified Modeling Language dictionary	*http://uml.tutorials.trireme.com/*

Books on Java, JBuilder, and Related Topics:

Charlie Calvert's Learn JBuilder 7	by Charlie Calvert and Margie Calvert Wordware Publishing
Learn Oracle 8i	by José Ramalho Wordware Publishing
Learn JavaScript	by Chuck Easttom Wordware Publishing
Advanced JavaScript, 2nd Edition	by Chuck Easttom Wordware Publishing
Developing Applications with UML and Java	By Paul Reed Addison-Wesley Publishing

Pure CORBA	by Fintan Boltan Sams Publishing
Instant Java Server Pages	by Paul Tremblet McGraw Hill

Appendix B

EJB Glossary

Activation – The process of re-activating a previously passivated bean and, if required, restoring state information.

API – Application Programming Interface. A set of functions in one object that are exposed to the external environment and which a programmer can utilize.

Application Server – An application that works as a container for EJBs.

AWT – Abstract Windowing Toolkit

AWTEventClass – The parent class for all of the specific AWT event classes. There are several AWT event classes to handle specific AWT events.

BDK – Bean Development Kit. The Sun Micrososystem's Free JavaBean Development Kit.

BeanBox – The standard Bean Builder tool that comes with the Java BDK.

Bootstrapping – A method for getting a reference to an EJB object.

Builder Tool – Any tool that is able to manipulate and help create JavaBeans.

COM – Component Object Model. This is another architecture for allowing remote procedure calls. It is commonly used with Microsoft development tools.

Conversation – The complete list of transactions between a client and an Enterprise JavaBean.

CORBA – Component Object Request Broker Architecture. A distributed architecture method that is quite popular with many Java and C++ programmers.

DCOM – Distributed Component Object Model. This is an enhanced version of COM used for machines that are in a remote location, perhaps even connected only by the Internet.

Delegation Model – The model that provides a standard mechanism for an event source to generate an event and send it to event listeners.

De-serialization – The process of restoring data to an object from a flat file.

DIL – Dynamic Interface Language. This is a client-side technology used when there is not enough information known about the server object when the client is compiled. It is a substitute for IDL.

DSI – Dynamic Skeleton Interface. This is the dynamic object that is analogous to the skeleton.

EJB – Enterprise JavaBean

Entity Beans – Enterprise JavaBeans that represent a data source.

Event Object – An object representing an event that is used as an argument for event listeners.

Exception – An unexpected interruption in the normal flow of your program's execution.

Externalizable – A form of persistence that gives the programmer more control over what variables are persisted.

Field – A single item in a record. In SQL server, this is called a column.

Finder Methods – Used by clients to locate entity beans.

GUI – Graphical User Interface

Helper Class – A class that is used to provide some needed functionality to the main class.

Home Interface – The home interface is the interface that provides methods for creating instances of the EJB.

IDL – Interface Definition Language. This is the language used to define the interface for the client in a CORBA application.

Inner Class – A class that is defined within another class.

Interfaces – These are used for clients to create instances of Enterprise JavaBeans and access those beans. There are two such interfaces — Home and Remote.

Introspection – The process whereby a bean exposes its functions for external use.

JAR – Java Archive file

JavaBean – A self-contained Java object that conforms to the JavaBean specification.

Java.io.NotSerializableException – The exception that is thrown if you attempt to serialize an object from a class that does not support serialization.

Java.rmi.Remote interface – This is the interface that is required for all use of RMI in Java.

JDK – Java Development Kit. This is Sun Microsystem's free Java development tool. It is command line based.

JMS – Java Message Service. This is the method whereby Java passes messages between components.

JNI – Java Native Interface. This is a method for allowing Java to communicate with COM objects.

JSP – Java Server Page. This is a web development technology that is used to separate the graphical presentation of the web page from the business logic. It is frequently used with EJBs as the business layer.

JVM – Java Virtual Machine. This is the actual Java environment that any Java component must run in.

ListenerInterface – An interface that, when implemented, allows a class to be a listener for a specific type of event.

Local Variable – Any variable declared within a function is considered a local variable, and its scope is limited to that function.

Logic Error – A flaw in the logic used to create your code. This could be a flaw in an algorithm.

Marshalling – The process of gathering together the arguments to be sent to a remote object.

MDB – Message-Driven Bean. These are beans that respond to messages sent by the Java Message Service. Those of you with a Microsoft background should try to remember that in the context of this book, MDB does not refer to MS Access databases.

Member Variable – A member variable is declared at the beginning of a class outside of any functions. Its scope extends throughout the class.

Message Beans – Enterprise JavaBeans that are used to process messages sent from the JMS.

N-tiered application – An application that consists of more than one layer. The letter *n* represents the number of layers actually present.

Object Serialization – The process of serializing object variables.

ORB – Object Request Broker. This is the part of CORBA that makes communication with remote server objects possible.

Passivation – The process of moving an Enterprise JavaBean to an inactive state and, if required, storing state information.

RAD – Rapid application development tool. Any tool used to ease software development by providing a graphical interface within which to program.

RDBMS – Relational Database Management System. This is a software package used to create and manage relational databases, often with a GUI interface.

Record – A collection of fields or columns that represent one coherent entry in the database.

Reflection – The process whereby a bean discovers its functions to expose.

RemoteException – The exception thrown by all remote procedure calls in Java.

Remote Interface – The interface with which the client will actually interact.

RMI – Remote Method Invocation. A methodology for invoking methods located remotely.

RPC – Remote Procedure Call. A call to a procedure that is running on another machine.

Run-time Error – An unexpected error that occurs at run time.

.ser Files – The flat files used to store serialization data.

Serialization – The process of saving data to a file.

Serialization Stream – The stream that is used to read and write serialization data to and from the flat file the data is stored in.

Session Beans – Enterprise JavaBeans that represent a single session with a client application. They can be either stateful or stateless.

SessionContext – The context within which the session bean interacts.

SQL – Structured Query Language. The language used by relational databases.

Skeleton – The server-side equivalent to the IDL.

Stateful – A session bean that retains state information between method calls.

Stub – A copy of the server component's code that only defines the interfaces. It has no implementation code.

Syntax Error – An error in the implementation of the programming language you are using.

Swing – This is a whole host of new classes; many of them are enhanced versions of classes you find in AWT.

Table – A collection of records that are logically grouped together

XML – Extensible Markup Language. This is a markup language, similar to HTML, that allows developers to create their own tags.

Appendix C

Answers to Review Questions

Chapter 1

1. What is the process whereby a JavaBean can reveal information about itself?

   Introspection

2. How do you start the BeanBox in a Microsoft Windows operating system?

   C:\bdk1.1\bin\run.bat

3. What does the Serialize Component drop-down menu option do?

   It saves the current state of the bean.

4. What is persistence?

   The ability to retain state information between invocations of a bean

5. Can standard JavaBeans be deployed as a stand-alone product?

   No

6. How do beans expose their features?

   Through properties

7. How do you alter a bean's internal information?

   Only through calling methods or properties

8. What class provides a standard way for bean development tools to learn about a bean?

   BeanInfo

9. What is a JAR?

   Java Archive file

10. How do you remove all the beans from the canvas?

    File ▸ Clear

Chapter 2

1. What interface must a bean implement in order to allow its properties to be saved?

   Serializable

2. What is a JAR file?

   Java Archive file

3. What is a manifest file?

   A text file listing the contents of the JAR

4. What does the x option cause the JAR utility to do?

   Extract the files from the JAR

5. What is a property?

   A method used to access instance variables of a bean

6. What is introspection?

   The process whereby a bean exposes information about itself

7. What is a bean container?

   Any application capable of hosting a bean. This includes bean development tools, such as the BeanBox.

8. What type of constructor must a JavaBean have?

   A no-arguments constructor

9. What does option M cause the JAR utility to do?

   Causes it <u>not</u> to create a manifest file

10. What is the first file in a JAR file?

    The manifest file

Chapter 3

1. What is an event?

   Events are mechanisms for propagating state change notifications between a source object and one or more target or listener objects.

2. How are events received by a component?

   By event listeners

3. What is the parent object of all events?

   EventObject

4. List the two subclasses of the InputEvent class.

   MouseEvent and KeyEvent

5. List four subclasses of the AWTEvent class.

   ComponentEvent, ActionEvent, ItemEvent, TextEvent, FocusEvent, AdjustmentEvent, WindowEvent, InputEvent

6. How do event sources identify themselves as sources for a particular event?

   By defining registration methods that conform to a specific design pattern and accept references to instances of particular EventListener interfaces

7. What class do all EventListener interfaces inherit from?

   java.util.EventListener

8. What is an adaptor class?

   An adaptor class provides empty implementations of all the methods defined in a given EventListener interface.

9. What is an inner class?

   An inner class is a class defined completely within another class.

10. What is an event state object?

    It is an object that is used to encapsulate the state associated with a given event.

Chapter 4

1. What is persistence?

   A bean's ability to retain information about its current state

2. What two interfaces allow you to implement persistence?

   Serializable and Externalizable

3. How would you make a particular instance variable not persist in a class that implemented Serializable?

   By declaring it as transient

4. What type of constructor must be used by classes that implement the Serializable interface?

   A no-arguments constructor

5. Are thread objects serializable?

   No

6. What package is the Serializable interface found in?

   Java.io

7. What two methods are used in object serialization?

   WriteObject and ReadObject

8. When should you implement Externalizable rather than Serializable?

   When you require greater control over the persistence process

9. What advantage does Externalizable have?

   It provides you with complete control over the persistence process

10. Are socket classes serializable?

No

Chapter 5

1. What is the primary difference between a standard JavaBean and an Enterprise JavaBean?

   A standard JavaBean is a component used to build applications. An Enterprise JavaBean is a deployable component used in multi-tiered architectures.

2. Where do Enterprise JavaBeans run?

   In an EJB container such as an application server

3. List the three types of Enterprise JavaBeans.

   Session, entity, and message-driven

4. How do remote clients pass parameters?

   By value

5. How do local clients pass parameters?

   By reference

6. Give a brief definition of a session bean.

   It is a bean that represents a single session with a single client.

7. What are the two mechanisms for handling persistence with entity beans?

   Bean-managed and container-managed

8. Do message-driven beans retain their state?

   No

9. Can an entity bean handle more than one client simultaneously?

   Yes

10. Can a session bean handle multiple clients?

    No

Chapter 6

1. What is RMI?

    Remote Method Invocation, literally a methodology for invoking methods located remotely

2. What is marshalling?

    Marshalling refers to the process of gathering data from one or more applications or sources in computer storage and making the data available to another application.

3. What is an RPC?

    Remote Procedure Call

4. What interface must be extended to use RMI?

    java.rmi.Remote

5. What causes a ServerException to be thrown?

    A ServerException is thrown as a result of a remote method call if the execution of the remote method on the server machine throws a RemoteException.

6. What methods are found in the RMI interface?

    None

7. List one method for obtaining a reference to a remote object.

    a.   An application can register its remote objects with RMI's naming facility, the rmiregistry.

    b.   The application can also pass and return remote object references as part of its methods.

8. What exception must all RMI objects throw?

    java.rmi.RemoteException

9. What is the purpose of the remote interface?

    The remote interface identifies interfaces whose methods may be invoked from a non-local JVM.

10. What is the purpose of the marshalled object?

The marshalled object represents the actual parameters to be passed to the remote object.

Chapter 7

1. What interface must all remote interfaces extend?

   java.rmi.Remote

2. What access modifiers can you use with the EJB class?

   Public only

3. Each method in the remote interface must match a method in what class?

   The enterprise bean class

4. What object is responsible for creating client instances of the EJB object?

   The home interface

5. What does an ejbCreate method return?

   The return type of the create method must be the enterprise bean's remote interface type.

6. What object must the home interface extend?

   EJBHome

7. What exception must all remote interfaces throw?

   java.rmi.RemoteException

8. Does a stateless session bean create method usually take arguments?

   No

9. What exception must all business methods throw?

   javax.ejb.EJBException

10. Is it possible to have an abstract session bean?

    No

Chapter 8

1. What method do you use to restore an EJB from persistent storage?

   getEJBObject()

2. What interface must all stateful session beans implement?

   javax.ejb.SessionBean

3. What method is executed just after a new bean instance has been instantiated and populated with state information from secondary storage?

   ejbActivate()

4. What are stages in a transaction's life cycle referred to as?

   transaction synchronization points

5. What three methods are required for session synchronization?

   afterBegin(), beforeCompletion(), afterCompletion()

6. What method notifies the bean instance that it is about to be removed from memory and its instance variables will be serialized?

   ejbPassivate()

7. During what process does the container recreate the session object in memory and restore the previously serialized state?

   The process of reactivation

8. What interface must a session bean implement if it wishes to be informed about changes in the state of any transaction in which it is involved?

   SessionSynchronization interface

9. The bean will remain in this "ready" status until one of three actions occurs. What are the three actions?

   Enters a transaction, is passivated, or is removed

10. Only stateful session beans using what type of transaction can implement SessionSynchronization?

    Container-managed transaction

Chapter 9

1. What is JDBC?

   Java Database Connectivity. The Java drivers for database connection.

2. What is a group of related fields called?

   A record

3. What is the purpose of the DriverManager class?

   To manage access to all of the database drivers on the system

4. Who invented SQL?

   Dr. Codd

5. List three classes found in the java.sql package.

   Statement, resultset, connection, DriverManager

6. What does the ORDER BY SQL statement do?

   Sorts the resultset according to the field you have selected to ORDER BY

7. What is ODBC?

   Open Database Connectivity, standard database drivers

8. Is it possible to search for items in a database that are only similar to a given criteria?

   Yes. Instead of using the = command, use the LIKE command.

9. After successfully getting a resultset returned to you from a statement object, what must you do before attempting to work with that result set object?

   Make sure you are pointing to the first record in the database, rs.next().

10. What is the purpose of the connection object?

    It represents the actual connection to the data source and is used to open and close that connection.

Chapter 10

1. What interface must all entity beans implement?

   The javax.ejb.EntityBean interface

2. What two types of persistence are there?

   Bean-managed and container-managed

3. What three states are there for an entity bean?

   Nonexistent, pooled, and ready

4. List any three methods of the EntityBean interface.

   ejbStore(), ejbLoad(), ejbActivate(), ejbPassivate(), ejbRemove(), EntityContext(), unSetEntityContext()

5. All ejbCreate() methods must have what type of access modifier?

   Public

6. All container-managed entity bean create methods must return what?

   Null

7. All bean-managed entity bean create methods must return what?

   An instance of the primary key class for the new entity object

8. All finder methods must have what in their name?

   A prefix of ejbFind

9. Can a finder method be static?

   No, finder methods cannot be static or final.

10. All ejbCreate() methods must have what corresponding method?

    All ejbCreate() methods must have a corresponding ejbPostCreate() method.

Chapter 11

1. List a circumstance where bean-managed persistence would be preferable to container-managed persistence.

   If you wish to persist only selected data based on some criteria, or if your application requires some complex data validation prior to saving the data

2. How do all EJBs specify their home interface ?

   By using the <Home> tag

3. What are the three data types that can be used for a primary key?

   Integer, string, and primary key class

4. What method must an entity bean with bean-managed persistence implement?

   ejbRemove()

5. What methods access the underlying database object?

   ejbStore, ejbLoad(), ejbCreate(), ejbRemove(), ejbFindByPrimaryKey()

6. After an SQL statement completes, what should the method do before returning?

    Close the database connection

7. Does the ejbLoad() method close the connection?

    No, it simply returns the connection to the connection pool.

8. Can a primary key class be shared by multiple entity bean classes?

    Yes, it can be specific to a particular entity bean class, or multiple entity beans can share the same primary key class.

9. Are there many similarities between bean-managed and container-managed entity beans?

    Yes, many facets of entity beans are common to all entity beans regardless of whether they use container-managed persistence or bean-managed persistence.

10. Must all database code be written directly in the methods that use it?

    No, you can create a database helper class that each of these methods use.

Chapter 12

1. What is a message-driven bean?

    A stateless, server-side, transaction-aware component that is driven by a Java message

2. What interface(s) must a message-driven bean implement?

    javax.ejb.MessageDrivenBean and javax.jms.MessageListener

3. What are the requirements for a message-driven bean's home interface?

    None. Message-driven beans do not have a home interface.

4. What are the requirements for a message-driven bean's remote interface?

    None. Message-driven beans do not have a remote interface.

5. What is passed to the onMessage() method as an argument?

    The full JMS message object is passed as an argument.

6. Where is the business logic placed in a message-driven bean?

    In the onMessage() method

7. How does a message-driven bean maintain its state?

   They don't. Message-driven beans are stateless.

8. What arguments must be passed to a message-driven bean's constructor?

   None. An MDB must have a no-arguments constructor.

9. How is a message-driven bean's life cycle managed?

   By the EJB container

10. What objects can be message consumers?

    The consumer is either a QueueReceiver or TopicSubscriber.

Chapter 13

1. Give a simple definition of Java Server Pages.

   Java Server Pages allow you to embed Java code into HTML documents.

2. What code in an HTML document is used to embed JSP code?

   <% and %>

3. What inherent JSP object is used to send output to the screen?

   Out

4. List five inherent JSP objects.

   Request, response, session, application, page

5. What is the primary advantage of JSP over ASP?

   JSP is platform independent.

6. What type of platform will Java Server Pages execute on?

   Any platform

7. What inherent JSP object is used to get information submitted from an HTML form?

   Request

8. What types of Java variables can you use in JSP?

   Both primitive data types and object data types

9. What is the primary advantage of JSP over JavaScript?

   JSP is server side, whereas JavaScript is purely client side.

10. Can Enterprise JavaBeans be used in conjunction with JSP?

    Yes. Both standard JavaBeans and Enterprise JavaBeans can be used with Java Server Pages.

Chapter 14

1. What are the three categories of UML diagrams?

    Structural, behavioral, and model

2. Which UML diagram is used to show the basic code for classes?

    The class diagram

3. What diagram shows the various entities/actors that might operate on a system?

    Use-case

4. What keyword is used to denote a method that is written for another language's library?

    Native

5. Native libraries are usually loaded in a _________ code block.

    Static

6. How many UML diagrams are there?

    12

7. UML standards are defined by _____________.

    The OMG

8. What does the # symbol in a class diagram indicate?

    private

9. What is always executed when the class is first loaded?

    Static code block

10. What exception will be thrown if the library fails to load?

    UnsatisfiedLineError

Chapter 15

1. What part of the CORBA architecture is used on the client side to define the methods in the remote object?

   The IDL (Interface Definition Language)

2. What portion of the CORBA architecture is used to manage communication between the client and the remote object?

   The Object Request Broker

3. What is OMA?

   Object Management Architecture

4. What four policies does OMA define?

   Shared Server Policy, Unshared Server Policy, Server-per-Method Policy, Persistent Server Policy

5. What protocol is used for communication in CORBA?

   IIOP

6. What is an Object Adaptor?

   The OA is the part of CORBA that handles communication between the server object and the ORB core.

7. What object in CORBA is responsible for the actual remote method invocation?

   The Object Adaptor is also responsible for method invocation.

8. What is the repository?

   A database that provides persistent storage of object interface definitions

9. How many free CORBA implementations are currently available?

   None

10. What allows interlanguage interoperability?

    IDL

Chapter 16

1. What two exception classes are specific to Enterprise JavaBeans?
   EJBException and RemoteException

2. Are the terms "error" and "exception" synonomous? Why or why not?
   No, an error is any flaw in your program's execution or compilation. An exception is a specific type of error — a run-time error.

3. What are the three types of errors?
   Syntax, logic, and run-time

4. What two classes do all exception classes inherit from?
   java.lang.object and java.lang.throwable

5. How many different constructors are there for the EJBException class?
   Three

6. What class does the EJBException class inherit directly from?
   java.lang.exception

7. How many different constructors are there for the RemoteException class?
   Three

8. What class does the RemoteException class inherit from?
   java.io.exception

9. What is the purpose of the printStackTrace() method?
   To display the contents of the call stack

10. Is the RemoteException class used with non-EJB classes?
    Yes, it can be used with any remote communication.

Chapter 17

1. What model is used for EJB security?

   The security model advocated by the EJB 1.1 specification is a declarative model.

2. In this model, who is responsible for EJB security?

   The person responsible for deploying the Enterprise JavaBean is responsible for its security.

3. Where are these security parameters established?

   In the ejb-JAR descriptor file

4. What two methods are defined in the custom security API?

   java.security.Principal getCallerPrincipal() and boolean isCallerInRole(java.lang.String roleName)

5. What three elements does the method element use to define method permissions?

   security-role, role-name, description

6. How many styles of method element declarations are permitted?

   Three

7. Every security role is identified by what?

   Every security role in the list is identified by the role-name element.

8. May a given security role appear in multiple method-permission elements?

   Yes, a security role or a method may appear in multiple method-permission elements.

9. Is there any case where you might place security logic within a business method?

   Yes, when using custom security

10. Give one reason why custom security may not be desirable.

    - *Placing security code into business methods makes the code less readable.*

- *Having security code spread throughout your bean makes maintenance more difficult.*

- *Handing security yourself leaves open the possibility that you will miss some critical portion of the security and leave a significant security hole in your application.*

Chapter 18

1. What are the four parts to the ACID test?

   Atomicity, consistency, isolation, and durability

2. What is a transaction context?

   A transaction context consists of all the participating components that uniquely identify a transaction.

3. Transaction isolation is essential for any operation that ______________.

   Involves modification of an underlying database

4. What is atomicity?

   In a transaction involving two or more discrete pieces of information, either all of the pieces are committed or none are.

5. Should Enterprise JavaBeans handle thread management?

   The need to keep transactions atomized and in separate threads is one of the reasons why EJBs should not initiate or manage their own threads.

6. What are the six transactional attributes?

   Not Supported, Supports, Required, Requires New, Mandatory, Never

7. Which transaction attribute prevents a bean from participating in a transaction?

   The Never attribute. If this attribute is set, the bean can never be part of a transaction.

8. What does the TransactionRequiredException exception indicate?

   You have attempted to use a bean with the Mandatory attribute outside of any transaction context.

9. What does the Requires New attribute do?

    This transaction attribute always starts a new transaction whether the client that called a method on this bean is part of a transaction or not.

10. What is the preferred method for defining transaction support?

    The preferred method for specifying transaction support is declarative.

Appendix D

The Java.Beans Package

The java.beans package contains classes related to JavaBeans development. Some of these classes are used by beans while they run in an application (i.e., at run time). For example, the event classes are used by beans that initiate events. However, most of the classes in this package are meant to be used by a bean tool. These classes help the bean tool create an interface that the programmer can then use to customize the bean.

To minimize the resources used by a bean, the classes used by bean tools are loaded only when the bean is being edited. These classes are not needed while the bean is running in an application and, therefore, they are not loaded.

Interface	Purpose
AppletInitializer	This interface is designed to work in conjunction with Java.beans.Beans.instantiate.
BeanInfo	A class can implement this BeanInfo interface and provide explicit information about the methods, properties, and events of its bean.

Interface	Purpose
Customizer	A customizer class provides a custom GUI for customizing a target JavaBean.
DesignMode	This interface is intended to be implemented by instances of java.beans.beancontext.BeanContext in order to propagate to its nested hierarchy of java.beans.beancontext.BeanContextChild instances.
PropertyChangeListener	A propertychange event gets initiated anytime a bean changes a "bound" property.
PropertyEditor	A PropertyEditor class provides support for user interfaces that want to allow users to edit a property value of a given type.
VetoableChangeListener	A VetoableChange event gets initiated when a bean changes a "constrained" property.
Visibility	Under some circumstances, a bean may be run on servers where a Graphical User Interface is not available.

Class	Description
BeanDescriptor	A BeanDescriptor provides global information about a bean.
Beans	This class provides some general-purpose bean control methods.
EventSetDescriptor	An EventSetDescriptor describes a group of events that a given JavaBean initiates.
FeatureDescriptor	The FeatureDescriptor class is the common base class for PropertyDescriptor, EventSetDescriptor, and MethodDescriptor, as well as other descriptorbeans.
IndexedPropertyDescriptor	An IndexedPropertyDescriptor describes a property that acts like an array and has an indexed read and/or indexed write method to access specific elements of the array.

Class	Description
Introspector	The Introspector class provides a standard way for tools to learn about the properties, events, and methods supported by a target JavaBean.
MethodDescriptor	A MethodDescriptor describes a particular method that a JavaBean supports for external access from other components.
ParameterDescriptor	The ParameterDescriptor class allows bean implementors to provide additional information on each of their parameters beyond the low-level type information provided by the java.lang.reflect.Method class.
PropertyChangeEvent	A propertychange event gets delivered whenever a bean changes a "bound" or "constrained" property.
PropertyChangeSupport	This is a utility class that can be used by beans that support bound properties.
PropertyDescriptor	A PropertyDescriptor describes one property that a JavaBean exports via a pair of accessor methods.
PropertyEditorManager	The PropertyEditorManager can be used to locate a property editor for any given type name.
PropertyEditorSupport	This is a support class to help build property editors.
SimpleBeanInfo	This is a support class to make it easier for people to provide BeanInfo classes.
VetoableChangeSupport	This is a utility class that can be used by beans that support constrained properties.

Exception Class	Description
IntrospectionException	This is thrown when an exception happens during introspection.
PropertyVetoException	A PropertyVetoException is thrown when a proposed change to a property represents an unacceptable value.

Appendix E

HTML Primer

Chapters 13 and 14 of this book show you how to use Java Server Pages and how to incorporate Enterprise JavaBeans into those pages. In order to use Java Server Pages, you will need a basic working knowledge of HTML. Most readers probably already have the requisite HTML skills; however, for those who do not or require a refresher, this appendix is offered.

HTML, or Hypertext Markup Language, is a relatively simple markup language that web browsers can use to display web pages. You can write HTML code in any text editor. I personally use Windows Notepad, at least when working on a Windows platform. Linux users who use the KDE interface might find the built-in advanced text editor to be a suitable choice. The choice of what text editor to use is purely one of personal taste. When you save the file, remember to save it as an .htm or .html file. The browser recognizes files with the .htm and .html extensions and will look in them for valid HTML code.

HTML has had a long history and has gone through a number of revisions. Each successive revision adds more functionality to HTML, and with the current version (as of publication) of HTML (Version 4.0), it is a very powerful language that can take some time to learn. Most browsers, however, don't yet support many of the HTML 4.0 tags. The HTML that is covered in this chapter should work in any browser that has been released since 1997. Fortunately, most work on web pages can be done with just the essentials of HTML, and that is what this chapter will teach you.

> **NOTE:** Many tags in HTML <u>must</u> be closed. The <B> tag must be closed with </B>. However, some tags, such as <TD> and <TR>, do not have to be closed. Some HTML programmers prefer to close them anyway. I do not. This is simply a style difference, but one you will see throughout this book. This seems to have been an annoying point for some HTML purists who have read my previous books, so I note the fact here (in order to save myself some unflattering e-mails).

The first question is, how do we get the web browser to know that our document has HTML codes for it to read? HTML code is composed of tags that let the browser know what is to be done with certain text. At the beginning of your document, place the command <HTML>, and at the end, use </HTML>; the web browser will know that the codes in between are supposed to be HTML.

```
<HTML>
  put HTML code here
</HTML>
```

You have to admit that this is pretty simple, but this web page won't do much of anything at all. So let's use the obligatory "Hello World" example that every programming book starts off with. It will demonstrate how to do text and some basic HTML.

```
<HTML>
<HEAD>
  <TITLE>My First HTML Page</TITLE>
</HEAD>
<BODY>
<P><CENTER>
  <B><FONT SIZE="+2">Hello World</FONT></B>
</CENTER>
</BODY>
</HTML>
```

Believe it or not, this little snippet shows you most of what you need to know about HTML. To begin with, note that everything is contained between the <HTML> and </HTML> tags. These two commands define the beginning and the end of the HTML document. The web browser will ignore any items outside these commands. Next we have a section that is contained between the <HEAD> and </HEAD> commands. This is the header portion of your HTML document. The <TITLE> and </TITLE> commands contain the title that will actually appear in the title bar of your browser.

Then we have the <BODY></BODY> commands. As you might have guessed, this is the body of your HTML document (where most of your web page's code is going to go). Inside the body section, we have some text that will define how the text will appear in the browser. The <P> command defines the beginning and end of a paragraph. The <B> and </B> commands tell the browser to make whatever text is between them bold. <FONT SIZE="+2"> tells the browser how big the text should be (there are a variety of methods for doing this). The </FONT> command ends the font section of the HTML code.

By now, I trust you have noticed a pattern. All the commands have an opening command and a closing command. This is true for all but a very few HTML commands. Just remember that you close the commands in opposite order of how you opened them. Notice in the example that I opened the commands before the text like this:

```
<P><CENTER><B><FONT SIZE="+2">
```

and closed them like this:

```
</FONT></B></CENTER></P>
```

This is important to remember. You can think of this as "backing out" of your commands.

Images and Hyperlinks

What we have so far gives you a very simple web page that displays one phrase in bold text. Admittedly, this is not very impressive, but if you understand the concepts involved with using these HTML commands, then you conceptually understand HTML. Now let's expand your knowledge of HTML. Usually, web pages contain more than simply a title and some text. Other items you might put in a web page include images and links to other web pages. Placing an image on an HTML document is rather simple:

```
<IMG SRC="imagepath\imagename" WIDTH=52 HEIGHT=88 ALIGN=bottom>
```

Simply provide the path to the image and the name of the image, including its file extension (such as .gif, .bmp, .jpg, etc.). The other properties in this command allow you to alter the placement and size of the image. You can alter its width and height, as well as its alignment.

You will also note that when you first place an image on an HTML page, it has a border around it. You can get rid of this by adding "border = 0" into the tag, as in this example:

```
<IMG SRC="somepic.gif" BORDER =0>
```

Putting a hyperlink to another web site or an e-mail address is just as simple:

```
<A HREF="http://www.wordware.com">
```

This link will connect to the URL (Uniform Resource Locator) contained inside the quotation marks. In order to use this methodology to create an e-mail link, simply use this:

```
<A HREF="mailto:sombody@somemail.com">
```

You simply have to change the "http://" portion to "mailto:". Notice that all three of the preceding methods have one thing in common; they do not close the command in the typical manner that other HTML commands are closed.

Now let's examine the source code for a simple but complete HTML document:

```
<HTML>
<HEAD>
   <TITLE>Test HTML Page</TITLE>
```

```
</HEAD>
<BODY BGCOLOR="blue">
<P>
<CENTER><B><FONT SIZE="+2">My First Web Page </FONT></B></CENTER>
<P>I am learning HTML ! I <B><I>LOVE</I></B> HTML!
<P><CENTER><IMG SRC="java.gif" ></CENTER>
<P>
<P><CENTER>You can e-mail me  at</CENTER>
<P>
<CENTER><A HREF="mailto:myemail@someemail.com">E-mail ME</A>
</CENTER><
<P><CENTER>Or go to this publisher's web site </CENTER>
<P><CENTER><A HREF="http://www.wordware.com">Wordware Pub-
lishing</A></CENTER>
</BODY>
</HTML>
```

Here are a few clarifications. You should note at the beginning a new command:

```
<BODY BGCOLOR="blue">
```

You can change the background color of your page using this command and any standard color. You can also set a background image for your HTML document with a similar command:

```
<BODY background="mypicture.gif">
```

I will be the first to admit that this sample web page is very trivial, but it does contain the basics of HTML. With the material we have covered so far, you can display images, text, links, e-mail links, background colors, and background images — not too bad for just a few short pages. You may also want to look in the Sample HTML folder from the downloadable files to see several sample HTML documents for various purposes. These can be used as templates for your own web pages. Examining these can give you a deeper understanding of basic HTML.

Colors and Backgrounds

Let's examine a few other simple items we can add to our HTML documents. The first is altering text color. You can set the default text color for the entire document and alter the color of specific text. You can alter the default text color for the entire document using a technique very similar to the one used to alter the background color of the document:

```
<BODY TEXT="blue">
```

This text simply tells the browser that unless otherwise specified, all text in this document should be blue. In addition to changing the default color of all text in a document, you may wish to simply change the color of a specific section of text. This is fairly easy to do as well. Instead of using the <BODY TEXT> command, we use the <FONT> command:

```
<FONT COLOR="red">This is red text</FONT>
```

This, like the other color commands, can be used with any standard color.

There are a wide variety of tags you can use to alter the appearance and behavior of texts and images. Consider the <BLINK></BLINK> tag, which, as the name implies, causes the text to blink (this is only supported by Netscape and will not work in Internet Explorer). Another example is <STRIKE></STRIKE>, which causes the text to appear with a line through it (a strike through). The tags we have covered so far are enough to allow you to accomplish what you need in HTML.

Tables

The next HTML command we are going to examine is the table. You frequently see tables on web pages, as they are a very good way to organize data. You can use the tables with or without a border, and I will explain the various reasons to use one method or the other.

First, I will show you how to create a table with a border:

```
<TABLE BORDER=1>
  <TR>
```

```
        <TD>
          <P>This
          <P>Is a
      <TR>
        <TD>
          <P>Table
        <TD>
          <P>With a border
    </TABLE>
```

By now, you should be able to recognize that the <TABLE></TABLE> tags actually contain the table. Each <TR> tag designates another row in the table. <TD></TD> creates a cell within that row (TD refers to Table Data). Using those three tags, you can create a table with any number of rows or columns you wish. Notice in the first line of this code that the BORDER property is set to 1. This means that the border has a width and is therefore visible.

In some instances, you may not want the border to show. Tables can be used simply to hold images and text in relative positions. In cases such as this, you may not wish the border to show. Below is an example of a table whose boarders will not show:

```
    <P><TABLE BORDER=0 CELLSPACING=0 CELLPADDING=0>
      <TR>
        <TD>
          <P>This
        <TD>
          <P>is a
      <TR>
        <TD>
          <P>Table
        <TD>
          <P>With no borders or padding
    </TABLE>
```

Notice that BORDER, CELLPADDING, and CELLSPACING are all set to 0. This causes the table itself to not be displayed. However, the contents of the table will display. You should also notice that in both examples, I have placed text in each cell.

Lists

It is common to present data in lists. With HTML, you have access to a variety of types of lists. The first we will discuss is the unordered list:

```
<UL>
  <LI> First Item
  <LI> Second Item
</UL>
```

The <UL></UL> tags define the code that lies between them as being part of an unordered list. The <LI> tags identify list items. An unordered list item will simply appear as a bullet.

An ordered list is not much different. The <LI> list item stays the same, but the <UL> is going to change somewhat:

```
<OL type = I>
  <LI> First Item
  <LI> Second Item
</OL>
```

The "type =" portion of the tag tells the browser what type of list this is. The capital "I" in our example will give you capital roman numerals for your list items.

Here is a table containing all the types of ordered lists and how they appear in your browser:

Type = I	I. First Item II. Second Item
Type = i	i. First Item ii. Second Item
Type = 1	1. First Item 2. Second Item
Type = a	a. First Item b. Second Item

Type = A   A. First Item
                    B. Second Item

Marquee

A very fascinating item you can add to your web page is the marquee. A scrolling marquee takes a message or an image and scrolls it across the screen. The basic format is:

```
<MARQUEE LOOP = INFINITE> Hey this is really cool </MARQUEE>
```

In addition to text, you can place an image in the marquee that scrolls across the screen:

```
<MARQUEE LOOP = INFINITE> <IMG SRC = "mypic.gif"></MARQUEE>
```

You can also change the direction in which the marquee moves. The direction tag will tell the marquee which direction to scroll to, not from.

```
<MARQEE LOOP = INFINITE DIRECTION = RIGHT>Hey this is a cool marquee
</MARQUEE>
```

You can choose from the following directions: Left, Right, Up, and Down. Marquees provide an interesting and relatively easy way to display very eye-catching information on your web page.

HTML Forms

Perhaps the most common method for getting a user to supply information is via a web form. Web forms are simply form elements that are placed on the web page using specialized form element tags. The tags are fairly simple. The most common elements are:

- Button
- Text field
- Text area
- Combo box

- Radio button (also called an Option box)

- Check box

The purpose of each of these is relatively self-explanatory. Let's take a look at a simple example of an HTML form:

```
<form>
  <input type = "textfield" name ="test" value ="Chuck"> <br>
  <input type = "button" name = "ok" value = "OK"> <br>
</form>
```

This very simple HTML form will display a text field and a button under the text field. Once you have filled in the data in the text field, click the button. The button click event can be used to call some JavaScript function, often defined in the head section of the HTML document. HTML forms by themselves are not particularly useful, but they can be when they are used in conjunction with JavaScript or JSP.

Index

L

listener interfaces, 73-76
local access client, 124-125
logic errors, 367-368

M

manifest file, 45-46
marker interface, 96, 140
marshalling, 136, 323
MDB, *see* message-driven beans
message-driven beans, 114, 122-123, 275-276
   characteristics of, 278-279
   class, 282
   creating, 282- 283
   creating with JBuilder, 287-291
   deploying, 286-287
   life cycle of, 127-128, 279
   reasons for using, 123
MessageDrivenBean interface, 280-281
MessageListener interface, 281
messages, 122, 276
   acknowledging, 285-286
Method Tracer window, 23
multi-tiered architecture, 321-322

N

non-transactional beans, 401
n-tiered architecture, 112-113, 321-322

O

Object Adaptor, 349
   policies, 349-350
Object Management Architecture, *see* OMA
Object Management Group, *see* OMG
object persistence, 101
Object Request Broker, *see* ORB
ObjectInputStream class, 98, 100
object-oriented programming, 2-3
ObjectOutputStream class, 98-99
objects, using, 302-304
ObjectStreamClass class, 98
OMA, 352-353
OMG, 348, 351-352
   Object Model, 348

onMessage method, 122, 284-285
ORB, 346-348, 352
out object, 300

P

page directive, 310-312
page object, 300
pageContext object, 300
passing by reference, 126
passing by value, 126
passivation, 128, 182-183
persistence, 11, 89, 232-234
   and JavaBeans, 89-90
   in Java 2, 97-98
   bean-managed, 119-120, 232, 255-256
   container-managed, 119-120, 232-233, 255-256
   example of, 93-96
   example of bean-managed, 257-263
Persistent Server Policy, 349-350
persistent session beans, *see* stateful session beans
primary key, 119, 204, 231, 233
Project Wizard, 168
properties, 11
   defining, 41-43
Properties window, 22-23

R

RDBMS, 204-205
receiver bean, 11
record, 204
reflection, 39-40
relational database, 204-205
Relational Database Management System, *see* RDBMS
relational database systems, 119-120
remote access client, 124-125
remote interface, 124, 139-140, 154-156
Remote Method Invocation, *see* RMI
Remote Procedure Call, *see* RPC
RemoteException class, 144, 373-374
RemoteObject class, 141

Extend Your Power.

***Borland Solution Partner Resource Guide* provides an opportunity for vendors of software products and services designed to extend the power of Borland developer tools and technologies to reach developers and IT professionals at the point of purchase.**

The primary means of distribution of *Borland Solution Partner Resource Guide* is its placement into every North American box of Delphi (for both Linux and Windows), C++Builder, JBuilder, Application Server, VisiBroker, and AppCenter from Borland Software Corporation. In addition, Borland Software Corporation and Informant Communications Group will distribute *Borland Solution Partner Resource Guide* at a number of leading industry trade shows.

When you advertise in *Borland Solution Partner Resource Guide*, you will also receive a FREE advertisement in the electronic version at www.BorlandSolutions.com. Traffic will be directed to this site from both the Borland and Informant Communications Group Web sites. Advertisements in the electronic version may be updated each month. Visitors to your online advertisement will be linked directly to your Web site. Your electronic advertisement will appear until the next edition of *Borland Solution Partner Resource Guide* is published.

No other publication will reach as many Borland development and IT professionals more quickly or efficiently.

2 Great Ways to Get Your Delphi Fix!

Delphi Informant Magazine: FREE Issue, FREE Web Site

Receive **one free issue** of **Delphi™ Informant®Magazine**, and a **FREE** 30-day **DelphiZine.com** Web site membership. If you choose to subscribe, you'll get 12 additional issues (13 in all) and a one-year Web site membership for the super low price of **$49.99**. If you don't, simply write "cancel" on the invoice and owe nothing.

With the first issue, you'll discover why **Delphi Informant Magazine** is the world's leading publication covering Delphi development. And you'll see why **DelphiZine.com** is the most comprehensive and valuable information resource on Delphi development in the world.

- ▶ Complete Delphi 6 coverage
- ▶ Ready-to-run code examples
- ▶ Real-world solutions

- ▶ Tips, tricks, and techniques
- ▶ Web and database development
- ▶ COM+, MTS, LDAP, and more

Delphi Informant Magazine Complete Works CD ROM

(1995-2000)

Get a jump on your Delphi skills with this comprehensive reference. The **Delphi Informant Magazine Complete Works CD-ROM** contains all content published in **Delphi Informant Magazine** from 1995-2000, including all supporting code and sample files. Order this unbelievable collection for only **$49.99** *(additional charges apply for shipping & handling)*.

The must-have ultimate reference source for Delphi developers *features*:

- ▶ Over 500 technical articles, product reviews, book reviews, and other content appearing in **Delphi Informant Magazine** from 1995 through 2000
- ▶ All supporting code, sample files, and utilities from each article

- ▶ Fast text searching across all articles contained on the CD-ROM
- ▶ Bookmarks for easy navigation
- ▶ ... And much more

CALL NOW!

YES! *I want to sharpen my Delphi™ programming skills...*

800-884-6367 x10

Outside the US dial (916) 686-6610

INFORMANT
COMMUNICATIONS GROUP